STEM Education: An Overview of Contemporary Research, Trends and Perspectives

Edited By:

Elliott Ostler

First Printed in 2015.
No subsequent editions, alterations, or derivative works in progress

Cycloid Publications, Elkhorn Nebraska, Des Moines, IA United States of America
STEM Education: An Overview of Contemporary Research, Trends, and Perspectives.
Ostler, E. (Ed.). One Volume

ISBN: 978-0-9966741-1-9

First Edition. Printed in the United States of America

Code Association: 3 4 7 9 2 8 1 6 9 9 3

STEM Education: An Overview of Contemporary Research, Trends and Perspectives

Preface

During the past two decades the acronym *STEM*, signifying the disciplines of Science, Technology, Engineering, and Mathematics has evolved into what is arguably one of the most popular trends in the history of American education. It is difficult to recall a time where so many new organizations with responsibilities in advancing research and practice in a specific nomenclature of education have emerged so quickly, and established such momentum. In fact, to call STEM a *trend* may actually misrepresent the attention it commands in today's educational and political arenas. At any rate, a statement we can make with some confidence is that nearly anyone having curriculum design or instructional responsibilities in mathematics, science, engineering, or technology, particularly within the past five years, immediately recognizes the significance of the term. STEM as an educational acronym has become so familiar, in fact, that you may even have grown tired of the introductory statements in STEM literature that reference the disciplines the acronym represents.

Yet, as is so common with educational trends, and in particular, trends that are embraced with such enthusiasm, our rush to participate often precedes the establishment of operational or conceptual definitions and goals. Many popular trends, regardless of the fields in which they emerge, are often more complex than we initially believe. As a result, we discover that functional definitions end up being somewhat elusive as we begin to wade through the salient issues. Such is the case with STEM, but perhaps to an even greater extent than other educational programs because the acronym itself presents a content integration model that appears to be self-explanatory. The problem is that now, nearly twenty-five years after its formal conception, there are significant disagreements about what STEM is and what the term actually implies. In fact, what was initially the National Science Foundation's (NSF) designation of four interrelated academic fields has become a unique series of dynamic and often passionate debates about teaching, learning, and the application integrated technical knowledge. Some professionals believe that we are farther from a common definition of STEM now than we were when the term first emerged, and they may be right. STEM has certainly become what more than one professional has called "messy."

One of the main reasons for this messiness is that numerous professions and perhaps even hundreds of job descriptions, at least tangentially involve one or more of the many aspects we have come to describe as "STEM related" content. Much of this messiness can also be attributed to the unpredictable applications of emerging technologies. If asked, professionals in many different career tracts would undoubtedly attach some importance to the STEM related skills necessary for success in their jobs. And yet, other professionals deeply invested in academic fields that are interpreted as more traditionally STEM (i.e. mathematics and science teachers) would probably not include the vast majority of those jobs in the nomenclature of what they call "STEM professions." This discontinuity, indeed, leaves some of us in the awkward position of compromising strongly held beliefs for the sake of progress in a common direction. So how do we work in a common direction without compromising what we individually believe is important about STEM? This is one of the many issues being addressed in the following pages.

In researching the topics needed for providing focus to this book, we have found that many definitions tend to misrepresent or, at the very least, marginalize STEM from some point of view, and so it seems appropriate to try to honor the perceptions of many different professionals by examining a diverse range of integrated STEM skills and academic preparation models rather than focusing on specific content knowledge. We believe one of the most effective ways to address the issue is to begin where all STEM professionals begin, and that is in STEM *learning*. Professional education, although not uniquely STEM in the purest sense, is probably the one profession that can naturally bring greater clarity to the curricular and instructional necessities of STEM better than any other. STEM education professionals everywhere are continually reevaluating what STEM content and instruction should look like in the classroom and there even seems to be a new dedication to conducting and disseminating research that is truly changing the way we think about STEM teaching and learning. With efforts to understand and better communicate STEM related ideas, beliefs about the appropriate form and implementation of STEM learning experiences remain tremendously diverse even among STEM education professionals. Clearly there is a great deal to learn and understand about each other's unique contributions.

It is within the scope of this book that we hope to describe emerging trends and perspectives in STEM learning with two primary goals in mind. First, we believe STEM can only be defined and understood by contextualizing it within clearly defined goals, thus creating many small *tactical definitions* rather than one broad conceptual definition. A *tactical definition*, sometimes referred to herein as a *strategic definition*, leverages a single way of viewing and describing the interrelatedness of the STEM disciplines for the explicit purpose of completing a goal related to one or more of those STEM disciplines. Second, STEM knowledge and skills are both adaptable to and supported by nearly every other discipline and profession, thus making it highly integrated beyond what the STEM acronym suggests; therefore, we believe that it is appropriate to capture the critical facets of STEM by focusing on the pedagogies of describing, knowing, verifying, adapting, and designing. Later on in this book, you will read more about the first goal and how we need to adopt smaller *tactical* definitions (again, sometimes referred to as *strategic definitions*) in understanding and defining STEM. Special attention is given to this point because today's education professionals, in mathematics and science especially, are so familiar with the common paradigm of instruction in these disciplines that it is often difficult for them to conceive of how or why STEM would need to be considered in different contexts. Popular standardized assessment tools in these disciplines no doubt contribute to the status quo as well. In some ways, convincing mathematicians and scientists that broader views of STEM can and must exist beyond the walls of classrooms and labs has been our greatest challenge. As we explore the rather complex landscape of STEM trends, perspectives, and research represented in this book, you will find that many STEM professionals, despite the noted differences in perceptions, actually share a fair amount of common ground. For example, what is apparent to nearly everyone with whom we have spoken is that the professional education community cannot continue to labor under the assumption that simply renaming traditional mathematics and science programs as "STEM programs" will change what our students experience in schools. We know with some certainty that meaningful 21st century STEM curriculum and instruction must look very different than the math and science classrooms of the past half century, but most of all, we agree that it must be assessed differently.

SCOPE

This book was designed to overview a number of different perspectives, and to describe some unique instructional profiles, all specifically relating to *STEM* systems *learning* and *pedagogy*. However, because of the vast differences in professional beliefs about STEM content, it is quite simply impossible to create a comprehensive resource for everyone. This book, instead, takes a look at how STEM research and perspectives inform teachers about their craft and ultimately influence what happens in classrooms and beyond. To accomplish this task, we believe that it was first appropriate to make some important semantic distinctions. For example, although the difference between *STEM learning* and *learning* in the *STEM disciplines* is subtle, our perception is that there is a clear difference in both content and purpose. Thus, the primary strategy for the essays found in this resource will be to look at the underlying principles and processes to help define the critical questions for *STEM learning*. In addition, we have included manuscripts that reflect the professional academic outcomes of STEM learning. Within this context, we place *learning* at the focus of our discussions, rather than the content topics of the specific disciplines involved in STEM. And so, within the context of *learning*, we will have created our first *tactical* definition. Finally, what you may have noticed is missing from this book are chapters specifically dedicated to STEM assessment. The reason for this decision is that we believe *assessment* is often a function of the context and the goals of any given STEM program and so we have included frequent advertent references to STEM assessment within the chapters themselves rather than dedicating a chapter to it.

STRUCTURE

STEM Education: An Overview of Contemporary Research, Trends and Perspectives, consists of a series of articles and essays, each written as a single chapter. Each chapter represents core beliefs held by educators and other professionals about how learning and learning systems should look in the context of STEM, but at a number of different stages. The book provides an overview of STEM learning from historical, semantic, instructional, programmatic, content, and innovation-based perspectives. Each chapter represents an independent set of ideas, (although there will certainly be substantial overlap) so the book does not need to be read in any particular order. Many of these ideas will hopefully challenge readers' beliefs about the values and benefits of traditional learning, but it is important to understand that the articles presented herein represent the perceptions of various professionals who have already established a context for how they view STEM. The chapters follow a progression of development that generally seek to describe how STEM was originally conceived, what it means from different professional and academic contexts (including ethical considerations), what it looks like in progressive classrooms, what successful STEM programs look like, what unique content is emerging, and finally, how STEM innovations are literally changing our world. Within the chapters are ideas that will hopefully generate new questions and unique considerations for professionals all across the country. The challenges we face in defining STEM are daunting to be sure, but we believe professionals from all areas of STEM are up to the task as long as they remain open-minded and are willing to consider broad views of STEM. We hope you will find this resource both informative and interesting, but most of all, we hope it will help facilitate further discussions on STEM Learning.

Annotated Table of Contents

Chapter 1: *The Conception and Evolution of STEM: A Brief Historical Perspective* 11
Author(s): Elliott Ostler

ABSTRACT: Chapter One provides a brief historical account of the evolution of STEM as an acronym representing Science, Technology, Engineering, and Mathematics, and the potential influences of STEM curriculum being designed within the context of an integrated meta-discipline. A number of questions are posed to provide a framework for the discussion. The history of the STEM disciplines is explored through an analysis of research documentation beginning with the *Report of the Committee of Ten at Harvard* and extending to contemporary research describing the development of STEM teaching and learning environments. Responses to the pending national *STEM crisis* are examined from historical perspectives as well. Finally, *engineering* as academic content is brought into focus as a way to tie the STEM disciplines to a common anchor for mathematics and science learning.

Chapter 2: *Ethics and Science/Technology/Engineering/Math (STEM) Education* 27
Authors(s): Harrison Means

ABSTRACT: Chapter Two considers STEM from a non-content specific system of ethics. As STEM education evolves, students will face challenging questions in the development and use of new science and technological discoveries. In particular, ethical codes are discussed in the context of specific examples of ethical transgressions, the contemporary meaning and uses of ethics by philosophers and social psychologists, and a classroom ready instrument designed for collecting data on student perceptions will be presented. The perspectives given within this manuscript are believed to be important to STEM learning in particular because of the challenges of rapid advances in technology and how beliefs about technology improving the human condition bump up against many systems of ethical codes.

Chapter 3: *Metasystems Learning Design Approach for STEM Teaching, Learning and Assessment* 52
Author(s): Elena Railean, Atilla Elci, Duygu Çelik, Alev Elci

ABSTRACT: Chapter Three addresses how globalization emphasizes the role of didactical models in cognitive systems research. Didactical models aim to describe understanding and construction of knowledge through ontology and semantics, i.e. metasystems. The innovation of metasystems thinking is in savoir-vivre structure of competence, viewed as core capability of learner to be more adaptive and accommodative in both real and virtual learning environments. The basis of this approach, which is coined as META-Era, emphasizes the role of educational data mining, participatory design, personalized curricula and diversity of processes common for cognitive systems. This research goes beyond constructivist learning theory and attempts to explain behavioral changes through personalization of learning objects. Consequently, this chapter investigates cross-principles towards highlighting metasystems thinking in learning mathematics, technology, and science.

Chapter 4: *The Many Faces of Inquiry Based Learning* 82
Author(s): Angie Hodge, Dana Earnst, Matt Jones, Stan Yoshinobu

ABSTRACT: Chapter Four provides the authors a way to define inquiry-based learning (IBL), briefly explain some evidence for IBL as a method of instruction in STEM courses, and explore the meaning of IBL in more detail by examining the specific structure of three mathematics courses taught by the authors: mathematics for elementary teachers, calculus, and introduction to proof. Finally, the authors introduce the IBL community. The narrative of this manuscript is informal to capture the nature of the class discussions and represent the nature of the classroom interactions.

Chapter 5: *Perspectives on Project Lead the Way (PLTW)* 96
Author(s): Rosemary Edzie, Dustin Driever, Lee Kallstrom , James Mayberger, & Julie Sigmon

ABSTRACT: Chapter Five is structured to provide an overview of a successful science, technology, engineering and mathematics (STEM) K-12 pathway program. The successful STEM program that we have focused on was implemented in the Omaha Public Schools (OPS) in 2003. This chapter is structured as follows. The reader is provided a report on the national status of STEM education. Next, past research on the impact of early exposure to STEM activities and curriculum programs is discussed. Third, there is a discussion of the OPS institutions that have implemented a STEM focused curriculum program. Then, the reader is exposed to the benefits of engaging students in STEM focused afterschool programs that compliment lessons learned in school. The chapter concludes with a discussion of what was learned and recommendations for implementing a similar program.

Chapter 6: *Preservice Elementary Teachers' Understanding of Inquiry-Based Instruction in Science* 121
Author(s): Kristin VanWyngaarden, Sheryl McGlamery, & Saundra Shillingstad

ABSTRACT: Chapter Six provides a contemporary overview of literature and data in inquiry-based science classrooms. The study was conducted with pre-service teachers at the elementary level. The research adopts a formal study format focused on the collection and analysis of data for three primary questions: 1) What are the understanding of pre-service elementary teachers about inquiry teaching and learning entering a science methods course, 2) What instructional experience is most useful to pre-service teachers in helping them understand inquiry, and 3) What experiences with inquiry-based labs are most useful to preservice teachers in helping them understand inquiry. Both quantitative and qualitative data analysis provided information about what was learned related to the research questions listed above.

ABSTRACT: Chapter Seven is focused on chronicling the efforts of a comprehensive teacher induction program as it tries to build beginning science and mathematics teachers' knowledge, skills and dispositions. Further, this research explores the implementation of a systematic reflection process that allows mentors to provide feedback on the beginning teachers' knowledge, skills and dispositions using the Plus/Delta instrument. The responses/reflections of both the mentors and beginning science and mathematics teachers are compared to see what areas of concern and success each reports after observing and reflecting on science or math lessons taught by the beginning teachers.

ABSTRACT: Chapter Eight provides a focused look at research on the early development of science concepts. Many of the research findings from contemporary literature suggest that young learners are interested, eager, and sensitive to statistical patterns in their observations. These early learners can infer causal relationships, and test informal "hypotheses." Research also indicates that at very young ages, children demonstrate an impressive array of scientific behaviors, suggesting they are capable of learning a great deal about the physical, biological, and psychological worlds around them. The primary focus of the research contained herein is related to the questions of, why when we assess what young children have learned as a result of science instruction in the United States, is their performance relatively poor in international comparisons.

ABSTRACT: Chapter Nine chronicles a detailed account of the development and implementation of a middle school course focused on *Invention and Innovation*. The chapter is written from a personal account of the challenges and benefits to both teachers and students, who function as co-participants in the developmental process of teaching and learning under the new paradigm described herein. The chapter uses an informal voice in the description to tell a story, but also better represent the nature of communication, research, and development in middle school education settings. Specifically, content and outcomes from a practical Design Cycle are overviewed.

ABSTRACT: Chapter Ten suggests that the fundamental content differences in the STEM disciplines have created differences in academic training that STEM teachers receive in order to gain their certification. The literature reviewed herein suggests that mathematics and science teachers tend to have well defined coursework leading to professional certification, particularly at the secondary level. Engineering and technology teacher training, however, has traditionally been more focused on applications of the curricular principles of engineering and technology within mathematics and science courses, and does not universally lead to teaching certification. The variations within the STEM disciplines and how they are taught makes the integration of these subjects difficult and yet, it seems that for most STEM practitioners the perception of a natural connection between the STEM disciplines exists. This natural connection has become one emphasis in current educational reform; namely, the push for integration of the STEM disciplines at all educational levels where STEM is viewed as a meta-discipline.

ABSTRACT: Chapter Eleven indicates several studies that have shown when teachers teach for conceptual and procedural understanding, rather than focusing solely on computational fluency, student achievement improves (Haycock, 2001; Knapp, 1995; Newmann & Associates, 1996). But because teachers themselves learned mathematics through a system that emphasized procedural fluency, many teachers currently lack the conceptual basis to teach in this manner. There is thus a need for high-quality professional development that gives teachers both the knowledge and the pedagogical tools to teach for deep mathematical understanding. This chapter describes one successful effort to develop and implement a professional development framework that models what teaching for understanding looks like while deepening teachers' own conceptual content knowledge.

In order to build a model for teaching mathematics with understanding and conducting professional development to promote this type of teaching in mathematics, we researched and identified instructional practices we wanted to observe in teachers' classrooms. From this theoretical framework for developing mathematical thinking, we proceeded to build a professional development model that helps teachers put these instructional structures into practice.

ABSTRACT: Chapter Twelve is a brief manifest relating the notation, syntax, and semantics of mathematics to the notation, syntax, and semantics of natural written English. Semiotics is the context used to describe the similarities in the processes and goals of both systems as methods of communication. The discussion of semiotics falls within three categories: 1) examining the parallel structures of written language and mathematics (syntax), 2) translating mathematical symbols, notation, and processes into meaning (semantics), and 3) exploring the nature and differences of mathematical versus standard written vocabulary and notation (pragmatics). Finally, the manuscript concludes by defining the term "STEMiotics" as a way to define the interplay in symbols used for communication between the STEM disciplines using natural language as an intermediary context.

ABSTRACT: Chapter Thirteen suggests that at some point in their careers science, technology, engineering, and mathematics (STEM) teachers all face the same question from their students; "When am I ever going to use this?" This question is relevant to students and deserves an answer that is credible and based in the real world. If an educator can answer this question, student engagement and learning is enhanced. This article reports on a professional development program for teachers of STEM called Project SHINE. Project SHINE addressed the paradigm related to teachers of STEM and their experiences with real world STEM applications by giving them the real world experience that they often lack.

Chapter 1

The Conception and Evolution of STEM: A Brief Historical Perspective

ABSTRACT: The article at hand provides a brief historical account of the evolution of STEM as an acronym representing Science, Technology, Engineering, and Mathematics, and the potential influences of STEM curriculum being designed within the context of an integrated meta-discipline. A number of questions are posed to provide a framework for the discussion. The history of the STEM disciplines is explored through an analysis of research documentation beginning with the *Report of the Committee of Ten at Harvard* and extending to contemporary research describing the development of STEM teaching and learning environments. Responses to the pending national STEM Crisis are examined from historical perspectives as well. Finally, *engineering* as academic content is brought into focus as a way to tie the STEM disciplines to a common anchor for mathematics and science learning.

Introduction

What is STEM? It is a popular question these days but it is nowhere nearly as rhetorical or as simple as it sounds. It is a question to which the answer is wrapped up in a complex mosaic of diverse and unique perspectives; and, it is a question that unfortunately does not have a single definitive answer. A number of professional organizations and professional researchers have tried to broadly define STEM but all of these attempts result in definitions that misrepresent STEM from one or more *perspectives*. Perspective, in fact, is an important idea to acknowledge when talking about STEM, and one that is specifically honored in the present chapter. We must remember that the conceptualization of STEM is actually a human endeavor and, therefore, the evolution of our understanding is subject to the various complexities of human perceptions. Historical perspective is what this introductory chapter intends to address. Simply put, I will argue that STEM does not now, nor ever will, be represented by a single unique identity. We, as human beings, must assign identifying structures to both STEM content and STEM learning. Within the context of human perception, this chapter will attempt to reveal the historical development of STEM by identifying the evolution of ideas that influenced how we have generated our current belief system and where we think that belief system will guide us in the future. With that in mind, I will begin this section with a humble admission that my opening question represents more of a path to an ongoing discussion than to a single definitive answer.

A cursory explanation of the four interrelated disciplines the acronym represent (Science, Technology, Engineering, and Mathematics *as if they still yet need to be identified*) tends to under-conceptualize what is really involved in STEM and STEM learning. We can easily identify these familiar content disciplines within STEM, but the STEM term carries with it a number of other assumptions and these assumptions are largely what causes STEM to take on different identities. On one hand the overlapping content bases of the STEM disciplines are being recognized in ways that, even two decades ago, would never have been considered. For example, who among us would have guessed that some of the most prestigious universities in the world would be offering content to 50,000 people at a time through Massive Open Online Courses? Almost daily, scientific findings, engineering models, and technological advancements are being leveraged into new product conceptions and operational systems that are quite impressive. On the other hand, the pedagogy offered within today's *STEM instructional culture* is neither reflected in those advances nor responsible for them. Secondary education, in particular, is simply not suited to developing the kinds of content specializations necessary for innovation on the cutting edge.

This chasm between scientific and technical advancement and STEM education remains an issue of heated debate, and for good reasons. The STEM movement is forcing education professionals and their constituents to re-conceptualize much of what we have grown accustomed to believing and practicing. In some sense STEM has sought to replace humanism with mechanism and large scale automation. In other ways it has forced upon us new ethical dilemmas related to ideas like stem-cell research, digital brain implants, biological weaponry, and even the search for *The God Particle*.

These dilemmas are accented by beliefs that the boundaries between the STEM disciplines as we know them from an educational context are becoming somewhat distorted as we try to understand the differences between factors that describe the natural *physical world* in which we exist versus those that describe the *engineered world* that we work so tirelessly to manipulate and constantly reinvent. These perceptions as well as other belief systems that represent similar ideologies explain much about why we have such difficulty in defining STEM. These varying but appropriate perceptions suggest that the popular definition of STEM as a "meta-discipline" does not honor some of the more unique interactions among the subjects it involves, nor does it alleviate the conflicting pedagogies and ideologies that are necessary for us to experience a balanced advancement as a world. So what does? Well, as is true in so many facets of life, it probably depends on the perspectives of those involved in the discussions. STEM means different things to different people and their beliefs about it are often the sum of their experiences, instincts, challenges, and successes. A concern that may emerge as we refine our belief systems, then, is that sometimes people harbor strong beliefs about STEM *learning* without very much real information and that fact was largely the motivation for writing a chapter addressing the historical evolution of STEM as a kind of living entity.

As a way to help establish new meaningful and useful conduits for STEM related discussions, the current chapter will begin with a search for consistent and hopefully factual information about the emergence and evolution of STEM and about the disciplines the acronym represent. I say "hopefully factual" because many of the original, compelling research sources cited herein actually contradict one another. That is not to say that the sources are incorrect or even that they have been irresponsibly collected. It is simply testimony of the difficulty of conducting accurate historical research in an era where so much information is available; moreover, the available information is presented from different perspectives and from different ideological standpoints.

Although our perceptions about the structure and implementation of STEM and STEM learning may be very different (depending on our unique perspectives), I would argue that a progressive exchange of ideas can only happen within a framework of factual information. Additionally, to establish a uniform information base for STEM discussions, we must first entertain a few more pointed questions. Hopefully these questions should help to give our search a productive context. For example, from where did the term STEM come? When was the acronym first coined? Who is credited with the idea? Why has it become so popular? Why now? And perhaps most importantly, what is *STEM learning* really supposed to look like inside and outside of schools and other professional settings? These are just a few of the questions being debated by various professionals now that the STEM movement appears to be here to stay.

As we investigate the history and evolution of STEM by trying to answer some of the questions just posed, what we are really doing is attempting to establish a system for identifying the most important issues, those that may lead to some useful *tactical* definitions. In fact, if there is a single theme that runs through this narrative, it is that *tactical* or *strategic* definitions of STEM may serve our localized STEM goals much better in the long run than a broader unified definition. At this point, adopting broad definitions often force us to compromise what we believe and how we choose to address our local needs. For this reason, the manuscript at hand will make no attempt to arrive at a single unified definition of STEM. Instead, the pages and chapters that follow will provide many ways to consider STEM curriculum and instruction as well as a foundation upon which to build meaningful perspectives about *STEM learning* and *STEM pedagogy*. To discover, or perhaps rediscover, facts about STEM from which reasonable perceptions can be leveraged into a positive exchange of ideas and research will be our quest.

Setting the Stage and Asking Questions

From where did the term STEM come? As we already know, STEM is really not a term, it is an acronym; although, it has essentially evolved into a term recently in much the same way *Google* has evolved into a verb. What I mean is, the last time you did a Google search you might have described it as "Googling" something. Of course, STEM fits differently into our everyday conversations than Google does, but the point is that when someone mentions STEM in professional conversations, the acronym carries with it a host of assumptions. We might assume that the movement toward using STEM as a *term* comes mostly from familiarity, popularity, and from the desire to communicate advanced strategic meanings about curriculum and instruction in technical disciplines. Many professionals who are familiar with STEM understand the interactive and interdependent nature of the STEM areas, which has led to the popular idea of describing STEM as a *meta-discipline* (Morrison, 2006). A popular definition based on how many professionals believe STEM should look is captured by Tsupros (2009), who suggests that STEM is an interdisciplinary approach that integrates academics and real world concepts in school, community and work based contexts. However, describing STEM in this way presumes a great deal about academic content, pedagogy, and the effective application of knowledge to solve problems. To be certain, these presumptions are often shaped by individual expertise and experiences, so be sure to keep an open mind as you read on through this chapter. Even if our own personal views of STEM are not uniquely meta-disciplinary, STEM still defines a kind of theoretical construct which, when used in conversation, links various curriculum and instructional nuances in one or more of the involved subjects. Again, the problem is that theoretical constructs depend largely on perceptions.

Let us now reconsider the primary question at hand; from where does the term STEM come? This might initially seem to be a simple point of interest question and not necessarily relevant to the critical *why* and *how* issues of STEM learning. On closer inspection, however, you will find that the question actually speaks to a couple of key factors in the evolution of American education.

The first factor is the emergence of *engineering* and *technology* as tangible extensions of mathematics and science curricula, and new questions about how schools should go about addressing this emergence. It may be useful to ask the question, when and why did this happen? In some sense STEM must have evolved from a need to expand upon traditional perennial academics (where the goal is to pass on the cultural ideals and knowledge of our communities and create students who are *thinking* people) to academic programs that include skills-based components which, unlike *classics-based* subjects, the information bases are not only non-traditional, but are constantly changing and growing at a rapid pace. This is not to say that a classics based education is not useful, nor is it an attempt to suggest that new ideas about the classics cannot emerge. Instead it is an acknowledgement that the STEM curriculum of the future is not set simply because many of the technologies of the future do not yet exist. The very foundation of the T and E of STEM are based on the fact that it is their nature to be in a constant state of change. If a classics based education is considered in some way Perennial, then engineering heuristics and technology advancements would have to be considered almost polar opposite. Schools will no doubt be asked to respond to preparing students to understand, use, advance, and re-conceptualize the ideas associated with emerging technologies simply because a static information base is so difficult to define. This is already happening to some extent with the emergence of engineering elements in the Next Generation Science Standards (NGSS, 2012). If new STEM curriculum and instruction is going to be effectively integrated into classrooms, it is going to have to look different in the next 20 years than it has in the past 20. This will be true even in traditional mathematics and science classrooms because the STEM acronym convincingly implies an integration of math and science content using engineering and technology tools and methods. Currently the kind of instruction focusing on developing an authentic marriage of academic and applied content is not being done on a broad scale, and particularly not in secondary mathematics classrooms. In fact, many education professionals, mathematics teachers in particular, would probably agree that mathematics and science, as secondary level subject disciplines, have both looked a lot like *perennial* content areas in American schools for the past100 years, primarily because of a combination of the instructional focus on procedural fluency and limited availability of authentic integrated STEM learning materials. Algebra, for example, is studied and practiced in secondary schools in a way that considers the content as a generalized series of rules that govern numbers. Application outside of what is already considered contextual algebra (a search for unknown values and patterns) is not often included in algebra courses. In addition, common standardized assessments used for broad based academic comparisons drive much of how mathematics and science content is selected and presented in secondary schools, which brings us to our next point.

The second key factor in the emerging STEM movement lies in the assumption that truly integrated STEM content and instruction will force us to reshape how school and student success is measured. Clearly if the preparation of students in STEM disciplines involves tangible products in a way that reflect the needs of the nation's economy and security, then accurate and unique ways of measuring STEM success are necessary as well.

Again, we must ask, how is this going to happen? And do the assumptions associated with STEM content address the need for looking at *success* in ways that are as innovative as the rest of our STEM considerations? Assessment of STEM learning will most probably remain one of the primary battlefields for debates in U.S. education, and the trend promises to remain fairly complicated. One of the primary reasons is that technological advancements and technology marketing systems are emerging at a rate that far outpaces the possibility of creating the assessment tools needed for measuring how students are appropriating and using these technologies. In short, the methodologies used for validating a single measurement instrument for a particular emerging technology may actually take more time than that particular technology's entire life span. By the time a validation process is completed, both the technology and the validation are essentially extinct. Most assessment development specialists will argue without hesitation that assessment instruments from which we can draw reasonable academic conclusions take time to build and refine. Unfortunately, those responsible for advancements in technology, especially when the technologies are relied upon as an economic force, have no interest in delaying new research and development efforts to see if academic gains are a byproduct of the tools they are developing. Their marketing and sales data is typically the barometer for success and as long as schools are purchasing their products, technology designers will probably have little interest in how their products contribute to learning. We are going to be forced to consider how academic information can be effectively gathered and tested in an environment that moves and changes as rapidly as we see digital technologies change.

Addressing Questions About STEM

Let us continue by addressing some of these questions in a bit more depth, beginning with *the beginning of STEM*. As far as the STEM term is concerned, there are a number of contradictory sources referenced on the web and in other professional publications both giving and claiming credit for the term. The most popular references suggest that it is a National Science Foundation designation that began around the turn of the 21st century, while other sources put the emergence of the term at about a decade earlier (Chute, 2009). Still other sources claim that the term was coined in the late 19th century in the Report of the Committee of Ten at Harvard (Eliot, et. al. 1894). Certainly they cannot all be absolutely correct but each does have accurate elements based on differing perspectives, so let us examine the sources and cross reference other information to see if we can establish some facts.

From one point of view, the idea of using acronyms like STEM as a basis for describing integrated curriculum and instruction has existed for quite some time in professional education but the STEM acronym itself, probably has not. The formally published acronym STEM, it appears, has only been around for a little over a decade; although, I did run across several unpublished research sources that informally flirted with the STEM acronym along with other permutations of the same letters nearly 30 years earlier. However, because these documents were never formally published there is really no way to verify their authenticity. We do know with some certainty that engineering based mathematics and science content were being considered regularly at the secondary level long before the formal STEM movement emerged, and that the use of digital technology was becoming commonplace in teaching secondary level mathematics and science (Petroski,1981). What this suggests is that the foundations of mathematics and science instruction were changing as a direct result of industry and commerce nearly 40 years ago, not just within the last decade and a half as so many of the experts are suggesting. The *STEM crisis*, as it is being called, is perhaps more pronounced, but the need for engineering and technology advancements to be addressed within mathematics and science curriculums is a seasoned idea that has a much longer history. The availability and affordability of digital technologies even 30 years ago made it possible for mathematics and science classrooms to look different than they ever had in the past. With this new *practical* or *applied* instructional potential, the trans-disciplinary nature of STEM was essentially being introduced into secondary level schools even though it was not yet being formally recognized as STEM.

Many sources suggest that the actual STEM acronym is generally credited to Dr. Judith A. Ramaley, who was the Assistant Director of the Education and Human Resources Directorate at the National Science Foundation from 2001 to 2004 (Chute, 2009). But it is clear, based on cited works, that the semantics behind what we now call STEM existed (at least in some form) long before Dr. Ramaley coined the acronym. Some sources even reference the idea of mathematics and science integrated instruction during the mid-1890's. During the early 1990's, however, the National Science Foundation was already using the acronym SMET with the same four disciplines, which made many of the same curriculum and pedagogical assumptions related to topic integration as the term we now know as STEM. According to some professionals the term SMET appeared to create an academic hierarchy associated with how the subjects should be valued based on the order in which they were listed in the acronym. In essence the occurrence of Science and Mathematics as the first two subjects placed them as the most important subjects. Dr. Ramaley reportedly thought the term SMET sounded distasteful and so she suggested that the letters be reorganized into STEM. In doing so, she also described science and mathematics as academic bookends to engineering and technology, which are both applied endeavors that she believed better represented how we actually experience the world. So ultimately it appears that the conception of science, technology, engineering, and mathematics as a meta-discipline was a product of the early 1990s (SMET) or earlier even though the reorganization of the letters into STEM didn't happen officially until about a decade later.

There are several other contemporary sources on the web suggesting that the STEM acronym was actually "coined" more than a century ago, in the *Report of the Committee of Ten at Harvard*. These references are fairly convincing at first, but evidence from the actual *Report* does not really support the claim. The *Report* is an interesting piece of education history and it does contain brief snapshots of how the committee viewed integrated learning, but the focus of this report is primarily rooted in the traditional intellectual development of the time. The committee's charge was to address preparedness issues for American secondary level students and the standardization of secondary level schooling. For the *Committee* to recommend intentionally cross pollinating the non-academic disciplines of *engineering* and *technology* would have been highly unusual for the time, particularly since the committee members were mostly from higher education institutions and steeped in traditional educational *Perennialism* and *Essentialism*. So, while it is possible that I may have overlooked something when researching this topic, I actually believe the 1890's reference is inaccurate as far as "coining" the STEM acronym is concerned.

The Report of the Committee of Ten at Harvard does address some basic premises of curriculum integration by making statements such as, *"... that while these nine*

Conferences desire each their own subject to be brought into the courses of elementary schools, they all agree that these different subjects should be correlated and associated with one another in the programme and by the actual teaching." (Report of the Committee of Ten: Main Report Section 16). The integration of mathematics and physics are also specifically mentioned, which may be where the STEM reference is implied. But, the reference can only be *implied* at best because there are no advertent references to engineering or technology (meaning engineering or technology described as academic disciplines) in any of the conference reports, which would effectively make the E and T in STEM nonexistent in the eyes of the Harvard Committee.

The Main Report of the Committee of Ten was actually a summary of a series of nine conference reports. Each of the conferences was held in a different location and each reported on a different academic nomenclature. In 1892, Charles W. Eliot, the president of Harvard University and a group of nine other men, mostly from higher education, were sanction by the National Education Association to look into the concept of standardizing secondary school student preparation. The language of the reports indicated that there was a fair amount of discussion on elementary schooling as well, but for the most part, the committees dealt with content that was designated appropriate for secondary schooling. The topics of each of the nine conferences were as follows: 1. Latin; 2. Greek; 3. English; 4. Other Modern Languages; 5. Mathematics; 6. Physics, Astronomy, and Chemistry; 7. Natural History (Biology including, Botany, Zoology, and Physiology); 8. History, Civil Government, and Political Economy; 9. Geography (Physical Geography, Geology, and Meteorology). Note that the primary disciplines of what we could currently consider STEM were actually separated into four different conferences, specifically, conferences five, six, seven, and nine. Given this fact, it is difficult to imagine that cross-curricular issues ranked among the highest of the Committee's priorities. So despite the previous reference indicating that the individual conference committees intended that the subjects support one another, little discussion was dedicated to how they intended for this to happen. Even considering the instruction of science as a method (i.e. the *Scientific Method*) was marginalized in the main report so it is difficult to determine how important the Committee thought it was for secondary school students.

Although it appears that the Report of the Committee of Ten did not intentionally include academic engineering in their recommendations, there were formal engineering education efforts happening at roughly the same time. In 1893, engineering educators from various universities formed the Society for the Promotion of Engineering Education (SPEE). This society slowly evolved into what is now the American Society of Engineering Education (ASEE) and represented the first professional society devoted specifically to improving education (Reynolds & Seeley, 1993). The efforts of the Society for the Promotion of Engineering, as they relate to STEM, do raise an interesting question. The formation of SPEE was significant in that it publicly defined a broadly shared belief that universities could and should institutionalize the training of engineers by developing and teaching engineering curricula that relied on the fundamental principles of mathematics and science. If the actions of the Society took as their goal the combining of formal mathematics and science with engineering principles, then should we consider these actions to be the first recorded efforts in STEM learning in the United States?

It appears, based on the recorded historical evidence, that STEM as we now use the term is a 21st century *invention*, but that the academic subject integration and articulation aspects of STEM have clearly been evolving for over a century. We can conclude, too, that the emergence of engineering and technology represent external influences on schooling that differ greatly from those that established the beliefs in Perennialism and Essentialism. Engineering was being considered as an educational product of the university system at the same time as secondary schooling was being standardized. Finally, we know that emergence of technologies, and in particular, digital technologies in the form of personal computers and graphing capable calculators, established an educational norm and ultimately a new way of describing the T in STEM.

The STEM Crisis

Why is STEM so important? The *STEM crisis,* strongly reminiscent of the *Sputnik Crisis*, as some are now referring to it, is unlike other modern educational imperatives because there is quite a lot of evidence that suggests the problems are real and substantial such as the National Academies Press release of *Rising Above the Gathering Storm* reports (NAP, 2005, 2007, 2010). But in the case of STEM the issues are not uniquely educational. They seem to be a product of global economic and national security concerns as much as they are a simple evolution of American secondary education, and this is not a unique phenomenon. Educational initiatives that support the learning of technical subjects have often emerged in response to direct threats to the nation's security and other geopolitical factors, ostensibly beginning with the launching of Sputnik in 1957. At that time, the fact that the United States trailed in a technology race that helped to define the Cold War was both sobering and frightening. One of the results was the National Defense Education Act (NDEA) in 1958, which was a conduit for millions of additional dollars to flow into the U.S. education system, mostly in support of science, but there were other needs being addressed as well. At that time there was a shortage of pure and applied mathematicians who were being recruited as programmers for a relatively new innovation known as the computer. During the late 1950's electronic computers were promising, not as household gadgets or even as educational tools, but as computing devices that would help shorten the time it would take for new mathematical theories to develop into practical applications. Though the NDEA was primarily focused on strengthening engineering and science, mathematicians were seen as necessary for developing the theoretical models needed for innovations in cryptography, medicine, and of course, weapons development. The focus on mathematics as a tool for technology is somewhat alive today as it is still common for math teachers to be recruited into computer science instruction in many secondary schools. From one perspective, it is possible to consider the NDEA's intent to promote the development of mathematical theories through the application of digital technology a critical first step toward understanding the part technology plays in improving formal technical academics.

Today the geopolitical climate has the education profession reacting to a STEM crisis that is nearly as unnerving as Sputnik, but it falls under the much more subtly threatening distinction of economic and political vulnerability. In other words, not everyone knows to feel threatened as they did with a Soviet satellite floating overhead emitting an ominous beep. As a nation, many of us are at risk of losing a lifestyle to which we have grown accustomed and, indeed, which we take for granted. The research evidence is abundant, and much of the data is well articulated in the President's Council of Advisors on Science and Technology (PCAST, 2010), Report to the President, Prepare and Inspire: K-12 Education in Science, Technology, Engineering, and Math (STEM) for America's Future. PCAST's *Report* to the President summarizes a number of alarming trends, few of which are surprising to today's STEM professionals, and none of which can be summarily dismissed as having a divisive or politically based agenda. Other reports such as *Rising Above The Gathering Storm* from the National Academies Press (NAP, 2005) and the follow up report, *Rising Above the Gathering Storm, Revisited: Rapidly Approaching Category 5* (NAP, 2010) present an alarming set of facts and figures that illustrate comprehensive failures in nearly all facets of American society. Add to this data the annual employment reports from the United States Bureau of Labor Statistics and the patterns become very convincing. I highly recommend reading all of these reports if you are genuinely interested in better understanding the critical factors of STEM preparation in the United States.

The statistics presented within these reports are eye opening and alarming to be sure, but even if you are prepared to be shocked by the reported loss of economic security and an uncertain future, you may still be surprised at the academic and professional apathy the statistics represent. In fact, one of the two main findings of PCAST's *Report* to the President indicates that many American students decide early in their academic careers that the STEM fields are too difficult, uninteresting, and unwelcoming. Because of these early decisions, students are often unprepared to take on the advanced academic challenges at a later point in time even if they become interested in following a STEM related path. The concern in this realization is not only that the workforce is becoming increasingly less aware and less concerned about technical needs and responsibilities, but that innovation itself is in jeopardy; that the engineering processes and foresights needed to lead us into the future are being stultified by lack of interest, imagination, and knowhow.

From a crisis standpoint, it is perhaps important to understand that innovation in engineering drives a large portion of the U.S. economy. Communication, transportation, health, safety, entertainment, the environment, sustainable energy, and other areas of human interest all benefit from advancements in engineering. Yet, secondary school exposure to the transferable content and heuristics of engineering is very limited because of the focus on traditional performance in content *Standards*. For the most part, perspective engineering students do not self-select an engineering path until they are in college, and the students that do, represent a small percentage of the college bound population. Part of the reason for this is that the ways in which the T and E of STEM fit into K-12 education is less understood than the how the perennial studies associated with science and mathematics fit. There are a few K-12 programs that focus on engineering, such as Project Lead the Way (PLTW) and the national attention on STEM is forcing education reformers to consider additional programs, but as a discipline with didactic content, engineering still is not considered to be on even ground with science and mathematics. Perhaps it is because we are still struggling to define what engineering education should look like at the secondary level. Most fields of engineering require previous exposure to advanced mathematics and science concepts, so many students would still not be able to participate in the formal engineering education approaches used by universities even if the curriculum was better defined.

So what exactly is engineering and how did it become part of STEM? This is a particularly interesting question in the context of American K-12 education, where engineering has never seen large scale inclusion in the curriculum. Some of the more theoretical answers to this question might take us all the way back to discussions about the purpose of schooling; however, while goal here is not to debate the nuances of what did and did not influence American schooling, it is worth acknowledging that the goals of schooling often reflect the needs and wants of contemporary society. American schooling has changed and is still changing, away from the responsibilities of language, literacy, and citizenship outlined in the *Report of the Committee of Ten* and toward a new form of citizenship and global literacy, and not because we want to but because we are being forced to. Engineering and technology innovations have surfaced as global titans because they drive such a large percentage of the world economy. To not participate to the fullest extent possible as a nation is to lose ground, and so as night must follow day, schools (universities in particular) are expected to find new ways to respond to this demand.

We also often hear engineering in K-12 settings mentioned in the context of innovation and creativity, which has brought a number of new perspectives about how the arts can be incorporated into STEM. The creative needs of STEM have even resulted in new acronyms like STEAM, where the A represents the creative arts. There are a number of educators in the arts and in the STEM fields alike who believe strongly that the creative components and pedagogies of the arts are needed to support STEM learning in the most unique and powerful ways. Other STEM reformists want STEM left alone, claiming that we cannot lose focus on the actual goals of STEM learning. What this discontinuity tells us is that we probably do not entirely understand the nature of academic articulation, especially since we are woefully underrepresented in a critical perspective, and that is of the engineering educator. Engineering educators, that is to say educators who hold academic degrees in an engineering field and also in professional K-12 education, are few and far between. To really understand how engineering can be taught and learned in K-12 schools would require the perspectives of these professionals. For example, engineers may agree that creativity is an important aspect of design and efficiency, but they might also suggest that engineering creativity looks very different than creativity in the arts. Artistic creativity allows the mind to freely express ideas in many different ways while engineering creativity must often happen within some very specific design constraints. The laws of nature, science, and even economics impose some very rigid parameters on scientific innovation. But artistic elements absolutely exist in the context of engineering in such fields as architecture and industrial design. Because of this, engineering that exists as a product of schooling needs to be considered carefully and with the perspectives of many knowledgeable scientists, mathematicians, engineers, and perhaps artists too, to create programs that address localized strategic goals. To better understand how engineering fits into strategic STEM learning paradigms, let us continue to explore STEM perspectives by taking a historical look at engineering.

A Brief History of Engineering

Although the STEM term assumes a number of inherent similarities and overlap in the study of engineering, mathematics, technology, and science, there are important differences to be defined as well. Science, for example, is often considered a way of knowing and defining information from facts and phenomenon that already exist in the natural world. Under this system of belief, scientific phenomenon is simply waiting to be discovered through an organized system of inquiry and testing. The discoveries described and governed by science are often nothing more than ways of expressing the categorization and use of natural phenomenon. Mathematics, then, provides a concise and comprehensive way to describe the knowledge, interactions, and processes of science, as well as having applications and natural phenomenon of its own. It uses patterns, notation, logic, and predictable relationships as its primary tools. Based on what we have already explored from the *Report of the Committee of Ten at Harvard*, we know that science and mathematics have long histories. They both have curriculums, standards, and common assessments associated with them. They are so familiar, in fact, that the term STEM is commonly considered shorthand for science and mathematics.

Engineering, on the other hand, is only now starting to gain an identity through standards in the K12 world, specifically in documents such as the Next Generation Science Standards (NAS, 2012). As a K12 academic discipline, engineering is really in its infancy. A joint research effort from the National Academy of Engineers and the National Research Council (2009) indicates that very few professional educators view engineering as a K12 discipline, and nationwide, very few teachers are involved in engineering education processes, which has essentially resulted in a limited number of students being exposed to bona fide engineering related activities in schools. The report also suggests that the engineering related curricula that does exist is unfocused and is largely designed around promoting familiarity with engineering careers, improving technological literacy, or improving skills in math and science. Rarely are the students exposed to pure engineering methodologies and expectations. This is not altogether unexpected because professional engineering is very difficult to quantify from a K12 education standpoint. It involves both invention and design heuristics, and thus, it requires processes that are both like and unlike the traditional science and mathematics that schools emphasize. Invention and design are also very difficult to quantify didactically within the K12 setting, which further begs the question of how to approach engineering education in K12 schools.

If we step away from viewing engineering through the lens of K12 schools for a moment, we can look at the intrinsic qualities of engineering as a professional pursuit. Engineering is often described as an applied process but it is much more than that. Engineers create solutions to the many problems that challenge us as human beings. Engineers expand on mathematical knowledge and scientific theories to help provide tangible products that improve the quality of our lives. Defined this way, it is not unreasonable to suggest that engineering in some form has existed since the dawn of humankind. After all, we have continually searched for creative solutions to daunting challenges. We have then tested, used, and improved the resulting products. This same improvement cycle has been used in education over the past century; however, as we have suggested previously, *engineering education* as a formal K12 academic pursuit has a much shorter history, at least here in the United States.

The word *Engineering* reportedly has its roots in the Latin word "ingenium" which is also said to be the derivative of such words and phrases as *ingenious*, *of clever thought, to devise in the sense of craftsmanship, ingenuity, of quality thinking, of rational expression*, and even one reference which literally quoted, "*...builder of war machines.*" Perhaps it is some combination of the interpretations listed, but as you can see, many of the linguistic sources I consulted do not agree completely. Strangely enough, the last quote may actually be closer to the truth than it appears because the first engineering school in the United States was actually the United States Military Academy at West Point in 1802. They were directly linked to the Army Corps of Engineers, and not surprisingly, the *curriculum* focused on military engineering. Although the study of engineering at West Point began in 1802, it was not actually systematized until 1817. Little by little the combination of westward expansion and momentum from the Industrial Revolution created a need for more engineers. New engineering schools mimicking the *engineering* *polytechnics* of France slowly emerged in response (Langins, 2004). But even back then, opinions varied greatly about the most effective way to structure academic programs for engineering.

For most of the first half of the 19th century, engineers were trained through apprenticeships. Even by the end of the century when universities had more clearly defined academic engineering programs, only about 30 percent of practicing engineers held academic degrees in engineering. By the mid-1800s, a number of universities had developed programs that treated engineering as two-to-three year parallel undergraduate tracks or as additional one-year graduate tracks that happened outside or in addition to the traditional four year Bachelor's Degree programs (Reynolds, 1993). At the time of this early program development in engineering, it is interesting to note that the professionals of the time debated many of the same issues that are contested today when discussing STEM learning. It initially struck me as a bit strange that a group of professionals who practice in disciplines, governed by math, science, and relatively similar design heuristics could be so polarized in their views about what engineering preparation and experiences should look like from the learner's standpoint. But then I ran across a joke when I was researching the history of engineering that helped me better understand that the perceptions varied because the design heuristics in the different fields are not as similar as I had initially believed. The essence of the joke was captured by comparing the following statements. Mechanical engineers believe that, "... if it doesn't move, it must be broken," while civil engineers believe that, "...if it moves, it must be broken." What a difference a single word can make in how we view the world! Certainly these statements are not always true, but the point is well taken. How we approach solving problems is often a function of the constraints of the problem. So, too, is the case in building programs for STEM learning.

Despite the differences in the beliefs about how engineers should be professionally trained, engineering schools (universities) began to emerge in earnest after the Civil War. At the same time, professional engineering societies were appearing. Among them were the American Society of Civil Engineers (ASCE) in 1865, the American Society of Mechanical Engineers in 1880, and the American Institute of Electrical Engineers in 1884 (NAE, & NRC, 2009). The presence of these professional engineering groups, which appeared to exist on a different level and for different reasons than the universities that trained engineers, actually created a kind of symbiosis between the professional world and the academic world that still exists today. These engineering societies had a strong influence on university engineering programs and also helped define new fields of engineering. They also developed ethical codes for their members and standards for industry (Reynolds, 1991).

As we examine the training of professional engineers, we see that the demands of a modernizing world have left a series of fingerprints on the history of engineering societies and also on the academic programs of professional training institutions. It appears that when trade disciplines (i.e. mining technology) and academic fields become *saturated* with usable information, *engineering* appears like a new life form gathering energy from the informational environment. For example, in 1871, a splinter group from the ASCE broke off to form the American Institute of Mining Engineers. This was in response to the need for innovative, safe, and reliable ways to harvest fuels. The information was available and the need was well established, and so a new engineering field emerged. This phenomenon appeared again 1908 when a group of industrial chemists formed the American Institute of Chemical Engineering.

As was mentioned earlier, the late 1950's was a time of great domestic concern, particularly about national security, and so mathematics and science took their turn in reshaping engineering education (Lucena, 2013). They were emphasized in engineering programs designed to bolster innovations in computer technology, cryptography, weapons, and military stratagem. Over the past two decades, the emphasis has again shifted in direct response to global communication and economic globalization. For more information on the technologies and perspectives that drive our global economy, an excellent book is, *The World is Flat* by Thomas L. Friedman (2005, 2006). Although most collegiate engineering programs still require substantial coursework in mathematics and science, some of the emphasis has shifted to the intellectual capacities needed for creativity, the ability to respond quickly to challenges, the ability to work in teams, and even to develop an understanding of how cultural differences affect perceived needs and technological uses of different societies (NAE, 2004).

In some ways the engineering profession's ability to foresee and shape the requirements of academic preparation in engineering could perhaps inform us about how to improve K12 STEM learning. The history of applied versus academic preparation in engineering is very telling and may help fuel the discussion about the hands-on nature of applied science and mathematics. A book chapter I read while researching the history of engineering recounted a story about how the theoretical and applied sides of engineering were brought together. It happened in response to some practical deficiencies of students in an engineering program, and it looked much like the calls to action we see today from mathematics reformist who demand more hands-on experiences for mathematics students. The story indicated that around 1870, Calvin M. Woodward, who was the Dean of the Washington University Engineering Department instituted *shop training* experiences for his students when he discovered that they were unable to develop the wooden models needed for demonstrating various mechanical principles. Apparently the president of M.I.T, John D. Runkle also introduced a shop-based training program after seeing demonstrations of Russian *manual-arts* training at the 1876 Centennial Exposition in Philadelphia. With leadership by Woodward and Runkle, intermediate and secondary level schools were established that combined liberal arts and manual training. By the early 20th century, this manual training had slowly evolved into what we now typically recognize as the Industrial Arts.

The difference between early 20th century industrial arts and what we know think of as industrial arts is that back then, the industrial arts represented a shift in thinking away from vocational education toward general education where all students studied how industry created value from raw materials in the context of producing industrial innovations. The curriculum required the use of industrial machines, tools, and equipment in a laboratory setting, not for the purpose of learning to use the equipment to its own end, but rather for the purpose of advancing formal studies in liberal arts, mathematics, and science (NAE, & NRC, 2009). Counter to this idea, the popular trend over the past few decades has been to separate college preparation coursework from the industrial arts. Students who are not considered to be college bound are often channeled into manual training experiences that are more suited to their academic interests. It turns out that these manual experiences are one, untapped possible solution to what is needed to solidify academic understanding of mathematical and scientific concepts. The STEM movement may actually justify the need for reestablishing mathematics and science curriculum and instruction that are materials (i.e. Industrial Arts) based. There are already a number of programs that cross over nicely into the realm of engineering education that follow a materials-based model of learning. Such programs include the National Academy of Engineering (NAE) Grand Challenges Partners Program, Mathematics Engineering and Science Achievement (MESA), and Engineering is Elementary (EiE). Although this chapter is about the history of STEM, the first of the programs listed above really represents both the past and the future of engineering, and by extension, some form of the evolution of STEM in schools.

The National Academy of Engineering (NAE) is a government sponsored institution that was founded in 1964 under the same legislative umbrella as the National Academy of Sciences, the Institute of Medicine, and the National Research Council. In 2008, the NAE created a list of 14 Grand Challenges for engineering in the next century that essentially address the nature of engineering in the future. They are as follows:

- Make solar energy economical
- Provide energy from fusion
- Develop carbon sequestration methods
- Manage the nitrogen cycle
- Provide access to clean water
- Restore and improve urban infrastructure
- Advance health informatics
- Engineer better medicines
- Reverse-engineer the brain
- Prevent nuclear terror
- Secure cyberspace
- Enhance virtual reality
- Advance personalized learning
- Engineer the tools of scientific discovery

These NAC engineering challenges capture the humanistic side of engineering as well as the technical side in that the solutions being sought represent our commitment to making the world a better place, as well as our desire to use technology to achieve that goal.

Conclusion

The history and evolution of STEM may not necessarily be the most interesting of the ongoing discussions about STEM learning, but the more information we are armed with, the better we will be able to communicate our individual needs and goals. In some sense, this chapter has been about discovering not only the history, but also the *culture* and evolution of the thinking behind STEM. By understanding our history and culture, we are better equipped to steer the proverbial ship as we determine which direction our individual goals need to take us. In the introduction of this article, a number of guiding questions were posed. We explored information about many of those questions, but perhaps the most important question, "what is STEM learning supposed to look like" may not really have been addressed to any level of satisfaction. But perhaps this is not surprising given that the education profession has been debating the issue of effective mathematics and science education for well over a century. It is unlikely that now, in the 21st century, we will have suddenly managed to figure it all out by adding engineering and technology into the mix. The inclusion of the E and T of STEM does actually provide clarity to parts of science and mathematics curriculum and pedagogy in that it provides tangible ways to *experience* those subjects, but at the same time, it creates a whole new set of questions, particularly in assessment.

Questions are a fact of life in any profession; in point of fact, questions are essential for growth. So, it is likely that you have more questions now than when you began reading this chapter. But, I would suggest that the ability to ask good questions indicates that some learning has occurred and that a *mental engineering* process is beginning. Asking good questions about STEM means that we are starting to define our own design constraints, and in some sense, we are beginning to develop our own tactical, or strategic, definitions of STEM.

References

Chute, E. (2009). STEM Education is Branching Out. Pittsburgh Post Gazette. Pittsburgh, PA. URL: postgazette.com/news/education/2009/02/STEM-education-is-branching-out.

Committee on Prospering in the Global Economy of the 21st Century (U.S.), & Committee on Science, Engineering, and Public Policy (U.S.). (2007). Rising above the gathering storm: Energizing and employing America for a brighter economic future. Washington, D.C.: National Academies Press.

Friedman, T.L. (2006). The World is Flat: A brief history of the 21st Century (Updated and Expanded). Farrar, Straus and Giroux: New York

Langins, J. (2004). Conserving the Enlightenment: French Military Engineering from Vaubam to the Revolution. Cambridge, Mass.: MIT Press

Lucena, J. (ed.), (2013). Engineering Education for Social Justice: Critical Explorations and Opportunities, Philosophy of Engineering and Technology, 10. ISBN: 9400763506

Morrison, J. (2006). Attributes of STEM education. TIES STEM education monograph series, Baltimore, MD: TIES.

National Academy of Engineering (NAE). (2010). Standards for K-12 engineering education. Washington, DC: National Academies Press.

National Academy of Engineering and National Research Council (NAE & NRC). (2009). Engineering in K-12 educaiton: Understanding the status and improving prospects. Washington, DC: National Academies Press.

National Education Association (1894). Report of the committee of ten on secondary school studies with the reports of the conferences arranged by the committee, New York: American Book Company

PCAST, 2010 President's Council of Advisors on Science and Technology (PCAST, 2010), Report to the President, Prepare and Inspire: K-12 Education in Science, Technology, Engineering, and Math (STEM) for America's Future: Washington, DC.

Petroski, H. (1981). *The Mathematics Teacher*. Reston, VA: NCTM

Reynolds, T.S. (1991)

Reynolds, T.S. (1993). The Education of Engineers in America before the Morrill Act of 1862. *History of Education Quarterly*. Spring, 1993.

Reynolds, T.S., & Seely, B.E. (1993). Striving for balance: A hundred years of the American Society for Engineering Education. *Journal of Engineering Education*, Vol. 82, No. 3.

Tsupros, N., Kohler, R., & Hallinen, J. (2009). STEM education: A project to identify the missing components, Intermediate Unit1 and Carnegie Mellon, PA.

Chapter Author(s)

Elliott Ostler is a Professor of Educational Leadership specializing in STEM Education at the University of Nebraska at Omaha. He has taught courses in mathematics, physics, statistics, pedagogical methods, and research design. His research interests are primarily focused on the paradigms of integrated STEM education and the use of mathematics as a language.

Chapter 2

Ethics and Science/Technology/Engineering/Math (STEM) Education

ABSTRACT: The following chapter considers STEM from a non-content specific system of ethics. As STEM education evolves, students will face challenging questions in the development and use of new science and technological discoveries. In particular, ethical codes are discussed in the context of specific examples of ethical transgressions, the contemporary meaning and uses of ethics by philosophers and social psychologists, and a classroom ready instrument designed for collecting data on student perceptions will be presented.

Introduction

I dislike starting off with an impertinent question but I have to ask, "Do you have an ethical code written down somewhere so that it could be readily printed and shared with an interested STEM colleague or student?" I predict the answer to be no. I further predict that anyone reading these words will be hard pressed to give me, orally, his or her six most important ethics principles through which a good life would be lived. I base these claims on the fact that I have asked 5028 undergraduates to write a code of ethics during the past 12 years and exceedingly few have a clue as to where to begin.

After instruction and coaching, most are able to successfully create a somewhat simplistic explanation of an ethical system. After study and more coaching, they can enhance the ethical code and apply various parts of it to ethical clashes. Most importantly, they are sensitized to their ethical responsibilities as future educators and as citizens.

As STEM educators, every act of our teaching is either an ethical or unethical act. We choose, unconsciously or consciously, to be ethical in our work but we often cannot articulate what is going on with our decision process. Sometimes, some of us choose unethical paths. We rarely have much time to deliberate about our ethical decision points and that can be troublesome. The same can be said about our STEM students and we need to help them because the ethical issues they will face can be career ending if they make the wrong decisions. I will give some powerful and authentic examples in just two more paragraphs and will sprinkle them throughout this chapter.

There was a time when ethics, a branch of philosophy, was owned by philosophers but more recently the social psychologists have put a claim on the territory. As a result, in this chapter, 1) I will explore some of the ethical transgressions in the various STEM disciplines, 2) examine some of the landscape now shared by philosophers and social psychologists, 3) and, I will propose a plan for STEM educators to implement while helping students become ethically aware.

Some Ethical Transgressions

On the face of it, having a highly functional ethical system seems as simple as doing the right thing instead of doing the wrong one. Of course, it turns out to be more complicated than that, just as there is many a slip betwixt the glance and the matrimonial vows. Some of the slips come about because of human frailties, others because of different world views and values, others because of special circumstances. For example, it is widely believed that telling a lie is unethical. Yet, would a person tell a lie to save his or her own life, if no one else would get hurt in the process? How about a lie to buttress one's reputation? Also, is there a difference between a small lie and a BIG lie?

These are not just hypothetical situations. According to Dan Charles of NPR, a researcher recently had all research privileges taken away for two years due to a lie. Here is the situation. An Institutional Review Board (IRB) approved study about the effects of "golden rice" crashed into the ethics wall. Golden rice is the result of biotechnology and genetically modified organisms (GMO) which are produced. The creation of yellow endosperm in ordinary white rice increases the beta-carotene in the part of the rice which is eaten. According to claims, a single bowl of this product will provide over half of a child's daily requirement of vitamin A. This vitamin is important in nutrition, especially among the children of the world who have marginal diets.

Half the requirement would be a substantial boost to nutrition but do children's bodies readily absorb the vitamin from the rice? In order to find out, the IRB at Tufts' University approved a study on children in China. We will return to the issue of who benefits in a moment—for now let's stay with the study. Guangwen Tang of Tufts and her team lied about the nature of the rice (withheld GMO information to parents consenting to allow their children to participate in the study). As a result, several of the Chinese researchers have lost their jobs and, after Tufts conducted a year of review on the study, it has banned Guangwen Tang from doing research on human subjects for two years and for two additional years any research she does will be under supervision (Charles, 2013).

This is why human subject research requires IRB approval and why the conditions are to be scrupulously followed. One particular reason is because it may be tempting for researchers to cut corners on ethical behavior in the energetic search for scientific answers. There are many other reasons. Unfortunately, the numbers of these ethical transgressions in scientific inquiry are staggering to contemplate. One of the most dramatic examples is the case of Diederik Stapel who manufactured data for approximately 50 scholarly articles and may have done so for his doctoral work. He did confess his transgressions and returned/renounced his doctoral degree (Levelt, 2014). The initial reports came out in September of 2011 and the full analyses of three commissions which investigated the unethical behaviors may be read at www.commissielevelt.nl

It is because of the many human research transgressions that the United States Department of Health and Human Services put in place the principles of the famous Belmont Report in April of 1979. The basic ethical principles are detailed under the concepts of Respect for Persons, Beneficence, and Justice. The full report can be obtained at the following web address: www.hhs.gov/ohrp/humansubjects/guidance/belmont.html but very briefly, from pages two and three of the report, the *respect for persons* provision requires that "individuals should be treated as autonomous agents, and second, that persons with diminished autonomy are entitled to protection." Under beneficence, "Persons are treated in an ethical manner not only by respecting their decisions and protecting them from harm but also by making efforts to secure their well-being." The idea of justice is captured by, "Who ought to receive the benefits of research and bear its burdens?" These principles and the supporting explications offer substantial guidance to Institutional Review Boards who oversee research on human subjects to determine whether or not the research will be conducted ethically (National Commission, 1979). They can also give STEM educators insights about ethical behavior for themselves and their students. If we think back to the "Golden Rice" study, who benefited? Was it the rice producer, the researcher, or the participants? It is likely the children bore too heavy a burden given the ethical transgressions.

How long have we humans have been struggling to work out our ethical behaviors? Would 2, 400 years be about right? That takes us back to the Hippocratic Oath which has supposedly been guiding medical doctors since it was proposed in about 400 B.C. It may predate Aristotle's work on ethics (publication dates and authors of ancient texts are a little uncertain). Translations of the Hippocratic Oath are very interesting. One of the best known advisories in the Oath is to do no harm. Another is to not have sexual relations with patients, whether they are male or female, free or enslaved. The code also speaks to the necessity of keeping in confidence all the personal information acquired while treating a patient (Tyson, 2001). Those statements seem quite modern though they are ancient.

It seems that humans have been facing deep ethical issues for thousands of years and we are still working on them and expanding the applications and are now moving our ethical inquiry to Science/Technology/Engineering/Math (STEM). STEM educators who are aware of past and potential ethical transgressions may wish to enhance their own sensitivity to ethics within STEM instruction. They may also choose to assist their students in doing so by causing them to write ethical codes for themselves and make use of them. I will give suggestions for that process later in the chapter but for now I turn from science to technology.

Technology and Ethics

Let's take another example—one from technology in the areas of Big Data and Little Data. Let's do the intersection of Big Data (BD) and Little Data (LD) first. (Big Data is a phrase in common use—Little Data, so far as I know, has been used the first time here.) The example is as follows. To what degree is the collection of personal information from our digital trails ethical? Some say it is legal but is it ethical just because it is legal? The National Security Agency is one collector and user of digital information and there were a lot of technical and math people writing algorithms to make it happen. We have recently heard that Google and other providers are often handing out information about us and they are using it themselves to serve their own interests. Even the local police are using personal digital trails.

In 2013, a murder suspect who was also a licensed MD traveled across several states and then allegedly murdered a man and a woman in their own home. He shot one and stabbed the other. Within days the police had tracked him digitally using cell phone records, credit card records, internet searches, and more. All the tracking was reported in the Omaha World Herald between May and September (O'Brien, Skelton, & Cooper, 2013). It was also reported on the local evening news programs.

As we all know now, aside from the other records mentioned, there are video records at many convenient stores, there are license plate scanners, and there is facial identification software in use. Most of this is available without a search warrant, according to authors Daniel Zwerdling and G. W. Schulz reporting for National Public Radio (NPR) and the Center for Investigative Reporting. This situation is often called living in the world of BD. The storehouses of BD are searched by many users and they reveal information about each of us, individually, as well as collectively. When users drill down through BD to the individual level, they are in LD. Generally, today, BD is seen as ethical while LD may not be, especially without legal permission or a personal release.

Even though most of us receive letter after letter claiming that our personal medical data, banking data, phone data, email data, and more are private; it is usually a lie, or at least a very special use of the word "private." Now the word lie is a very strong word and it means there is intent to obscure the truth. It is unethical to pretend to protect private data and then hand it out at the slightest pretext of legitimacy. NPR reports that Google will, with a court order (not a warrant) provide "your name, IP address, the dates and times you're signing in and out, and with whom you're exchanging emails" (Zwerdling & Schulz, 2013).

In the same article, NPR reports that, "The Electronic Communications Privacy Act of 1986 was designed to protect Americans who at the time were using the Internet increasingly to communicate. But the government has interpreted the law to mean that once your emails are opened or older than 180 days, no warrant is required" (Zwerdling & Schulz, 2013). Search warrants, court orders, or subpoenas are supposed to be required to do searches of private information. Those are legal requirements but also not completing one of the requirements carries ethical implications and those implications tie back to the technology side of STEM. It may be that making a profit from the sale of such information, or making uses of it that were never intended, will be judged to be unethical while protecting the information from unintended uses will be labeled as ethical.

The technological people of today and the near future will decide these issues and they ought to make the decisions from a strong ethical base. Who are these people? Perhaps they are the students STEM teachers educate.

They are also people who specialize in data analytics but one big business (ConAgra) has renamed it "customer analytics," and there are others (Soderlin, 2013). Now, supposedly they are working in BD but they do drill down to shopper #2980001 and other individual shoppers. The idea is to use individual customer shopping data to refine product creation, product management, and to enhance sales (profits). Whether individuals are protected is open to question but the ethical answer is, yes, they must be. Maybe they are—ethical persons in the field of data analytics should make sure of it while they apply their ethical codes.

As for how they make sure of it—working within the system is the first step but whistle blowing seems to be the most productive path. That is the reason for laws protecting them. For example, we are as yet uncertain about whether Edward Snowden will be judged as an ethical whistle blower or as a criminal. Nevertheless, his situation may be instructive. Mr. Snowden revealed what he considered to be criminal activity by the United States government, along with British and Israeli governments, in their uses of secret surveillance programs operated partly by the NSA. He seems to have adopted his ethical principles from various sources, including the United States Constitution.

Jeffrey Toobin, a lawyer and journalist wrote an article on Snowden. Toobin said, while introducing a quote by Snowden, "Snowden provided information to the *Washington Post* and the *Guardian*, which also posted a video interview with him. In it, he describes himself as appalled by the government he served:

> [These are now Snowden's words] The N.S.A. has built an infrastructure that allows it to intercept almost everything. With this capability, the vast majority of human communications are automatically ingested without targeting. If I wanted to see your e-mails or your wife's phone, all I have to do is use intercepts. I can get your e-mails, passwords, phone records, credit cards. I don't want to live in a society that does these sort (sic) of things… I do not want to live in a world where everything I do and say is recorded. That is not something I am willing to support or live under" (Toobin, 2013).

Apparently some European leaders do not want to live under such conditions of surveillance either since the USA has taken considerable heat from them for having done surveillance there using the NSA. I raise this issue to show how complex ethical decisions can be. Is the greater good of no terrorist attacks more important than individual privacy? Are there ways to have both? Was Snowden doing the ethical thing when he blew the whistle? It is this sort of scenario than can be useful to STEM educators when they want their students to discuss complicated ethical problems.

Ethics and Engineers

There are at least four groups of engineers and their work in moving society forward is legendary. They are the American Society of Civil Engineers (ASCE), the American Institute of Electrical Engineers (AIEE), the American Society of Mechanical Engineers (ASME), and the American Institute of Mining Engineers (AIME). Three of the groups have specific ethical codes. AIME does not.

Part of the stimulus for codes were the numerous disasters involving bridge failures, building collapses, and other structural issues. Here are three events which are common knowledge among most citizens and certainly among most engineers. One of the most famous early disasters related to engineering is the Boston Molasses Disaster of January 1919. A tank storing over two million gallons of molasses burst and sent waves of molasses down streets and into buildings. Over 50 people and many animals died. Apparently, the rivets holding the panels of the tank failed. Who was responsible? Perhaps the weather but engineers who designed the tank accepted some of the blame.

A second famous event occurred with Columbia where seven NASA astronauts died upon re-entry into the atmosphere of the earth due to a structural failure of the space shuttle. A third is the Hyatt Regency Hotel walkway collapse where two walkways collapsed onto people in the lobby. One hundred fourteen people were killed and over 200 were injured. Apparently, inadequate steel support rods were the cause of the failure, along with the design of the walkway. Were these design failures, construction failures, or something else for engineers to worry about?

What are the ethical clashes here? Engineers have a huge responsibility for designing structurally sound buildings, bridges, and more. The questions always are compelling: Is the design correct? Are the specified materials appropriate? Is the structure put together properly? Are the limits to the structure clearly known and specified (load limits on bridges for example)? How long will the structure last and remain strong enough to do what it was designed to do? How much damage will cause it to fail? From an ethical perspective, all those questions need definitive answers before a structure is released for human use. Also, a time specification for length of use is desirable but is a very challenging question to answer precisely.

I am not sure how many groups of engineers there are. Perhaps no one knows and, in any case, there are new ones being created all the time. I know of automotive engineers, ballistic engineers, agricultural equipment engineers, and would you believe it…food engineers. I will spare the reader a longer list but will probe the ethics related to food engineers.

The food engineer has many problems to solve and the one that involves the most profit is how to make food taste good, really delicious, so that the grocery shopper will develop brand loyalty and will want to purchase large amounts of a particular food and consume it. In order for this to occur, the bliss point needs to be sought and achieved—this requires food engineering, or optimization. These terms come from various people and are reported in Michael Moss's (a winner of the Pulitzer Prize) book: Salt, Sugar, Fat (Random House, 2013). Bliss point is attributed to Robert McBride on page 11. According to Moss, McBride said, "For all ingredients in food and drink, there is an optimum concentration at which the sensory pleasure is maximal. This optimum level is called the bliss point" (Moss, 2013). Now the ethical problem is do, or can, bliss point foods which are highly processed also provide superb nutrition? Or, are they by their very nature unhealthy? If they are inherently unhealthy, should they be sold for human consumption?

There is a wonderful or horrible, depending on one's point of view, ethical clash in the word optimization. Optimization is part of the process in finding the bliss point. Moss notes on page 29 of his book, "Grocery products have lots of attributes that make them attractive, chief among them color, smell, packaging, and taste. In the craft called optimization, food engineers alter these variables…with the sole intent of finding the most perfect variation…" (Moss, 2013). Moss reports on a famous food engineer named Howard Moskowitz who spends his time and the time of his employees finding the bliss point for grocery items. Moss explained some of the ethical issues in the form of health problems related to high intakes of salt, sugar, fat, such as obesity and heart disease. Moss reports on page 31 that Moskowitz, "… said he had no qualms about his own pioneering work on the bliss point or any of the other systems that helped food companies create the greatest amount of crave." Then Moss quotes Moskowitz directly. Moskowitz said, according to Moss, "There's no moral issue for me," he said flatly. "I did the best science I could" (Moss, 2013).

Well, there you have it. Ethical decision points are all around us and even engineers have to make ethical or unethical decisions—their work is not neutral. As STEM educators, we can help our students think about ethical issues and be aware of the absence of neutrality. Before I leave this food engineering category, let me look at one simple ingredient—SUGAR!

In the *National Geographic* of August, 2013 there is an article on sugar that gives a fascinating account of the growth in human consumption of sugar and the unhealthy implications of it. Rich Cohen reports in the article, "Sugar Love: A Not So Sweet Tale" (p. 78) that USA citizens consume nearly 23 teaspoons a day, partly because it is dumped in great volumes into our food. Humans love sugar and one reason is how it affects our brains. We can become addicted to it. Cohen reports that endocrinologist Robert Lustig of the University of California, San Francisco says, "Sugar is a poison by itself when consumed at high doses" (p. 96). Sugar is what creates and/or contributes to obesity, diabetes, high blood pressure and other food related diseases, according to Cohen and his sources.

In March of 2014, the World health Organization called for a substantial reduction in sugar consumption to six teaspoons a day. The American Heart Association is already on record recommending nine teaspoons a day for men and six for women (Jaslow, 2014). Now, given what the average USA citizen consumes and what is recommended, it seems the food engineers (optimizers and bliss pointers) have some explaining to do and may need to revisit their ethical codes. Moskowitz's best science needs to be integrated with best health practices or food damage to humans may occur, or may continue to occur.

Math plus Technology and Ethics

STEM educators are working with students who are learning to integrate the disciplines and use them in solving problems. Mathematicians have the skills to create algorithms to solve complicated math and technology related issues. It is possible that such an algorithm might appear to be neutral. That is, it is value free. I am not sure if mathematicians have a highly tuned channel for values or for ethics—probably some do and some do not but let me take an example to illustrate the issues that STEM educators may wish to address.

Let's suppose that a person with the skills to do so creates an algorithm or a string of them that will be used in what is called an Onion Router, or anonymizing Tor network. This is a special network of computers using a series of algorithms to confound the Internet addresses of the computers and to bounce content from one computer to another. This makes it nearly impossible to track the path of the messages on the computers. Exactly this process has been recently used to disguise the origin of transactions on the Silk Road website. This site marketed illegal products and used Bitcoins, a virtual currency that can be bought and stored online, to allow purchases to take place. That way anyone who purchases the illegal products cannot be tracked through charge cards or bank accounts. Federal agents decided this was an illegal activity making millions of dollars for its alleged creator, Ross Ulbricht, a former physics major at The University of Texas at Dallas. So, they arrested him (Leger, 2013).

Here is the ethics question—is it acceptable for a math/computer person to create algorithms which can be used in Onion Routing computer traffic on the Internet?

Let me draw an everyday comparison. Is it ethical to create a knife? It could be an object of art, a kitchen utensil, or a murder weapon. Is it ethical to create a knife if the creator knows, after it is sold, it will be used to commit a murder? The idea here is the tool may be innocent but the user may or may not be ethical. Creators of instruments using STEM expertise may not be able to control the uses to which the tools will be put. Nevertheless, they need effective protective systems in place or they could be held accountable for misuses. Also, they might decide that the potential for harm is so great that the algorithm or tool should not be distributed. It is very hard not to want to share a brainchild but the ethical issues should at least be considered.

Universal Human Ethic

There is another ethical issue in the rice example mentioned a few paragraphs earlier…who benefits from Genetically Modified Organisms--people or companies? I will not go too deeply into this at the moment but it is a world view issue, along with being a Belmont Report issue.

What is a world view? It comes back to one's philosophy of life and it also always comes back to a value system. Some of our values are given to us by important people in our lives and some are acquired when we choose to adopt them.

In philosophy there are three branches of inquiry tied to three basic questions. 1) What is the nature of reality (metaphysics)? 2) What is the nature of knowledge (epistemology)? 3) And, what is the nature of values (axiology)? Under the values branch comes ethics. Our philosophical system guides our world view. Our value system has the largest impact on our ethical behavior and that system often operates sub rosa, under or almost under one's radar. Let us leave the exploration of philosophy there for a moment and return to the marketing ethics issue compared to the universal human ethic, as hinted at in the preceding paragraph and along the way we can consider values. We must also keep in mind the social context of ethical and unethical behavior which seeps into the minds of STEM educators and STEM students. The social context may corrupt STEM students' minds and warp an existing value system and budding ethical code.

Paulo Freire, in his book, PEDAGOGY OF FREEDOM: Ethics, Democracy, and Civic Courage (1998), delineates the differences between the two ethical approaches. The marketing ethic is focused toward the ethics within the business model oriented primarily toward making a profit. Profiting off the backs of those living without adequate nutrition would not be acceptable, according to Freire's perspective (p. 23). It would be unethical from a universal human ethics standpoint but could be ethical from a marketing ethics perspective. Even the marketing perspective is supposed to remain inside legal boundaries.

Should a STEM researcher be a servant to a company poised to make a huge profit from a GMO? Will the gain in a healthful diet counterbalance the profit motive and profit making/taking? These are not easy ethical questions when the diversity of human interests is taken into account. Simply making a profit is not a crime but making a profit unethically may be criminal as well as immoral.

As for the legal side of things, the record is quite dismal. Business is a STEM concern since companies hire educators, scientists, computer programmers, engineers, and mathematicians. It seems that the biggest businesses occasionally have little concern for legalities and we can infer there are few concerns for the greater good of society (an ethical principle). That means there is little interest in worrying about the components of a universal human ethic like that advocated by Freire.

For example, JPMorgan has agreed to a $13 billion fine for its role in the 2008 financial crisis which harmed so many citizens in the USA and elsewhere in the world. The crime was violating Federal securities law by selling bad mortgage securities (rt.com, 2013).

There is more— Johnson and Johnson, which advertises itself on its webpage as having the credo: "The values that guide our decision making are spelled out in Our Credo. Put simply, Our Credo challenges us to put the needs and well-being of the people we serve first." (Johnson and Johnson, 2013) That sentence sounds like a component in a universal human ethic, and the words might be worth incorporating into an ethical code written by STEM students. Yet, the company was fined 2.2 billion dollars in November of 2013 for marketing drugs for unapproved uses and for paying doctors and nursing homes bribes to prescribe those drugs (ABC News, 2013).

Another example from the business world causes me to imagine there is a low interest in being ethical and having the public good in mind—Steve Cohen's SAC Capital will pay a record 1.8 billion dollar fine because the company is guilty of criminal insider trading. According to money.cnn.com, Cohen and company fostered a culture of insider trading "that was substantial, pervasive, and on a scale without known precedent." The quoted words come from language by the Federal prosecutors in their indictment, as reported by O'Toole and Isidore (O'Toole & Isidore, 2013). It is possible that Mr. Cohen himself and others in the company may face prosecution. Furthermore, the company will no longer manage money for outside investors.

Given this unethical cultural context in the USA, and given the rampant transgressions against a universal human ethic within the country by researchers, businesses, and others, we must consider to what degree STEM educators are being sensitized or desensitized regarding a system of universal human ethics, or even any ethical system. These same ethical issues permeate STEM activities and instruction and they permeate the lives of those who practice in one or more of the STEM disciplines. There are plentiful numbers of transgressions to report in every discipline and branch of society but are there advisories like the Hippocratic Oath in STEM areas? The answer is yes and I list some of them in the following section.

Standards and Ethics

Many performance standards for educators and subject area specialists declare that ethical behaviors are required. A reading of the InTASC (Interstate Teacher Assessment and Support Consortium) and ISTE (International Society for Technology in Education) standards reveal that both require ethical behaviors of educators. For example, InTASC Standard #9 says, under Critical Dispositions 9 (o): "The teacher understands the expectations of the profession including codes of ethics, professional standards of practice, and relevant law and policy" (Council, 2013, p. 41).

ISTE standard VI notes that there are standards for social, ethical, legal, and human issues which need to be met by all educators. These are tied specifically to computer and other technologies (ISTE, 2000).

The separate disciplines of Science, Technology, Engineering, and Math each have published ethical codes which present standards for ethical behavior. In the interest of illustrating a few of the codes, I have given some in toto or excerpted from them and noted the sites, usually online, where they can be found. There are many more than I have listed below so the listing is simply an illustration of the efforts professional organizations have made. STEM students can use them as stimulants for their thinking but must also create personalized and customized codes to meet their particular needs. This is so because the code a person develops is tied to a genuine, personal belief system and will be more likely than a professional society's to operate when it is needed. Even so, codes from professional societies are useful and can stimulate the thinking required for formulating a personal code. I have listed codes below from Science, Technology, Engineering, and Math.

Science. These ethical guidelines are from Sir David King of the United Kingdom where he is the government's chief scientific advisor. They were referenced in *The Guardian*, March, 2007 and archived in August, 2007.
"Rigour, respect and responsibility: A universal ethical code for scientists"
This is a public statement of the values and responsibilities of scientists. They are intended to include anyone whose work uses scientific methods, including social, natural, medical and veterinary sciences, engineering and mathematics. It aims to foster ethical research, to encourage active reflection among scientists on the wider implications and impacts of their work, and to support constructive communication between scientists and the public on complex and challenging issues.

Individuals and institutions are encouraged to adopt and promote these guidelines. It is meant to capture a small number of broad principles that are shared across disciplinary and institutional boundaries. They are not intended to replace codes of conduct or ethics relating to specific professions or areas of research.

Rigour, respect and responsibility: A universal ethical code for scientists
Rigour, honesty and integrity

- Act with skill and care in all scientific work. Maintain up to date skills and assist their development in others.
- Take steps to prevent corrupt practices and professional misconduct. Declare conflicts of interest.
- Be alert to the ways in which research derives from and affects the work of other people, and respect the rights and reputations of others.

Respect for life, the law and the public good

- Ensure that your work is lawful and justified.
- Minimise and justify any adverse effect your work may have on people, animals and the natural environment.

Responsible communication: listening and informing

- Seek to discuss the issues that science raises for society. Listen to the aspirations and concerns of others.
- Do not knowingly mislead, or allow others to be misled, about scientific matters. Present and review scientific evidence, theory or interpretation honestly and accurately" (King, 2007).

Technology. These commandments are from (computerethicsinstitute.org):

The Ten Commandments
1. Thou shalt not use a computer in ways that may harm people.

2. Thou shalt not interfere with other people's computer work.
3. Thou shalt not snoop around in other people's computer files.
4. Thou shalt not use a computer to steal.
5. Thou shalt not use a computer to false witness.
6. Thou shalt not copy or use proprietary software for which you have not paid.
7. Thou shalt not use other people's computer resources without authorization or proper compensation.
8. Thou shalt not appropriate other people's intellectual output.
9. Thou shalt think about the social consequences of the program you are writing or the system you are designing.
10. Thou shalt always use a computer in ways that ensure consideration and respect for your fellow humans" (Computer Ethics Institute, n.d.).

Engineering (Fundamental Canons)

Engineers, in the fulfillment of their professional duties, shall:

1. Hold paramount the safety, health, and welfare of the public.
2. Perform services only in areas of their competence.
3. Issue public statements only in an objective and truthful manner.
4. Act for each employer or client as faithful agents or trustees.
5. Avoid deceptive acts.
6. Conduct themselves honorably, responsibly, ethically, and lawfully so as to enhance the honor, reputation, and usefulness of the profession" (NSPE, 2006).

The Fenn College of Engineering at the Cleveland State University held the first ceremony on the Order of the Engineer in 1970. Here are the declarations.

"I am an engineer, in my profession I take deep pride. To it I owe solemn obligations. Since the stone-age, human progress has been spurred by the engineering genius. Engineers have made usable nature's vast resources of material and energy for humanity's benefit. Engineers have vitalized and turned to practical use the principles of science and the means of technology.

Were it not for this heritage of accumulated experience, my efforts would be feeble. As an engineer, I pledge to practice integrity and fair dealing, tolerance, and respect, and to uphold devotion to the standards and the dignity of my profession, conscious always that my skill carries with it the obligation to serve humanity by making the best use of Earth's precious wealth.

As an engineer, [in humility and with the need for Divine guidance,] I shall participate in none but honest enterprises.

When needed, my skill and knowledge shall be given without reservation for the public good. In the performance of duty and in fidelity to my profession, I shall give the utmost.

- The Obligation of the Engineer" (Fenn College, 2013).

Math. The American Mathematical Society (AMS) has the following ethical guidelines.

"ETHICAL GUIDELINES OF THE AMERICAN MATHEMATICAL SOCIETY
Adopted by the Council of the American Mathematical Society in January 2005…

I. MATHEMATICAL RESEARCH AND ITS PRESENTATION

The public reputation for honesty and integrity of the mathematical community and of the Society is its collective treasure and its publication record is its legacy.

The knowing presentation of another person's mathematical discovery as one's own constitutes plagiarism and is a serious violation of professional ethics. Plagiarism may occur for any type of work, whether written or oral and whether published or not.

The correct attribution of mathematical results is essential, both because it encourages creativity, by benefiting the creator whose career may depend on the recognition of the work and because it informs the community of when, where, and sometimes how original ideas entered into the chain of mathematical thought. To that end, mathematicians have certain responsibilities, which include the following:

To endeavor to be knowledgeable in their field, especially about work related to their research; To give appropriate credit, even to unpublished materials and announced results (because the knowledge that something is true or false is valuable, however it is obtained); To publish full details of results that are announced without unreasonable delay, because claiming a result in advance of its having been achieved with reasonable certainty injures the community by restraining those working toward the same goal; to use no language that suppresses or improperly detracts from the work of others; To correct in a timely way or to withdraw work that is erroneous.

A claim of independence may not be based on ignorance of widely disseminated results. On appropriate occasions, it may be desirable to offer or accept joint authorship when independent researchers find that they have produced identical results. All the authors listed for a paper, however, must have made a significant contribution to its content, and all who have made such a contribution must be offered the opportunity to be listed as an author. Because the free exchange of ideas necessary to promote research is possible only when every individual's contribution is properly recognized, the Society will not knowingly publish anything that violates this principle, and it will seek to expose egregious violations anywhere in the mathematical community.

II. SOCIAL RESPONSIBILITY OF MATHEMATICIANS

The Society promotes mathematical research together with its unrestricted dissemination, and to that end encourages all to engage in this endeavor. Mathematical ability must be respected wherever it is found, without regard to race, gender, ethnicity, age, sexual orientation, religious belief, political belief, or disability.

The growing importance of mathematics in society at large and of public funding of mathematics may increasingly place members of the mathematical community in conflicts of interest. The appearance of bias in reviewing, refereeing, or in funding decisions must be scrupulously avoided, particularly where decisions may affect one's own research, that of colleagues, or of one's students. When conflicts of interest occur, one should withdraw from the decision-making process.

A recommendation accurately reflecting the writer's views is often given only on the understanding that it be kept confidential; therefore, a request for a recommendation must be assumed to carry an implicit promise of confidentiality, unless there is a statement to the contrary. Similarly, a referee's report is normally provided with the understanding

that the name of the writer be withheld from certain interested parties, and the referee must be anonymous unless otherwise indicated in advance. The writer of the recommendation or report must respond fairly and keep confidential any privileged information, personal or mathematical, that the writer receives. If the requesting individual, institution, agency or company becomes aware that confidentiality or anonymity can not be maintained, that should be immediately communicated.
Where choices must be made and conflicts are unavoidable, as with editors or those who decide on appointments or promotions, it is essential to keep careful records that would demonstrate the process was indeed fair when inspected at a later time.

Freedom to publish must sometimes yield to security concerns, but mathematicians should resist excessive secrecy demands whether by government or private institutions. When mathematical work may affect the public health, safety or general welfare, it is the responsibility of mathematicians to disclose the implications of their work to their employers and to the public, if necessary. Should this bring retaliation, the Society will examine the ways in which it may want to help the "whistle-blower", particularly when the disclosure has been made to the Society.

No one should be exploited by the offer of a temporary position at an unreasonably low salary and/or an unreasonably heavy work load" (AMS, 2005). In addition, the society has guidelines for III Educating and Granting Degrees, and IV Publications which I have omitted due to space considerations.

A worthwhile exercise for the STEM educators and students is to seek commonalities among the codes from these societies. They can then be tied back to the Belmont Report and other published statements on ethics. Those insights can then be used as aids in the development of each STEM educator's ethical code.

Too Much Unethical Behavior

So, now we have an introduction to ethics and some illustrations, which hint at STEM education issues. STEM educators need to be aware that many of the aspects of Science, Technology, Engineering, and Math are laced with ethical issues. Because scientists and technical people often tend to view their work as neutral (unbiased), they may imagine it, and they, are less likely to fall into ethical traps. Nothing could be more distant from reality, as I have endeavored to illustrate.

Now, simply reading an organization's listing of ethical codes is not the same as personally internalizing a full range of ethical behaviors. Knowing something is wrong does not always prevent someone from doing wrong. Does Lance Armstrong come to mind? Another illustration is the Enron mismanagement and the resultant convictions, which authenticate the existence unethical behaviors on the part of numerous executives in the company. Another is the Tuskegee fiasco labeled research by the U.S. Public Health Service headed by Dr. Taliaferro Clark— hundreds of syphilis infected men were left untreated from 1929 to 1972 and they were not informed of their infection. The government eventually admitted wrong doing, paid a $10 million settlement, and promised lifetime medical benefits to survivors and their families. Unfortunately, a half a century of unethical behavior passed before all that occurred. The Tuskegee case is not unique.
A similar case occurred in Guatemala in the 1940s but was only recently reported. Mike Stobbe gives the following information.

"The Guatemala experiments are already considered one of the darker episodes of medical research in U.S. history, but panel members say the new information indicates that the researchers were unusually unethical, even when placed into the historical context of a different era.

"The researchers put their own medical advancement first and human decency a far second," said Anita Allen, a member of the Presidential Commission for the Study of Bioethical Issues" (Stobbe, 2011).

Quite simply, there is too much unethical behavior and our students need personalized, customized ethics codes to guide their professional lives. I will now make some suggestions for enabling that to occur.

Creating a Personal Ethics System

When a person begins to think seriously about an individualized ethical code, a statement in essay form or bullet form, which captures one's ideas about ethical, moral, and righteous behavior, he or she may wonder where such a thing may be found. Is it pre-packaged in one's mind at birth? Is it acquired by directive from authority figures such as parents, teachers, or religious leaders? Perhaps it is simply learned by living. Perhaps there are little bits from all of those areas, and others, too, such as professional organizations.

There is some evidence emerging that suggests we are born with an understanding of good and bad. Of course, the understanding is undeveloped and unprepared for the complexities of life. So, those enhancements must be acquired. Kelly Wallace reports on the Yale University's Infant Cognition Center and the Center's work on morality. Wallace writes and quotes as follows:

"Humans are born with a hard-wired morality, a sense of good and evil is bred in the bone," wrote Paul Bloom, Yale's Brooks and Suzanne Ragen professor of psychology, in an opinion piece for CNN.com.

Bloom, author of the new book "Just Babies: The Origins of Good and Evil," collaborated on the research with his wife, Karen Wynn, a professor of psychology at Yale University.

"We are naturally moral beings, but our environment can enhance -- or sadly, degrade -- this innate moral sense," Bloom said (Wallace, 2013).

Unfortunately, our inborn sense of right and wrong appears to be quite immature, and may, over time, be degraded by living in an unethical society or by poor thinking. So, we as STEM educators have our work to do.

Maybe the philosophers are right that the ethical code comes from values but where do humans get values? Also, how strong are the values in directing behavior? How much does guilt come into play? Is guilt always present and always corrective?

Along with philosophers we have bioethicists and we have social psychologists who can give us insights. Let me suppose that all STEM educators want to do right and not do wrong. Rightness and wrongness are problematic as the practitioners who wrote the Belmont report realized. Yet, problems have solutions and sometimes consensus is present. The consensus was to agree on three broad principles (mentioned earlier) and to insist upon IRB approval. Even so, in the day to day lives we participate in, we may not have time to convene our personal IRB committee before we make decisions!

To what extent does each of us have an IRB inside of us to approve plans for living, for teaching, for working? I hope all those questions have been illuminating, but let me turn to some very powerful flashlights which can give us guidance on our development of a code and then I will explain the process I recommend for producing an individualized and customized ethical code which should pass inspection and be useful to keep people out of jail and from harming other persons. Such a code may even guide a person toward virtuous behavior.

Let me recommend an online activity and two books which can serve as illuminating flashlights. The online activity is a survey, which is safe and private. No data are collected from any participant. Persons who take the survey receive the gift of a report on philosophical preferences, which may be printed out. Knowing one's philosophical labels will help a person know how his or her value system works and whether it is absolutist or relativist. An example of an absolute value could be life and whether it is ever acceptable, even in self- defense, to kill another human. If the answer is that killing is never right—not in self-defense, not in a time of war, never—then it is absolute. Relativists would say that under certain extreme circumstances, killing another human would be acceptable.

Upon completing the survey, which has been validated by its use within an undergraduate course by over 5000 students, each participant will know how he or she ranks on the four main philosophies—idealism, realism, pragmatism, and existentialism. Persons who answer the prompts truthfully are always correctly labeled. Most of the time persons who lean toward idealism or realism also lean toward absolute values. Those who learn toward pragmatism or existentialism will lean toward relativistic values. The URL for the website is: coeportfolio.unomaha.edu/philosophy It was created by Dr. Harrison Means and Dr. Paul Clark (Be sure to go all the way down to the bottom to see the calculate survey button. If the website is not working, there is a "paper and pencil version at the end of this chapter.) Having an understanding of one's philosophical preferences is useful in creating a record of one's ethical system. I will present more on that later, along with some procedures for writing a philosophy statement.

Now, let me turn to the books. The first book, which acts as an illuminating flashlight, is Taking Sides Clashing Views on Bioethical Issues by Carol Levine. In this 14th Edition (McGraw Hill, 2013), Levine has prepared a superb introduction on the sources of ethics. It is a short course on the history and players in the creation of ethical systems. Equally important are the 22 bioethical issues with advocates for and against. The deliberations show, if nothing else, that ethical issues usually are very complicated.

One of the first issues she explores is Truth Telling. It is issue number two and begins on page 23. The question is one most people can readily understand. Put in practical terms, does the doctor owe the patient the truth about terminal cancer? "Telling the truth, the whole truth, and nothing but the truth..." has a long tradition in western society but for generations most doctors withheld the truth from cancer patients and their families. Some still do. More recently, Levine says on pages 23-24 in her introduction to the scenario, "...what must be balanced in this decision are two significant principles of ethical conduct: the obligation to tell the truth and the obligation not to harm others..." (p. 24). Clearly, this illustrates the complexity that STEM educators should be aware of while they guide their students toward a meaningful ethical system. The book is full of stimulating scenarios and discussions and they are helpful for stimulating ethical thinking among STEM educators even though bioethics may not be a person's first interest.

One final point which I wish to draw from Levine comes in this quotation from her introduction (p. XIX), "Professional codes of ethics, to be sure, offer some guidance, but they are usually unclear and ambiguous about what to do in specific situations." I agree and that is the reason I recommend creating an individualized, personalized ethical code. So, what do you want from your doctor, or your mentor, or your teacher, or your students? Do you want the whole truth…? Of course, it is complex but each of us must have a sentence, or a paragraph, or a page to explain our ethical behavior for Truth Telling in our ethical code, in my opinion.

Now let me turn to the second book I recommend. It is Jonathan Haidt's, The Righteous Mind, Pantheon Books, 2012. As a social psychologist, Haidt is interested in empirical data about ethical decision-making and the sources from which it derives. He and his associates have collected a lot of it and use the data to formulate a Moral Foundations Theory (p. 124). There are six pieces and each piece ties into evolutionary psychology as well as the data. They are Care/harm, Fairness/cheating, Loyalty/betrayal, Authority/subversion, Sanctity/degradation, and Liberty/oppression. Haidt argues that these six cognitive modules are what guide our moral behaviors and they are more reactive than rational. He says the righteous mind responds intuitively to care, fairness, loyalty, authority, sanctity, and liberty. The cognitive modules also react to the opposites. For example, we may be repulsed by physical manifestations of disease or what we perceive as dirtiness (degradation). Our repulsion may interfere with our desire to provide care or equitable treatment. Haidt's explication of the modules is far more detailed than I can reconstruct here.

Still, it is through these modules that STEM educators may wish to guide students into an enhanced understanding of the buried codes they need to surface (bring to consciousness) so they can understand themselves and others better. Then they may be able to catch themselves before they fall into an unethical act. Too late realizations are not soon enough for ethical decisions. Just in time realizations are more protective.

Haidt says (p. 190), "…we care more about *looking* good than about truly *being* good. Intuitions come first, *strategic* reasoning second. We lie, cheat, and cut ethical corners quite often when we think we can get away with it, and then we use our moral thinking to manage our reputations and justify ourselves to others. We believe our post hoc reasoning so thoroughly that we end up self-righteously convinced of our own virtue." (Haidt, 2012) Haidt also says that picture of humans is true but it is not complete and our group identities and teamwork skills reveal a capacity for group interests over self-interest. This, Haidt believes, gives humans a mixture of selfishness and selflessness. I say it gives us a pathway to ethical behavior and the creation of an ethics system.

The Plan

Given these three flashlights to illuminate our way, I believe we can turn to a plan for creating a personalized and customized ethical code (system). An optional step can be to write a philosophy statement using information from the philosophy survey and other sources. This gets the students thinking about the three philosophical questions, plus their values, and whether or not they have absolute or relative values. Some of the values students often list are family, honesty (truth telling), trust, fairness (equity), love of country, duty, love, friendship (similar to family members), freedom, and others of a similar nature.

I do not believe having a philosophy statement with values listed and explained is an <u>absolute</u> requirement for success in ethics code construction but it will make it easier for students to transition into ethics because they will have some insights into philosophy and values as precursors to ethics.

An activity for constructing a set of philosophical preferences is available at online (coeportfolio.unomaha.edu/philosophy), as mentioned earlier. If the online version is not available, I have a "paper and pencil version" at the end of this chapter. Upon completing the Philosophy Preferences Survey, the student will have a label for four philosophies. Some hints at what the philosophical leanings mean are in the questions used to create them. Specific thumbnail definitions for the four philosophies may be found at plato.stanford.edu. There is a search box in the upper left hand corner of that website and the student can type in idealism, realism, pragmatism, and existentialism to read descriptions of the philosophical schools. Press return after typing in the name of the philosophy and there will be many documents to read. After reading and thinking about the survey, the STEM students may, and probably should, construct an essay which meets the following requirements.

Philosophy Essay Requirements

1. The first task for you is to analyze/synthesize and evaluate the data you collected about yourself when you took the Philosophy survey. You should decide whether your answers to the survey and the bar graph which is created from them are accurately labeling you as an idealist, realist, pragmatist, or existentialist. Only you can determine whether you have been accurately labeled. Nevertheless, if you are in touch with who you are and answer the questions truthfully, you will be correctly labeled.
2. Based on my philosophy survey results, it appears that I believe the nature of reality is: Explain what your survey results reveal. Make some statements, defend them, and give some concrete examples of how your philosophy translates into your view of reality.
3. After looking at the results of my philosophy survey, it looks like my beliefs regarding the nature of knowledge, and how I create knowledge inside my own mind, are: Make some statements, defend them, and give some concrete examples of how your philosophy translates into your view of knowledge.
4. My philosophical preferences lead me toward the following system of values: State at least seven values which are essential to you and explain why they are important to you. Explain where these values came from--did you make them up for yourself or get them from family, school, society, your religion, or someplace else?
5. My current thoughts (insert the date) on how my educational philosophy will translate into my future classroom approaches are as follows: Here you should try to make sense of what you have reported in 1, 2, 3 and 4 above and explain what kind of teacher you imagine you will be as a result of your philosophy.
6. My ethical code, which I will develop later, is part of my value system and my philosophy, but it will be maintained as a separate document.
7. After you have completed the text for items 1-5 above and completed your essay, you should write a one or two paragraph summary statement of your philosophy and

theory of education. Label the summary as an ABSTRACT. Think of it as an executive summary which will be meaningful for busy Human Resource people or Administrators who may be reviewing your applications for work in a particular school district or elsewhere. Place the Abstract at the beginning of your Philosophy statement and label it as an abstract. Be sure to name both your philosophy AND your theory of education in the abstract.

If you are an idealist or realist, predominantly, then your theory is likely to be perennialism/essentialism. If you are a pragmatist, predominantly, then your theory is likely to be progressivism/constructivism. If you are an existentialist, then you are likely to use the theories of constructivism and existentialism. The philosophy specification and values listing will be of assistance in preparing your ethics statement.

Preparing the Ethical Code

I created the following plan and have used it with over 5000 students and, when the students give it serious thought, they end up sensitized to ethics and have a written document to remind them of their ethical obligations. First I present a visual (Figure One) that shows the five steps to developing a code. The "View Ethics Portfolio" button number "6" signifies that the product is complete and the students can view all the components in the ethics activity. The students follow the directions as provided and I give more detail following the visual labeled Figure One.

Figure 1: Ethics Navigation

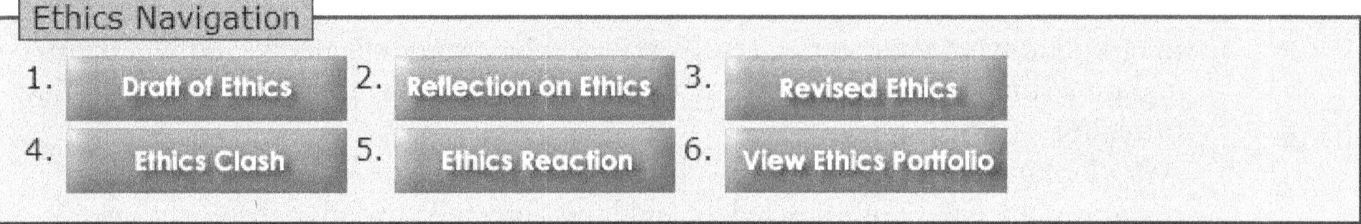

<u>Step one</u> is a draft of ethics. I coach the students by giving them ethical clashes in class or online to analyze. For example, Mrs. Cortez who was a third grade teacher was arrested after police discovered she was selling methamphetamines. She had about $27,000 in cash in her apartment. She had controlled substances on hand. She had a client list. I ask my students to discuss the ethical issues here in this scenario. They usually mention right away that the teacher is involved in an illegal activity (selling drugs). It takes a while before the students come up with the idea that she is putting her students at risk for harm in the event one of her drug customers comes to school, armed or not, and insists on getting his supplies right now—can't wait until later and after school. Or, perhaps they will raise the idea that she is a hypocrite in telling her students not to use drugs while she is a dealer and a user herself. If she is a regular user, it seems fair to ask if she always fully competent to care for her third grade students and whether she is fit for duty as a teacher.

I have another clash on a science teacher in Florida who asked his students to do experiments in chemical reactions. The particular reaction is to produce a remote controlled explosion and make a video recording of it. The activity may be motivating for adolescent males and it may qualify as a chemical reaction, but my students are quick to point out that the instructor may cause the students to be arrested for terrorist activities (bomb making) and blowing up an improvised explosive device (IED). Furthermore, the activity puts the students at risk of being harmed or harming others. There is disrespect for the law (authority) and more to discuss.

Once students develop a sense for what ethical and unethical behavior is through discussion, then they are ready to write. The first draft is usually somewhat underdeveloped because the students have not given much thought to ethical behavior during their lives. They have not brought ethics to the surface of their intellectual awareness even though they have been using a rudimentary ethical system for years.

Step two is reflection after having studied some other ethical systems. This is where the STEM educator collects some codes and asks the students to study them to extract some specifics to assist in the creation of personal guidelines for their own ethical system. The Belmont Report, codes from various professional societies in STEM disciplines like the ones shown earlier in this chapter, videos from state organizations, and books or chapters from books like the Haidt and Levine books are very useful. Obviously, the readings need to be concise where possible. Nevertheless, some reading is helpful in enabling the students to write an improved code. Here are two online sites I recommend: www.ethics.ubc.ca/papers/invited/colero.html (Colero, 1997) and josephsoninstitute.org/MED/MED-2sixpillars.html (Josephson, 1987)

There are also six online videos developed by the Nebraska Department of Education. They explore a variety of ethical issues and can be viewed at: **nppc.nol.org**—when arriving at the website, simply click on the video section and that will take you to the links to view the online videos (Nebraska, n.d.). (If the links do not work then search the Internet using the information in the references section or sometimes using a different browser will solve the problem.)

The improved code is step three. After studying, viewing, discussing, and thinking, each student should be in a position to expand and enhance his or her ethical code. Be sure to have the students be ethical in their use of sources and provide the proper citations in their essay. That will allow them to avoid the ethical transgression of plagiarism.

Steps four and five are to use the code. This works best if the student finds a clash to respond to and specifically references the written ethical system. I sprinkled such clashes throughout this chapter and my students have never had difficulty finding one to react to because they are everywhere and in every part of the social structure of the nation, including government and government officials. An online search will turn up thousands of clashes. The idea here is to cause each student to use his or her code to react to a genuine ethical clash.

Conclusion

In conclusion, let me say we cannot conduct our lives or our professional efforts without using our ethical systems and our philosophy. It is worth knowing what our ethics are and worth making serious efforts to refine them as we grow as professionals. This is equally true for us as educators and for our STEM students. I hope your journey toward cognitive growth in ethics is fruitful and that your written code is a useful guide in your personal and professional life. I also hope that each STEM educator is able to assist his or her students in creating a useful code of ethics.

References

ABC News. (2013, November 5). *Johnson and Johnson fined $2.2 billion for faulty drug claims, kickbacks*. Retrieved from http://ww.abc.net.au/news/2013-11-05/jj-fined-22bn-for-faulty-drug-claims-kickbacks/5070346

American Mathematical Society (AMS). (2005, January). *Ethical guidelines of the American mathematical society.* Retrieved from http://www.ams.org/about-us/governance/policy-statements/sec-ethics

Charles, D. (2013, September 17). *Golden Rice Study Violated Ethical Rules*. Retrieved from http://www.npr.org/blogs/thesalt/2013/09/17/223382375/golden-rice-study-violated-ethical-rules-tufts-says

Cohen, R. (2013, August). Sugar love: A not so sweet tale. *National Geographic, 2249*(2), 78-97.

Computer Ethics Institute. (n.d.) *Ten commandments of computer ethics.* Retrieved from http:// computerethicsinstitute.org

Colero, Larry. (1997). *A framework for universal principles of ethics*. Retrieved from http: www.ethics.ubc.ca/papers/invited/colero.html

Council of Chief State School Officers. (2013, April). Interstate Teacher and Support Consortium in InTASC *Model core teaching standards and learning progressions for teachers 1.0: A resource for ongoing teacher development*. Washington, DC: Author.

Fenn College. (2013, November*).* *Order of the engineer*. Retrieved from http:// en.wikipedia.org/wiki/Order_of_the_Engineer

Levelt Committee, Nort Committee, & Drenth Committee. (2014) *Flawed science: Fraudulent research practices of social psychologist Diederik Stapel*. Retrieved from http://www.commissielevelt.nl

Freire, P. (1998). *PEDAGOGY OF FREEDOM: Ethics, democracy, and civic courage*. New York, NY: Rowman & Littlefield Publishers, Inc.

Haidt, J. (2012). *The Righteous Mind.* New York, NY: Pantheon Books.

ISTE (International Society for Technology in Education). (2000). Retrieved from www.iste.org/docs/pdfs/nets_for_teachers_2000.pdf?sfvrsn=2

Jaslow, R. (2014, March 5). World Health Organization lowers sugar intake recommendations. *CBSnews.com.* Retrieved from http://www.cbsnews.com/news/world-health-organization-lowers-sugar-intake-recommendations

Johnson and Johnson. (2013, November). *Our credo*. Retrieved from http://www.jnj.com/about-jnj/jnj-credo

Josephson, M. (1987). *Josephson Institute Six Pillars*. Retrieved from josephsoninstitute.org/MED/MED-2sixpillars.html

King, D. (2007, August 8). *Rigour, respect, and responsibility: A universal ethical code for scientists*. Retrieved from http://webarchive.nationalarchives.gov.uk/+/http:/www.dti.gov.uk/science/science-and-society/public_engagement/code/page28030.html

Leger, D. (2013, October 3) End of the Road for 'Silk Road.' *USA TODAY*, 1A.

Levine, C. (2013). *Taking sides: Clashing views on bioethical Issues*. (14th ed.). New York, NY: The McGraw Hill Companies, Inc.

Means, H. & Clark, P. (2012) *Philosophy preferences survey*. Retrieved from http://coeportfolio.unomaha.edu/philosophy

Moss, M. (2013). *Salt, sugar, fat.* New York, NY: Random House, Inc.

National Commission for the Protection of Research Risks. (1979). *The Belmont Report: Ethical principles and guidelines for the protection of human subjects for research.* Washington, DC: Government Printing Office. Also available at www.hhs.gov/ohrp/humansubjects/guidance/belmont.htm

National Society of Professional Engineers (NSPE). (2006, July 24). *Code of ethics for engineers* . Online Ethics Center for Engineering, National Academy of Engineering. Retrieved from www.onlineethics.org/Resources/ethcodes/EnglishCodes/9972.aspx)

Nebraska Professional Practices Commission. (n.d.) *Videos*. Retrieved from nppc.nol.org

O'Brien, M., Skelton, A., & Cooper. T. (2013, August 15) Creighton slayings: Garcia's internet searches, DNA evidence help build case. *Omaha World Herald.* Retrieved from http://omaha.com/article/20130814/NEWS/130819514/1690

O'Toole, J., & Isidore, C. (2013, November 4*).* SAC Capital to plead guilty to insider trading charges. *CNN.com*. Retrieved from http://money.cnn.com/2013/11/04/investing/sac-settlement

Online Ethics Center for Engineering. (2013, November 7). *National society of professional engineers (NSPE) code of ethics for engineers*. Retrieved from www.onlineethics.org/Resources/ethcodes/EnglishCodes/9972.aspx

rt.com. (2013, October 20). *JPMorgan 'agrees' to tentative $13 billion penalty for role in 2008 financial crisis.* Retrieved from http://rt.com/business/morgan-deal-crisis-us-453

Toobin, J. (2013, June 10). Edward Snowden is no hero. *The New Yorker*. Retrieved from http:// www.newyorker.com/online/blogs/comment/2013/06/edward-snowden-nsa-leaker-is-no-hero.html

Tyson, P. (2001, March 27). *The Hippocratic oath today*. Retrieved from www.pbs.org/wgbh/nova/body/hippocratic-oath-today.html

Soderlin, B. (2013, October 1). Drilling deep in data 'Gold Mine'. *Omaha World Herald*, 1D-2D

Stobbe, M. (2011, August 29). *Guatemala experiments: Syphilis infections, other shocking details revealed about US medical experiments*. Retrieved from www.huffingtonpost.com/2011/08/29/guatemala-experiments_n_941284.html

Wallace, K. (2014). What babies know. *CNN.com*. Retrieved from http://www.cnn.com/2014/02/13/living/what-babies-know-anderson-cooper-parents

Zwerdling, D., & Schulz, G. W. (2013, September 30). Your digital trail and how it can be used against you. *NPR.org*. Retrieved from www.npr.org/blogs/alltechconsidered/2013/09/30/226835934/your-digital-trail-and-how-it-can-be-used-against-you

Appendix A
The "paper and pencil" version of the philosophy survey activity is printed below:

PHILOSOPHY PREFERENCES SURVEY
by
Harrison Means, Ph. D.
©
1992 and 2012 (revised)

Directions: This questionnaire is divided into eight sections of five statements each. You are to rank order the questions in each section using the following: 5 = statement with which you most agree; 3 = your second choice; 1 = your third choice and 0 = your fourth choice.

I. THE TEACHER

The teacher is ...

_____ 1. the model of the knowledgeable person we want students to become.
_____ 2. the director who focuses the student's attention to the world around them.
_____ 3. both a participant in the learning process with the child and a guide for the process.
_____ 4. the facilitator who helps each child choose what is individually important for them to learn.

II. REALITY

The real world for which we educate children is...

_____ 5. a world in which permanent natural laws are the source of knowledge.
_____ 6. a world in which activities of the mind are the source of knowledge.
_____ 7. the world in which social experience, in which we all participate, is the source of knowledge.
_____ 8. a world of individual choice and individual choice is the source of knowledge

---

III. REASONS FOR SCHOOLS

The primary reason schools exist is to...

_____ 9. provide experiences to foster societal improvement.

_____10. facilitate self-awareness of the individual student.
_____11. develop the student's ability to engage in intellectual activities.
_____12. develop an understanding of the orderly process in the natural environment.

IV. PEDAGOGY

The most effective instruction stresses...

_____13. choosing one own responses to the world.
_____14. finding solutions to problems that are real to the learner.
_____15. absorbing ideas through language and mastery of symbols.

_____16. the mastery of facts and information through direct observation.

V. THE STUDENTS ROLE IN THE SCHOOL

The student's role is to...

_____17. acquire knowledge about the natural laws that govern the world in which we live.

_____18. expand his/her mental capacity to grasp the intellectual ideas that lead us toward true learning.

_____19. determine what is truly meaningful; learning for one's self.

_____20. experience the process of learning from which all knowledge develops.

VI. TRUTH

Truth is...

_____21. found in intellectual contact with great ideas not in everyday experience.

_____22. what works to solve real problems for real people.

_____23. the discovery of natural laws that operate in all of nature, including the affairs of man.

_____24. what we individually determine it to be.

VII. THE CURRICULUM

The curriculum should be based on...

_____25. the information we have attained in a pursuit of the laws governing thee natural world.

_____26. the experiences that assist the learner in determining their own unique response to world.

_____27. the ideals and concepts that have stood the test of time.

_____28. activities that will help the learner understand that truth is the result of the collective experiences of the society.

VIII. VALUES

Values are...

_____29. the answers that yield the most satisfactory solutions for the majority of the society.

_____30. identified through the operation of natural laws in the affairs of man.

_____31. not found in the everyday experiences of man but are derived from a higher realm through the development of the intellect.

_____32. determined by each of us through the process of choosing value.

Go to the next page to tally the rankings….

Scoring Procedures for the Survey of Philosophy Preferences
Place the value you assigned to each item in the survey in the area for the item in the chart below. The total for each column indicates how your choices agree with the different philosophic positions.

Idealism	Realism	Pragmatism	Existentialism
1______	2________	3_________	4__________
6______	5________	7_________	8__________
11_____	12_______	9_________	10_________
15_____	16_______	14________	13_________
18_____	17_______	20________	19_________
21_____	23_______	22________	24_________
27_____	25_______	28________	26_________
31_____	30_______	29________	32_________
________ Total Idealist	__________ Total Realist	___________ Total Pragmatist	___________ Total Existentialist

Chapter Author(s)

Harrison J. Means – is a Professor of Teacher Education at the University of Nebraska at Omaha. He has worked extensively with Pre-service and practicing teachers in the area of Human Relations and is one of the universities leading experts in the implementation of ethical systems in teacher education and pedagogy. His efforts in the area of ethics in instruction and curriculum development have extended across the globe. He spent time in Pakistan assisting Afghan educators in developing a strategic plan to rebuild an educational system ravaged by a decade of war. His experiences have given him new insights and sensitivities to contributing in the area of ethics to emerging educational structures such as STEM learning.

Chapter 3

Metasystems Learning Design Approach for STEM Teaching, Learning and Assessment

ABSTRACT: Globalization emphasizes the role of didactical models in cognitive systems research. Didactical models aim to describe understanding and construction of knowledge through ontology and semantics, i.e. metasystems. The innovation of metasystems thinking is in savoir-vivre structure of competence, viewed as core capability of learner to be more adaptive and accommodative in both real and virtual learning environments. The basis of this approach, which is coined as META-Era, emphasizes the role of educational data mining, participatory design, personalized curricula and diversity of processes common for cognitive systems. This research goes beyond constructivist learning theory and attempts to explain behavioral changes through personalization of learning objects. Consequently, this chapter investigates cross-principles towards highlighting metasystems thinking in learning mathematics, technology, and science.

Introduction

Over the past centuries human society embraced the linear thinking paradigm. Rudic (2011) notes that majority of modern people are brought up in a linear style of thinking, whose main objective is to develop, implement and manage step by step instructions. Mathematical models of linear thinking prove *Scholastic Learning*, which often takes the form of *Explicit Disputation*: a topic drawn from the tradition is broached in the form of a question, opponents' responses are given, a counterproposal is argued and opponent's arguments rebutted. There are theories and models aimed to prove linear thinking. For example, *Theory of Operant Conditioning* suggested looking only at the observable causes of behavior. In case of programmed textbook, development emphasizes 'practice the correct responses, reinforce the right answer, and with minimum delay of reinforcement while taking successful small steps with hints'. Knowledge, acquired by learner, is controlled by immediate feedback. Learning is a change of probability between antecedents, operant responses, and consequences.

Negative effects of linear thinking were commented by many prominent researchers. Mainzer (2004) observed that linear thinking may be dangerous for non-linear reality with social networks, both real and virtual, in which learners are more 'homogeneous' than in formal schooling and where learning objects embody formalized concepts.

In opposition to linear thinking, system thinking is based on interdependences between input, output and environment. The systems can be open or closed. Mebratu (2001) describes systems thinking based on the premises of system composition consisting of a group of things or parts working together in a regular relationship. In contrast to cause-effect relationship, systems thinking model describes relationships between parts or entities which add positive or negative aspects to outcomes. A cause can lead to more than one effect (multifinality), while a number of causes can independently lead to an identical effect (equifinality).

Mora, Gelman, Cervantes, Mejía andWeitzenfeld (2003, p. 4) note that systems approach is a paradigm that emerged in the early 1940s. As noted it aimed to study phenomena characterized by extraordinary complexity, high level of interaction of its parts, and possession of properties that are lost if the whole phenomenon is considered partially isolated from its environment. Systems approach to instruction was advanced by Stolurow (1965) who noted that the proposed model described a tutorial system with: a) Pre-tutorial decisions which match individual differences among learners; b) Tutorial decisions which are implementation of a specific set of rules and c) Changing of tutorial decisions which involve the substitution of a set of rules whenever the previous set fails to produce the desired performance. As was noted by Edwards (2011), the systems thinking is the continual process of viewing, studying or otherwise observing a system. Elements within the system influence one another and external elements influence internal elements both directly and indirectly.

Toward Metasystems Thinking

Two schools of thought have challenged linear and systems thinking: *Quantum Psychology* (Oshins, 1989; Wilson, 1990) and *Knowledge Management* (Koulopoulos & Frappaolo, 2001), together leading to *Metasystems Learning Design* approach. According to Oshins (1989) the quantum psychology processes involve thoroughly specifying a collection of questions that have empirically distinguishable answers; specifying criteria by which observations pass and fail the test of the questions and, then, attempting to ask the questions of the relevant observation set. In quantum psychology, empirical truth is distinguished by whether or not the answer satisfies the agreed upon criteria. The term 'empirical logic' is sometimes used for formulation of facts and it is subject to indeterminacies and uncertainties of any empirical facts. Moreover, knowledge management strategies are used in order to strengthen learning, social networks and knowledge sharing. Knowledge management models provide rules for creation, retention and transfer of knowledge; and they are focused on meta-data, metacognition, meta-knowledge. In order to develop knowledge in learning environments focus is on metasystems thinking.

The fundamentals of metasystems thinking were laid by Capra (2004), Demetrovics, Knuth, and Rado (1982), Garber (2010), Hall (1987) and Turchin (1977). Theoretically, the idea of 'Metasystems' was coined by Klir (1990), who notes that Meta *X* is something, which occurs after *X* or is prerequisite for Meta *X*. The expression 'Meta *X*' denotes that *X* has been changing and it is used as a common expression for this fact. Meta *X* is used as name of things, which is smarter than *X* in the sense that it is more organized, has higher logical type or it is analyzed in more general sense. Metasystems describes the conversion – replacement of one system by another and vice versa. The transition from one stage to the next stage occurs by multiplication and integration of systems into a single whole.

Following the metasystems transition theory, we can assume that the carchitecture of knowledge, described in terms of Foucauldian terminology as *Savoir;* evolve to concept of competence, described in modern terminology as *Savoir–Vivre complex* (Railean, 2012, p. 242). The metasystems learning design principles relate to philosophy, pedagogy, cybernetics, psychology, knowledge representation and management. The metasystems approach aims to develop *Metasystems Thinking.* This idea is valid when *synergistic effect* is established. Such a result could be obtained through computerized self-assessment method, which allows calculating the coefficient of assimilation. Traditionally, this method allows measuring knowledge, skills, attitudes, or to promote learning and reduce forgetting. The idea to use the coefficient of assimilation as a measure for self-regulated learning was coined by Bespalco (2007). From the author's point of view, the coefficient of assimilation (K_a) is equal to $K_a = a/p$ where a corresponds to the number of test operations resolved correctly and p is the total number of such test operations. K_a is stabilized within the range $0 \leq K_a \leq 1$. In cases where $K_a \geq 0.7$ the teaching process is considered to be completed, the learner achieves self-regulated competence, thus the synergistic effect occurs. In all other cases, teaching can be improved by algorithmic and heuristic methods.

The main idea of metasystems learning design is *a total functional* cognitive *mechanism*, which includes learner cognitive mechanisms and learning environment, which are both real and virtual. There is a significant shift in terms of strategies, processes, interconnections and exchanges with multicultural learning environments, designed for future competitive, adaptable, and accommodative specialties. Pervasiveness of such shifts is in the focus and the driving force behind the metasystems thinking aimed at achieving professionalism, planetary thinking and cultural pluralism. Learning 'how to learn' is the most significant cognitive achievement learners have to develop in order to be sensitive to global challenges. Learning 'how to learn' engages learners to build on prior learning and life experiences in order to use and apply knowledge and skills in a variety of contexts: at home, at work, in education and training. Motivation and confidence are crucial to an individual's competence" (Fidel, 2007). A range of new technologies and educational approaches have been developed to support learning 'how to learn', as random application of technologies without sufficient knowledge on methodology is likely produce chaos.

Metasystem learning design provides norms for learning viewed as complex processes of students' understanding and constructing own competence. Its ontological framework provides semantics tools and components that network with existing *Information and Communication Technologies* (ICT). This allows designing more effective technology enhanced learning environments with information, communication, cognitive and assessment processes. While the current cohort of students, variously called as X- / Y-generations, are far more competent in ICT than previous generations, their short attention span and multimedia expectations make them harder to reach educational objectives via conventional pedagogical means. As noted by Karadeniz and Bayram (2010) students would engage with learning material, if they could understand abstract / difficult concepts with ease and relate new information and knowledge to what they already know. Students learn through formal schooling or through individual or/and collaborative projects provided by global learning environment. That is the point when learning occurs: as students get the opportunity to create and self-assist understanding, and as they evaluate their outcomes in real learning environment.

Internet provides a convenient environment for learning, however, the success of education depends on self-regulatory skills (for *savoir-vivre* architecture of competence). As was observed by Mihand Mih (2011) self-regulated training has positive effect on learning achievement. Self-regulated training emphasizes the role of *Concept Mapping.* This technique "makes concepts, and propositions composed of concepts, the central elements in the structure of knowledge and construction of meaning" (Novak & Gowin,

1996, p. 7). That finding strengthens the case for inclusion of the *Semantic Web* technology which is an early scheme in the family of semantics-based approaches. Semantic Web is a kind of semantic structuring of content with well-defined ontological annotation based on pre-declared concepts. The integrated structure of concept mapping and semantic infrastructure could be embodied in novel *Learning Management Systems* (LMS). Such a prototype will not only include the traditional syntactic-based search queries which limit the utility of the search results but essentially provide semantics rich searching. Therefore, it is clear that querying of content through semantic-based approaches would render LMS to provide more relevant results for users. Queries are then semantics-based and this enables the system to make meaningful inference in human-computer interaction and in educational data mining. Semantic approach can be applied in learning objects, processes, and performance monitoring of learners. One idea is to propose the system architecture based on semantic technology that performs semantic-based searches through an intelligent software agent in order to seek and plan learner-centered choice of teaching materials automatically as a result of student's performance in the course of a semester (Çelik, Elçi, & Elverici, 2011).

Next section introduces the research methodology, basics of the semantic approach, and the semantic infrastructure designed. Section 4 provides the design aspects of the META-Era API, the unique core component of the *Metasystems Learning Design* approach, details of and its use in learning design with concrete examples.

Methodology of Research

Our research methodology is based on *Metasystems Learning Design* principles. The methods used are structure–context methodology based *e-textbook* and *e-portfolio*, semantic technology and agent-based educational data mining.

Firstly, we introduce the *e-textbook* and *e-portfolio* concepts. According to Porter (2010) e-textbooks, also known as digital texts, e-texts, e-books, electronic books, and hypertext books, represent a marriage of a hardcopy book within an electronic environment with software, such as Adobe Acrobat PDF, XML, SGML, HTML files, and hardware, such as a Palm Reader, E-Reader, Sony Reader, and Amazon's Kindle among others. Secondly, the idea of integration technologies of e-textbooks with electronic portfolio is explored. This idea is based on a constructivist approach of integration dynamics and flexible instructional strategy in *savoir-vivre* structure of competence. E-textbook will serve as tool for self-regulated teaching aimed at personalization of core concepts, providing self-assessment tests and progress monitoring. The role of e-portfolio is to keep all resources in one place (for both teachers and learners). The concept of *Personal and Professional Learning Portfolios* is applied to resolve and support particular needs of individual learners in their individualized learning processes (Sherry, Havelock &Gibson, 2005). The methods are such that students build all-inclusive e-portfolios during learning process and construct their own collection of work with record of achievements. The learning portfolios include: a) *Base Framework* aimed at providing guidance (e-glossary, calculator, formulae, periodical table, etc.); b) *Informational Framework* in order to provide and personalize information with semantic structure and c) *Operational Framework* designed for purposes of self-assessment. It is composed of items, which are immediately evaluated with feedback. The learner receives feedback as correct / incorrect answer or percent of correct answers. Each test is composed of 20-25 items and lasts for 15-20 minutes. Once all frameworks are personalized, s/he will integrate all structures into a whole, add table of contents and convert into PDF or EPUB. The personalized e-textbook can be disseminated. The main problem here is how to elaborate the personalized informational framework.

In further highlighting the semantic infrastructure of the personalized informational framework, an LMS is re-considered vis-à-vis the teacher and learner roles. In the way of explaining its parts, the following features are noted. The infrastructure behaves as a frontend user interface playing go-between the learner and Learning Objects (LOs). '*Learning Object*' is meant to signify each smallest independent structural experience containing an objective, a learning activity and an assessment (Polsani, 2003 with reference to L'Allier 1997). Essentially LOs reside in an industry-standards-compliant LMS (Elçi, 2005). Particulars of LOs with respect to metasystems learning and semantics will have already been seized and saved within the ontologies in the repository of the META-Era semantic infrastructure. Likewise, the infrastructure would have already built up a unified semantic base for learning activities, interactions, outcomes, learner integration, and learning methods, models, and techniques. The custom-built Application Program Interface (API) for this purpose is composed of internals to properly handle the ontology repository. Thus, semantic, cognitive, affective and psychomotor integration of parts is achievable. Figure 1 displays an overall view.

Figure 1. Conceptual interface layout of the META-Era Infrastructure

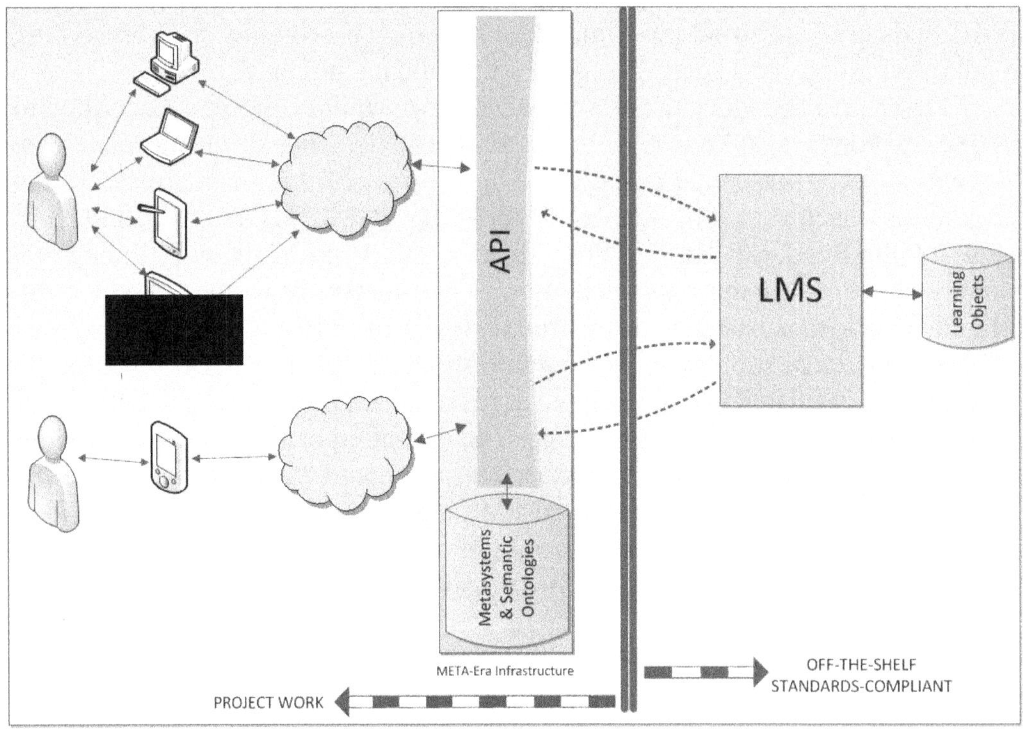

The infrastructure will actually be a layered cake of descriptive protocol layers as depicted in Figure 2. LOs of LMS are placed in the first layer at the bottom, which is an interface layer. Each LO is defined semantically in the second layer in accordance with the upper ontology knowledge base. The upper ontology keeps concepts, properties and relations of learning activities, models, and methods of LOs (Elçi, 2005). Additionally, it is possible to infer new solutions starting with the learning needs and the prevailing performance of the learner; this is done through the predefined semantic-based learning rules in the fourth layer, i.e. one of generating a study plan, finding suitable material or recommending preparation of a new LO. The API also provides a set of functions used during programming phase while preparing a user interface design so that the users, students and resource persons alike, could access the LMS using several different kinds of terminals over interconnected networks.

Figure 2.Layered representation of Meta-Era Infrastructure.

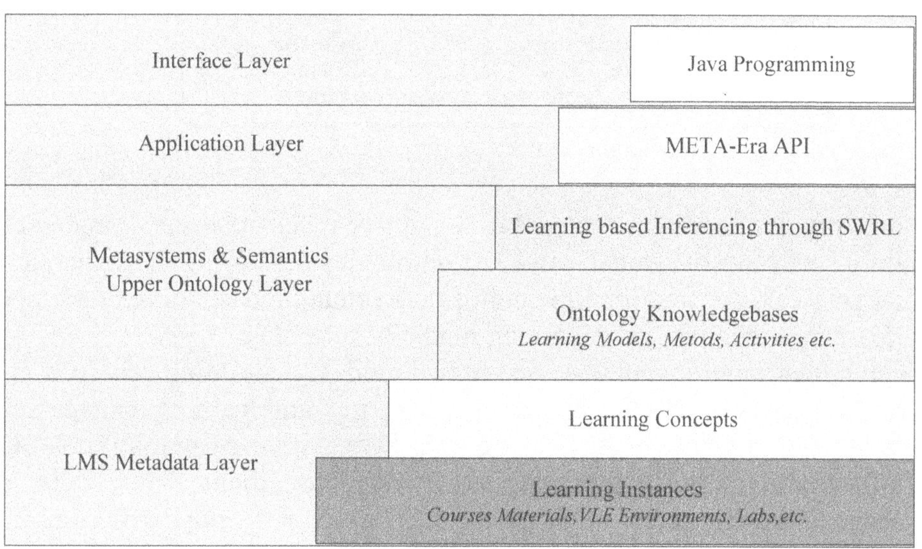

The custom-built API itself is, as noted already, composed of internal modules based on semantics and software agent technologies. The design of user interface is based on metasystems principles. These modules and their inter-operations are the subject of Figure 3.

(Figure 3 is shown on the following page)

Figure 3. API Functions

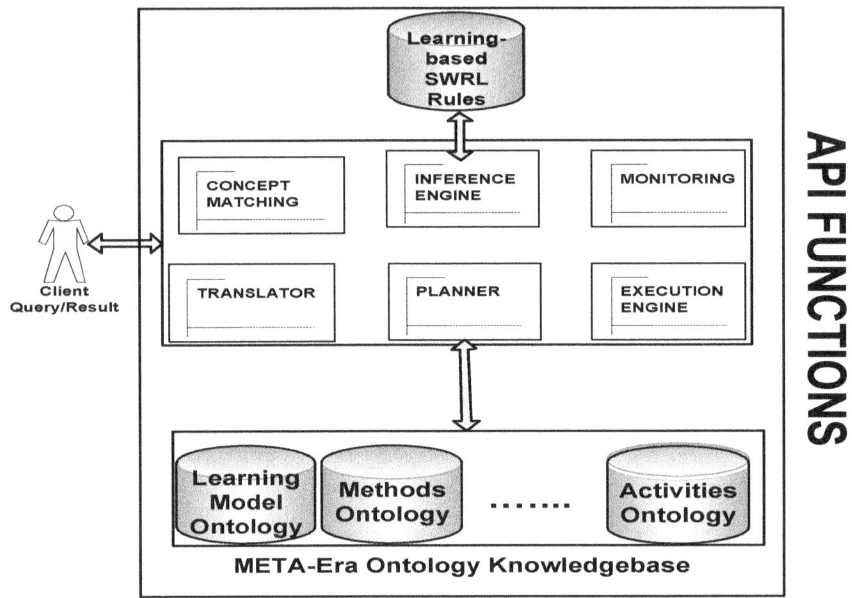

The infrastructure combines semantics, cognitive mechanisms and processes. Whereas so far others have developed disparate ontologies describing the semantics of learning, this framework for the first time builds up a semantic base for expressing learning interactions, learning outcomes, new learning methods, and LOs.

Such an infrastructure would be used in two modes: in building new LOs, it will help the builder to express semantics of learning, teaching, and learning management by building them in to an LO; and, in utilizing existing LOs, a trainer can map such LOs to META-Era infrastructure terms without necessarily recreating them.

The semantic infrastructure performs as an envelope for a standards-compliant LMS for both modes; it is generic with ease of integration to any industry-standards-compliant LMS and utilizable in any area of study as long as relevant domain ontology is made available.

Meta-era API for the Metasystems Learning Design

This section describes the functionality of META-Era API in the learning design of e-textbooks. Semantically rendered LOs are kept in an LMS repository and serve the following purposes: *The teacher* can perform the main role of identifying core concepts, constructing the adjacency matrix of a weighted knowledge graph, building knowledge graph and designing e-textbook structure. *The learner* takes an active role in building the personalized content and subsequently using it.

META-Era API provides the following important functionalities to the teacher role:

- *Learning standards*: Maintaining standard requirements for learning.
- *Problem definition or recognition*: Understanding the request for content or problem (for example, this may be *'generating e-textbook tasks in a laboratory study for a student or a group'*).
- *Generating solution paths* or *graphs*: A semantic-based software agent can advise the system to produce, possibly a multitude of, solution paths (graphs). Such solution paths may be full or partial solutions in response to the request.
- *Decision making*: The agent may help the LO developer to decide which path would provide suitable solution for a specific problem. Such solution paths are generated based on standard learning models.
- *Generate an e-textbook core structure*: The agent proposes a specific unit together with the relevant core concepts. The system may search through its ontology knowledge base (OKBs) and extract necessary concepts and relationships for the topic (say, of the laboratory study, the specific unit or related ones). Then, it may search LO repository of the host LMS, specify related pages through URLs, then propose suitable content.
- *Control mechanism* and *evaluation*: Teacher users are able to propose the generated e-textbook to a student or a group. The system can evaluate the performance of students after the laboratory study (delayed feedback) or propose a subsystem for self-assessment (immediate feedback).

The META-Era API for an LMS supports students in the same way as that of an LO developer albeit with some role-based limitations as indicated below:

- The same facilities as those given above for teacher role are supported for generating e-textbook except evaluation or testing parts. A student may want to generate a study plan or search a suitable LO such as a section of an e-textbook for use in preparing for an exam, a course study, quiz, laboratory study, etc.
- The crucial point here is that, through an upper ontology knowledgebase, META-Era based system is able to understand the semantic descriptions of the contents, be it of an exam, a course study plan, quiz, laboratory study, etc. found in the LMS repository.
- After specifying a topic and its units for meeting student requirement, META-Era based system is able to extract and infer suitable concepts, properties and relationships information among entire materials of that topic in an LMS.
- In the next level, the system may start to consider *'How can the materials be organized?'* and also *'Which organized path is suitable?'*
- META-Era based system can manage learning models according to metadata models. To do this, task flow of learning models may be defined as in the form of graphs or flow diagrams. Semantic descriptions of the models are to be defined in the upper ontologies included in the upper ontology knowledgebase of META-Era based system.
- META-Era based system monitors and keeps records on the performance of students individually. This data could be presented in the form of text, tables, diagrams, and concept maps.

Various kinds of LOs, such as e-documents, HTML, MS Word, MS PowerPoint, etc., can be further enriched semantically by representing them and their attributes in connection with ontologies. The question of “How would Semantic Web and Ontologies help here?” can be answered as: “Through semantically annotating all types of e-materials (video, text, test, presentation, html, audio, and others)”.

META-Era semantic infrastructure includes an ontology knowledgebase of methods, concepts, and inference rules, units for study, a generator of units, and an intelligent evaluator of student’s answers. A materials upper ontology would include all concepts, properties and relationships about all LOs contained in LMS. A small declarative portion of such type of an upper ontology that contains commonly used concepts and properties of LOs is depicted in Table 1.

Table 1.Labels of Class, DataProperty, and ObjectProperty in material ontology (in OWL 2)

```
1  <?xml version="1.0"?>
2  Ontologyxmlns=http://www.w3.org/2002/07/owl#
3  xml:base="http://.../OKB/2012/Material.owl"
4  <Declaration><Class IRI="#Book"/></Declaration>
5  <Declaration><Class IRI="#Material"/></Declaration>
6  <Declaration><Class IRI="#Presentation"/></Declaration>
7  <Declaration><Class IRI="#Test"/></Declaration>
8  <Declaration><Class IRI="#Video"/></Declaration>
9  <Declaration><ObjectProperty IRI="#Covered_by"/></Declaration>
10 <Declaration><ObjectProperty IRI="#Covers"/></Declaration>
11 <Declaration><ObjectProperty IRI="#Previous_Material"/></Declaration>
12 <Declaration><ObjectProperty IRI="#Next_Material"/></Declaration>
13 <Declaration><DataProperty IRI="#Interactive_Content_Property"/></Declaration>
14 <Declaration><DataProperty IRI="#Visual_Content_Property"/></Declaration>
15 <Declaration><DataProperty IRI="#Material_Address"/></Declaration>
16 <Declaration><DataProperty IRI="#Material_Language"/></Declaration>
17 <Declaration><DataProperty IRI="#Material_Author"/></Declaration>
```

Through use of ontologies, it is possible to define properties of LOs and other materials, activities, methods for LMS systems. To do this, an upper ontology needs to contain *“ObjectProperty”* and *“DataProperty”* of OWL language (http://www.w3.org/TR/owl-features/). For instance, the semantic definitions of *“ObjectProperty”* in an upper ontology of materials in LMS are indicated by*“#Covered_by”, “#Covers”, “#Previous_Material”* and *“#Next_Material”* (see Table 1, Appendix 1 at lines 9-12). The *“#Covered_by”* and *“#Covers”* properties associate a particular part of a material withanother material. Likewise, the *“#Previous_Material”* and *“#Next_Material”* properties associate a student individual to a material individual. Additionally, such an upper ontology provides basis for analyses of common LOs. As an example to show the contribution of a META-Era based approach to an LMS system, the LMS may keep its own metadata for the LOs in its repository linked to upper ontology knowledgebase; this would provide grounds to infer or generate a suitable study plan for an e-textbook according to user requirements. For instance, a META-Era based LMS can advise better didactical remedial materials in response to queried requirements for a weak student. A generated lower level ontology of some LOs for an LMS system is given in Table 2.

Table 2.Creation and definitions of the material of course and existing units (partial content)

```
1   <ClassAssertion>
2   <Class IRI="#Presentation"/>
3   <NamedIndividual IRI="#01_Math101_01_005"/>
4   </ClassAssertion>
5   <DataPropertyAssertion>
6   <DataProperty IRI="#Material_Address"/>
7   <NamedIndividual IRI="#01_Math101_01_005"/>
8   <Literal datatypeIRI="&xsd;URI">../lms/courses/math101</Literal>
9   </DataPropertyAssertion>
10  <DataPropertyAssertion>
11  <DataProperty IRI="#Material_Author"/>
12  <NamedIndividual IRI="#01_Math101_01_005"/>
13  <Literal datatypeIRI="&xsd;Name">Prof.Dr. John Smith </Literal>
14  </DataPropertyAssertion>
15  <ObjectPropertyAssertion>
16  <ObjectProperty IRI="#Covered_by"/>
17  <NamedIndividual IRI="#01_Math101_01_005"/>
18  <NamedIndividual IRI=="#01_Cal102_01_001"/>
19  </ObjectPropertyAssertion>
20  <ObjectPropertyAssertion>
21  <ObjectProperty IRI="#Next_Material"/>
22  <NamedIndividual IRI="#01_Math101_01_005"/>
23  <NamedIndividual IRI="#01_Math101_02_001"/>
24  </ObjectPropertyAssertion>
25  <DataPropertyAssertion>
26  <DataProperty IRI="#Question_Number"/>
28  <NamedIndividual IRI="#01_Math101_01_005"/>
29  <Literal datatypeIRI="&xsd;integer">12</Literal>
30  </DataPropertyAssertion>
```

Let's take the case of the LO unit 01_Math101_01_005 at line 3 in Table 2. This is the material numbered as 005 of the freshman mathematics course, Section/Unit 1 (i.e. *Grade_CourseName_Unit_MaterialID*). The semantic declaration (class assertion) of this material is defined as an *owl:individual* (through *'NamedIndividual'*) in this ontology (lines 1-4). One can see the semantic relations between this and other course materials. For instance, the material 01_Math101_01_005 is covered by the material 01_Cal102_01_001 (lines 15-19). In *Data Property* assertions part, it is seen that the number of the questions of this material is 12 (lines 25-30). The author of it is Prof. Dr. John Smith, and its level is the 1st year (lines 10-14). The address information is also present in order to facilitate search and allow accessibility by a semantically developed smart agent. The address of this material includes a URL information showing that it is in Math101 file in the LMS courses repository (lines 5-9). The relationship between the fifth material of section 1 of the first grade Math 101 course (that is, 01_Math101_01_005) and the first material of the section 2 of the same course (01_Math101_02_001) is 'the next material'. Namely, the materials required in sequence can be defined by using the "#Next_Material: Object Property" (lines 20-24). An intelligent software agent uses such semantic annotations of materials in seeking and planning student-based automatic scheduling of course documents according to student's requirements during a semester. The partial ontology shown in Table 2 is also depicted in the graph of Figure 4.

Figure 4. 'Next Material' of "owl:ObjectProperty" feature defined for two materials (individuals) in the Materials.owl ontology.

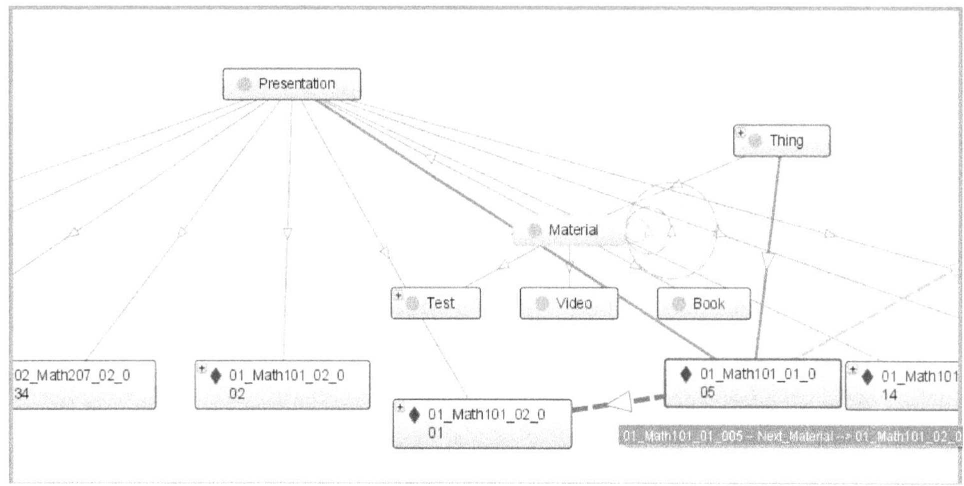

Inference rules are semantically defined by using the Semantic Web Rule Language(SWRL; http://www.w3.org/Submission/SWRL/) for learning model rules. The SWRL rules also apply to predefined criteria to find a suitable LO for a particular field or requirement.

Let's study a couple of examples as the first case study in order to demonstrate the utility of SWRL queries and META-Era API. According to a pedagogical scenario, a learner logs in to a META-Era API-cum-LMS system using credentials, say ID & password, and chooses the code of the lesson for which a work plan is needed. META-Era API reaches all information related to both the course and the student in the LMS repository. Two SWRL based example rules as shown in Figure 5 are developed to be used during the following discussion. OWL declaration of the first rule in Figure 5 is depicted in Table 3.

TABLE 3. SWRL SYNTAX IN OWL FILE FOR FIRST SWRL RULE EXAMPLE ABOVE:

```
<DLSafeRule>
<Body>
<ClassAtom><Class IRI="#Student"/><Variable
IRI="urn:swrl#s"/></ClassAtom>
<ObjectPropertyAtom>
<ObjectProperty
IRI="http://aydin.edu.tr/2011/Material.owl#Previous_Material"/>
```

```
<Variable IRI="urn:swrl#s"/><NamedIndividual IRI="#01_Math207_01_003"/>
</ObjectPropertyAtom>
<ObjectPropertyAtom>
<ObjectProperty IRI="#hasEducationDegree"/>
<Variable IRI="urn:swrl#s"/><NamedIndividual IRI="#College"/>
</ObjectPropertyAtom>
<ObjectPropertyAtom>
<ObjectProperty IRI="#hasFocusedTopic"/>
<Variable IRI="urn:swrl#s"/><NamedIndividual IRI="#Sets"/>
</ObjectPropertyAtom>
<ObjectPropertyAtom>
<ObjectProperty IRI="#hasSuitableMaterialType"/>
<Variable IRI="urn:swrl#s"/><NamedIndividual IRI="#Presentation"/>
</ObjectPropertyAtom>
<ObjectPropertyAtom>
<ObjectProperty IRI="#hasTakenCourse"/>
<Variable IRI="urn:swrl#s"/><NamedIndividual IRI="#Math101"/>
</ObjectPropertyAtom>
<DataPropertyAtom>
<DataProperty IRI="#hasStudentLevel"/>
<Variable IRI="urn:swrl#s"/><Variable IRI="urn:swrl#l"/>
</DataPropertyAtom>
<BuiltInAtom IRI="http://www.w3.org/2003/11/swrlb#greaterThanOrEqual">
<Variable IRI="urn:swrl#l"/><Literal
datatypeIRI="&xsd;double">2.0</Literal>
</BuiltInAtom>
</Body>
<Head>
<ObjectPropertyAtom>
<ObjectProperty IRI="#Next_Material"/>
<Variable IRI="urn:swrl#s"/><NamedIndividual IRI="#01_Math207_01_004"/>
</ObjectPropertyAtom>
</Head>
</DLSafeRule>
```

The use of SWRL rules during inference phase for building relations among materials was pre-meditated as a work plan is prepared. Therefore, in this work, SWRL has been applied to the types of *owl:Class, owl:Object Property* (*Covered_by, Covers, Previous* and *Next_Material,*etc.),and*owl:DataProperty*(*Interactive_Content_Property, Visual_Content_Property, Material_Address,* and *Material_Author*, etc.)in order to detect the order of the relations among relevant materials and develop a material-based work plan corresponding to student needs.

Let's consider the case of a learner with a *College* degree, who takes *Math101*, needing to focus on unit *Sets*, having *level ?l* where the level value is greater than *2.00* out of 4.00 and suitable learning material type for that student is *Video*. Then, it is better to advise taking*01_Math207_01_003* as a suitable next material. The formulation of the SWRL rule and the reasoning leading to that entailment goes as follows (the second rule in Figure 5). The conceptualization of a learner and a college can be captured from OWL classes called "Person" and "University". The college degree, focused unit, student level,

level value, currently considered course and suitable material type conditions for that student can be expressed as *has Education Degree, has Focused Topic, has Student Level, has Suitable Material Type, has Taken Course* and *Next_Material*object properties. These rules could be written as follows where '?s' stands for a variable (atom) whose value will be obtained from the matching data records of the database, and the implication operator '->'helps establishing the consequence (the right hand side expression) for those data points satisfying the antecedent (all of the left hand side terms):

SWRL Rule 1:
Student(?s), hasEducationDegree(?s, College), hasFocusedTopic(?s, Sets), hasSuitableMaterialType(?s, Video), hasTakenCourse(?s, Math101), hasStudentLevel(?s, ?l), greaterThanOrEqual(?l, 2.0) ->Next_Material(?s, 01_Math207_01_003)

Another similar SWRL rule example is given below. This is the same case as above except this time *Presentation* instead of *Video* is the most suitable learning material type for the considered unit of the course. Additionally, taking the previous material studied by the student as *01_Math207_01_003* and the student level value as *3.00*, then, the system would recommend *01_Math207_01_004* as a suitable next material for that student (SWRL code of the rule is depicted in Table 3 and the first rule in Figure 5).

SWRL Rule 2:
Student(?s), Previous_Material(?s, 01_Math207_01_003), hasEducationDegree(?s, College), hasFocusedTopic(?s, Sets), hasSuitableMaterialType(?s, Presentation), hasTakenCourse(?s, Math101), hasStudentLevel(?s, ?l), greaterThanOrEqual(?l, 2.0) ->Next_Material(?s, 01_Math207_01_004)

Figure 5: Rule syntax from SWRL Tab of Protégé Framework and asserted data for the student id '00001'.

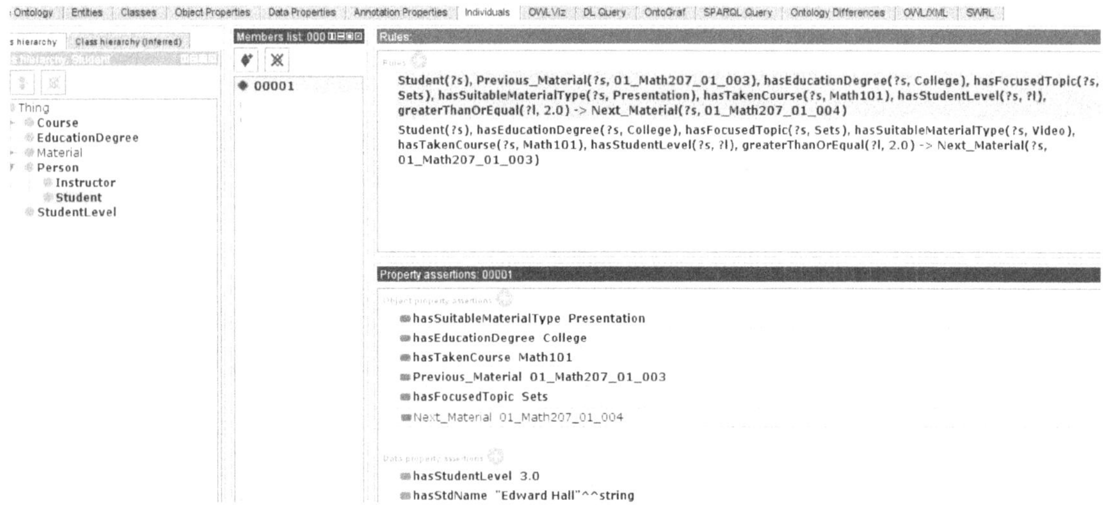

Initially, the system does not have any idea about the next material for the student named Edward Hall (see Figure 6). Executing the SWRL Rule 2 (depicted in Function 1, Appendix 4, by clicking the FIND NEXT MATERIAL button) the reasoner of the system infers a suitable next material: *01_Math207_01_004*. That is, the answer of the system for the student having id *'00001'*, whose suitable learning material type being Presentation, concerning the *Math101* course, according to his level being *3.0* and also his *Previous_Material* being 01_Math207_01_003, then, for that student (Line 7 in Function 1) the outcome is printed output as *01_Math207_01_004*. Let's note that before the inference task, the student's *Next_Material* property value is depicted in Figure 6 as 'null'. Figure 7 displays that outcome.

Figure 6: Before inferring the Next_Material data from the asserted data for the student (Std_ID is 00001, Edward Hall) through SWRL Rule 2.

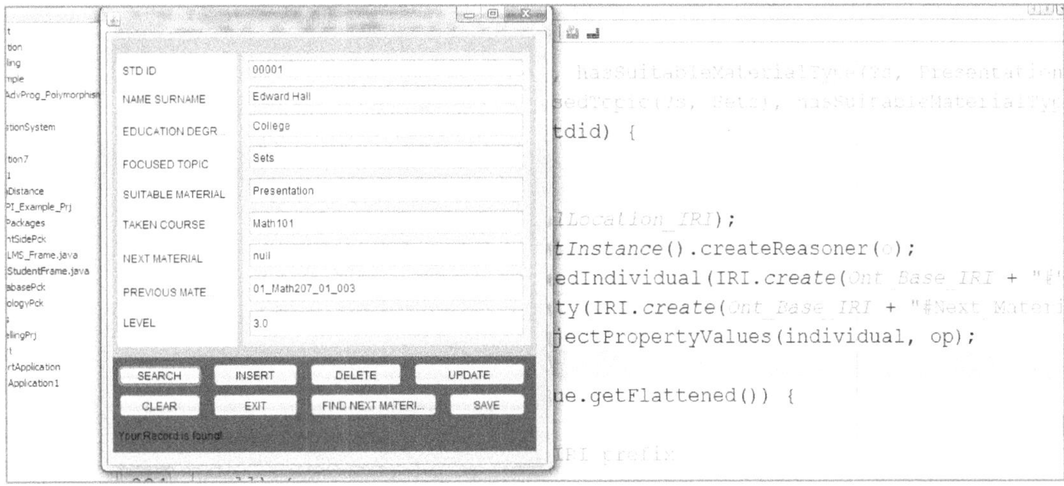

Function 1: This function infers the result of the SWRL Rule 2.

```
1    public List getAnObjectProperty() {
2     List<String> list = new ArrayList<String>();
3      try {
4       o = m.loadOntologyFromOntologyDocument(localLocation_IRI);
5    PelletReasoner r = PelletReasonerFactory.getInstance().createReasoner(o);
6    OWLNamedIndividual individual =
     f.getOWLNamedIndividual(IRI.create(Ont_Base_IRI + "#Std_ID"));
7    OWLObjectProperty op =
     f.getOWLObjectProperty(IRI.create(Ont_Base_IRI + "#Next_Material"));
8    NodeSet<OWLNamedIndividual> value = r.getObjectPropertyValues(individual,
     op);
9       String result=null;
10       for (OWLNamedIndividualrangeVal : value.getFlattened()) {
11         result = result + ", " + IRI_Cut(rangeVal.toString());
```

```
list.add(result);
        }
m.removeOntology(o);
    } catch (Exception e) {
System.out.println("Could not create ontology: " + e.getMessage());
    }
    return list;
  }
```

According to the SWRL Rule 2 shown above, for all members of OWL Class Student, which satisfies all the conditions, the Next_Materialproperty is inferred as 01_Math207_01_004 by the system inference engine (Figure 7).

Figure 7: System infers the Next_Material data from asserted data for the student (Std_ID is 00001) through SWRL Rule 2

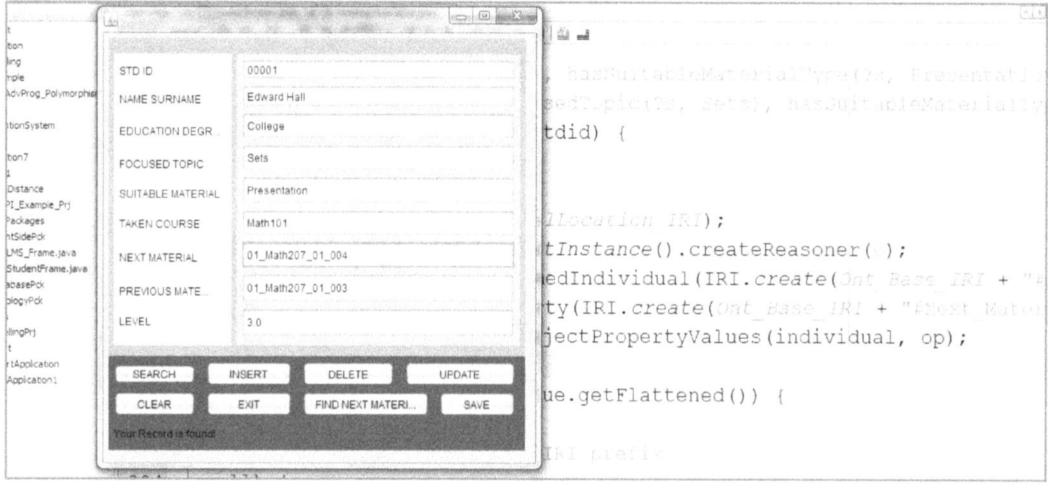

Let's study a couple of complete case scenarios through Protégé Framework.

CASE STUDY: Scenario 2: An instructor uploads a test material to the database and updates the ontology knowledge base of LMS for the same. These steps are needed in order to generate a suitable e-textbook according to the student's characteristics via ontology through the semantic based LMS. The descriptive properties of the material are added to the system's knowledgebase in the machine understandable form (in OWL 2.0). Each instructor has own account to upload the test material. In the case study below, the test material numbered*01_Math101_01_006*is added to the LMS system by its creator*(Prof.Dr.Atilla Elci) (depicted in Figure 8).*

Figure 8: A material by instructor's account is being added to the semantic based LMS in machine understandable form.

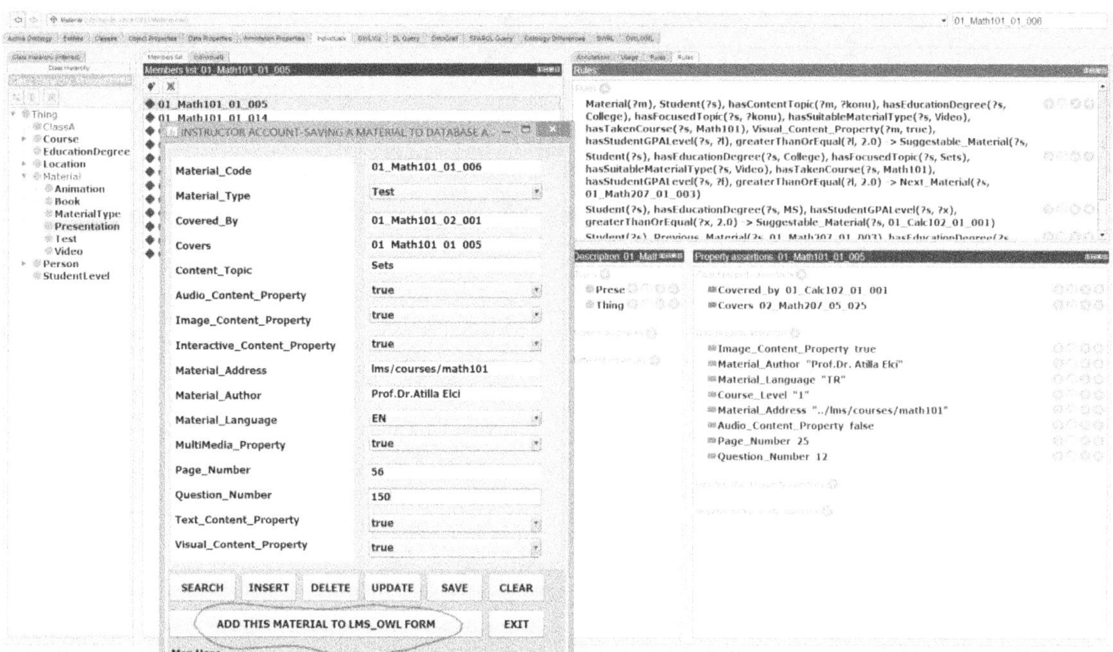

The instructor adds the material to the ontology knowledgebase of the LMS system through the above interface (Figure 8). In addition, Figure 9 presents the ontology form conversion of the document after the instructor inserts it to the material pool. Here, the aim is to cater for the need for descriptive properties of materials to be understood by machines (semantic based LMS) to generate suitable e-textbooks in future according to the student characteristics.

According to the scenario, the *01_Math101_01_006* material covers its previous material '*01_Math101_01_005*' which also contains same topic that is about *'Sets'*.

However, the newly added *01_Math101_01_006* numbered material is a 'Test' which also contains several other descriptive properties given below:

Material_Author=Prof.Dr.Atilla Elci
Interactive_Content_Property=true,
Text_Content_Property=true,
Image_Content_Property=true,
Visual_Content_Property=true,
Audio_Content_Property=true,
Multimedia_Property=true,
Material_Language=EN,
Question_Number=150,
Page_Number=56,
Material_Address=lms/courses/math101.

Figure 9: The Protégé Editor displays the test material in OWL form after inserting it to the LMS using instructor account.

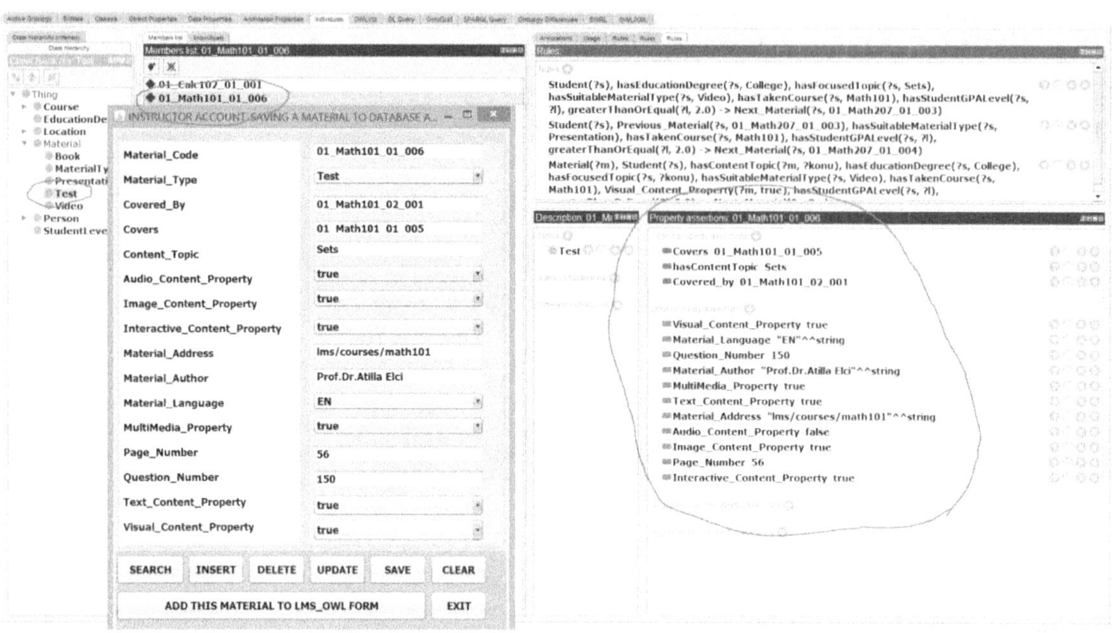

Table 4: After inserting the 01_Math101_01_006 test material to the system pool, then OWL 2.0 conversion is automatically performed and saved to the ontology knowledgebase of the LMS system.

```
<ClassAssertion>
<Class IRI="#Test"/>
<NamedIndividual IRI="#01_Math101_01_006"/>
</ClassAssertion>
<ObjectPropertyAssertion>
<ObjectProperty IRI="#Covered_by"/>
<NamedIndividual IRI="#01_Math101_01_006"/>
<NamedIndividual IRI="#01_Math101_02_001"/>
</ObjectPropertyAssertion>
<ObjectPropertyAssertion>
<ObjectProperty IRI="#Covers"/>
<NamedIndividual IRI="#01_Math101_01_006"/>
<NamedIndividual IRI="#01_Math101_01_005"/>
</ObjectPropertyAssertion>
<ObjectPropertyAssertion>
<ObjectProperty IRI="#hasContentTopic"/>
<NamedIndividual IRI="#01_Math101_01_006"/>
<NamedIndividual IRI="#Sets"/>
</ObjectPropertyAssertion>
<DataPropertyAssertion>
<DataProperty IRI="#Audio_Content_Property"/>
<NamedIndividual IRI="#01_Math101_01_006"/>
<Literal datatypeIRI="http://www.w3.org/2001/XMLSchema#boolean">false</Literal>
</DataPropertyAssertion>
<DataPropertyAssertion>
<DataProperty IRI="#Image_Content_Property"/>
<NamedIndividual IRI="#01_Math101_01_006"/>
<Literal datatypeIRI="http://www.w3.org/2001/XMLSchema#boolean">true</Literal>
</DataPropertyAssertion>
```

```
<DataPropertyAssertion>
<DataProperty IRI="#Interactive_Content_Property"/>
<NamedIndividual IRI="#01_Math101_01_006"/>
<Literal datatypeIRI="http://www.w3.org/2001/XMLSchema#boolean">true</Literal>
</DataPropertyAssertion>
<DataPropertyAssertion>
<DataProperty IRI="#Material_Address"/>
<NamedIndividual IRI="#01_Math101_01_006"/>
<Literal datatypeIRI="http://www.w3.org/2001/XMLSchema#string">lms/courses/math101</Literal>
</DataPropertyAssertion>
<DataPropertyAssertion>
<DataProperty IRI="#Material_Author"/>
<NamedIndividual IRI="#01_Math101_01_006"/>
<Literal datatypeIRI="http://www.w3.org/2001/XMLSchema#string">Prof.Dr.Atilla Elci</Literal>
</DataPropertyAssertion>
<DataPropertyAssertion>
<DataProperty IRI="#Material_Language"/>
<NamedIndividual IRI="#01_Math101_01_006"/>
<Literal datatypeIRI="http://www.w3.org/2001/XMLSchema#string">EN</Literal>
</DataPropertyAssertion>
<DataPropertyAssertion>
<DataProperty IRI="#MultiMedia_Property"/>
<NamedIndividual IRI="#01_Math101_01_006"/>
<Literal datatypeIRI="http://www.w3.org/2001/XMLSchema#boolean">true</Literal>
</DataPropertyAssertion>
<DataPropertyAssertion>
<DataProperty IRI="#Page_Number"/>
<NamedIndividual IRI="#01_Math101_01_006"/>
<Literal datatypeIRI="http://www.w3.org/2001/XMLSchema#integer">56</Literal>
</DataPropertyAssertion>
<DataPropertyAssertion>
<DataProperty IRI="#Question_Number"/>
<NamedIndividual IRI="#01_Math101_01_006"/>
<Literal datatypeIRI="http://www.w3.org/2001/XMLSchema#integer">150</Literal>
</DataPropertyAssertion>
<DataPropertyAssertion>
<DataProperty IRI="#Text_Content_Property"/>
<NamedIndividual IRI="#01_Math101_01_006"/>
<Literal datatypeIRI="http://www.w3.org/2001/XMLSchema#boolean">true</Literal>
</DataPropertyAssertion>
<DataPropertyAssertion>
<DataProperty IRI="#Visual_Content_Property"/>
<NamedIndividual IRI="#01_Math101_01_006"/>
<Literal datatypeIRI="http://www.w3.org/2001/XMLSchema#boolean">true</Literal>
</DataPropertyAssertion>
```

SWRL Rule 3:

Student(?s), Test(?m), hasEducationDegree(?s, College), hasFocusedTopic(?s, ?topic), hasContentTopic(?m,?topic), hasSuitableMaterialType(?s, Test), hasTakenCourse(?s, Math101), hasStudentGPALevel(?s, ?l), greaterThanOrEqual(?l, 2.0) ->hasSuggestedMaterialToStudent(?s,?m)

After inserting a test material to the system, any instructor can automatically assign such material to the suitable students who is a ***College*** student***, Suitable Material Type*** is ***Test,*** current course is ***Math101,*** where last GPA level is above ***2.0.,***etc. as an homework or as an exam. Figure 10 below depicts the situation where the system infers and suggests the newly added test material to a student (***00003***) who has satisfied all conditions for taking it. The SWRL rules are automatically generated by the system. Rules may as well defined/modified by instructors or LMS admins through a similar approach (namely rule defining forms of instructors such as in Figure 8 or Figure 9). In this scenario, the SWRL rule 3 says:

If '?s'→ is a Student and
If '?m'→ is a Test material and
If '?s' is a College student and
If '?s' has a focused topic that is '?topic' and
If the material '?m' in the LMS DB contains the '?topic' and
....
Then,
Result: suggested the test material to such type of similar students in the class '?s' who are able to solve the such type of similar test materials'?m' in the LMS pool.

Figure 10: Inference phase of the scenario.

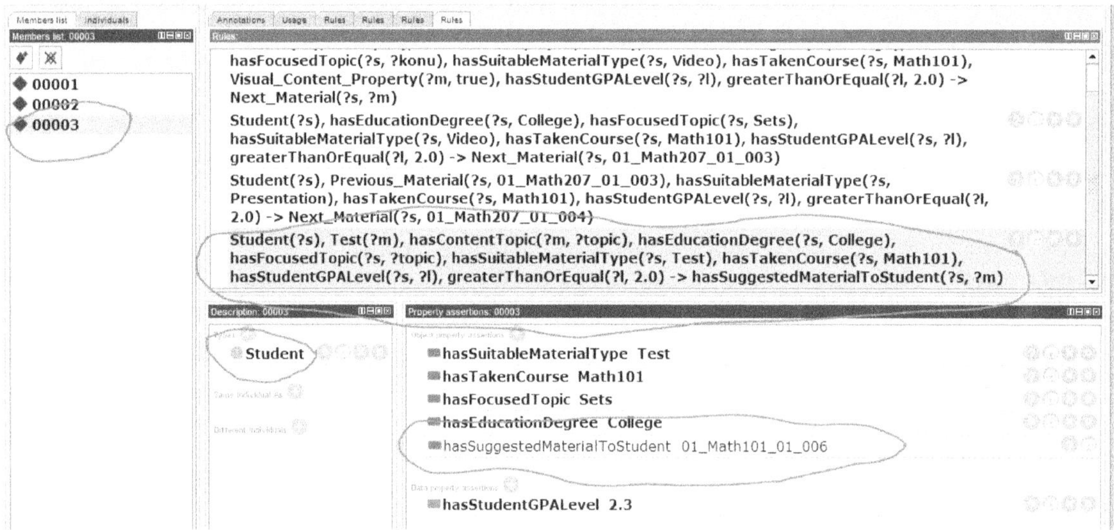

As mentioned above, the SWRL rules are automatically generated by the system. The rules are also defined/modified by instructors or LMS admins through a similar approach (namely rule defining forms of instructors such as in Figure 8 or Figure 9).

CASE STUDY: Scenario 3: An instructor creates a learning rule through the interface. The rule is generated automatically by the system and then inserted in SWRL form to the ontology knowledge base of LMS (see Figure 11 and Figure 12).

SWRL Rule 4:
Student(?s), Test(?m), hasContentTopic(?m, Sets), hasEducationDegree(?s, College), hasFocusedTopic(?s, Sets), hasSuitableMaterialType(?s, Test), hasTakenCourse(?s, Math101), hasStudentGPALevel(?s, ?l), greaterThanOrEqual(?l, 2.0), Audio_Content_Property(?m, true), Image_Content_Property(?m, true),

Interactive_Content_Property(?m, true), MultiMedia_Property(?m, true), Text_Content_Property(?m, true), Visual_Content_Property(?m, true), Material_Language(?m, "EN")->hasSuggestedMaterialToStudent(?s, ?m)

The rule states that:

All students in the class whose currently focused topic is 'Sets', education degree is 'College', suitable material type is 'Test', who is currently taking the course 'Math101', with GPA greater than '2.0', are suggested to assign any 'Test' type materials in the LMS materials pool which by the way may contain Audio, Image, Interactivity, Multi Media, Text, Visual content properties. The body section of the SWRL Rule 4 is depicted before the implication '→' symbol above. This is converted to OWL 2.0 form shown in the lines 2 through 33in Table 5(<body>…</body>). The head section of rule is depicted after the '→' symbol above which mentions ***hasSuggestedMaterialToStudent*** property that is converted to OWL 2.0 form as well (<head>…</head>) in the lines 34 through 37 in Table 5).

Figure 11: The SWRL Rule 4 for the scenario is generated by the instructor using the above visual interface.

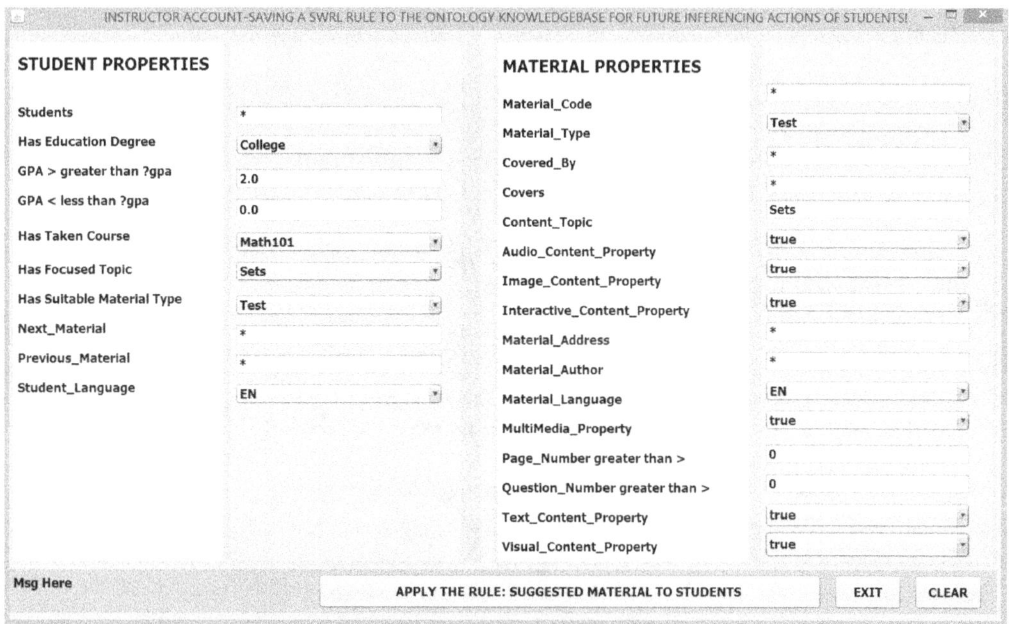

Table 5:The OWL 2.0 form of the SWRL Rule 4 after adding in the rule set is depicted below (see Figure 11).

```
1  <DLSafeRule>
2  <Body>
3  <ClassAtom><Class IRI="#Student"/><Variable IRI="urn:swrl#s"/></ClassAtom>
4  <ClassAtom><Class IRI="#Test"/><Variable IRI="urn:swrl#m"/></ClassAtom>
5  <ObjectPropertyAtom><ObjectProperty IRI="#hasContentTopic"/>
6  <Variable IRI="urn:swrl#m"/><NamedIndividual IRI="#Sets"/></ObjectPropertyAtom>
7  <ObjectPropertyAtom><ObjectProperty IRI="#hasEducationDegree"/>
8  <Variable IRI="urn:swrl#s"/><NamedIndividual IRI="#College"/></ObjectPropertyAtom>
9  <ObjectPropertyAtom><ObjectProperty IRI="#hasFocusedTopic"/>
```

```
<Variable IRI="urn:swrl#s"/><NamedIndividual IRI="#Sets"/></ObjectPropertyAtom>
<ObjectPropertyAtom><ObjectProperty IRI="#hasSuitableMaterialType"/>
<Variable IRI="urn:swrl#s"/><NamedIndividual IRI="#Test"/></ObjectPropertyAtom>
<ObjectPropertyAtom><ObjectProperty IRI="#hasTakenCourse"/>
<Variable IRI="urn:swrl#s"/><NamedIndividual IRI="#Math101"/></ObjectPropertyAtom>
<DataPropertyAtom><DataProperty IRI="#Audio_Content_Property"/>
<Variable IRI="urn:swrl#m"/><Literal datatypeIRI="&xsd;boolean">true</Literal></DataPropertyAtom>
<DataPropertyAtom><DataProperty IRI="#Image_Content_Property"/>
<Variable IRI="urn:swrl#m"/><Literal datatypeIRI="&xsd;boolean">true</Literal></DataPropertyAtom>
<DataPropertyAtom><DataProperty IRI="#Interactive_Content_Property"/>
<Variable IRI="urn:swrl#m"/><Literal datatypeIRI="&xsd;boolean">true</Literal></DataPropertyAtom>
<DataPropertyAtom><DataProperty IRI="#Material_Language"/>
<Variable IRI="urn:swrl#m"/><Literal datatypeIRI="&rdf;PlainLiteral">EN</Literal></DataPropertyAtom>
<DataPropertyAtom><DataProperty IRI="#MultiMedia_Property"/>
<Variable IRI="urn:swrl#m"/><Literal datatypeIRI="&xsd;boolean">true</Literal></DataPropertyAtom>
<DataPropertyAtom><DataProperty IRI="#Text_Content_Property"/>
<Variable IRI="urn:swrl#m"/><Literal datatypeIRI="&xsd;boolean">true</Literal></DataPropertyAtom>
<DataPropertyAtom><DataProperty IRI="#Visual_Content_Property"/>
<Variable IRI="urn:swrl#m"/><Literal datatypeIRI="&xsd;boolean">true</Literal></DataPropertyAtom>
<DataPropertyAtom><DataProperty IRI="#hasStudentGPALevel"/>
<Variable IRI="urn:swrl#s"/><Variable IRI="urn:swrl#l"/></DataPropertyAtom>
<BuiltInAtom IRI="http://www.w3.org/2003/11/swrlb#greaterThanOrEqual">
<Variable IRI="urn:swrl#l"/><Literal datatypeIRI="&xsd;double">2.0</Literal></BuiltInAtom>
</Body>
<Head>
<ObjectPropertyAtom><ObjectProperty IRI="#hasSuggestedMaterialToStudent"/>
<Variable IRI="urn:swrl#s"/><Variable IRI="urn:swrl#m"/></ObjectPropertyAtom>
</Head>
</DLSafeRule>
```

Reference Table 5, the rule is automatically converted into OWL 2.0 form that is performed and saved to the ontology knowledgebase by the LMS.

Figure 12: The new SWRL Rule 4 generated for the scenariois added to the ontology that is displayed by Protégé.

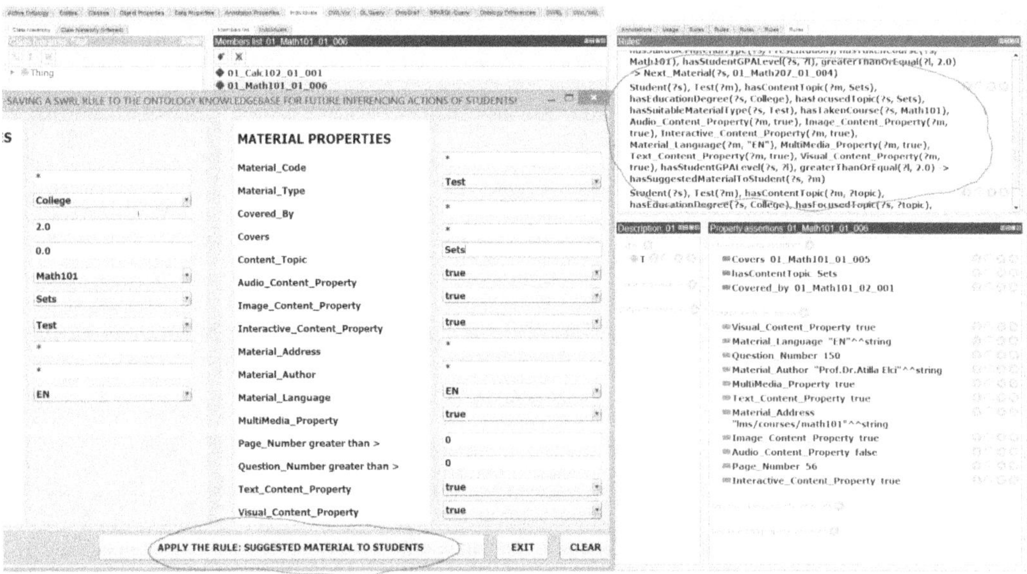

Reference Figure 12, Rules window shows the rule set of the system that contains SWRL Rule 4 in red on upper right.

Several examples and case scenarios considered above provide clues to how a Meta-Era-based learning system help materialize the principles of learning. The principles of learning are naturally cross principles which may be identified according to metasystems approach. Teaching, learning and assessment strategies and methods will integrate the proposed principles into e-textbook design using the model of competence pedagogy. This model subsumes *savoir-dire, savoir–faire* and *savoir–etre* components. According to Minder (2003, p.42)*savoir–dire* (which is equivalent to *savoir*) represents theoretical and verbal knowledge, *savoir–faire* represents methods, techniques, procedures, and learning strategies, and *savoir–etre* represents wishes, affectivity, emotions, and motivation.

Consequently, the principles of metasystems learning design are the following:

- *Principle of self-regulation* – automatic regulation of learning process through activation of metacognition using didactical and psychological methods, cybernetics techniques and management systems;
- *Principle of personalization* – individualization of learning objects through increasing formation of the individuals as a self and as a member of global learning community;
- *Principle of feedback diversity* – electronic education context needs to be evaluated through immediate and delayed feedback;
- *Principle of clarity* – formation of structural skeleton of the content with powerful interconnected concepts;
- *Principle of dynamism and flexibility* – active inclusion of the learner in elaboration of the content in order to provide the competence development skills; and,
- *Principle of ergonomics* – computer-based learning and assessment are guided by ergonomic interfaces and take place in an ergonomic work place.

Future Research Directions

The META-Era approach to e-textbook learning design is squarely addressing the issue of learner control towards creating a personalized and customized learning object for STEM teaching and learning. This work is ultimately linked to learner autonomy, ownership and empowerment in personal learning environments. Personal learning environments represent, "a shift away from the traditional model of technology-enhanced learning based on *knowledge transfer* towards a model based on *knowledge construction*" (Buchem, 2014) which has been pointed out in this chapter. Many of the papers included in this special issue are related to this chapter's topic. Contrasting especially the one by Rahimi, van den Berg and Veen (2014) proposing a Web 2.0 based framework to the META-Era approach can be worthwhile.

Even if the term 'Web 2.0' is quite vague with considerably varying connotations depending on its uses and users, it would be safe to assume that it alludes to Web Technology and furthermore to Semantic Web (http://www.w3.org/standards/semanticweb/). Both of these technologies are in the bases of

META-Era approach. Thus, design and development of VLEs firmly based on META-Era approach would be serving to materialize the aspirations for and the principles of learner autonomy, ownership and empowerment.
Learner attitudes towards electronic LOs such as e-textbook as learning tools are not considered in this chapter but may be another important dimension in creating successful learning environments. Liaw and Huang (2014) provide some insight into learner satisfaction, usefulness, behavioral intention and learning effectiveness also proposing a conceptual research model based on the activity theory approach.

Conclusion

This chapter proposes a novel approach to e-textbook learning design coined as META-Era approach. The foundation of this approach rests on instructional dynamics and flexible strategy, educational data mining, flexible personalized curricula, generated structure of customized, personalized, and semantically-annotated contents, and various learning environments. This approach benefits from complex interdisciplinary research conducted in metasystems learning design embodying data mining, learning theory, operational research, knowledge representation and management, Web technology, and metadata-based semantics-enhanced learning environments. The need for metasystems thinking, the concept of e-textbook in electronic portfolio, the nature and utilization of semantic infrastructure META-Era API in metasystems learning design are explained. Especially the semantic tones of META-Era are taken up and SWRL examples are provided highlighting utility and advantage of semantic annotations in personalized learning.

In catering for needs of learners changing by time e-textbooks can be used for delivering information, receiving constituent information from e-libraries, and for purposes of developing metacognition and self-regulation skills. Future availability of learning objects can be enhanced through META-Era metasystems learning design with semantics. Learning materials can be prepared on the go to fit the requesting individual's particular needs and learning styles for delivery on digital devices, and through ubiquitous access. This chapter addressed some of the issues in relation to design and development of META-Era also providing detailed realistic examples to highlight its use and benefits.

META-Era approach relies on a framework infrastructure operating on the foundation of semantics, ontology engineering and semantic agent technologies. The framework builds up a semantically annotated unified base for learning activities, interactions, outcomes, learner integration, learning methods and models, learner skills, and progress. META-Era aims at combining thinking with educational and cognitive aspects of learning in order to empower the learner, the designer of learning objects, and the learning environment. All advanced features of META-Era including semantic annotation referring to ontologies of topic and environment manifest themselves in the end-product, the e-textbook. Effective utilization of this approach involves research on how well taking advantage of educational technologies on the one hand, and evolution of frameworks for intelligent analysis of information and assessment on the other.

References

Bespalco, B. (2007). Parameters and criterions of diagnostic aim. *Learning Technologies* (In Russian),19-34.

Buchem, I. (2014). Editorial for the special issue on Personal Learning Environments. *Journal of Literacy and Technology*, Special Edition: 15(2), 2-13.

Capra, F. (2004).*The hidden connections* (In Russian). Moscow: Sofia.

Çelik, D., Elçi A., & Elverici E. (2011). Finding suitable course material through a semantic search agent for Learning Management Systems of distance education.*6th IEEE International Workshop on Engineering Semantic Agent Systems* (ESAS 2011) in conjunction with the 35th Computer Software and Applications Conference (COMPSAC 2011) Proceedings (pp. 386-391). Munich, Germany

Demetrovics, J., Knuth, E., &Rado, P. (1982). Specification meta systems. *Computer*, 15 (5), 29-35.

Edwards, M. D. (2011). *Fundamentals of software company operations*. Raymong Swart, Karigon (Pvt) Ltd. e-book conversion. Willie Hooykaas Baldwin Kindle.

Elçi, A. (2005). A metadata for e-Learning coordination through Semantic Web Languages. *Turkish Online Journal of Educational Technology*, 4 (3) 12-17.

Fidel, J. (2007). Key competences for lifelong learning - European Reference Framework0 2007. Retrieved May 11, 2014, from http://ec.europa.eu/dgs/education_culture/publ/pdf/lllearning/keycomp_en.pdf

Garber, I. (2010).Meta-approach to psychology (In Russian). Saratov: Saratov news.

Hall, A. (1987). *Metasystems methodology: a new synthesis and unification*. Pergamon Press.Retrieved June 11, 2014, from http://www.panarchy.org/vonbertalanffy/systems.1968.html

Karadeniz, B., & Bayram, H. (2010).Effect of computer aided teaching of acid-base subject on the attitude towards science and technology class. *Social and Behavioral Sciences*, 2 (2), 2194-2196.

Klir, G. (1990). *Architecture of systems problem solving*.(In Russian).New York and London: Plenum Press.

Koulopoulos T. & Frappaolo C. (2000).*Smart things to know about knowledge management*. Padstow, Cornwall: T. J. International Ltd.

Liaw, S. & Huang, H. (2014). Investigating learner attitudes toward e-books as learning tools: based on the activity theory approach. *Interactive Learning Environments*. doi: 10.1080/10494820.2014.915416.

Mainzer, K. (2004).*Thinking in complexity: the computational dynamics of matter, mind, and mankind*. Berlin, Heidelberg, New York: Springer-Verlag.

Mebratu, D. (2001). The knowledge dimension of the sustainability challenge. *International Journal of Economic Development*, 3(1).Retrieved May 1, 2011 from http://www.spaef.com/file.php?id=1051.

Mih, C., &Mih, V. (2011). Conceptual maps as mediators of self-regulated learning, *Social and Behavioral Sciences,* 29, 390-395.

Minder (2003, p.42).Functional didactics: Objectives, Strategies, assessment (in Romanian). Chisinau: Cartier Educational.

Mora, M., Gelman, O., Cervantes, F., Mejía, M., &Weitzenfeld, A. (2003).*A systemic approach for the formalization of the Information Systems concept:why Information Systems are systems?*Hershey, PA, USA: IGI Publishing .

Novak, J., &Gowin, D. (1996).*Learning how to learn*. New York: Cambridge University Press.

Oshins, E. (1989). Quantum psychology of nots. In Jones, E. (ed.), *Proceedings of the 5th annual ANPA West meeting*. Carmel Valley, CA: Alternative Natural Philosophy Association.

Polsani, P. R. (2003). Use and abuse of reusable learning objects. *Journal of Digital Information*, 3(4).Retrieved June 18, 2014, from http://journals.tdl.org/jodi/index.php/jodi/article/view/89/88.

Porter, P. (2010). *Effectiveness of electronic textbooks with embedded activities on student learning*. Unpublished doctoral dissertation, Minnesota, United States: Capella University.

Rahimi, E., van den Berg, J.,& Veen, W. (2014).A pedagogy-driven framework forintegrating Web 2.0 tools into educational practices and building Personal Learning Environments. *Journal of Literacy and Technology*, 15 (2), 54-79.

Railean, E. (2012). Issues and challenges associated with the design of electronic textbook. In B. H. Khan (Ed.), *User Interface Design for Virtual Environments: Challenges and Advances* (pp. 238 – 256). Hershey, PA: IGI Publishing.

Rudic, G. A. (2011). How we think today, so we will live after 15 years. (in Russian). Retrieved April 20, 2012 from http://www.pedagogiemoderne.ru/blog/vaucherno_modulnaja_sistema_v_povyhenii_valifikacii_uchitelej/2011-04-18-4.

Sherry, L., Havelock, B., & Gibson, D., (2005). The personal and professional learning portfolio: an online environment for mentoring, collaboration, and publication. In Roberts T. (Ed.), *Computer Supported Collaborative Learning in Higher Education*(pp. 201-217). Hershey: Idea Group Publishing.

Stolurow, L. (1965). Systems approach to instruction. Retrieved June 18, 2014, fromhttp://oai.dtic.mil/oai/oai?verb=getRecord&metadataPrefix=html&dentifier=AD0619186.

Turchin, V. (1977).*The phenomenon of science: A cybernetic approach to human evolution.* Retrieved May 11, 2014, from http://pespmc1.vub.ac.be/POSBOOK.html.

Wilson, R. (1990). *Quantum psychology: how brain software programs you &your world.* USA: New Falcon Publications.

Additional Reading

The concept of personalized learning seems to defy definition. Bray and McClaskey provide a wholesome guide stressing learners' ability to actively participate in the design of their learning by selecting appropriate LOs for their mission:

Bray, B., &McClaskey, K. (n.d.). Personalized Learning Chart [Online]. Retrieved May 5, 2014, from https://sites.google.com/site/personalizedlearningtoolkits/

META-Era, aiming at empowering learner, designer of learning objects and learning environment, is thus likely to help towards evolving a personal learning environment (PLE). As Buchem (2014) discovers, both learner control and ownership in relation to the learning environment are the key defining characteristics of PLEs "revealing what "personal" in PLE may really mean."

Semantic Web is for rendering Web content equally usable by both human and machines (that should mean, software) through judicious annotation in connection to domain ontologies. The World Wide Web Consortium, W3C for short, states the vision and the technologies making up the Semantic Web authoritatively: Semantic Web (n.d.). Retrieved 12 June 2014, from http://www.w3.org/standards/semanticweb/.

Inner working of Semantic Web is inherently dependent on availability of domain ontology. Ontology is a set of vocabulary defining "the concepts and relationships (also referred to as "terms") used to describe and represent an area of concern" (http://www.w3.org/standards/semanticweb/ontology). OWL Web Ontology Language is a set of standards defining the most prominent form of ontology "is designed for use by applications that need to process the content of information instead of just presenting information to humans. OWL facilitates greater machine interpretability of Web content … by providing additional vocabulary along with a formal semantics" (*http://www.w3.org/standards/techs/owl#w3c_all*).

Ontologies constitute basic building blocks used in inference techniques on the Semantic Web. The Semantic Web Rule Language(SWRL;*http://www.w3.org/Submission/SWRL/*) is used for semantically defining learning model rules. The SWRL rules also apply to predefined criteria to find a suitable LO for a particular field or requirement. Very briefly, a SWRL rule is a conditional statement: the IF part states the conditions that must be satisfied forming the premises in order for the THEN part to come true. The IF part, called as the antecedent or the body of the rule, computes the atomic terms by also using the instance data in the ontology and maybe performing basic computations. The THEN part, that is the head or the consequent of the rule, contains only the assertions that will come true once the antecedent computes true.

Combining semantics and e-learning, as the case is in this chapter, leads to a semantic interworking of e-learning so called "Semantic E-learning Theory". A short introduction is presented in:

Yli-Luoma, P., &Naeve, A. (2006). Towards a semantic E-learning theory by using a modeling approach. In A. Naeve, M. Lytras, W. Nejdl, N. Balacheff& J. Hardin (Eds.), Advances of the Semantic Web for E-learning: Expanding Learning Frontiers. Special Issue of the British Journal of Educational Technology, 37(3), 445-459. Retrieved 20 May 2014 from http://kmr.nada.kth.se/papers/TEL/Semantic-eLearning-theory.pdf.

META-Era does not favor a particular e-learning model whereas other frameworks and PLEs inherently assume one.META-Era operates around a content-based metadata model for e-learning environments. The lack of and the need for such a model for the benefit of the learner was noted in connection with the IEEE Learning Technology Standards Committee's the Learning Technology Systems Architecture(LTSC LTSA)a decade ago (Elçi, 2005). Further detail on the LTSC LTSA may be reached at *http://ieee-sa.centraldesktop.com/ltsc/*.

Of all the e-learning frameworks Badrul Khan's for institutions is the most complete. A short overall introduction to the Eight Dimensional E-Learning Framework is available at *http://en.wikipedia.org/wiki/Eight_Dimensional_E-Learning_Framework*.That reference identifies the dimensions, mentions of several other successful e-learning frameworks, and provides links for further information.

The International Digital Publishing Forum (IDPF) has the EPUB® as the key standard for distribution and interchange format for digital publication media. Providing for representation, packaging and encoding semantically annotated Web data, EPUB is for distribution in a single-file format (*http://idpf.org/epub/*). The EPUB ecosystem for the community is reachable at *http://epubzone.org*.EPUB 3, the new version specification developed by the IDPF, is likely to change e-learning. Being based on Web standards, switch to HTML5 and use of W3C Open Web Platform facilitate interactivity, mobility, platform and terminal device independence, inclusion of semantics and personal preferences for EPUB 3. IDPF, W3C (*www.w3.org/*) and the IMS Global Learning Consortium (*www.imsglobal.org/*) have set up an alliance called EDUPUB in exploiting EPUB 3for use in the next generation learning content for developing a profile for the education sector. EDUPUB, presenting a comprehensive model for the interchange and deployment of educational content, is set to change how e-textbook is formed and presented (*http://www.imsglobal.org/edupub/*). See also:

Belfanti, P., &Gylling, M. (2014). What is EDUPUB? Presented in EDUPUB 2 Workshop, Salt Lake City, 12-13 February 2014. Retrieved June 10, 2014, from http://www.imsglobal.org/edupub/WhatisEdupubBelfantiGylling.pdf.

In some resemblance to META-Era API, ADL Initiative has come up with the Experience API (xAPI; *http://www.adlnet.gov/tla/experience-api/*). xAPIrenders textbooks dynamic and interconnected through links to the Internet of Things, containing real-time data and collaborative content. It also provides the infrastructure needed for learning analytics across the cloud data. The IEEE LTSC is now standardizing xAPIto employ it in connection with EPUB 3 in the IEEE LTSC's new project called the IEEE "Actionable Data Book." ADBis expected to provide a revolutionary approach to making learning material. See the following leads:

Richards, T., & Robson, R. (2014). The next disruption in digital learning [*Computing Now* blog online March 12, 2014]. Retrieved June 8, 2014, from *http://www.computer.org/portal/web/Musings-from-the-Ivory-Tower/content?g=7512968&type=article&urlTitle=the-next-disruption-in-digital-learning. http://www.gtn-quebec.org/wp-content/uploads/2014/03/Tyde-Richards-IEEE-ADB-Montreal.pdf. https://ieee-sa.centraldesktop.com/adb/.*

Key Terms and Definitions

- **Learning Management System (LMS)**is an information system for administration, documentation, delivery, planning, implementing, and maintaining of e-learning courses, training programs, related material and operational data as well as tracking, assessing and reporting of learner progress.

- **Learning Object (LO)**is an educational resourcecontaining an objective, a learning activity and an assessment. An educational resource is likely to be a collection of items for content, practice, and assessment based on a single learning objective. The term LO is employed in realm of technology-supported learning. An LO can be any resourceused for learning such as an electronic text, a simulation, a Web site, a .gif graphic image, a QuickTime movie, a Java applet.

- **E-textbook** represents embedding of a hardcopy book within an electronic environment. Various software such as Adobe Acrobat PDF, XML, SGML, HTML files, and personal devices such as a smart phone, Palm Reader, E-Reader, Sony Reader, and Amazon's Kindle among others are employed in utilizing it. It comes in many names such as digital texts, e-texts, e-books, electronic books, and hypertext books. It can serve as a tool for self-regulated teaching with purposes of personalization of core concepts, providing self-assessment tests and progress monitoring. Compare with e-portfolio.

- **E-portfolio** is for keeping all learning resources in one folder for both teachers and learners. The concept is employed in supporting particular needs of individual learners in their individualized learning processes. Learners build all-inclusive e-portfolios during learning process by and construct their own collection of work with record of achievements.

- **E-learning (or eLearning)** is teaching and learning conducted via electronic media and information and communication technologies (ICT). E-learning uses various forms of educational technology to create a virtual learning environment (VLE) by providing equivalent technology-enhanced access to classes, content, homework, tests, assessments and grades.

- **Framework for e-Learning** is a foundation of technology enhanced teaching and learning systems including various dimensions that guide design, development and implementation of e-learning curriculum.

- **Concept map** is a schematic drawing used in organizing and structuring knowledge. It depicts the relationships among concepts or even propositions about them. A concept map is an abstraction of a system of concepts. Concept mapping may be used together with semantic technology to enhance semantic aspects of *Learning Management Systems* (LMS).

- **Ontology** is a conceptualization of a domain of interest by stating the concepts, relations among concepts, and assertions about the domain. Ontology of a domain reflects the personal views of the ontologist creating it. Ontology can be used to extract entailments, that is, all deducible knowledge that does not invalidate any other stipulation in the ontology. Inference rules may as well be stated to draw conclusions based on the ontology.

- **Software agent** is a computer program or a part of a software system acting on behalf of a user, say a learner, or another program. It works autonomously and continuously in its environment, usually dormant until awakened by a trigger event. The so-called intelligent ones are able to learn from their experience.

Chapter Author(s)

Elena Railean - Ph.D in Sciences of Education, IANUS Erasmus postdoctoral fellow at Ioan Cuza University of Iasi (Romania), senior researcher at Academy of Sciences of Moldova and senior lecturer at University of European Studies of Moldova. Dr. Railean is author of 1 book, 5 IGI chapters and more than 60 articles in theory and methodology of learning design. Research interests include philosophy of learning, cybernetic pedagogy, computerized assessment, knowledge management, quantum psychology and mathematical modeling. The focus of her research is to investigate the metasystems approach of learning processes, principles of writing and assessment in digital semantic workplaces, and learning theory and design. Elena Railean is author of didactical model for electronic textbook use and development, which affordance is to develop competence through dynamic and flexible instructional strategy. Main publications: Methodology of educational software; Knowledge Management Model for Electronic Textbook Design; Issues and challenges associated with the design of electronic textbook; Trends, issues and solutions in e-books pedagogy; Digital Textbook in Personal Learning Portfolios: A Case of Interdisciplinary Pedagogical Innovation for Sustainability and Instructional dynamic and flexible strategy: integrity of effective methods for engaging all learners in classrooms.

Atilla Elçi is a Professor and Chairman of the Department of Electrical and Electronics Engineering at Aksaray University, Aksaray, Turkey, since August 2012. He was a full professor and chairman of computer and educational technology at Süleyman Demirel University, Isparta, Turkey (May 2010 - June 2012). He served as full professor of computer engineering, the founding director of the Graduate School of Science and Technology, and the dean of Engineering Faculty at Toros University, Mersin, Turkey (July 2010 - June 2011). He also served in various universities and the International Telecommunication Union since 1976. He has been organizing IEEE Engineering Semantic Agent Systems Workshops since 2006, Security of Information and Networks Conferences since 2007; and, IJRCS Symposiums 2007&9. He has published over a hundred journal and conference papers; co-authored the book titled Composition of OWL-S based Atomic Processes; edited the book titled Semantic Agent Systems (Springer 2011), and Theory and Practice of Cryptography Solutions for Secure Information Systems (IGI 2013); proceedings of SIN 2007, 2009 - 2013 by ACM, ESAS 2006-14 by IEEE CS, and IJRCS 2009; special issues. He was the program chair for the 36th IEEE COMPSAC (2012). He is an associate editor of Expert Systems: The Journal of Knowledge Engineering and editorial board member of several other journals. He obtained B.Sc. in Computer/Control Engineering at METU, Ankara, Turkey (1970), M.Sc. & Ph.D. in Computer Sciences at Purdue University, USA (1973, 1975).

Duygu Çelik is an Assistant Professor in Computer Engineering Department, Istanbul Aydın University. Her research topics are related to Web and Semantics, Composition of Semantic Web Services, Discovery of Semantic Web Services, Semantic Search Agents. She is one of organizers of two international workshops: "IEEE International Workshop on Engineering Semantic Agent Systems" and "Security of Information and Networks". She also supervises a number of researches and development projects supported by the university, government and industrial companies. She has published almost several publications at numerous international/national journals and conferences about the topic of Semantic. She also has published a book 'Composition of OWL-S based Atomic Processes' and an international book chapter on Semantic Agent Systems-Foundations and Applications (SASFA).

Alev Elçi got her undergraduate and graduate degrees respectively from Hacettepe University Mathematics and METU Computer Engineering departments in Ankara, Turkey. She has got doctoral degree in Educational Sciences from Eastern Mediterranean University, Gazimağusa, Northern Cyprus. She had worked in private companies such as Unisys and Oracle in Turkey, Pakistan, China, and Kuwait for 15 years giving software support and training to customers. She has been teaching in academia for the last 16 years, as a part-time instructor in Bilkent University and as a senior instructor in Information Technology Department, Eastern Mediterranean University. She currently works as Asst.Prof.Dr. in Department of Management Information Systems, Aksaray University. Her main research areas are faculty development, technology enhanced learning, educational technology, learning communities, animation and game based learning, internationalization, and HCI. She has a book titled "Faculty Beliefs and Needs: Opening the Gate to ICT-based Professional Development in Teaching and Learning". She has been teaching digital storytelling with animation and games, project management, ethical and social issues in IT, and database management.

Chapter 4

The Many Faces of Inquiry Based Learning

ABSTRACT: In this chapter, the authors define inquiry-based learning (IBL), briefly explain some evidence for IBL as a method of instruction in STEM courses, and explore the meaning of IBL in more detail by examining the specific structure of three mathematics courses taught by the authors: mathematics for elementary teachers, calculus, and introduction to proof. Finally, the authors introduce the IBL community. The narrative of this manuscript is informal to capture the nature of the class discussions and represent the nature of the classroom interactions.

Inquiry-Based Learning (IBL)

IBL is a pedagogical framework. Researcher Sandra Laursen and her colleagues define IBL as having two essential components: students deeply engage in meaningful problems, and students collaboratively process ideas (Laursen, et al., 2011). Although this chapter uses mathematics courses as examples in which IBL can be implemented, IBL works similarly in any STEM area where you wish for students to solve problems collaboratively.

Does IBL work

Evidence in favor of some form of active engagement of students is strong across STEM disciplines (Freeman, Eddy, McDonough, Smith, Okoroafor, Jordt, & Wenderoth, 2014). Freeman and colleagues conducted a meta-analysis of 225 studies of various forms of active learning, and found that students were 1.5 times as likely to fail in traditional courses as compared to active learning courses, and students in active learning courses outperformed students in traditional courses by .47 standard deviations on examinations and concept inventories.

For IBL specifically, Laursen (2011) and her colleagues studied IBL across more than 100 mathematics course sections at four universities, with courses including lower- and upper-division mathematics major courses, as well as courses such as mathematics for elementary teachers. Among their findings, they reported that in comparing students who came in to the study with GPAs below 2.5, those who took IBL math-track courses outperformed comparison low-GPA students in subsequent courses, raising their grades by between .3-.4 on a 4.0 scale, while the comparison students earned grades that were *lower* by more than .4 (for a between-groups difference of .8 grade points). Students in math-track courses also took a pre-course and post-course survey. The survey (Student Assessment of Learning Gains in Mathematics, SALG-M) asked students to respond on cognitive domain measures, such as mathematical thinking and problem solving, affective measures, such as confidence, persistence, and attitude about mathematics, and collaborative measures, on the value of working with others, seeking help, and appreciating different perspectives. On a pre-to-post comparison of math-track students' gains, IBL students improved significantly more than non-IBL students across these three domains of cognitive gains, affective gains, and collaborative gains.

How do I know if I am using IBL

Because of its historic roots in the method of R.L. Moore, there are some practices that are commonly associated with IBL that are not necessary conditions for a course to be IBL. For instance, Moore dedicated class time to students presenting their work (Coppin, Mahavier, May, & Parker, 2009). Moore also prohibited most forms of collaboration by students, with the exception being questions for a presenter at the board. Many current practitioners of IBL continue to spend large amounts of time with presenters at the board. However, for other IBL instructors, presentations need not be the primary focus of class time. Instead, in many IBL classes, collaboration may take the form of partners or small groups working together for significant amounts of time. In the authors' view, a class is IBL if the students are the focus of classroom activity, if the students are working on making sense of problems, and if there is discussion and sharing of mathematical ideas.

How does IBL differ for courses at different levels or for different audiences

The success of an IBL course depends on students making progress with the mathematics in the course. For this reason, it is important to design both the problem sets of the course and the grading incentives in ways that enable and encourage students to work hard to develop their understanding. The specifics of these elements will also depend on the particular students at the institution where the class is taught. As a group, the authors have taught at a wide range of institutions, including places where the students are traditional recent high school graduates, living on or near campus, but also places where the students may come from under-resourced high schools, and where the students are non-traditional, commuter students, balancing college with demands of full-time work and family.

In the following sections, we describe three implementations of IBL in different courses at different institutions. These instantiations of IBL should serve to illustrate some of the variety in how IBL courses are organized and operate on a day-to-day basis.

An IBL Mathematics for Elementary Teachers course: Jones

This course is the first in a two-course sequence for those interested in teaching elementary school. In practice, it is often the case that students may also take this course as part of their preparation for certification in teaching middle school mathematics. The course material ranges over K-7 arithmetic, from understanding base ten, through basic operations with whole numbers, integers, fractions, and decimals, and including working with per cents and proportions. This course is taught in sections of 25-35 students, many of who are non-traditional students on a commuter campus. Further, as a course for non-math, non-science majors, many of the students have a negative view of mathematics.

The problem set for the course (Jones, 2013) has been refined over several iterations. A few key points about the problem set: the problems are designed to broaden students' understanding of arithmetic by helping them discover algorithms previously unknown to them, such as the common-denominator method for division of fractions, or by providing alternate algorithms, such as the lattice method for multiplication, and asking them to analyze methods to determine whether they are correct, and why. The work of discovering new ways of doing arithmetic and of analyzing and understanding algorithms are fundamentally different from typical school mathematics activities that emphasize performing calculations accurately, but without understanding why the methods work. This problem set also illustrates that when IBL is defined as working to make sense of problems, the problems need not be "real-world"; they can be purely mathematical, as long as the students have a way to work to understand them.

Here is a typical week of instruction. The class meets twice weekly, 75 minutes per meeting. For purposes of illustration, suppose the class meets on Mondays and Wednesdays. On Monday, class begins with a brief discussion of the homework due, and possibly a presentation of a homework solution or two. Then we move to an introduction of a new topic. Often, I introduce a manipulative that students are expected to use as a tool to understand the mathematics for the week. For instance, I may introduce base ten blocks when we begin to work on understanding addition, early in the semester. My introduction generally serves to identify the names of the manipulatives, and to establish how the physical work with the manipulatives is to be recorded on students' papers. Students are then asked to work in groups on the problem section for the week. In this class, early in the semester, the groups are self-selected, but I usually change the groups every 3-4 weeks. My goal in changing groups is for students get to know their classmates, and to ensure that the students do not fall into patterns where only some students do the thinking while the others follow along. Once groups have begun working, my job is to monitor progress. I also work to ensure that all members of a group are participating and collaborating.

As I walk around the room, groups sometimes ask for clarification, or they ask, "Is this right?" While I may offer clarification, I tell students that part of their job is to find ways to verify their own answers. Other times, students have a question, and I redirect them to talk to their partners in the group. As the groups are working, I list a few problem numbers on the board. These problems are generally pre-selected to bring out the most important points of the section. However, if a problem not on the list is causing problems for most of the class, then that may be added to the list. As I see that students have completed these problems, I carry a notepad around the classroom and solicit specific students to sign up as presenters for the problems. There are two main considerations in selecting presenters: first, presentations are a requirement of the course, with a minimum of 3 presentations required for a passing grade on that component of the course, so that I try to ensure that every student has a roughly equal number of presentations at any given time; second, I am looking for particular approaches to some of the problems, and so I look for students who have taken those approaches whenever possible. Note that I sometimes purposely select a solution that is incorrect because I feel that it will lead to a fruitful mathematical discussion. Also, when there are multiple solution ideas among the students, there may be more than one presenter for some problems.

Depending on the particulars of the problems to be presented and the pace at which students are working, the last 25-45 minutes of class will be spent on student presentations. The particulars of the presentation norms vary each time I teach the course, but frequently, students come to the board while the class is still working in groups and write their solution. Then the class stops to listen as the presenter explains her or his work, and sits down. The class is then encouraged to ask questions, and I moderate the discussion, while also injecting questions of my own. Sometimes, I ask the groups to apply what they have learned to a follow-up task, which we then discuss briefly. We then proceed to the next presentation. Finally, students are asked to work on a few more problems before we meet again on Wednesday.

On Wednesday, since students have worked on an assignment, we usually begin presentations of selected problems within a few minutes of the start of class. Depending on the topic, after presentations, we either begin a new section, or students are asked to finish the problems from the current section. If we are continuing to work in the same section, then students may be assigned a group presentation. A group presentation means that students must work on a specific problem and, when everyone in the group is satisfied that they understand the solution, they call me over to present their work to me (not to the whole class). When the group is presenting, any group member may begin explaining the solution, but I will interrupt the presentation, and then ask someone else to take over the presentation, and I ask questions to ensure that the entire group understands their work. If anyone in the group gets stuck or cannot answer a question to my satisfaction, the group is told to discuss their work some more and call me back when they are ready. If we are beginning a new section, then I will introduce the topic and manipulatives, as appropriate, and then students begin working, and class will end with presentations.

In any IBL class, the instructor is getting more information about student understanding on a day-to-day basis than in a standard lecture course. For this reason, I prefer to limit the number of quizzes and exams. I give one quiz a few weeks into the term, two exams, and one final. In this course, my current grading scheme is: Homework, 10%; Journals, 5%; Quiz, 5%; Presentations and Group Work, 25%; Exams, 25%, Final, 30%. Homework for this class is collected weekly. As described above, homework is worked on in class and at home. Most of the homework grade (6 out of 7 points) is given for showing evidence of an attempt at all the assigned problems, while the last point is given for a correct solution to one or two particular problems. Journals are writing assignments, typically 8 of them in a semester, in which students are asked to read an article, usually from the journal Teaching Children Mathematics, and to respond to specific questions about the article. One major purpose of the journals is to help the students confront their negativity toward mathematics, and to begin to think about mathematics in new ways. A second purpose is to reinforce some of the concepts from the class, e.g., by reading about alternate methods of performing arithmetic that have been discussed in class.

For presentations, students are given a rubric (see Table 1). For group work, I record whether the students successfully presented their work, attempted but did not complete a presentation, or did not present. Generally, if students have made 4 good presentations and about 6 group presentations, they earn an A for this part of the course.

Table 1: Rubric for Presentations in Mathematics for Elementary Teachers.

10	Complete solution and explanation
9	Solution and explanation with minor issues resolved at the board
8	Solution and explanation with issues resolved at the board
7	Incorrect or partial solution that is not resolved by the class discussion
0	Little or no demonstrable progress toward a solution

An IBL Calculus course: Hodge

This course is a standard calculus course taken mainly by engineering majors, mathematics majors, and other STEM majors. It is usually populated by university freshman about half of who have taken a calculus course in high school. It is taught in sections of 40 students at a large metropolitan university. The course is five credits and meets for four 65-minute periods for 16 weeks. The topics of limits, derivatives, applications of derivatives, and basic integration techniques are all covered in the course using a traditional textbook for homework problems.

At a glance, this may seem like a very traditional calculus course. However, the way it is structured allows for student exploration of ideas, deep engagement with the mathematics, and collaboration with other students in the course.

Classroom setup. The atmosphere in the room sets the tone for a collaborative learning experience from the moment students walk into the classroom. There are 10 tables with 4 seats at each table in the room. They are arranged in a way so that it is nearly impossible to know which part of the room is the "front." Whiteboards and chalkboards cover 3 of the 4 walls in the classroom, with the fourth wall being windows. The tables let the students know that they will be working with each other on a regular basis. If you have a room with standard desks, I would suggest moving them together *before* students arrive on the first day of class, if possible. Then let them know that they should move the desks into this arrangement as soon as they arrive. Either pairs or groups of four seem to work best for a calculus course.

Typical day. On a typical day, the instructor would begin class with student presentations of 1-4 homework problems that students seemed to have difficulty completing. Problems are written on the whiteboards and as the students arrive they write up solutions to the problems on a first-come, first-serve basis. Then all of the problems are presented with the instructor acting as a coach and the students critiquing/complimenting each other's work.

After homework problems are presented, one of two things usually happens: (1) students work on an activity in pairs or groups of four or (2) students listen to a mini-lecture and then work on problems in their groups. No matter what, students are actively engaged in mathematics each and every day of the course.

Activities were designed to be hands-on "experiments" to help students either learn new concepts or reinforce topics they have already studied, but need help solidifying. Sample activities can be found with instructions at: http://math.colorado.edu/activecalc1/. These activities were created by the University of Nebraska Omaha Mathematics Department in partnership with the University of Colorado Boulder Mathematics and Education Departments.

If no activity has been designed for the daily topic, then I usually start with a mini-lecture introducing the topic. I keep these to a maximum of 5-10 minutes, just long enough to give the students something to work with on their own. Then the students are given calculus problems to work on in their groups. I always have a wide range of problems so that all students can do something and the stronger students are also still challenged.

During both the activities and problem solving sessions, I walk around the room constantly. I am always moving around checking for student understanding. If there is a common misconception, I will stop the group and have a short group discussion. As much as possible, I keep these discussions student-led (or have a student present a problem to help clear up any misunderstandings). On an average day roughly three more presentations are given throughout the hour. An ending summary/debrief is also created by the class at the end of most class periods so that all students know what they "should have taken" from the problem set or activity.

Logistics. Student grades in this course are determined according the following grade break down: four tests (14% each), homework (7%), quizzes (12%), participation/presentations (5%) and a comprehensive final exam (20%). I will explain each portion of this grade.

Homework is assigned and collected daily. My homework policy is similar to Ernst's homework policy except I call my weekly homework a quiz. Students are allowed to work with others on this weekly homework/quiz.

Exams are given four times during the semester and are very similar in nature to standard calculus exams. There are two parts to each exam: (a) an in-class individual portion in which no calculator is allowed and (b) a take-home group portion in which students can use a calculator and can work collaboratively with other classmates. The in-class part of the exam counts for two-thirds of their exam grade and the take home part counts for the remaining third of their exam grade. Final exams are all individual and given in class. One part of the final exam is printed on colored paper and a calculator is allowed on this portion of the exam.

Participation is an important part of such an active classroom atmosphere. Hence this paragraph is included in my syllabus:

> "This class will be a highly interactive one. You must come to class prepared to do problems, discuss ideas and strategies, and occasionally present material to the class. If you haven't looked at the material previously, this will be difficult to do. You must do at least three classroom presentations during the semester (with at least one in between each test). These will be presentations of problems/concepts to the class. You do not have to be 100% correct with your work. The class will work cooperatively to look at each other's work and to examine content and procedures. We will always be helping each other, and encouraging each other. We will learn from each other's mistakes; we don't learn anything if we're always right. We learn far more from our mistakes, so don't be afraid to try all problems! In order to receive full credit for presentations, you must also show interest in mathematics outside of regularly scheduled class hours. There are several ways to do this, which I will discuss."

In a class of 40, most students typically present 3-5 times per semester. I have them complete self-evaluations related to their participation two times during the semester. The students rank themselves on a scale of 0-10 (with 10 being the best) on what grade they would give themselves for participation and write a page on why they would give themselves this grade. They are usually very honest about this grade and also show improvements after writing a mid-semester reflection on their participation.

Tips for calculus (or any larger class). In any class where group work is the focus of the course, with student presentations being secondary, I strongly recommend going out of your way to help the students feel comfortable. Learn the students' names, learn something about each student, and learn to be very mobile in the classroom (move around constantly). Also let students "shop around for groups" until they find people they feel comfortable working with. Let the students know that you will not tell them the answers, but you are there to help them succeed. Be available to help them outside of class as well as in class. Lastly, have fun! IBL lets you have fun and watch your students bloom as problem solvers. Enjoy it!

An IBL Introduction to Proof course: Ernst

This section describes the nuts and bolts of one possible implementation of an IBL approach in an introduction or transition to proof course. Essentially a modified-Moore method, the approach described here is what I have converged on after several iterations. My expectation is that readers will envision ways to modify and even improve upon what is described here. We refer the reader to articles by D. Chalice (Chalice, 1995) and W.T. Mahavier (Mahavier, 1997) for additional information.

My experience is limited to classes involving 10-45 students and typically includes a mixture of mathematics and mathematics education majors, as well as the occasional non-mathematics major. In larger classes, some modifications are likely necessary.

The topics covered in an introduction to proof course vary from institution to institution, but in my case the topics include an introduction to logic, number theory, set theory, topology of the real line, mathematical induction, infinitude of the primes, irrationality of the square root of 2, relations, partitions, functions, and order relations. In addition, I have several goals that transcend the content of the course. In particular, I want students to be able to:

- Produce examples/counterexamples,
- Make conjectures,
- Validate arguments,
- Produce valid proofs,
- Write technical prose in the context of mathematics,
- Persist on difficult tasks,
- Call upon their own prodigious mental faculties to respond in flexible, thoughtful, and creative ways to problems that may seem unfamiliar on first glance.

In order to nurture these goals, students should as much as possible be responsible for guiding the acquisition of knowledge and validating the ideas presented. That is, the instructor should not be the sole authority. My goal is to get out of the way and see what my students can do.

In a standard introduction to proof class, students are taught the skill of producing valid mathematical justification. To write proofs well, students must become skeptical consumers of their own work. They must learn how to look at their own writing as if it were written in someone else's hand and ask, "Am I convinced?"

On a day-to-day basis, students are responsible for digesting new material outside of class by completing assigned tasks from the course notes that are specifically designed for IBL. The tasks are a combination of exercises aimed at developing understanding of the relevant concepts together with statements of theorems that students are supposed to prove. These tasks make up the Daily Homework, which is assigned at the end of each class meeting and is due the next class meeting. Nearly all class time is then devoted to students' presenting their proposed solutions/proofs from the assignment that is due that day.

The student-led presentations form the backbone of the class as this is what we spend the bulk of time on each day. The norm is to have one student at a time presenting to the class. Having experimented with different methods, the approach I usually take is to have students write out their proposed proofs/solutions as they present. That is, presenters should explain their reasoning as they go along, not simply write everything down and then turn to explain. While this may seem painfully slow to the instructor, I believe it provides for a much richer experience. The audience has time to process and it allows speakers to practice their presentation skills as opposed to rushing through a pre-written solution. However, if there are several easy exercises to present, I may have multiple students go to the board at once to simultaneously write down their solutions and then take turns discussing them.

The number of problems presented in a 50-minute class meeting varies, but the norm is roughly five. For proofs, presenters are also required to write in complete sentences and use proper grammar. This provides plenty of opportunities to discuss the finer points of formal composition in the context of mathematics.

The expectation is that at the beginning of class volunteers write their names on the board next to the problems they are willing to present. If multiple students volunteer for the same problem, the student with the fewest number of presentations to date has priority. If no student volunteers, an attempt will be made to call on a student, or possibly, the problem will be saved for small-group work at the end of class. In addition, I allow the students to call on me to present up to three times during the semester.

It is the job of the students in the audience to determine the validity of a presented proof/solution, as well as make comments related to the eloquence of the proof itself. A student's presentation may be interrupted at any time by questions or comments from the class, and the presenter is expected to act as the discussion leader for the problem being presented.

The best presentations are the ones that contain subtle errors or interesting mistakes. Of course, I do not want students to make mistakes on purpose nor not strive for quality, but I make it clear to the class that there is a lot to learn from mistakes. It is important to create a safe environment where risk taking is encouraged and mistakes are not stigmatized.

In a standard lecture-style course, the students diligently copy down the material being presented. In my experience, it is often the case that students do not question the validity of what is being said by the instructor. The reason for this is that the instructor is a trusted authority. However, if a student is presenting, the other students in the audience are much more likely to process the argument being presented while asking, "Is this true?" This engages the student with the material on a much deeper level.

Presentations are graded using the rubric given in Table 2. In practice, students almost never receive a grade below 2 and the most common grade is a 3. I often break the rubric into half-point increments (e.g., a score of 2.5 may be given). It is important that the rubric not deter students from presenting. If an individual has an idea about a proof that he or she would like to present, but is concerned that the proof is incomplete or incorrect, that student should be rewarded for being courageous and sharing creative ideas. For this reason, a student's overall presentation grade is predominately a function of how many times he or she came to the board as opposed to the average of their presentation scores. Yet, students should not come to the board to present unless they have spent time thinking about the problem and have something meaningful to contribute.

Table 2: Rubric for Presentations in an introduction to proof course

Grade	Criteria
4	Completely correct and clear proof or solution. Yay!
3	Proof has minor technical flaws, some unclear language, or lacking some details. Essentially correct.
2	A partial explanation or proof is provided but a significant gap still exists to reach a full solution or proof.
1	Minimal progress has been made that includes relevant information & could lead to a proof or solution.
0	You were completely unprepared.

In addition, each student should strive to present a few challenging problems as opposed to only tackling easier problems. Do not be afraid to provide feedback to individual students about the frequency with which they are presenting and the difficulty level of the problems they are choosing to present. I make it clear that earning a 3 on a difficult problem that generated lots of discussion is more valuable to the class as a whole than scoring a perfect 4 on an easy exercise.

Because I am taking volunteers for presentations, it is important that I provide some structure for the students so that no one tries to wait until the last week of the semester to start presenting. The details of the scaffolding that I provide differ depending on the number of students I have and the number of exams that I plan to give, but in general the scheme goes as follows. Let's assume that there are two midterm exams and a cumulative final exam. In order for a student to receive a passing grade on the presentation portion of his or her grade, that student must present at least twice prior to each exam for a total of at least six times during the semester. A student's overall presentation grade is determined by taking into account the number of times the individual presented, the average of the presentation scores, the level of difficulty of the problems that the student chose to present, as well as the level of interaction during others' presentations. A student's overall presentation grade is worth 30% of his or her overall grade.

Within reason, I allow students to request mini-lectures on topics at any time. The typical length of a mini-lecture is 5-10 minutes. With experience, one can begin to anticipate when these requests will occur. Students need to be appropriately supported, but instructors must take care not to immediately default back to lecturing when students are struggling. Otherwise, students may become dependent on the instructor rather than themselves and each other. On the other hand, you have to make sure that the students feel supported and are not struggling too much. Sometimes the class honestly needs assistance; so do not be afraid to give it to them.

One advantage of doing mini-lectures upon request is that students have to take ownership of what they are struggling with. If I lecture on a topic before the students have struggled with the material, it is easy for them to be lulled into thinking they can figure things out later. In contrast, if the students struggle with the material on their own first, their misconceptions and weaknesses are exposed. Moreover, the students tend to hang on every word I say during a mini-lecture because they have already attempted to understand the relevant material, but failed. In the students' view, the mini-lecture may be their last chance to grasp the material.

I give two types of homework assignments (Daily and Weekly), each with an intended purpose. My structure is one possible solution to an optimization problem that all instructors are faced with: maximize the quality of the experience for the student, as well as the usefulness of feedback for the student, while minimizing the amount of time spent grading. In a typical semester, I assign 30-35 Daily Homework assignments and about a dozen Weekly Homework assignments. A student's overall homework grade is worth 25% of his or her final grade.

As mentioned above, Daily Homework is assigned each class meeting, and students are expected to complete each assignment before walking into the next class session. Since this is their first point of contact with new material, the work done on these assignments is not necessarily intended to be perfect. Students are allowed–in fact, strongly encouraged–to modify their written work in light of presentations made in class; however, they are required to use a colored marker pen that is provided at the beginning of each class. Students can annotate their work as much as they like and there is no penalty for using the colored pen. At the end of class, students submit their work and the assignments are then graded on a ✓-system. Whether a student receives a ✓-, ✓, or ✓+ depends on how much work he or she completed before walking in the classroom.

There are several advantages to this approach to Daily Homework. First, students are encouraged to attempt every problem, but are not severely punished for making an error on their first attempt to learn new material. At the end of each class, students have at least a sketch of a proof/solution for most of the assigned problems. When they look back at their notes, they see their comments about what they were thinking together with their corrected mistakes. Moreover, I know which problems were attempted before class began versus what annotations were made during class. In addition, the grading of the Daily Homework requires minimal effort, and as a result, Daily Homework is easily returned the next class session.

Each week, some subset of the problems from the Daily Homework assignments that are due that week are marked with a star. The starred problems are typically theorems that require more than a trivial proof. For the Weekly Homework, students are required to submit formally written proofs for two of the starred problems from the previous week. I require my students to typeset their proofs using LaTeX, but this is just a personal preference.

One advantage of this approach is that students are forced to reflect on the previous week's work and it allows them another opportunity to learn the material if they did not master it the first time. In addition, students are forced to incorporate multiple rounds of revision. Since students are essentially completing a problem for a second time, the quality of the work is quite good. As a consequence, the grading of the Weekly Homework goes smoothly and at the same time I feel comfortable holding high standards. The Weekly Homework assignments are subject to a 0–4 point rubric that is a slight modification of the one given in Table 2.

In a typical semester, there are two midterm exams and a cumulative final exam. Each exam is worth 15% of a student's overall grade and consists of both an in-class portion and a take-home portion. The weights of the in-class versus take-home portions vary, but roughly 75% and 25%, respectively, is common.

What do we learn from these instances of IBL

Our hope in describing three courses in some detail is to let readers observe the variety in the details of courses that we consider to be IBL. Earlier, we stated that a class is IBL if the students are the focus of classroom activity, if the students are working on making sense of problems, and if there is discussion and sharing of mathematical ideas. From the examples of Jones, Hodge, and Ernst, we see that how student activity and discussion is organized can vary significantly, from students spending more than half of the class time in groups, to students spending nearly all of the time focused on student presentations. We also see that class time may be used to introduce new ideas, but that a lot of time is used for students to share their thinking after having worked outside of class. Across all of these examples, students make sense of the problems through working on their own, through their interaction with their peers, and with coaching from the instructor.

These examples also show how incentives can vary. No system is perfect, but over time, the authors have found ways to balance the competing needs of giving students feedback and having reasonable documentation of students' learning, without overwhelming the instructor with grading, and to value students' efforts and failures as part of the learning process while also holding students accountable for achieving the course goals. Next, we will describe the community of IBL instructors and how this community supports individuals committed to advancing student learning.

The IBL Community

Ongoing community support for IBL instructors is a key component of the IBL movement. A driving force of the IBL movement is the aggregate effort of members of a growing community of IBL practitioners, who contribute in a variety of ways to helping one another, sharing ideas, and grappling with implementation issues. This section provides a brief overview of the nature of the IBL community and the kinds of support programs available for instructors.

The skills and practices necessary for successful IBL implementation are significant; therefore, mentoring, access to IBL training, course materials, and opportunities for continual professional development can significantly improve the initial and ongoing IBL experiences for students and instructor alike. Further, IBL methods are being employed in a larger number of types of classes and in a variety of different settings. Implementation challenges vary across courses, institutions, and class parameters (e.g., number of students in a course). As IBL is implemented in a wider range of courses and institutions, new opportunities and challenges emerge, and the community has grown and adapted to meet these challenges to the extent that available resources are available.

The present day IBL community has its roots in the immense efforts made by Harry Lucas, Jr. and the foundation he created: The Educational Advancement Foundation (EAF). Using his personal fortune, Harry Lucas, Jr. established the EAF and funded a variety of efforts to promote the use of IBL methods, including the annual Legacy of R. L. Moore and IBL Conference. This conference is an annual event for the IBL community to meet, share, and learn from one another. A student of R. L. Moore himself, Harry Lucas, Jr. found the educational experience personally transformative and applicable to his life and career. Wanting to help provide this experience for students across the nation, Mr. Lucas, Jr. has guided and supported efforts to expand the use of IBL by funding projects, organizing the first generation of IBL practitioners, and providing funding and initial organization of the annual conference.

Over the course of nearly two decades several outreach programs were created by EAF to support new IBL instructors and departments. These programs include a small grants program, a mentoring program, the visiting speakers bureau, the Journal of Inquiry Based Learning in Mathematics (www.jiblm.org), and summer workshops. These programs were created and organized by the community, where needs and obstacles were identified, and solutions were created to address them. An important fact to recognize is that these programs were developed and cultivated by the community to address the needs of members of the community. Hence, the programs are a result of grassroots efforts to address real-world implementation challenges.

In 2010, some of these programs were consolidated under one umbrella organization, the Academy of Inquiry Based Learning (www.inquirybasedlearning.org) or AIBL. AIBL is an organizational front to an existing IBL community and fosters many (but not all) of the inclusive efforts to support math faculty in learning about and disseminating IBL methods. The primary mission of AIBL is to support, sustain, and grow the IBL community.

The small grants program offers IBL instructors support for summer stipends or possibly course load reduction. The initial workload to create an IBL course and learn the skills and practices needed are significant, and small grants provide one strategy for providing much needed resources to faculty and external validation for their efforts. Small grants can be awarded to new IBL instructors, who work with a mentor. Other categories exist for more experienced IBL instructors to provide support for development of new IBL course materials, to prepare course materials for publication, and to pair new and experienced IBL instructors to teach the same course.

Mentoring is a major activity within the community. Mentoring is organized between individuals and also via groups that form around a particular course, topic, or workshop experience. Mentoring is a way for new IBL instructors to connect with more experienced practitioners in the community. This informal network is a major component of the IBL community, and a way for people to interact with one another regularly.

Members of the IBL community have been able to offer intensive summer workshops to help faculty, particularly those new to IBL. In the workshops, instructors observe and discuss video of other IBL instructors, learn critical skills involved in planning and facilitating IBL courses, get acquainted with existing IBL resources, especially course materials, and plan the particulars of their own courses with assistance from more experienced IBL instructors. These workshops have been responsible for increasing the size of the IBL community substantially in the last 10 years.

Social networking, email distribution lists, and blogging have been used to further support and promote exchanges of ideas. Social networking sites, such as Facebook and Google+, have been useful in bringing together faculty via a mostly informal setting. People interact on these sites primarily for social or other reasons, but occasionally information is shared or discussions about specific teaching issues occur. Email distributions lists (similar to listserve) are organized more formally, where members in each group are there for a specific purpose, such as interest in a specific course or part of a workshop cohort. Lastly, blogging is used to "push" information, teaching tips, and commentary on articles and news. Blogging is an informal way to send to the community ideas and information on regular intervals and share ideas in formats less formal than a peer-review publication. Often bite-size nuggets of wisdom are difficult to package in a full article, but play extremely well in the blogosphere.

If you would like to learn more about IBL, there are many websites available to get you started. We also provide links to access resources for your own STEM classroom.

Links:
The Educational Advancement Foundation, http://eduadvance.org
The Academy of Inquiry Based Learning, www.inquirybasedlearning.org
IBL Workshops, www.iblworkshop.org
The Journal of Inquiry Based Learning in Mathematics, www.jiblm.org
The IBL Blog, http://theiblblog.blogspot.com
The Math Switch, http://themathswitch.blogspot.com
Math Ed Matters, http://maamathedmatters.blogspot.com
Active Learning Materials for Calculus, http://math.colorado.edu/activecalc1/

References

Chalice, D. R. (1995). How to Teach a Class by the Modified Moore Method. *Amer. Math. Monthly*, *104*(4), 317–321.

Coppin, C. A., Mahavier, W. T., May, E. L., & Parker, G. E. (2009). The Moore Method: A Pathway to Learner-Centered Instruction. Washington, DC: Mathematical Association of America.

Freeman, S., Eddy, S.L., McDonough, M., Smith, M.K., Okoroafor, N., Jordt, H., & Wenderoth, M.P. (2014). Active learning increases student performance in science, engineering, and mathematics. *Proceedings of the National Academy of Sciences, 111 (23),* 8410-8415.

Jones, M. G. (2013). Mathematics for elementary teachers: Real numbers. *Journal of Inquiry-Based Learning in Mathematics, 32.*

Laursen, S., Hassi, M.-L., Kogan, M., Hunter, A.-B., & Weston, T. (2011). *Evaluation of the IBL mathematics project: Student and instructor outcomes of inquiry-based learning in college mathematics* (Report to the Educational Advancement Foundation and the IBL Mathematics Centers). Retrieved from http://www.colorado.edu/eer/research/ documents/IBLmathReportALL_050211.pdf

Mahavier, W. T. (1997). A Gentle Discovery Method: (The Modified Texas Method). *College Teaching*, *45*(4), 132–135.

Chapter Author(s)

Angie Hodge
University of Nebraska at Omaha
Omaha, Nebraska
USA

Dana Ernst
Northern Arizona University
Flagstaff, Arizona
USA

Matt Jones
Austin Peay State University
Clarksville, Tennessee
USA

Stan Yoshinobu
California Polytechnic
San Luis Obispo, California
USA

Chapter 5

Perspectives on Project Lead the Way (PTLW)

ABSTRACT: The following chapter is structured to provide an overview of a successful science, technology, engineering and mathematics (STEM) K-12 pathway program. The successful STEM program that we have focused on was implemented in the Omaha Public Schools (OPS) in 2003. This chapter is structured as follows. The reader is provided a report on the national status of STEM education. Next, past research on the impact of early exposure to STEM activities and curriculum programs is discussed. Third, there is a discussion of the OPS institutions that have implemented a STEM focused curriculum program. Then, the reader is exposed to the benefits of engaging students in STEM focused afterschool programs that compliment lessons learned in school. The chapter concludes with a discussion of what was learned and recommendations for implementing a similar program.

Introduction

Declining student interest in collegiate science, technology, engineering, and mathematics (STEM) degree programs is a nationwide concern. The American College Testing (ACT) organization reported that " from the 2010–2012 national ACT-tested graduating classes (N = 1,167,221), just over 1 in 10 graduates indicated interest in a STEM major or occupation" (American College Testing, 2013, p. 19). The U.S. Department of Commerce (2011) estimated that STEM careers would grow 17 percent by 2018, which is nearly double the growth for non-STEM fields. It is projected that by 2018, the U.S. will have more than 1.2 million unfilled STEM jobs because there will not be enough qualified workers to fill them (U.S. Department of Commerce, 2011). Of particular concern are the low numbers of females entering the STEM workforce. An insufficient number of females graduating from collegiate STEM degree programs results in workforce demands for diversity not being met, as more than half of all bachelor's degree graduates are female. This study aimed to explore the factors that influence and motivate female students to enroll and persist in collegiate STEM programs. The results of the study suggest that by providing increased access to pre-collegiate STEM activities, instilling confidence in female students, and establishing student and industry-based mentoring programs so that students can learn about STEM career pathways, more female students will enroll and persist in collegiate STEM degree programs.

Effects of Pre-Collegiate STEM Programs on Collegiate STEM Enrollment

In addition to providing high school students with exposure to advanced math and science courses, pre-collegiate STEM programs are designed to act as a pipeline to collegiate STEM degrees. Researchers have argued that increased levels of exposure to pre-collegiate math and science lead to higher self-efficacy, which may then lead to an increased likelihood for enrollment in and persistence through a collegiate STEM degree program (Fantz, Siller, & DeMiranda, 2011; Jenson et al., 2011; Hackett, 1985; Zeldin et al., 2008).

In one qualitative study, Dave et al. (2012) explored the reasons for a lack of females in the STEM fields. The researchers hypothesized that females were more likely to consider collegiate majors and careers if they believe these majors and careers make a positive impact on society and if they are exposed to female role models. The investigators tested their hypothesis with high school sophomores and juniors in a weeklong math- and science-focused summer camp. Fifteen participants were engaged in hands-on activities with female teachers and college-age mentors as part of the Math Options Summer Camp. The activities emphasized teamwork, design, and ergonomics in addition to mechanical engineering, steel cutting, electrical engineering, and plastic engineering workshops. The summer camp provided the participants with practical experience, the foundation to gain a better understanding of the hard sciences, and an opportunity to build confidence in their ability to succeed in a collegiate STEM degree program. Dave et al. (2012) found that participants benefited from interactions with the college student mentors, which increased their level of comfort with science. As a result of the additional exposure to math and science, many of the participants indicated that they would take math or science courses even if they were not required, and agreed that it is important for everyone to have a basic understanding of the STEM fields. The study reported that females were not as encouraged as males to consider collegiate STEM degree programs. The researchers concluded that female students gained a better understanding of the specific STEM disciplines as a result of the camp. For participants who had an interest in pursuing a STEM field, the camp solidified their decision, and for participants who did not know much about STEM, it was a mind-opening experience (Dave et al., 2012).

In the study by Fantz et al. (2011), the researchers looked at the student experience by considering the relationship among pre-collegiate engineering factors (e.g., outreach programs, field trips, exposure to engineering colleges, summer camps) and engineering students' self-efficacy. In particular, the researchers wanted to know if there were some types of pre-collegiate engineering factors associated with higher self-efficacy than others. The researchers hypothesized that the more rigorous the pre-collegiate experience, the more likely a student would possess a higher self-efficacy in math and science, resulting in an increased likelihood that the student would enroll in and persist through a collegiate engineering program.

Fantz et al. (2011) measured the students' engineering self-efficacy by administering the Motivated Strategies for Learning Questionnaire (MSLQ) to participants. MSLQ is a tool used to assess students' level of motivation to persist in a degree program and their likelihood of using different learning strategies for collegiate study. The MSLQ was administered to first year undergraduate students (N=332) who were enrolled in an engineering college. Of the 332 students who participated in the study, 81% were male (N=269) and less than 20% were female (N=62).

The results from the questionnaire led to two comparison groups: those who did not experience pre-collegiate engineering activities and those who did experience pre-collegiate engineering activities. Fantz et al. (2011) further drilled down the two comparison groups so that there were two sub-categories for those who did experience pre-collegiate engineering activities: formal experiences and informal experiences. If a student indicated that he/she did experience pre-collegiate engineering activities, the researchers considered the type of experience as either formal or informal. Formal pre-collegiate experiences were defined as "…middle school or high school courses, summer and out-of-school programs, and single-day field trips" (Fantz et al., 2011, p. 606). Informal pre-collegiate experiences included "…work experience and personal experiences with toys and hobbies" (Fantz et al., 2011, p. 606).

These researchers found that there were significant differences in engineering students' self-efficacy resulting from the types of pre-collegiate engineering experiences they had. Of the 53 types of pre-collegiate engineering experiences considered by the researchers, seven had significant differences in self-efficacy scores. Of the seven pre-collegiate activities (technology class, engineering class, programming as a hobby, electronics as a hobby, robotics as a hobby, model rockets as a hobby, and production of video games as a hobby) that displayed significant differences in self-efficacy scores, five were categorized as informal experiences (programming as a hobby, electronics as a hobby, robotics as a hobby, model rockets as a hobby, and producing video games as a hobby). Fantz et al. (2011) attributed higher levels of self-efficacy to pre-collegiate activities that were described as hobbies because they called upon the student to have: "…self-motivation, use of problem solving strategies, hands-on application of complex subject matter, use of computer applications, and immediate feedback on success of effort" (p. 100). Does this mean that informal pre-collegiate engineering activities lead to higher engineering self-efficacy and are more likely to result in enrollment in collegiate engineering colleges? Fantz et al. (2011) found that hobbies and formal classes with structured curricula (e.g., technology and engineering classes) were also associated with higher levels of engineering self-efficacy in participants. Furthermore, students who had pre-collegiate experiences (formal and informal) were associated with higher self-efficacy in engineering than their peers who did not have these experiences, which would lead to a greater likelihood of enrolling in and persisting through collegiate engineering programs.

Fantz et al. (2011) concluded with a call for more resources to be focused on developing pre-collegiate STEM experiences for K-12 students, as they lead to higher self-efficacy in students and a greater likelihood for enrollment in and persistence through a collegiate STEM major. The findings are not surprising as it seems obvious that students who are participating in pre-engineering classes, engineering summer camps, math and science hobbies, and so on are more likely to enroll in and persist through collegiate STEM programs than students who have not had those experiences. The researchers called for more rigorous pre-collegiate engineering activities that include higher levels of mathematics and engineering and targeting of students who display an interest in these courses through their hobbies.

In one quantitative study, Espinosa (2011) looked at the effects of pre-collegiate activities, experiences in college, and institutional setting on the persistence of females (N=1385) in collegiate STEM majors. Espinosa's (2011) research revealed that females were more likely to enroll in and persist through collegiate STEM programs if they had the opportunity to engage with their peers and participate in STEM-related student organizations, and if they were made aware of altruistic career opportunities. The findings from the study called for developing cohort STEM programs that provide female students with a greater sense of community, increasing the number of student organizations related to STEM fields (e.g., Society of Women Engineers), and providing female students with real world experiences that demonstrate how a career in STEM can influence environmental, social, and economic problems.

With regard to increasing K-12 resources and access to pre-collegiate STEM programs, organizations such as American College Testing (ACT) encourage secondary institutions to align their academic standards with higher education institutions and provide more college readiness opportunities so that students are better prepared for collegiate STEM programs. Consequently, ACT recommended that educators raise expectations of students so that they develop strong math and science skills by requiring that all students complete three years of a rigorous math and science course sequence (American College Testing, 2006). Another advocate of pre-collegiate STEM curricula is the non-profit organization Project Lead the Way (PLTW). PLTW is a national provider of pre-engineering and technology education curricular programs for middle and secondary schools committed to preparing students for the global economy by increasing access to and preparation for collegiate STEM degree programs. PLTW was established in 1997 to prepare students to be innovative and productive leaders in Science, Technology, Engineering, and Mathematics (Project Lead the Way, 2013). Since its inception, PLTW has served as an effective tool for increasing collegiate enrollment in STEM degree programs. In a survey of PLTW (2009) seniors, it was found that more than 90% intended to pursue a four-year degree as compared to the national average of 67%. Consequently, 70% of PLTW high school seniors indicated that they intended to study engineering, technology, or computer science. PLTW reported that "college students, who took PLTW courses in high school, study engineering and technology at 5 to 10 times the rate of those students who did not take PLTW courses in high school and also have higher retention rates in their fields of study" (PLTW, 2009). PLTW partners with high schools and institutions of higher education to provide a rigorous, relevant STEM education to K-12 students. Higher education institutions are involved in the process of educating both students and their teachers, as they serve as trainers to high school teachers in math and science in their preparation for teaching the PLTW curriculum.

Nebraska Project Lead The Way (PLTW) – Rosemary Edzie

In 2006, the University of Nebraska-Lincoln joined the PLTW network. The College of Engineering at the University of Nebraska-Lincoln enthusiastically embraces its unique role as the singular intellectual and cultural resource for engineering and technology instruction, research, and outreach within the State of Nebraska. The College of Engineering provides the people of Nebraska with comprehensive engineering and technology academic programs to fulfill their highest aspirations and ambitions Project Lead The Way, University of Nebraska – Lincoln, College of Engineering, 2014).

The College of Engineering works with Nebraska schools in the national Project Lead the Way initiative. PLTW's curriculum includes hands-on and project-based engineering courses for elementary, middle, and high school students. The curriculum is founded in the fundamental problem-solving and critical-thinking skills taught in traditional career and technical education, while integrating national academic and technical learning standards and STEM principles. Currently, there are 17 high schools, 1 middle school and 1 elementary school in Nebraska involved. Table 1, *2013 Secondary School PLTW Enrollment*, provides an enrollment overview for the 2013-2014 academic year.

Table 1 2013 Secondary School PLTW Enrollment

NE Secondary School PLTW Enrollment	
High School	Number of Students
Kearney High School	54
Lincoln East High School	53
Lincoln Northeast High School	20
Lincoln Southeast High School	45
Millard North High	73
Millard South High	31
Millard West High School	92
North High School	195
Northwest High School	66
Papillion-La Vista High School	90
Papillion-La Vista South High School	80
Southwest High School	38
Total	837

The American Psychological Association reported that by second and third grade, many students begin to lose interest in learning. Past research shows that students make career and curriculum choices that can influence their future postsecondary and education career paths (Akos, Lambie, Milsom, and Gilbert, 2007). Knowing that secondary school curriculum choices drive postsecondary career paths, focus will be placed on outreach to middle school populations. Hands-on, pre-collegiate STEM programs provide exposure to advanced math and science courses and act as a pipeline to collegiate STEM degrees. Researchers argue that increased levels of exposure to pre-collegiate math and science will lead to higher self-efficacy, which may then lead to an increased likelihood for enrollment in and persistence through a collegiate STEM degree program (Fantz, Siller, & DeMiranda, 2011; Jenson et al., 2011; Hackett, 1985; Zeldin et al., 2006).

Omaha Public School district has committed to excellence and equitable education for all students in the classroom through its 40-year implementation of magnet schools. OPS' magnet schools develop unique curriculum in themed areas attracting students from across the metropolitan area. At Skinner Magnet Elementary, engineering, mathematics, technology and the arts are the themes that make this school a one of a kind choice for parents in the Omaha metropolitan area. Elementary students at Skinner experience blended learning lessons taught by specialist teachers. This magnet curriculum experience continues at McMillan Magnet Middle School through PLTW's Gateway to Technology middle school program in grades 7 and 8 and concludes at Omaha North High School with PLTW's Pathway to engineering high school program. Throughout this K-12 Magnet Pathway, OPS continues to demonstrate its commitment by providing resources in terms of teachers and supplies to prepare our students for the ever-evolving, engineering-rich international global economy. The following image demonstrates the strong pathway to

STEM relationship that exists amongst Skinner Magnet School, McMillan Magnet Middle School, and Omaha North High School. OPS' investment in PLTW benefits not only the students in the district, but also the teachers who have an opportunity to participate in professional development training as they prepare to teach new courses.

Teacher Professional Development. The PLTW Professional Development model is designed to create dynamic learning experiences for teachers through robust and flexible instructional support and ongoing professional community. PLTW teachers participate in a three-phase professional development model. The model provides teachers with learning opportunities that emphasize proper preparation, in-depth training, and continuing education. The three phases of the model are Readiness Training, Core Training, and Ongoing Training (Project Lead The Way, Engineering - Professional Development, 2014).

Readiness Training focuses on preparation and awareness to ensure that teachers have basic technical and content knowledge prior to participating in pedagogy, skill, and knowledge enhancement training experiences.

Core Training focuses on building awareness and confidence related to STEM education; activity-, project-, and problem-based learning; the roles of the teacher and student as they relate to instruction; and course-specific STEM content. Core Training is a collaborative, in-person training experience offered at PLTW Affiliate Universities across the nation and facilitated by PLTW Master Teachers.

Ongoing Training consists of self-paced and live online e-Learning resources that provide knowledge enhancement opportunities and ongoing learning for educators. Ongoing Training encourages teachers to move beyond baseline knowledge and skills related to both content and pedagogy to deepen their understanding. Teachers also have access to training resources related to course updates and new releases.

Working with Pathway Members

For the last few years, the Omaha North Magnet High School's National Society of Black Engineers (NSBE) student organization has made bimonthly visits to Skinner Magnet Center and McMillan Middle School with the goal of introducing younger students to engineering and provide partner/peer mentoring to those students. Now that Skinner and McMillan have become part of the PLTW family we expect this peer tutoring effort to increase to the benefit of both groups of students. Additionally, students participate in competition presentation practice and tutoring between the high and middle schools, providing students the opportunity to join with students of different ages to work together to grow their programs and projects. Teachers and staff at the schools collaborate in an effort to bring the programs together into a STEM pathway. Since major competitions include both levels students anticipate continuing their participation in those activities.

Figure 1 OPS PLTW Pathway Program with Afterschool STEM Activities
Skinner Magnet Center - Dustin Driever

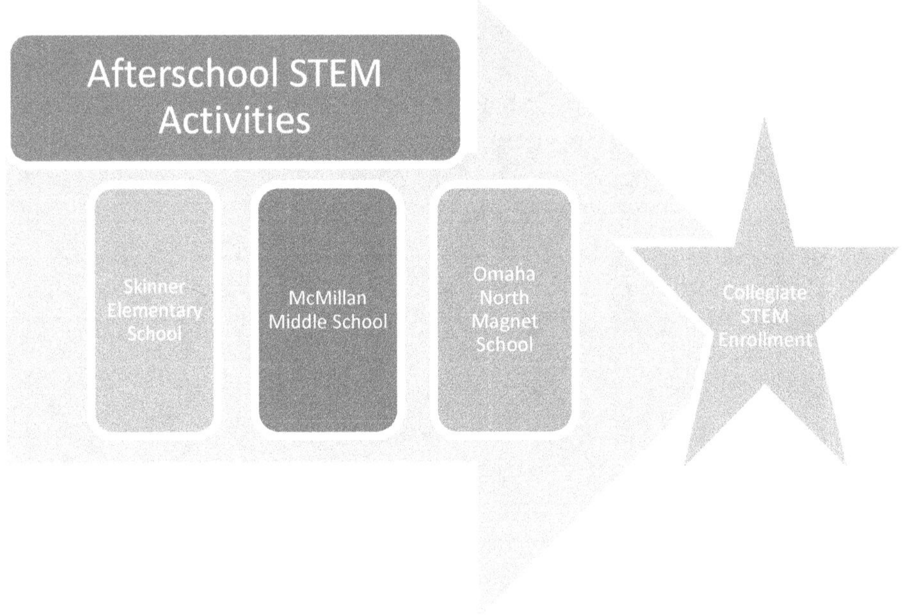

STEM History

Established in 1996, Skinner Magnet Center's mission is to provide consistent academic, social, and emotional growth utilizing discipline alternatives through the focus areas of the magnet program. It is our vision to create an environment that allows each student to develop his or her academic potential, promoting a genuine appreciation of human worth and dignity, as well as creating an atmosphere where one's contributions are recognized and rewarded (Omaha Public Schools –Skinner Magnet Center, 2009).

School Demographic

In the 2013-2014 academic year, 415 students were enrolled with an eight to one student teacher ratio. Of that amount, 91% of the students are free and reduced lunch, 7% are learning English as a second language learner, 17% are enrolled in special education and 15% are gifted. The school's pre-K-6 curriculum emphasizes Math, Technology and Performing Arts. For the 2013-2014 academic year, the school had a total student enrollment of 432 students with a little more than half (N = 223) being male and 209 females. More than half of students, 64.6% are African American with the second highest student ethnicity reported as Hispanic (15%), Caucasian (9%), Multi-racial (6%), Asian (3%) and Pacific Islander (.5%).

Why PLTW

In the spring of 2006, the three "pathway" schools (Skinner Magnet Center Elementary, McMillan Magnet Middle School, and Omaha North Magnet High School) started to the conversation that led to the establishing of a STEM pathway for Omaha Public Schools. At the time, Omaha North and McMillan were already a part of PLTW. The initial thought was to speak to PLTW and see if it would be possible for Skinner to join the PLTW team at the elementary level. Unfortunately, at that time, the PLTW curriculum was only implemented in middle and high school. As a result, I was forced to develop my own STEM focused curriculum that would challenge my elementary students and prepare them to be successful for the PLTW program that they would receive in middle and high school. My goal was engage my students so that they were critical and creative thinkers who also liked to problem solve. Through the help and guidance of my colleagues, Mr. James Mayberger and Dr. Lee Kallstrom, at McMillan Middle School and Omaha North High School respectively, I was able to take the concepts they were teaching to their students, simplify them, and teach them to my students.

Initially, I rolled out the engineering classes to my second grade students. At the time, Skinner didn't a budget that could support the hiring of a full-time engineering teacher, but I would not allow limited funds to keep my students from being exposed to engineering and I wanted to fulfill the school's mission to be a school of excellence that offers a real life problem-solving curriculum to its students. In addition to the engineering classes with the second grade students, during my plan time, I worked with a group of fifth and sixth grade students during their science and math block. I had the fifth and sixth graders work on simple machine concepts using K'Nex blocks. We started with levers building and testing the Seesaw, Balance, Wheel Barrow, Hockey Stick, and Scissors. We then moved to other concepts including pulleys, wheels and axels, inclined planes, and bridges. The students loved the hands on projects and were excited to do the work. Gradually the engineering curriculum evolved and the school administrators began to see how important this program was for kids. Through leadership and staff request I became Skinner's full time engineering teacher the following year. With the insight and support of my building administrators I was able to purchase many engineering manipulatives including, K'Nex blocks and the Academy of Engineering and Academy of Robotics Kits. I had to have courage and take chances and upset some people with schedules but in the end the students are learning. They are engaged in problem solving situations that require collaborative, creative and critical thinking. I was able set up a time to see every class of students who were in the second through sixth grade once a week for 45 minutes where I continued my simple machines lessons: second grade students were studying levers and pulleys; third grade students were learning about wheels, axels, and inclined planes; fourth grade students were exposed to bridges; fifth grade students learned about gears; and, sixth grade students studied real bridges. In addition to the class time that was dedicated to learning about engineering, the engineering students at Omaha North Magnet high school mentored my students through a weekly meeting.

In 2008, engineering was implemented as part of the students schedule so I would meet with enrolled students on a consistent weekly basis. This was the first year we also incorporated electives into our school during the last hour of the school day. The specialist teachers, and some grade level teachers, wrote units for anything from origami to Claymation to engineering. Students were able to choose which class they wanted to take for a six-week period of time. Needless to say, engineering was always the first to reach enrollment capacity. In 2008, the elementary school students were also involved in their first big project with their secondary school mentors at Omaha North Magnet. The students studied inventions by African American inventors then recreated and improved them to fit today's society. We decided to have a wax museum to show off our inventions. We held an after school event and invited parents and other members of the community. Our guests pushed a button that brought my students to life. They shared a short story about the inventor and the invention before shutting down. Students need to see the connection to their community and their culture. They were able to develop their presentation skills and see that engineering is not only connecting disciplines but also connecting life skills. It was a tremendous success and the students felt immediate gratification.

In 2010 the demand for inclusion of kindergarten and first grade became evident. I developed a curriculum for these students based on their age that would allow them to actively engage in the STEM process. My kindergarten students studied shapes and structures and built with Legos. My first grade students studied Levers allowing me to have my second grade students' focus on Pulleys. The inclusion of these two grades meant that Engineering had now reached every student in our building. In the next few years engineering continued to grow at Skinner. The addition of a Vex Robotics club in 2012 was a high point. We were able to have four teams of four students design and create their own remote control Vex robot and compete with it in tournaments throughout Omaha. The Vex tournaments call for the students to work independently while integrating engineering into multiple disciplines as demonstrated through a written report, presentation and the building of the robot. In our first year we had a team not only go to Nationals but take second place. We continued our Robotics club in 2013 and actually bested the previous year and had a team finish first in Nationals.

Implementing Launch Elementary PLTW Program

The 2013-2014 school year was hands down our most exciting year yet. We applied and were chosen to be a part of the PLTW Launch Pilot. Through PLTW Launch program for kindergarten through fifth grade, students become problem solvers. Students use structured approaches, like the engineering design process, and employ critical thinking. They apply STEM knowledge, skills, and habits of mind, learning that it is OK to take risks and make mistakes. Through PLTW Launch students become problem solvers. Students use structured approaches, like the engineering design process, and employ critical thinking as they apply STEM knowledge, skills, and habits of the mind, learning that it is OK to take risks and make mistakes (Project Lead The Way Launch, 2014). We had 200 students go through a rigorous and relevant curriculum designed to challenge each student at every grade level second through fifth. Many schools are taking more tests trying to get students to be engaged in learning. At Skinner, we are testing solutions to real life problems that surround us every day.

STEM History at McMillan Middle School - James Mayberger

McMillan opened in 1958, in mid-1980 McMillan became the Omaha Public Schools first magnet junior high school featuring special courses in computers and mathematics. Ninth graders were moved up to the high schools in the late 1980's. The Vision of McMillan Magnet Center is to: (1) collaborate with school, family, and community-based partners; (2) provide an innovative, project-based, cross-curricular school setting; and, (3) integrate components of Science, Technology, Engineering, Arts, and Math through Project Lead the Way (PLTW) (Omaha Public School, McMillan Magnet Middle School, 2008).

School Demographic

In the 2013-2014 academic year, there were approximately 580 students enrolled at McMillan with a 12:1 student teacher ratio. Of that amount, 74% of the enrolled students were eligible for free or reduced-price lunch program. McMillan is a magnet school, focusing on technology, mathematics, engineering, and communication arts. In the spring of 2004, McMillan Magnet Center became the first middle school in Nebraska to offer PLTW's Gateway classes. PLTW Gateway provides engineering and biomedical science curriculum for middle school students that challenges, inspires, and offers schools variety and flexibility. Students get rigorous and relevant experiences through activity-, project-, and problem-based learning. They use industry-leading technology to solve problems while gaining skills in communication, collaboration, critical-thinking, and creativity (Project Lead The Way Gateway Program, 2014). McMillan was the Omaha Public Schools district's Math and Technology magnet, serving as a feeder to North Magnet High School, which had begun the PLTW classes in 2003 so it was a logical fit. For McMillan, it seemed like a great opportunity to create middle to high school STEM pathway program by offering PLTW Gateway Program.

Implementing PLTW Gateway Program: McMillan began a three-tiered program for offering STEM based classes, with the goal of enrolling as many students as possible in one of the Tiers (see Figure 2 McMillan Middle School STEM Tiers). Students select their specific tier based on ability and interest in engineering fields.

Figure 3 McMillan Middle School STEM Tiers

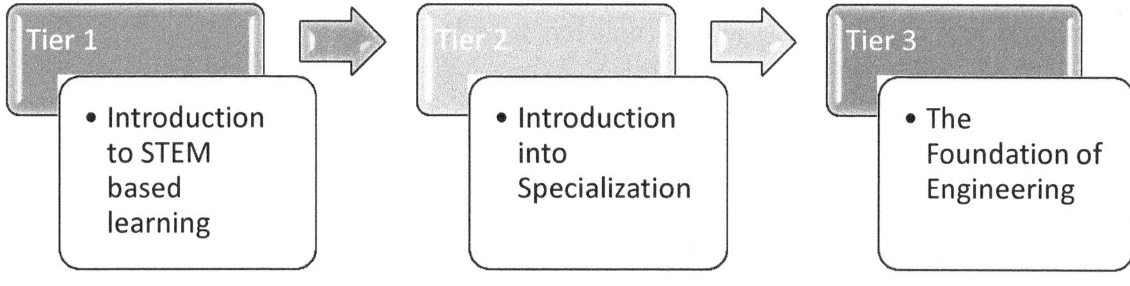

Introduction to STEM based learning. This is an exploratory, modular set up which combined traditional Industrial Technology and Family and Consumer Classes. McMillan offers 48 computer modules (24 for seventh graders and 24 for eighth graders) where students would select 8 modules that interested them and would work for two weeks on each before rotating to the next module. The curriculum offered hands on learning with the curriculum developed by Synergistic and Pitsco. The modules had a variety of interest with 6 focusing in on engineering themes.

The Industrial Technology and Living is the initial launching point for student exposure to STEM-centric, hands-on activities and provide real-world learning opportunities, engaging students in careers in science, technology, engineering and math. The modular learning environment would be the beginning of our Project Based Learning (PBL) as students would work for 10 schools days to accomplish a goal. After the 10 days students rotate to new module with a new learning goal. The dedicated lab time offered student-directed and teacher led foundation to STEM learning. The Technology and Living classes also gives the students the opportunity for collaborative learning as all modules required groups of two students helping them to develop their 21st century soft skills of teamwork and communication.

In addition to serving as an introduction to STEM based learning course, Technology and Living is offered to all students as a one-semester elective. Students can take Technology and Living each semester so a student could take the class four times in their two years as a student McMillan. Since 2004, nearly 85% of McMillan students have taken at least one of these courses. The modules have been dynamic and they reflect current issues as they relate to engineering, space and flight, and architecture. The lab component of the course provides students with exposure and an introduction to STEM based modules. In addition to the academic component, students are educated on careers pathways that can be achieved through enrollment in a collegiate STEM degree program. Because the modules change every two weeks students learn about a spectrum of STEM degrees and career paths.

Introduction to specialization. In 2004, three McMillan teachers developed an Architecture course that focused on applied mathematics, design process and technology. Later in 2004 PLTW, released four core classes: Design and Modeling, Automation and Robotics, Science of Technology and Magic of Electrons. McMillan teachers determined that students would benefit from a transitional class between the exploratory Technology and Living and the engineering foundational classes. The new class would be a specialization class that combines elements of the other two tiers (Introduction to STEM based learning and The Foundation of Engineering Classes).

As a math magnet middle school, McMillan, included advanced Algebra and Geometry classes in the seventh and eighth grade curriculum. For teachers leading these classes, it was often heard from their students, "when am I ever going to use this?" Additionally, some of the teachers expressed concern with teaching the advanced courses, as they did not have the proper training. In order to effectively address the student and teacher concerns, the PLTW course, Introduction to Architecture, was implemented as a one-semester course that all students could register for. The course focuses on applied mathematics, design process and technology.

Introduction to Architecture provides students an avenue to use architectural scales to create scaled drawing, floor plans and perspective drawings. The idea was that real world applications, creating of scaled drawings and floor plans would give students insight into how math skills are important in areas of building design, interior design and construction. The class also incorporates cross-curricular ideas throughout the lessons: (1) History is used to tell the story of buildings and structures, (2) Art is used in the design of the buildings and (3) English is used in the presentation of student projects. Students are expected to draw scaled buildings and structures with a majority of the grade on precision and accuracy of the designs. Students create landscape, interior, and perspective drawings as well as scaled floor plans of buildings and houses. Students use architectural scales to learn fractions and spatial relationships. High-rises would be drawn to 200' to 1", houses would be drawn to 5' to 1" and floor plans would be drawn to1' to ¼ inch scale. The amount of repetition and the variety of drafting activities would reinforce the concepts learned in math class. The class time dedicated to drawings and the use of rulers is substantially more than a regular math class which helps students who traditionally need extra time and attention when working on projects. Integrating scales into the assignments provides students with extra exercises that focus on fractions, students learn about real world applications for math, and students get excited about math! Floor plans provide an opportunity for students to use math concepts such as area, perimeter, spatial relationships, symmetry, fraction to decimal conversion, and general layout.

PLTW's Introduction to Architecture course incorporates technology into the curriculum through use of Autodesk. Autodesk has a variety of Computer Aided Design (CAD) software in multiple engineering disciplines. Revit is the Autodesk architectural software. Revit is building information modeling (BIM) which allows for 2D drafting elements to turn into 3D models and finally 4D capabilities track time in the various elements in design, building lifecycle and construction. The use of technology and specifically CAD programs is paramount for 21st century learners. Technology programs are the great equalizer for student designers. Students are adept at using technology and 3D modeling, as students are accustomed to seeing objects in gaming or computer applications. CAD programs also allow students to change designs, experiment, and practice with a few clicks instead of hours of hand drawings.

McMillan has offered four to six semester sessions of Introduction to Architecture each year since 2005 and 60% of the student population will complete the course before graduation. The popularity of Introduction of Architecture, the specialization of the class, and the fact that in 2012 PLTW offered a specialization course to its middle school Gateway program called Green Architecture contributed to McMillan offering a second Architecture class also called Green Architecture.

(Figure 4 Mastercraft Building Omaha, NE shown on the following page)

Figure 5 Mastercraft Building Omaha, NE

By adopting the Green Architecture at McMillan, students not only have a new course in their already math intensive curriculum, but they also have access to local business partners and engineering mentors. McMillan recently received grant funds to support student exposure and activities at the local Mastercraft Building. This building is run by a joint operation between the Omaha Chamber of Commerce and small business entrepreneurs. Students from Skinner Magnet Center, McMillan Middle School and Omaha North Magnet School will be using this site as a place to create, develop and house physical models of houses.

The ideology is to get underrepresented students into a business setting, to work with business mentors, and community partners. One of the tenants, Tack Architecture, is working closely with the students to create physical models and acts as mentors in the field of Architecture. The building itself has been remodeled from its original 1941 industrial function design into a modern eye-popping art deco office building. The remodel included many green features, such as natural lighting, Structural Insulated Panels and heat pumps. The vision of the developers was to restore rather than destroy, and to use the assets that the building possessed such as brick façade, high ceilings, clerestory windows, and rough sawn lumber joists. This idea made the Mastercraft the ideal site to have extension lessons for our students. The building is three blocks long (about 900 feet) and about 2/3 is renovated, so students will see actual construction and design elements every time they go to the building. McMillan is planning on taking students to the building for twenty hours throughout the semester.

The activities at the Mastercraft building will be hands on 3D modeling. The offsite building will allow for supplies and work areas to be in a designated place. The set-up, prep, and clean up time will be decreased because only the Green Architecture students will be using this space, therefore the time working on the projects will be increased. The room will have the feel of an office rather than a classroom. The unique feel and atmosphere will allow students the ability to feed off the environment to have a more creative energy, plus a sense of *I am doing something special that others are not*. Students' opportunities to see real world application of STEM, to see the diversity of careers and to guest speakers from actual businesses is greatly increased because of the variety of tenants in the building. The building houses more than 20 different careers including some of the more exciting careers such as: electrical engineers, laser engravers, architects, video production, nail art through using imaging technology and structural engineering. To get this type of real world exposure at one site would require a career fair and you still would not get the diversity of occupations. As stated earlier this does not include the careers in construction that the students see with the continued renovation of the site. Because it is in a working office space with a multitude of small business, the willingness of mentors to help on projects has increased. We are coming to them and they can come on their own schedule.

The Green Architecture class is going to our model class for future STEM classes and learning. This class is a joint venture between three schools at three different grade levels, the district's central office, PLTW, community partners, business partners and educational grants. With the changing climate of education and costs of such programs, this type of career readiness training and career academy learning will become increasingly the norm for school programs. The cooperation between the vested entities and the blurring on educational lines will strength programs. Working with business partners will greatly aid in the development of curriculum and project based learning assignments.

Foundation of engineering. The third tier of classes at McMillan is the PLTW engineering foundation. Students get challenging and real world experiences through activity-, project-, and problem-based learning. Students are exposed to Autodesk software technology to solve problems while gaining 21st century skills in communication, collaboration, critical-thinking, and creativity. We offer three one-semester classes: Design and Modeling, Automation and Robotics, and Science of Technology. The PLTW curriculum calls for nine-week courses but we have expanded the classes an additional nine weeks to include competitions and team projects.

Design and Modeling. This course focuses on the design process, virtual modeling, and solving real world problems by using creativity and innovation. Students learn parametric modeling, applied geometry, applications of Cartesian coordinates, and relationship between virtual and physical design. The design process is vital in understanding that there is more than one correct answer to a problem, research of past, present, and future trends will aid your design, that the constraints of time, resources and money influence many decisions, that teamwork and collaboration are keys to successfully completing problems and sometimes the best ideas need to be re-designed.

Automation and Robotics. This course focuses on the mechanical systems, gear ratios, simple machines, energy transfer, machine automation, and computer control systems. Students design, build and program a variety of simple machines and real world objects that solve problems. Automation and Robotics incorporates STEM throughout every lesson. Science concepts of simple machines, energy transfer and forces acting upon items are taught in each lesson. Technology is used in the control of the robot and in the automation of the design. Engineering concepts are taught in the build and design of the robot. Mathematics is used in both the build and program phases to compute the gear ratios, torque versus speed and in the automation phase in setting up the control variables. Designing relates to the first five steps of the design process where student need to define the problem, brainstorm ideas, research possible solutions, develop ideas, and choose the best idea. Students again learn about collaboration, communication and teamwork as they go through these steps as time and resources limit them. Building of the models allows the students hands on creativity and gives students insight on how fluid design plans can be when in the construction phase. Finally program brings the technology and control aspects to life.

Science of Technology. This course focuses on building of simple machines, exploration of electricity and the behavior of atoms, concepts of physics, chemistry and nanotechnology, and basic circuitry design. This class like the other two foundation classes provides a one-semester project based curriculum. The foundation courses are all PLTW classes so they have a common core.
Common core means the standards are:

- Research and evidence based
- Clear, understandable, and consistent
- Aligned with college and career expectations
- Based on rigorous content and the application of knowledge through higher-order thinking skills
- Built upon the strengths and lessons of current state standards
- Informed by other top-performing countries to prepare all students for success in our global economy and society

STEM Focused Competitions

McMillan students would are registered or completed a foundation class, I invited to participate in long-term engineering focused project based competitions. There are three competitive teams in our school: 1) Vex robotics; 2) SAME; and 3) Future Cities. The long-term project based teams require the students to work on a project for 6 to 8 months. They require students to work after school, weekends, to go on outside school day field trips, meet with mentors, and attend outside school day workshops. Students in these projects have developed a sense of ownership and are more than willing to spend the extra time on these projects.

Vex Robotics. The Vex robotics team is an extra-curricular activity that requires students to design, build and program a robot to compete in a game like challenge to compete against schools throughout the world. The students are required to use all prior engineering classes to design a robot, with guidance from their teachers and mentors, with the aim to build the most innovative robots possible and work together to obtain the most points possible.

Society of American Military Engineers (SAME). SAME provides student an opportunity to participate in the Student Imitative Mentoring Program (SIMP) competition. Student try to solve a real world community problems using engineering techniques of team work, sustainable design, presentation skills, use of graphic materials, model development, cost estimating, and creative, persuasive and technical writing. Students are required to research the project, write a 20 page technical document, create virtual and physical models, and give a 15 minute oral presentation to local engineers explaining their project, and 5 minute question and answer session.

Future Cities. This program is a competition that allows students to design and build futuristic cities. The students use the principles of engineering and architecture to build scaled models with recycled material, use a software program to build a virtual city, and present their findings to a panel of judges. All three competitions allow for the core STEM concepts and 21st century soft skills of applied math and science concepts to real-world issues, develop writing and technical writing skills, public speaking, problem solving, time management skills, research and propose solutions to engineering challenges, and develop strong teamwork skills.

Outcomes

The success of our engineering program and the PLTW course work has altered the thinking around our building. Beginning in 2014, our school has adopted a project based learning (PBL) STEM-centric curriculum throughout the building. Where in the past our classes where either stand-alone or supported the core curriculum, now our classes are going to be the lead classes in the school. PBL is a changing dynamic classroom where student look at real world problems and challenges to reach a higher level our understanding. The engagement level of students in the engineering classes, the hands on, design process, multiple solution and applied math and science were contributing factors in the school adopting PBL across the board.

McMillan has partnered with local university, engineering and business firms to provide mentoring, hands-on activities, and career fairs. University of Nebraska – Lincoln (UNL) has provided McMillan with the opportunity to showcase our program at the annual Engineering Fair. UNL has taken our students to the campus for hands on building activities and tour of the engineering facilities. Kiewit Corporation has set up engineering day activities in our school. The Kiewit engineers have a series of hands on activities where student work on math skills needed in the engineering field. Schnabel Engineering has provided office tours and on site learning extension for our students.

Our Science department is the first to offer a PLTW specialization course called Medical Detectives. With the popularity of crime scene shows this class will look at DNA evidence, genetic testing for diseases, possible future health problems, and prevention of contagious diseases. Like the other PLTW courses this class will have hands-on projects and labs, investigate how to measure and interpret vital signs, and learn how the systems of the human body work together to maintain health. The class will have a common core and will be aligned with national standards.

The McMillan philosophy has changed over the last ten years for offering a few electives in a tiered system, to now have the PBL learning throughout the curriculum. The goal is that every student will leave McMillan with at least two engineering classes and will have participated in at least one Project Based Learning project.

School History of Omaha North Magnet High School - Lee Kallstrom

Omaha North High Magnet School is a public high school located in Omaha, Nebraska. The school is a STEM magnet school in the Omaha Public Schools district. North has won several awards, including being named 2007 Magnet Schools of America "Magnet School of Excellence". The STEM focused curriculum program engages more than 400 students in STEM activities that are problem-based, hands-on learning in science, technology, engineering, and math. The goal of the STEM program is to help college-bound students achieve a well-rounded education with an emphasis on STEM.

School Demographics

In 2014, Omaha North Magnet High School reported a total student enrollment of 1900. The student to teacher ratio is 12:1, with 160 full-time teachers on staff. Of the total student enrollment, 412 students are registered for an engineering PLTW course. The majority of PLTW students are males (N=294) with less than half of students female (N=118). Since 2011, 1498 students have enrolled in an engineering focused course. Female enrollment continues to increase; however, it remains half of the male enrollment as displayed in Table 2, *Omaha North Magnet High School PLTW Enrollment*.

Table 2 Omaha North Magnet High School PLTW Enrollment

PLTW Course Enrollment by Gender			
	Male	Female	Total
2011	257	100	357
2012	257	112	369
2013	256	104	360
2014	294	118	412
	1064	434	1498

In 2003, Omaha North Magnet School implemented the PLTW secondary school engineering curriculum Our association with Magnet Schools of America and Project Lead The Way led our school to make all of our engineering classes honors level offerings. Our elective status making all of our classes optional helped bring to our program students who were really interested in the material or in becoming engineers, architects, etc. This simple fact raised the level of production from our students, and with a bootstrap effect, also raised the output of students and the program as well. All of these considerations have led to an increasing market for our students as they continue their post-high school education.

Currently, we serve magnet students selecting our school from across the city for our unique engineering, biomedical and most recently computer science programs. We are also serving neighborhood individuals who have attended our middle and/or elementary pathway partners. This population continues to grow as the pathway programs also grow and expand their curriculums.

As the current push for an improved hard science background has become part of the national effort to improve our student's skills and educational backgrounds in science, technology, engineering and math our programs have grown exponentially. With the growing need for employment in the above areas and increased potential for better employment opportunities as well as pay scale a greater population of qualified students are filling our classrooms. Since the PLTW courses are structured as electives in the course curriculum, our students want to be in our classes rather than being forced to take them as requirements. This fact improves the overall attitude of the department and provides a ready group of students to help raise the standards, status, and reputation of the program. We have consistently had the majority of the top ten students in the school at all levels. In the last four years we have had class officers, two Presidents of senior classes, two Valedictorians, and several student council members at all levels. Many of our students are also recognized as ambassadors for our school providing tour, assisting with open houses, and acting as spokespersons for the department. These types of students make our efforts to communicate the successes of our programs and secure placement of our students at colleges and universities of their choice, a much easier task.

In 2010, we instituted the Medical Biology program. Although in its infancy, data from the classes is included for comparison sake. It is apparent that this growing program, see Table 3 - Omaha North Magnet High School PLTW Enrollment for enrollment numbers, will take its place as a viable course selection along with engineering. At the high school level we have approximately three hundred students taking one or more of our classes each year. Below is a graph showing course involvement, yearly attendance, and progression through our program.

Table 3 Omaha North Magnet High School PLTW Enrollment

All PLTW Course Enrollment					
Course	2011-12	2012-13	2013-14	2014-15	Total
Biological Engineering	NA	NA	NA	12	12
Biomedical Innovations	NA	9	7	14	30
Biotechnical Engineering	11	NA	NA	NA	11
Civil Engineering & Architecture	47	52	56	44	199
Computer Science & Software Engineering	NA	NA	13	50	63
Digital Electronics	14	19	16	22	71
Engineering Design & Development	31	34	39	55	159

Human Body Systems	17	21	32	14	84
Intro to Engineering Design	118	97	87	100	402
Medical Interventions	9	12	18	19	58
Principles of Bioscience	40	42	34	22	138
Principles of Engineering	70	83	58	60	271
	357	369	360	412	1498

PLTW Implementation at Our School

In all of our classes, our students are encouraged to work independently and in small and large groups to complete prototype designs of products to assist any primary or secondary stakeholder. Our staff assists as facilitators to help the student complete their projects. Wherever possible, products are the result of perceived needs determined by our students. These products may take the form of a music stand attachment for a first chair violinist to a solar powered scoreboard for our school. In 2010 we moved into a new engineering addition at North as shown in Figure 5, *Omaha North Magnet High School Engineering Wing*. The first academic edition in the history of the district completely funded by private gifts. This unique building was the creation of one of our PLTW Civil Engineering and Architecture (CEA) classes in 2002. The team recognized that we as a department were scattered all over the building and with the influx of new students, approximately 150 they wanted a place to call their own. Several iterations of the design took place. Different student groups and teams contributed not only to the design but also to presenting to individuals and groups to ask for help funding the project. What began as a two-story facility turned into a four-story masterpiece with science labs, multimedia and music and video production rooms, an electric car garage, state-of-the-art wrestling area as well as our fully equipped engineering and architecture classrooms and laboratories.

Figure 6 Omaha North Magnet High School Engineering Wing

Preparing students in the overall skills and experiences that are most sought after at the post high school level we focus student deliverables in our classes on developing four skills as they are applicable in our various curricula: Problem Solving, Leadership, Team Membership, and Communications. Our students are expected to work in teams as often as working individually and when leadership opportunity presents itself the student is expected to be responsible, accountable, and proactive in guiding a group or team as well as they can. All of the projects completed by our classes include presentation of the information informally in the classroom as well as formally to outside professionals whether from the school or mentors brought in to assist in developing a completed project.

Engineering Afterschool Opportunities. Students will find their afterschool activities complement lessons learned in school time. PLTW students participate in outside workshops, volunteer service and service learning activities, competitions, and various community-based activities. Some of the extra-classroom activities are short-term, project based while others can span an academic year.

TEAMS. This is a student competition sponsored by Technical Students Association (TSA) hosted at the University of Nebraska that provides teams of up to eight students to compete at the state and national levels. In 2014 a team of four placed second in the nation in problem solving and tenth in the written portion of the national competition held in Washington, D.C. Our students commented that their training having had a course in principles of engineering and AP Physics gave them backgrounds to successfully complete this activity.

Society of American Military Engineers (SAME). This organization began an outstanding mentoring program through its Omaha Post. Students are provided with an opportunity to work with mentors on long term and real life problems in a team based environment for an entire academic year. Student teams submit a twenty-page paper and present a twenty-minute summary of their project to a group of four engineers, architects, corps of engineer professionals and university professors. Many of these projects are also advanced in other local, regional or national programs. A few have become multiyear projects. Over the years, our students have received the Post President's award five times and produced more winners than any other school entering the competition. Mentoring is an integral component of our programs. Professionals from across the city help our students in all of their projects. The variety and extent of their involvement and expertise adds immeasurable quality to the output and education of our students.

Haddix EngineeringWing. Students participating in the SAME competition developed the Haddix Engineering wing at Omaha North Magnet High School, as shown on the previous page in Figure 5, *Omaha North Magnet High School Engineering Wing*. The project entailed several groups of student's during a four year time period contributing various aspects of the design and development of our eight million dollar addition. During all aspects of the design process of the building our students observed the complexities of stages of construction of the complex, contributed ideas to the LEED requirements, recognized constraints posed by building codes and generally oversaw the completion of the addition. The building attained a Silver LEED award which was the highest an addition of its size was eligible for.

Rocket Stoves for Madagascar. This program provided engineering second school students with an opportunity to work on a real world problem in Madagascar. Rocket Stoves for Madagascar, addressed the reforestation concerns while working with Henry Doorly Zoo which is located in Omaha, NE. *Rocket Stoves for Madagascar,* In conjunction with the Madagascar Biodiversity Partnership which has an outreach program in Kingavato, Madagascar, and Conservation Fusion, a nonprofit providing educational service to the country, we were asked to help design a cooking system for rural communities throughout the country to help with reducing deforestation in rainforest regions of the country. This project resulted in a design for an inexpensive rocket stove, briquette development system, and hand-operated grinder for utilizing forest debris for alternative fuel production.

Engineering students at Omaha North Magnet School are also participating in NASA - Space Science Student Involvement Program, Real World Design Challenge and Simulation Exploration Experience competitions; collaborating with local universities such as the University of Nebraska at Omaha and University of Nebraska – Lincoln on STEM focused programs; engineering Ability One Design Challenge – Goodwill Industries; and volunteering through Service Learning, Habitat for Humanity and University of Nebraska at Omaha's Three and Seven Days of Service. Additionally, students are engaging with local engineering firms such as Union Pacific Railroad, Kiewit Construction Company, Clean Solutions for Omaha, Renaissance Design Group Design, and many others, providing them with real life examples and application of STEM focused coursework.

Student Perspective – Lee Kallstrom and Jewel Rodgers

In 2010, the first class that had started in the OPS Pathway Program enrolled at Omaha North Magnet High School. One of the standouts in this group of students was a young lady who enjoyed engineering and architecture from the beginning. In fall 2014, Jewel Rodgers enrolled at the University of Nebraska – Lincoln to pursue a college degree in Architecture. Before she left for school, Jewel took the time to share her experiences in the K-12 STEM curriculum program and how they shaped her studies. Jewel shared how her first experiences with STEM were as a fifth grader at Skinner Elementary School, commenting "…that experience certainly was good for me in directing my time in middle and high school. And now here I am going to the University with a major in architecture". At Omaha North Magnet High School, Jewel continued her interest in architecture and she took an independent study in design. During her junior year she entered a competition designing a facility that provided office and home needs. She won first place for the City of Omaha and overall award, The McCallister Award. As a senior, Jewel continued her architectural passion designing a community football stadium for the high school. She continues to receive wonderful public responses from the community and the media on her contributions and successes in engineering and STEM. Provided below is an excerpt from our conversation about how having had a STEM education beginning in elementary school influenced her academic and career goals.

Jewel Rodgers, Skinner Elementary School 08', McMillan Magnet Middle School 10' and Omaha North Magnet High School 14'. I've had the honor of being involved in the STEM program since grade school. I can honestly say that without this experience, I would not be where I am today. Very early on, I was able to establish a desire for design even though I was never sure of my career path until my junior year in high school. Since then,

I've won the McCallister award for architectural achievements, and received a paid internship at Meyer & Associates, Architects. [Additionally,] I have had my designs featured in the Omaha Star newspaper and have been featured for my overall achievements, including architecture, in the Omaha World Herald.

Skinner Elementary School. During grade school, I loved the STEM related courses. It was never too challenging, but allowed me to conceptualize a general idea of innovative design and building practices. I was able to understand what it meant to be "innovative". This is an extremely important thing to understand, considering STEM is all about innovation, good design, and problem solving. All of which, I was able to be exposed to as early as the age of 5 (I skipped Kindergarten). It's a very special program because it brings your mind into another realm of thinking. For instance, instead of thinking about the color of the cool you want to design, you're now thinking about the shape, the size, the gas mileage, the aerodynamics, how you can make it run on natural energy etc., all starting at the age of 5! (I'm sorry, I never really thought about how much the STEM program helped me until now! Woo, sure glad I was involved!). All I really did was build bridges and simple little motor cars with things like K'nex but they always allowed the student the ability to problem solve which is what STEM is really all about. I remember they wanted us to come up with just a cool idea. And I wanted a car that used no gas and I came up with 1,001 (figuratively speaking) things that would substitute for gas. Now, were all of these things plausible? Probably not. Of course you can't expect a kid to design and build this groundbreaking contraption BUT to get the child just thinking about it, is what really matters. I cannot stress enough how the STEM program really makes a student think. It's amazing because you start to think about things that people you're age aren't even dreaming about! (Jeez I'm glad I was part of this program!) When you already start off at a "higher level of thinking" imagine the possibilities, the capacity for growth that you acquire! After being exposed to the K'nex, I made my mom take me to TOYS-R-US to buy me K'nex. I ended up building a moving Ferris wheel. It was super cool…

McMillan Middle Magnet School. Middle school allowed for a more challenging approach. It involved more technologies and the use of computers and shop equipment to begin forming all these ideas I had rambling in my head since grade school. However, at this time I was more focused on sports than anything so I don't have too much to say about the middle school days but man oh man when I got to high school.

Omaha North Magnet High School. The STEM program at Omaha North High really allowed me to branch out and discover what I wanted to do with the STEM knowledge I'd acquired through my schooling. During my junior year, I discovered my passion for Architecture. My class was entered into a competition. The fact that students are entered into competitions is amazing. It gives a feel for the competitiveness of STEM related fields, as it would be searching for a job in the real world. It allows the student to take on bigger issues and responsibilities with real consequences and rewards. You start to begin understanding that not only do you need to have the idea, you then have to prove the idea, make the idea reality and then present the idea. You leave having a good understanding of how to successfully present a well thought out idea. That is what I think is the most important part of this program. The STEM program helps shape the student and prepares them for real world issues and expectations. From an early age, you already are starting to think big, to think innovative. When a student is able to participate in the STEM, program, start to finish, that student already has an edge because for so long, they've been exposed to problem solving and presentations and competitors and real world issues etc. So when you get out there (life happens, college, jobs etc.) you already have a decent understanding of what is expected of you and how you can exceed those expectations. That is truly the first step to a very successful STEM future.

I am immeasurably grateful that I was a part of the STEM program. Without this program, I probably wouldn't have any idea what I wanted to do in college. The best thing I could come up with is probably *I want to make stuff look cute*. But instead, I know that I want to and will be one of the architects that people remember. The best thing I can come up with now is *I want to make some of the most iconic structures our generation has ever seen.* After winning my first competitions, I began investing in the field of my chosen profession, hoping to acquire as much knowledge as I could about design. Instead of asking for an iPad or clothes for holidays, I began asking for sketchbooks, or a laptop powerful enough to run Revit and CAD so I could teach myself more about the programs. I began buying books introducing American vernacular, building types, drawing and model making, history and theory, monographs and even religious architecture in hopes to explore not only the history of Architecture but the trends that clients tend to follow. Without the STEM program, the very thought of looking into Architecture the way I do now, would have never surfaced as quickly and as dramatically as it did. Bottom line: STEM is amazing. The program played a huge role in shaping who I am as a student and who I am as a person. Eventually I'll be able to add, *and who I am as an Architect*

STEM Education in Afterschool Setting - Julie Sigmon

Beyond School Bells is a non-profit organization that is dedicated to improving access to and quality in Nebraska's Expanded Learning Opportunities programs by building partnerships with local schools and organizations. Expanded learning opportunities (ELOs) have the potential to be the great equalizer in American education. Regular participation in high quality before and after school learning, and enriching summer school programs have been shown to help low-income students succeed academically on par with their more affluent peers. These programs, characterized by strong school-community partnerships, can also help high-performing students stay engaged and achieve even greater levels of understanding (Beyond School Bells, 2014).

Beyond School Bells is very much aware of the national concern that too few students are enrolling and persisting in collegiate STEM degree programs. For students in grades K through 12, the formal school day and classroom teachers are at the forefront of the effort to not only increase the number of children and youth who have access to STEM learning opportunities but to do so in an equitable manner that will reach and equip a diverse group representative of the nation's population. But because children spend less than a quarter of their waking hours in school, out of school-time experiences such as afterschool programs—and the institutions and people who provide them—need to be essential partners in this effort. We need both the additional time offered by afterschool programs and the opportunity to diversify the ways that students experience STEM learning (Afterschool: A Vital Partner in STEM Education, 2011). In response to this national concern, at a local level, we have partnered with organizations and schools to host afterschool programs that are focused on STEM. These STEM activities are meant to be more than just content—they are designed to motivate and excite youth so that they will be interested in pursuing STEM activities and eventually careers beyond the life of any one activity or program.

Our STEM afterschool program participants often spend more time out of the classroom completing the activities in the real world. This change of paradigm is sometimes criticized as breaking tradition. Our experience has taught us that these kinds of learning procedures are the ones that are most memorable and positive for the students. Tasks are often more strenuous and require much teaming and leadership. High school aged teens vigorously approach the hardest of challenges and complete them with gusto. As our program has developed over the last fourteen years there has been a significant increase in requests from engineering firms, city departments, and individual/groups requesting our assistance in completing tasks in which they are involved. It is possible on many occasions to incorporate the needed task with some aspect of our curriculum. This affords us educational opportunities as well as community communications which expands our importance for student involvement in our city. Our classes consistently encourage repetitions of these projects, as they are meaningful and rewarding. Making these activities available and coordinating them with class requirements gives our students many opportunities for growth in preparation for university entrance and successes at those levels.

In addition to the afterschool activities that Beyond School Bells leads, an intermediary organization, Collective for Youth, is dedicated to creating quality partnerships between Omaha Public schools and community organizations. As an intermediary agency, their purpose is to create lasting partnerships between critical partners that promote STEM afterschool programs as well as provide professional development to staff that results in high quality STEM programs integrated with the formal school science content. Collective for Youth current manage 29 Community Learning Center sites at Omaha Public Schools, serving over 3,500 students, including Skinner Magnet Elementary School and McMillan Middle School. Their goal, to provide quality STEM programming at all sites, is a perfect reflects and emphasizes the mission and goals of Project Lead The Way.

References

In-text citations available only

Chapter Author(s)

Rosemary L. Edzie, Ph.D.
University of Nebraska, Lincoln
Lincoln, Nebraska
USA

Dustin Driever
Skinner Magnet Center
Omaha Public Schools
Omaha, Nebraska
USA

Lee Kallstrom, Ph.D.
Omaha North High School
Omaha Public School
Omaha, Nebraska
USA

James Mayberger
McMillian Middle School
Omaha Public Schools
Omaha, Nebraska
USA

Julie Sigmon, Director
Beyond School Bells
Omaha, NE
USA

Chapter 6

Preservice Elementary Teachers' Understanding of Inquiry-Based Instruction in Science

ABSTRACT: The article at hand provides a contemporary overview of literature and data in inquiry-based science classrooms. The study was conducted with pre-service teachers at the elementary level. The research adopts a formal study format focused on the collection and analysis of data for three primary questions: 1) What are the understanding of pre-service elementary teachers about inquiry teaching and learning entering a science methods course, 2) What instructional experience is most useful to pre-service teachers in helping them understand inquiry, and 3) What experiences with inquiry-based labs are most useful to preservice teachers in helping them understand inquiry. Both quantitative and qualitative data analysis provided information about what was learned.

Introduction

Education reform lauds the introduction of inquiry-based education in the classroom. It is often regarded as a more effective manner in teaching students science and mathematics concepts in a memorable fashion. According to Bigger and Forbes (2012), the following aspects comprise inquiry-based education: (1) students must ask scientific questions; (2) students must utilize evidence; (3) students must understand evidence in order to formulate an explanation and future research questions; (4) students must reflect on explanation and alternatives; (5) students must be able to justify and clearly communicate findings.

According to Bell, Smetana, & Binn (2005), there are four separate levels of inquiry: (1) confirmation, (2) structured, (3) guided, and (4) open. As students have a better understanding of the subject matter, hypothetically, they should advance through the levels of inquiry, ultimately using more science process skills. The first level of inquiry (confirmation) is teacher-directed. During this level of inquiry, students are given step-by-step instructions and given the results prior to experimentation. As students' knowledge-base increases, teachers are able to move on to the next level of inquiry: structured inquiry. During this level, students are given research questions and the procedures to set up an experiment, while the data collection, results, and conclusions must be completed by the students. This allows students to use more science processing skills, providing them the opportunity to discuss the outcomes of the experiment, what they did correctly, and areas of challenge during the experimentation process (i.e., in what ways did the experiment not go as expected). As students perfect this level, they are able to move on to guided inquiry, where the research question is given, but the student must generate the experimental procedures, collect data, and report results and conclusions. Students are able to organize their own experiments, yielding different outcomes for individual experiments. This process allows students to account for variables (i.e. time, temperature, measurements, etc.)

that may impact their experiment. Lastly, students may engage in open inquiry, where they are left to formulate their own research questions, organize their own experiments, and draw their own conclusions. This type of inquiry is the most student-centered, allowing students to act as scientists and researchers, resulting in them figuring out the unknown. During this level of inquiry, students are able to discuss their results with the classroom teacher and analyze the effectiveness and efficiency of their procedures.

Statement of Problem

Inquiry-based teaching methods are hard for elementary teachers to enact, and appears to be even more difficult for preservice elementary teachers to utilize (Biggers & Forbes, 2012). Some may regard inquiry-based teaching methods as inefficient because it takes more time to plan and enact an inquiry based lesson plan than traditional teaching methods (Biggers & Forbes, 2012). Preservice teachers often express ideas about inquiry-based teaching that are not congruent with science education reform, often regarding all hands-on activities as inquiry-based, which is erroneous (Biggers & Forbes, 2012). Another issue is that teachers often believe that science inquiry produces correct answers, which makes it hard to use inquiry-based teaching methods. Instead, inquiry is about the exploration of questions and concepts. This means that there may not be a "right" answer.

Evidence also suggests that inquiry-based teaching or variations of inquiry-based instruction is important for early learners, since early learners tend to learn through inquiry (Wang, Kinzie, McGuire, & Pan 2010). According to Wang, et al. (2010), inquiry-based methods are recommended, especially since young learners do so spontaneously. Children are naturally inclined to explore, because exploration offers children a mode to learn. This natural inclination presents itself as innate inquiry-based learning. Young children naturally use inquiry-learning during development in order to discover the world around them and develop necessary skills essential to further them in their academic and personal evolution (Wang, et al., 2010). Therefore, young children are already using this process, which is why this teaching method should be employed at young ages.

While inquiry is a natural process for young learners, attitudes and perceptions are also formulated at young ages (Perry, 2011). During this time, teachers may inadvertently sway the attitudes of young students by unintentionally sending messages about their perceptions of science, technology, engineering, and mathematics (STEM) based subjects (Perry, 2011). Perry (2011) wrote that students learn to like or dislike mathematics, an area of STEM that directly relates to science. This learned behavior correlates with teachers' perceptions (Perry, 2011). Therefore, positive perceptions of these content areas may be critical to a willingness to continue learning STEM-based material.

Since inquiry-based teaching is an effective method when teaching students, it is important that preservice elementary students teach using this method (Tessier, 2010). Inquiry-based instruction is currently recommended as the most beneficial teaching practice. While it is expected that science methods courses teach new teachers inquiry-based methods to use in their classroom, research indicates that teachers tend to maintain old methods, rather than change (Hayes, 2002). Unfortunately, changing how a teacher practices seems futile, and school constraints and culture make it difficult to implement new teaching strategies (Ozel & Luft, 2013).

While engaging students in inquiry is a problem, an even greater problem is that preservice elementary teachers do not understand what inquiry-based instruction is (Hayes,

2002). Inquiry-based teaching is often interchanged with similar teaching methods (Hayes, 2002). This lack of understanding makes it hard for preservice elementary teachers to engage in inquiry-based instruction when it has not been clearly defined. With a lack of understanding, some preservice elementary teachers are unable to effectively teach STEM subjects (Neija, 2011).

Operational Definition of Terms

- Inquiry-Based Teaching Methods- involves using science process skills and questions to explore scientific concepts, theories, and natural phenomena. In addition, inquiry-based instruction assists students to construct understandings about science content through experimentation, data collection, and data analysis. Further, inquiry methods demonstrate how scientists obtain information about the natural world and provide students with the critical thinking skills to be independent learners and researchers.
- Science Process Skills- Process skills are thinking skills such as observation, classification, inference, measurement, hypothesizing, etc.
- Understanding - Preservice teachers' ability to operationally define a term.

Assumptions, Limitations, and Delimitation

Assumptions:

It is assumed by the researcher that:

1. Preservice elementary teachers read articles regarding inquiry-based education as assigned.
2. Preservice elementary teachers complete assignments as assigned.

Limitations:

1. Preservice elementary teachers may not read articles regarding inquiry-based education, which may affect treatment.
2. Preservice elementary teachers may not complete assignments.

Delimitations:

1. This study is delimited to undergraduate preservice elementary teachers enrolled in the elementary science and mathematics methods courses at a midsized, Midwestern University.

Research Questions

1. What are the understandings of pre-service elementary teachers about inquiry teaching and learning entering a science methods course?
2. After experiencing the following instructional methods regarding inquiry: lecture, discussion, reflective writing and assigned readings; what instructional experience is most useful to pre-service teachers in helping them understand inquiry?
3. After experiencing inquiry labs in the following settings: field teaching experiences using inquiry labs, participation in inquiry labs, and designing inquiry-based

teaching and learning; what experiences with inquiry labs are most useful to pre-service teachers in helping them understand inquiry?

Review of Relevant Literature

This section will review journal articles regarding information about preservice elementary teachers understanding of inquiry-based education in science, technology, engineering, and mathematics (STEM). The purpose of the literature review is to investigate previous studies regarding inquiry-based education. The literature review will address the following:

1. Effectiveness of Inquiry-Based Education
2. Perceptions of Inquiry-Based Education
3. Preservice Elementary Teachers' Understanding of Inquiry-Based Education

Effectiveness of Inquiry-Based Education

Education reform lauds the introduction of inquiry-based education in the classroom. Inquiry-based education reform is currently recommended as the most beneficial teaching practice (Hayes, 2002). It is often regarded as a more effective manner in teaching students concepts in a more memorable fashion than traditional teaching methods, since it allows the student to take part in the process of discovery, whether the discovery be independent or a scaffolded experience. Due to the nature of science education, inquiry may be an effective tool to help facilitate learning (due to the active nature of the scientific process).

According to Leonard, Barnes-Johnson, Dantley, & Kimber (2011), many early education and elementary teachers avoid teaching science courses. This may be in part to preservice elementary teachers' emotions toward the scientific process. Biggers and Forbes (2012) suggested that many preservice elementary teachers harbor negative emotions toward science, resulting in low efficacy and low content knowledge. Unfortunately, these negative emotions do a disservice to early education and elementary students, whose teachers demonstrate low efficacy when teaching scientific content. Since preservice elementary teachers often avoid teaching scientific content, Leonard et al. (2011) introduced inquiry-based instruction to preservice elementary teachers. Using 16 participants, the researchers gathered data about the effectiveness of using inquiry-based instruction, specifically in regards to teacher efficacy of teaching scientific content.

Yager & Akcay (2010), found that while students are able to master material using traditional teaching methods, students are able to better master material when exposed to the material through inquiry-based education. The researchers linked an increased mastery of materials when using inquiry-based education to students' hands-on exposure. Additionally, they found that teachers gained confidence teaching inquiry-based lessons the more they used inquiry.

Singh Raghav & Upadhyaya (2010) found that both males and females had higher achievement scores when being taught using the inquiry model, than those who were taught using traditional methods. Inquiry-based education appears to correlate with higher science aptitude scores. Furthermore, inquiry education led to developed or increased problem solving awareness.

Jones (2003) also studied the effects of inquiry-based education and student outcome expectancies. Jones (2003) specifically researched the impact of inquiry-based education on standardized testing scores. Since standardized tests have become a more prominent component of the American educational system, understanding the most successful way to teach students standardized material should also be examined. Jones (2003) examined both non-inquiry and inquiry-based methods of instruction when compared to standardized tests. After looking at both teaching methods, Jones (2003) found that students scored better when the teacher used non-inquiry methods; however, these improvements were not significant. Conversely, some students did not have to take the standardized test and often times were less successful in the class, indicating that they may perform worse on standardized tests. According to Jones (2003), this may skew results. These students were more likely to be a part of the non-inquiry cohort. Moreover, Jones (2003) found benefits to using inquiry-based instruction that may be more beneficial than standardized test scores. Students who were taught using inquiry based methods were more successful in their physical science courses, receiving higher marks. Students taught using non-inquiry based methods were more likely to receive D's and F's (58%) than students taught using inquiry (37%). Additionally, students taught using inquiry-based education were more likely to take the standardized examination, less likely to give up on the learning process, and more likely to attend class. The overall participation level was substantially better for students that were taught using inquiry-based education, indicating that it may be a worthwhile teaching method to employ. Furthermore, inquiry-based instruction led to higher universal academic achievement (i.e., more students succeeded when inquiry-based instruction was used). Inquiry-based instruction appears to be helpful in developing interest in science learning among students while also benefiting less successful students. Inquiry-based education appears to benefit students by creating an interest in the subject matter; however, it may not result in higher standardized scores. According to Biggers and Forbes (2012), using inquiry-based education is especially beneficial for early learners. This may be in part due to the fact that early learners best understand a concept through the means of asking questions and hands-on interactions.

Additionally, inquiry-based instruction is student-centered, allowing the teacher to individually tailor the lesson to their students. For example, Heilbronner (2013) wrote that men often learn material faster than women; however, they do not learn material as indepth as women. Additionally, Heilbronner (2013) asserted that men outperform women in the SAT-Mathematics subtests and men exhibited higher self-efficacy for STEM related fields. Understanding nuances between different learning styles assists in allowing students to independently discover at a level that is appropriate while helping the student in areas they may struggle. Therefore, inquiry-based instruction could be used to help females learn material faster (since the experimentation is hands-on) and could help males delve further into the material (since they are expected to understand and make inferences about the results). Inquiry-based learning allows the student to make discoveries, while tailoring that experience to that particular student's learning style.

While the majority of literature and experts suggest that inquiry-based education is the most effective method to employ while guiding students through the learning process, some researchers disagree. Kirschner, Sweller, and Clark (2006) suggested that minimal guidance means of instruction are ineffective and do not benefit students as much as guided and structured approaches to education. The researchers suggested that empiricism has built a case against the use of inquiry-based education (and other minimal guidance instruction methods). While the researchers wrote that empirical experiences have made a case for why minimal guidance forms of instruction are malproductive, the researchers stated that current research provides insight into why direct guidance may be more beneficial for students.

As cited by Kirschner, Sweller, and Clark (2006), Moreno (2004) suggested that students learn better through "strongly guided learning than from discovery" (p. 79). The researchers suggested that minimal guidance instruction methods, such as inquiry-based education leave students with ambiguous understanding of the topics presented and that it presents with negative results for students when teachers use that form of guidance. The researchers argue that strongly guided learning experiences are most beneficial for students, providing students with the most effective learning experience.

Kirschner et al. (2006) made statements regarding minimal guidance instruction is a failed approach; however, they did not provide quantifiable evidence supporting their claims. The researchers advocated that using minimal guidance methods is a flawed response to pedagogy. Additionally, the authors claim that making clear connections and using strongly guided inquiry allows students to better understand the meaning of content. In congruence with Kirschner, Sweller, and Clark (2006), other researchers also hold negative opinions of inquiry-based education. Crawford (1999) suggested that inquiry-education is not a realistic method of instruction. Crawford insinuated that inquiry-based education is a challenging method and may be difficult for even teachers lauded as experts in their field.

While the dissenters of inquiry-based education make valid arguments regarding the use of inquiry, it is important to note how inquiry is used in education. Without a solid background on topic material, the learning process may be chaotic. This is why it is important to note inquiry begins as a verification process (D'Costa & Schlueter, 2013). Students are taught material on a continuum and as needed. Therefore, students should have an effective knowledge base to employ inquiry at the selected level. Additionally, inquiry is individualistic, indicating that students will be on different levels of the inquiry continuum. Understanding where a student falls on the inquiry continuum is essential to mitigate maladaptive behaviors and entropy.

Perceptions of Inquiry-Based Education

Inquiry-based education is hard for teachers to enact, and appears to be even more difficult for preservice teachers (PTs) to utilize. Some may regard inquiry-based inefficient because it takes more time to plan and enact a lesson plan than traditional education. Biggers and Forbes (2012) conducted a study in order to better understand PT's perceptions of inquiry-based education. They found that in a pretest, PT's perceived inquiry-based education as idealistic and used more traditional methods. During treatment, the PTs started using inquiry-based education, switching the focus from teacher-directed to student centered. As time passed, it was evident that there was value in both teacher-directed and student-directed inquiry. This exposure to the inquiry continuum changed PT's perceptions. PTs also found that lessons can be both teacher and student-directed. PTs also concluded, that while it took longer to plan and enact inquiry-based instruction, it was a more effective means of communication.

In congruence with Biggers and Forbes' findings, Hreptic, Zeller, Talbott, Taggart, & Young (2006) investigated PT's perceptions of inquiry. Like Biggers and Forbes, as PTs neared the end of the semester, they had more positive perceptions of inquiry. Initially, PTs did not enjoy being taught through the use of inquiry, but as the semester went on, they became excited about the learning process and grew to appreciate inquiry. The preservice teachers were also more able to use inquiry-based methods of instruction as the semester continued.

While many preservice elementary teachers appear to have positive opinions regarding the use of inquiry-based methods, some do not have a positive perception of inquiry. Some preservice elementary teachers feel that inquiry is too idealistic; therefore, it is not practical to use inquiry-based instruction (Hayes, 2002; Biggers & Forbes, 2012).

Preservice teachers' negative perceptions regarding employing inquiry while teaching appears to be overshadowed by some experts' perceptions regarding preservice teachers' ability to effectively use inquiry-based education. Some professionals believe that it is unrealistic to expect preservice teachers to successfully utilize inquiry-based education.

Preservice Elementary Teachers' Understanding of Inquiry-Based Education

While engaging students in inquiry is a problem, an even greater problem is that preservice elementary teachers do not understand what inquiry-based education is (Hayes, 2002). Inquiry-based education, to many, does not have a solid definition, abating preservice elementary teacher's understanding of the process. While the definition of the term is abstract, some students express ideas about inquiry-based education that are not congruent with science education reform (Biggers & Forbes, 2012). Mosley and Ramsey (2008) suggested that many teachers use inquiry-based curricula, but have not fully developed an operationalized definition of what inquiry-based education is. While Mosley and Ramsey (2008) reflected on teacher's understanding of inquiry instruction, they found that teachers generally had an unspecific definition of the term and focused much of the definition focused on problem solving, discovery, and other similar terms. Inquiry-based education is often interchanged with similar teaching methods (Hayes, 2002). This lack of understanding may make it difficult for preservice elementary teachers to engage in inquiry-based education when it has not been clearly defined. With a lack of understanding, preservice elementary teachers are unable to effectively use inquiry education, even though it is regarded as one of the most successful teaching styles.

Hayes (2002) identified that preservice elementary teachers' understanding of inquiry-based instruction is poor, and the exact definition of inquiry-based education is often interchanged with other, similar methods of instruction. One method of teaching science is using a hands-on approach, which often times, students think is inquiry (Biggers and Forbes, 2012). While teaching science using hands-on experimentation with lecture is not a bad way to introduce science topics, this method is not inquiry-based (Bonnsetter, 1998). In order to examine preservice elementary teachers' understanding of the concept, Hayes (2002) evaluated 22 individuals. Each individual was enrolled in the author's science methods course and a mathematics method course. Data were collected through the use of qualitative means by having preservice elementary teachers journal and write self-reflections. Each journal entry was around three to five pages in length and offered information on the students' perspective and understanding of using inquiry-based instruction during a field experience.

Data were encoded by separating the journal content into several descriptive categories. Journals indicated that preservice elementary teachers had positive perceptions of the idea of inquiry-based instruction. While their perceptions of inquiry-based education remained positive, preservice elementary teachers also indicated that they believed this method was idealistic and that using this method for education was not possible due to the constrictions of a classroom. While the preservice elementary teachers believed that this instruction method was not feasible to use when confined to the boundaries of a classroom, students also were worried about behaviors that may be associated with using inquiry-based education. They believed that off-task behaviors may increase due to the nature of using hands-on, inquiry-based instruction. Furthermore, data indicated that preservice elementary teachers lacked knowledge of the content area and therefore were concerned with their own understanding of scientific material in order to effectively use inquiry-based instruction. Reflection on defining what inquiry-based education is and how to effectively use it appeared to helpful for the students in Hayes' study.

Reflection appears to be a successful approach in helping students define and truly understand what inquiry may be. Moseley & Ramsey (2008) had 15 teachers reflect on the meaning by informally defining inquiry formally on the first day of class and informally throughout the semester through class discussions. These reflective experiences led to a deeper understanding of what inquiry meant individually to each student. Initially, the teachers had unsophisticated definitions of the term, but as their understanding deepened, they were able to formulate a more accurate definition. The teachers identified that inquiry-based education is a process and falls on a continuum. As the teachers gained familiarity with the idea, they were able to identify that inquiry is not always open, as many originally suggested. With greater comprehension, the teachers understood that inquiry may range from confirmation to open and therefore exists on a continuum. Additionally, reflection helped students recognize that inquiry is a process that is sequenced by logical actions to create the most adaptive and effective learning environment. While students were able to understand inquiry through the process of reflection, Moseley and Ramsey (2008) noted an important limitation of the study: it was unclear if the students' understanding of inquiry affected the students' future practice.

Moseley and Ramsey's (2008) participants were, for the most part, unable to make connections between inquiry and the constructivist model of education. Only one participant was able to identify the similarities between the two teaching models. According to the participants, inquiry is defined by constructivist methods. Constructivist methods of learning allow for students to engage at an individual level (Moseley & Ramsey, 2008).

Methods and Instrumentation

The present study investigates preservice-elementary teachers' understanding of inquiry. The following section will outline the participants artifacts used for analysis. Afterward, the research design of the present study will be discussed, followed by the general procedure used for data collection and analysis. This section will also review the instrumentation used to obtain data and describe the data collection procedures used. The data analysis will also be reviewed in this section.

Participants

The present study involves a more detailed performance analysis of a 52-participant data set (3 males; 49 females). Participants include 52 preservice elementary teachers attending a mid-sized university in a Midwestern city. Each participant was enrolled in an undergraduate science methods course. All students enrolled in the course participated in the study. Furthermore, all participants completed the study.

Research Design

The research design used for the research project was a mixed methods design using both qualitative and quantitative methods. All data collected were coded for trends and patterns in the responses using the constant comparative method (Bogdan & Biklen, 2008; Denzin & Lincoln, 2000). Where appropriate, the responses were quantified.

General Study Procedures

Each participant was asked to define inquiry-based education on the first day of class. Students were able to write as little or as much as they felt was necessary to answer this question. This open-ended question served as a baseline to determine participants' understandings.

The authors engaged the pre-service teachers in inquiry-based science experiments during each class for five weeks, explaining the level of inquiry used and why this particular level was chosen. Additionally, the authors gave presentations to pre-service elementary teachers regarding what inquiry-based instruction was and reasons for using this method of instruction.

The pre-service elementary teachers were then assigned to read three separate articles on inquiry-based education (specifically: Bell, Smetana, & Binns, 2005; Eick, Meadows & Balkcom, 2005; Fay & Bretz, 2008). These papers served as the basis for writing a paper which posed four separate questions: (1) What is inquiry-based education? (2) How can inquiry be used to encourage student learning? (3) Why does a teacher need to be able to assess the inquiry level of an activity or lab; and (4) What is the relationship between inquiry and science process skills? This paper was graded only for completion and coded with a rubric, as to obtain adequate data regarding participants' actual understanding of inquiry. Furthermore, students were given four weeks to complete this assignment and heard the author's presentations regarding inquiry and had completed eight inquiry-based experiments. This paper served as the mid-point check of understanding, as students received consistent treatment for operationalizing the term inquiry-based instruction.

In the second phase of the study, each of the pre-service elementary teachers participated in a five week field experience, whereby they taught children science using inquiry-based instruction. The preservice elementary teachers were asked to turn in their lesson plans and reflective journals to the authors for data collection and analysis. In the documents, the level of inquiry of the lessons and the reflective journals were coded to determine if the teachers could evaluate the learning experienced by the children. Furthermore, data was obtained about the perceived effectiveness of the inquiry-based instruction from the pre-service elementary teachers' perspective.

In the third and final phase of research, the preservice elementary teachers were asked to design inquiry-based labs appropriate for elementary age children to carry out.. The preservice teachers were asked to select a researchable question over a science topic and then demonstrate their knowledge of inquiry through designing an experiment to answer the selected question. The preservice elementary teachers worked in groups of two or three to accomplish the task. Each lab was written up as a lesson plan, and each group performed the experiment and reported their findings. The final labs were collected and coded to determine if the teachers were able to identify the level of inquiry, control for the appropriate variables and determine the science process skills used in the lab.

General Data Sources Used and Data Collection

The following is a list of all data sources used to identify trends and respond to the research questions:

1. What is Inquiry? (pre-assessment) An open-ended question was posed and pre-service elementary teachers wrote about their understandings of inquiry instruction.
2. Science Biography (self report): Pre-service elementary teachers reported completed high school and college science and mathematics courses. They also described the type of learning experiences they had in the science and mathematics courses.
3. Pre-service teachers experienced presentations on inquiry-based teaching methods and engaged in discussion questions about inquiry based instruction.
4. Participation in Inquiry Labs (eight labs total): Each week for the first five weeks of the course, the students performed an inquiry-based lab in class. Following the field experience, the in-class labs resumed for three weeks.
5. Inquiry Reflection Paper: Participants wrote a paper indicating their understanding of inquiry-based instruction after the fifth week of class.
6. Field-based teaching of inquiry-based labs (structured level) in a school setting: The pre-service teachers taught inquiry based science labs to children in 2nd through 6th grades for five weeks. There were eight lessons taught total per pre-service teacher (four science and four math).
7. Preservice elementary teachers constructed inquiry-based labs given only researchable questions (guided level): After the field experience and during the last four weeks of the course, preservice elementary teachers were given questions about science and asked to design an inquiry-based lab experiment for elementary age children to complete. The pre-service teachers had to select the researchable question, phrase the question, identify the variables, and write the procedure for the experiment. Subsequently, they performed the experiment, gathered data, graphed their data, and reported their findings and conclusions.

Data Analysis

After each data collection session, the data sources were coded for common themes/trends. Where appropriate the assignments were also scored using rubrics. These scores were triangulated with other data sources for reliability. The Table 1 shows the data sources used to triangulate the assertions. Coding of the data was completed by two researchers. Each coded assignment was prepared separately and then the researchers compared their results. Before drafting assertions all researchers came to consensus about the coding scheme and how it should be interpreted.

Table 1: Data Sources for the Assertions - Triangulation Table

Assertion #	What is inquiry ?	Science Biography	Presentations in class	Labs	Inquiry Reflection Paper	Field Experience Teaching Inquiry	Designing Inquiry Labs
1	X	X					
2	X	X	X	X			
3				X		X	X
4		X		X	X		
5	X	X			X		
6	X	X	X				
7					X	X	X

Assertions

Assertion #1

Generally, only 10 students out of 52 **(19%)** were able to define inquiry instruction on the pre-assessment question. In addition, no participant was able to articulate the levels of inquiry instruction or connect inquiry instruction to science process skills.

Most students indicated that inquiry involved the use of questions and asking questions, as evidenced by the following example:

- "Inquiry is all about asking questions. Children always have questions so they would make the best natural scientists." Pre-service teacher 15
- "The goal of inquiry is to ask questions and follow up with an experiment. The reason for doing the experiment is to answer the question posed, or explore the data collected and try to come to some conclusion." Pre-service teacher 22

While most students' understanding of inquiry was **limited**, it provided insight. Many students' explanations of inquiry focused on hands-on learning.

- "In order to participate in inquiry, students have to be involved in a hands-on learning experience." Pre-service teacher 9

Others regarded inquiry as the scientific method, noting that inquiry was the process of hypothesizing, testing, analyzing, and concluding. Student number 19 wrote, " Scientific Method – hypothesis, test, analyze/reflect, conclude as an investigative strategy/tool."

While the scientific method offers an explanation of what inquiry may be, it does not capture the true definition.

The vast majority of students provided incomplete explanations of inquiry-based education; 19% of students provided accurate definitions. For example, student 27 described inquiry as this, "Trial and error; experiments; research; discussions/interviews; prepared problem solving activities." This definition encapsulates the idea of inquiry-based learning. Learning through inquiry methods should be student led and provide students with the opportunity to experience success and failure.

Assertion #2

Participation in class labs that exhibited inquiry-based teaching methods were necessary, but not sufficient to allow pre-service teachers to understand the need to use inquiry to teach science. Instead, labs needed to be offered in conjunction with other experiences. The role of the inquiry lab was to offer preservice elementary teachers the opportunity to experience various levels of inquiry instruction.

- "I never really considered the levels of inquiry before. This idea of inquiry having levels and degrees of student input and further being able to control the level of inquiry used in instruction was all new to me." Pre-service teacher 4
- "Being able to manipulate the inquiry level of a lab was a different concept. I did not have a lot of experience with inquiry levels other than structured and confirmation. Seeing how to change the level of the labs we did in class helped me see how I could use the level of inquiry to assist my students in learning science in a more scaffolded way." Pre-service teacher 32

Not all of the preservice elementary teachers had experienced inquiry instruction at the various levels of inquiry (confirmation, structured, guided and open). Especially, guided and open levels were not generally experienced by our 52 pre-service teachers. Only five of the 52 (9.6%) teachers reported consistent experience at the guided level and some experience at the open level of inquiry.

The inquiry labs completed in class were used to assist the preservice elementary teachers in beginning to construct meaning from the presentations about inquiry. Therefore, inquiry labs were used as the experiential basis for further discussion.

" Doing the labs in class and seeing first hand, how the levels of inquiry and the process skills are connected is an important connection for any teacher to see and understand. The inquiry discussions we have had made more sense with the lab experience added." Pre-service teacher 19

Assertion # 3

Teaching inquiry lessons to children in the field was effective in helping pre-service elementary teachers identify the components of inquiry-based teaching and evaluate the effectiveness of such teaching strategies.

Ninety eight percent of pre-service teachers were able to identify the level of the inquiry used in lessons taught to their groups of children in the field. Further, they were able to evaluate the components of the lessons that were most effective in producing student learning. The connections with student learning and inquiry were stated in 68% of responses.

- "The inquiry level we used in lesson 3 was structured inquiry. The students really enjoyed collecting their own data and were able to summarize their findings in a table we filled out together. I asked the students to tell me why their circuit was successful? They responded by showing the completed circuit and told me why the light bulb lit up. Experiencing the experiments for themselves and collecting their own data and coming to their own conclusions is powerful learning. The children don't forget it as easily as just hearing about it." Pre-service teacher 42.
- "The children remember the lesson when they have opportunity to find their own answers." Pre-service teacher 35

Assertion #4

Readings combined with reflective essay, where language was assigned to learning was effective in helping pre-service elementary teachers identify the components of inquiry-based methods of instruction while connecting inquiry teaching strategies with learning outcomes.

Pre-service teachers rated this assignment as most useful, when combined with example inquiry labs. The pre-service elementary teachers were able to discuss the components of the inquiry labs and identify the level of inquiry of the lab, and how many science process skills a student would use if they participated in the lab.

- "I liked the readings and reflection writing about the inquiry labs. The labs made the components of the inquiry process concrete. The learning outcomes were very easy to identify and assess whether or not the students had learned." Pre-service teacher 46
- "I learned the most when participating in the labs and writing about the learning process...that was very useful for me. The discussion in teams, after the lab also worked well." Pre-service teacher 32

Assertion #5

Prior experience with inquiry learning in their own educational process was helpful in understanding inquiry. Specifically, pre-service elementary teachers who studied chemistry, physics, or advanced mathematics came into the class with a more developed understanding of inquiry-based education than other pre-service elementary teachers who had not enrolled and completed the aforementioned courses.

Out of 52 the preservice elementary teachers, five (9.6%) participants had taken chemistry or physics, and/or advanced mathematics at the collegiate level. These additional experiences allowed the participants with more inquiry experience, afforded by problem-based inquiry coursework, an advantage in understanding the process of inquiry. The personal inquiry learning of the teacher candidates helped the pre-service teachers to see the need to have children experience inquiry based learning.

- "In college I had the opportunity to learn using inquiry in most of the chemistry and physics classes I enrolled in for the bachelor's degree. The opportunity to problem solve and run experiments has given me an appreciation for the inquiry process. The children we taught in the field really made me realize the advantages students have when given the opportunity to learn using inquiry. I know my group of students learned the most about electricity when they were given the chance to set up the circuits and test their ideas. ....When we finished each session, the students would ask me if they could set up another experiment, they wanted to pose their own questions and wanted to see if they were right. It was exciting to see how engaged they were in the (inquiry) process." Pre-service teacher 53.

Most Pre-service elementary teachers participating in our study enrolled in Biology, Geology, or Food Science courses for the 8 hours required in science as part of the general education courses for the bachelor's degree in elementary education. No additional mathematics beyond the required courses were taken.

- "Going back to my own exposure to inquiry…I don't remember very many labs in high school, and college labs were probably structured level. We did collect data, but we followed the procedures we were given." Pre-service teacher 16

Assertion #6

Direct instruction regarding inquiry-based instruction was necessary; however, it was not sufficient to assist some pre-service elementary teachers in constructing an understanding of inquiry. Specifically, 46% of the pre-service teachers in the elementary science methods course could not articulate a complete definition of inquiry instruction after lecture presentations alone.

Assertion #7

During the field experience, pre-service elementary teachers (98%) were able to identify student learning levels (Bloom's taxonomy) and connect the student learning level to the level of inquiry used in the activity. Further, the preservice teachers were able to relate the number and kind of science process skills used to the level of inquiry employed in the lesson they taught.

- "In lesson 2 of the genetics unit the students worked with Punnett squares and solving simple dihybrid crosses. The level of the lesson lab was structured and the process skills used included all but measurement...Once we finished, the students wanted to explore their own proposed crosses and we extended the lesson to accommodate their requests. The questions they asked were higher order (synthesis and analysis level). This moved our subsequent lesson to the guided level." Pre-service teacher 39
- Table 2 Class Assignments, Percentage Completion and Learning Mode Utilized by Pre-service Science Teachers

Table 2: Percent of students who demonstrated knowledge from task

Class Assignment Activity	Number of Teachers	Percent of Pre-service Teachers who meet the Learning Target	Mode of Learning Demonstrated
What is inquiry?	52	19%	Written response to writing prompts
Science Biography	52	100%	Written response to writing prompts
Presentations/Class	52	100%	Participation in class

Discussions			
Labs	52	74%	Completion of lab and lab report
Inquiry Reflection Paper over Inquiry Articles	52	86%	Written essay responding to questions and readings
Field Experience Teaching Science	52	98%	Lesson plans and Journals about field teaching
Lab Activity Design	52	97%	Lesson plan written after designing an inquiry activity lab for children; given a topic question

Discussion

The majority of the participants in this study were female; therefore, taking a closer look at male preservice elementary teachers understanding of inquiry-based instruction male yield interesting and different results. Researching male participants' understanding of inquiry-based instruction would lead to more generalizable information that would be beneficial in determining effective learning experiences for preservice elementary teachers' understanding of inquiry as a whole. Since there are nuances in how males and females learn (Heilbronner, 2013), evaluating males' understanding would benefit instruction of inquiry-based learning. Further, best teaching practices (e.g., reflection, teaching using inquiry-based instruction, designing own experiments, lectures, etc.) for presenting information about this process would be utilized for males and females alike.

While the field experience employed by the elementary science methods course offers exposure to inquiry-based methods of teaching, it may be beneficial to assess students' use of inquiry-based instruction outside the methods course (i.e., evaluate their instruction during their student teaching experiences). Evaluating their teaching methods during their student teaching experience may be beneficial in determining how the students generalized information presented in the elementary science methods course in a more independent teaching environment. Tracking this data may be beneficial in determining their likeliness to use inquiry-based instruction when the preservice elementary teachers begin teaching in their own classroom (when they begin their teaching career).

While understanding the differences between males and females using inquiry-based education may provide understanding regarding the best methods of teaching, it may also be beneficial to research advanced courses in mathematics and science and its correlation to using inquiry-instruction. This was not implicitly researched; however, it may provide insight into students' understanding.

Additionally, implicit to the design of the research study, multiple modalities were used to assess the most effective method regarding the introduction of inquiry to students. Since multiple modalities were used to provide pre-service teachers with the opportunity to understand inquiry, it is clear where students cemented their understanding of inquiry-based education. While results indicated that the majority of students (86%) understood the process of inquiry after phase I of the research project, the opportunity to have direct experience with the application of inquiry based teaching and learning (Phase II field experience) produced the most change in pre-service teacher learning (98%).

Pre-service teachers report the following instructional experiences with inquiry (i.e., teaching in the field) as most helpful. This may be due to their ability to connect inquiry to real life experiences. These experiences, which may be categorized as inquiry-based, offered a hands-on perspective, providing pre-service teachers the opportunity to experience teaching inquiry first hand. Providing students with the opportunity to utilize inquiry offers them a guided understanding of teaching inquiry, allows them to understand the importance of the process (evidenced by 98% of participants understanding the definition of inquiry-based education through experiences).

While experience provided the opportunity for pre-service elementary teachers to use inquiry, taking advance science courses provided pre-service elementary teachers with the opportunity to experience inquiry at the collegiate level. Pre-service teachers who have undergone prior experience with inquiry-based science and mathematics classes prior to the methods course were better able to construct a definition of the concept of inquiry. Experience with inquiry and successfully completing advanced science-based courses appeared to aide in pre-service teachers' understanding of inquiry. In addition, the use of multiple teaching and learning opportunities and modalities appear to be necessary in order to provide pre-service teachers with the essential skill set to define and utilize the inquiry process. Only until provided multiple experiences were some preservice teachers able to provide an adequate and full definition of inquiry. Will the understanding and experience with inquiry result in pre-service elementary teachers using inquiry based instruction in their classrooms? It is unclear. More research is needed to confirm if the exposure and learning opportunities provided were enough to influence teacher practice long term.

References

Bell, R. L., Smetana, L., & Binns, I. (2005). Simplifying inquiry instruction. *Science Teacher*, *72*(7), 30-33.

Biggers, M. & Forbes, C.T. (2012). Balancing teacher and student roles in elementary classrooms: Preservice elementary teachers' learning about the inquiry continuum. *International Journal of Science Education, 34*(14), 2205-2229.

Bogdan,R.C., & Biklen, S.K. (2007). *Qualitative research for education: An introduction to theory and methods* (5rd ed.). Boston, MA: Allyn & Bacon.

Bonnstetter, R.J. (1998). Inquiry: Learning from the past with an eye to the future. *Electronic Journal of Science Education, 3*(1).

Choi, S., & Ramsey, J. (2009). Constructing elementary teachers' beliefs, attitudes, and practical knowledge through an inquiry-based elementary science course. *School Science and Mathematics, 109*(6), 313-324.

Crawford, B.A. (1999). Is it realistic to expect a preservice teacher to create an inquiry-based classroom? *Journal of Science Teacher Education, 10*(3), 175-194.

D'Costa, A.R., & Schlueter, M.A. (2013) Scaffolded instruction improves student understanding of the scientific method & experimental design. *The American Biology Teacher, 75*(1), 18-28.

Denzin, N.K., & Lincoln, Y.S. (1998). *Strategies of qualitative inquiry.* Thousand Oaks, CA: Sage Publications, Inc.

Eick, C., Meadows, L. & Balkcom, R. (2005). Breaking into inquiry. *Science Teacher,* 72(7), 49-53.

Fay, M. E., & Bretz, S. (2008). Structuring the level of inquiry in your classroom. *Science Teacher*, *75*(5), 38-42.

Hayes, M.T. (2002). Elementary preservice teachers' struggles to define inquiry-based science learning. *Journal of Science Teacher Education, 13*(2), 147-165.

Heilbronner, N.N. (2013). The STEM pathway for women: What has changed? *Gifted Child Quarterly, 57*(1), 39-55

Hrepic, Z., Adams, P., Zeller, J., Talbott, N., Taggart, G., & Young, L. (2006). Developing an inquiry-based physical science course for preservice elementary teachers. *AIP Conference Proceedings, 818*(1), 121-124.

Jones, M.G. (2003). Relationships between inquiry-based teaching and physical science standardized test scores. *School Science and Mathematics, 103*(7), 345-350.

Kirschner, Sweller, & Clark (2006). Minimal guidance during instruction does not work: An analysis of the failure of constructivist, discovery, problem-based, experiential, inquiry-based teaching. *Educational Psychologist, 41*(2), 75-86.

Leonard, J., Barnes-Johnson, J., Dantley, S.J., & Kimber, C. (2011). Teaching science inquiry in urban contexts: The role of elementary preservice teachers' beliefs. *Urban Review, 43*(1), 124-150.

Mosley, C., & Ramsey, S.J. (2008). Elementary teachers' progressive understanding of inquiry through the process of reflection. *School Science and Mathematics, 108*(2), 49-57.

Nejla, Y. (2011). The predictors of pre-service elementary teachers' anxiety about teaching science. *Journal of Baltic Science, 10*(1), 17-26.

Ozel, M. & Luft, J. (2013). Beginning secondary teachers' conceptualization and enactment of inquiry based instruction. *School Science and Mathematics, 113*(6), 308-316.

Perry, C.A. (2011). Motivation and attitude of preservice elementary teachers toward mathematics. *Social Science & Mathematics, 111*(1), 2-10

Singh Raghave, R.S. & Upadhyaya, A.K. (2010). Effectiveness of inquiry training model on scientific aptitude of students a secondary level. *International Journal of Education and Allied Science. 2*(2). 161-168

Tessier, J. (2010). An inquiry-based biology laboratory improves preservice elementary teachers' attitudes about science. *Journal of College Science Teaching, 39*(6), 84-90.

Wang, F., Kinzie, M.B., McGuire, P., & Pan, E. (2010). Applying technology to inquiry based lessons in early childhood education. *Early Childhood Education Journal, 37*(5), 381-389.

Yager R.E., & Akcay, H. (2010). The advantages of an inquiry approach from science instruction in middle school. *School and Mathematics, 110*(1) 5-12.

Chapter Authored By

Kristin VanWyngaarden, M.S.
Speech Language Pathologist
Millard Public Schools,
Omaha, Nebraska
USA

Sheryl Mcglamery, Ph.D.
University of Nebraska at Omaha
Omaha, Nebraska
USA

Saundra Shillingstad, Ph.D.
University of Nebraska at Omaha
Omaha, Nebraska
USA

Chapter 7

Reflection, Growth, and Mentoring of Science and Mathematics Teachers

ABSTRACT: The article at hand is focused on chronicling the efforts of a comprehensive teacher induction program as it tries to build beginning science and mathematics teachers' knowledge, skills and dispositions. Further, this research explores the implementation of a systematic reflection process that allows mentors to provide feedback on the beginning teachers' knowledge, skills and dispositions using the Plus/Delta instrument. The responses/reflections of both the mentors and beginning science and mathematics teachers are compared to see what areas of concern and success each reports after observing and reflecting on science or math lessons taught by the beginning teachers.

Introduction

Research completed to date confirms that beginning science and mathematics teachers face many challenges, and must master numerous areas of teaching proficiencies in order to demonstrate competence in teaching (EunJin, Kern, Luft, & Reohrig, 2007). Luft (2003) reports that fewer than 20% of mathematics and science teachers have access to mentoring or induction programs of any kind. Most beginning math and science teachers will face the initial year of practice with little or no access to an induction program targeting their content areas (Luft, 2009). Research further suggests that science and math teachers left without critically needed guidance, a comprehensive induction program could provide, often develop practices that do not allow their students to participate in inquiry activities (e.g. labs, simulations, problem solving, research projects (Luft, Roehrig, & Patterson, 2003). Instead the beginning science and math teachers persist with teacher centered teaching strategies (e.g. lecture, presentation, recitations) that may not be effective or engaging to their students. Further, helping beginning science and mathematics teachers to reach higher levels of teaching competence is shown to be possible and very effective through comprehensive induction programs of mentoring (Gilles, Davis, McGlamery, 2009; Simmons et al, 1999; Luft, 2009).

The focus of this paper is to chronicle the efforts of a comprehensive teacher induction program as it tries to build beginning science and mathematics teachers' knowledge, skills and dispositions. Further, this research explores the implementation of a systematic reflection process that allows mentors to provide feedback on the beginning teachers' knowledge, skills and dispositions using the Plus/Delta instrument. The responses/reflections of both the mentors and beginning science and mathematics teachers are compared to see what areas of concern and success each reports after observing and reflecting on science or math lessons taught by the beginning teachers.

Literature Review

Many articles have discussed the looming teacher shortage that our nation will be facing in the next decade. The National Center for Education Statistics (NCES, 2011) reported that between the fall of 2008 (the last year of actual public school data) and the fall of 2020, the number of qualified teachers needed in elementary, middle and secondary schools is projected to rise. The projected shortage has been brought on by the growing enrollment of students, teacher retirement, as well as teachers exiting classrooms due to high-stakes testing. Teachers of science and mathematics are no exception to the trend. Their numbers are unstable because of rising attrition rates. For example, national statistics show the attrition rate out of teaching for mathematics and science teachers is 50% within 3 years of the start of their teaching careers (NCES, 2011).

In order to stem the tide of attrition out of teaching, reformers and policy-makers have called for induction programs for beginning teachers. "The first years of teaching are an intense and formative time in learning to teach, influencing not only whether people remain in teaching but what kind of teacher they become" (Feiman-Nemser, 2001, p. 1026). Professionals have documented and argued that key factors in retaining beginning teachers are related to high-quality preparation, induction, as well as comprehensive mentoring programs (Berry & Hirsh (2005); Darling-Hammond (1997b); & Johnson & Birkeland (2003). Luft (2009) takes it a step further to suggest that science and mathematics teachers need not only a comprehensive program, but one focused on the needs of the content specialist.

As early as the 1980's educators identified the need to support the philosophical, professional and pedagogical needs of beginning teachers. During the past two decades a large body of research has been conducted on the benefits of mentoring and induction programs for beginning elementary, middle level, and secondary teachers. "Mentoring" refers to a master teacher providing the novice teacher with one-on-one assistance. "Induction" refers to a more comprehensive program to include expertly trained mentors that guide novices with content-specific needs, assistance in filling in gaps with content (knowledge), as well as management and assessment tools (skills). Teacher induction is the process of supporting the work of beginning teachers so that they adjust well (dispositions) into the new teaching environment and social system of the school, understand their responsibilities, and become professionally competent as quickly as possible (Gilles, Davis, & McGlamery, 2009; Gregory, 1998; Tisher, 1982; McDonald, 1980, Evey, 1956).

Across the literature it has been documented that the induction needs of secondary teachers vary from their elementary colleagues (Luft, 2009). Content needs are varied among new secondary teachers. Secondary teachers need to be proficient in their academic disciplines, have knowledge of how to differentiate curriculum to reach all students, as well as knowledge of a how to effectively manage and assess student learning (EunJin, Kern, Luft, Roehrig, 2007). "Induction, done well, has the potential to act as a professional incubating system that cultivates excellence among this country's secondary teachers" (Gschwend & Moir, 2007, p. 2).

To address the needs of beginning teachers' higher education has collaborated with school districts to design induction programs with mentoring support for the first year of teaching. Gold (1996) reported that programs for beginning teachers influenced their retention. A critical component of effective on-site induction programs is mentoring.

Research literature supports that quality teacher induction programs include particular components. Gschwend & Moir (2007) identified nine key components that most effective induction programs use a comprehensive system of support are marked by: (1) high-quality, carefully selected mentors; (2) expertly trained, fully released mentors; (3) authentic mentoring processes where teachers routinely reflect on their practices as measured against teaching standards; (4) rigorous and comprehensive use of an effective, research-based, formative assessment system; (5) a standards-based seminar series for new teachers; (6) collaborative inquiry; (7) district/site/professional partnerships; (8) supportive working conditions, including realistic workloads; and (9) administrative support (p. 21).

Mentoring is one component of quality teacher induction programs. The mentor is a teacher, advisor, sponsor, guide, coach, and confidante (Daloz, 1986; Kram, 1983; Ostroff & Kozlowski, 1993). In the California Mentor Teacher Program, for example, mentors represent an outstanding group of teachers who have the training and expertise necessary to help newcomers (Schulman & Colbert, 1985). Beginning-teacher induction programs with mentors in key roles refer to a planned program intended to provide systematic and sustained assistance, specifically to beginning teachers for at least one school year (Huling-Austin, 1990).

Investigations into mentoring indicate numerous benefits for the new teacher, as well as for the veteran teacher (Cochran- Smith, 1991; Feiman-Nemser et al., 1993). For example, Fox & Singletary (1986) found that successful assistance provides "new teachers with skills that will assist them in developing methods for problem-solving and transferring the theories learned in preservice training to appropriate teaching practices" (p. 14). By promoting observation and conversation about teaching, mentoring is believed to help teachers develop tools for reflection on and continuous improvement of teaching practice.

According to the literature, beginning teachers progress through various stages of development (Darling-Hammond & Bransford, 2005; Feiman-Nemser, 2001). As beginning teachers move through the various stages of development, their thinking about teaching becomes more complex and reflective, thus informing their teaching practices. How can we influence this reflection? How about the mentoring of science and mathematics teachers, are their concerns the same as other beginning teachers?

Research Setting

This paper focuses on research conducted with the CADRE Project at the University of Nebraska at Omaha. The CADRE Project is a collaborative teacher induction effort between higher education and K-12 practitioners. The Metropolitan Omaha Educational Consortium (MOEC), comprised of the 12 metropolitan Omaha public school districts and the University of Nebraska at Omaha College of Education, coordinates this project. This project is a true collaborative effort involving public school superintendents, university administrators and faculty and staff from both entities. The acronym CADRE refers to the overriding goal of Career Advancement and Development for Recruits and Experienced Teachers, and the project creates a framework of growth and development within the teaching profession; thus building a CADRE of outstanding teachers.

The project, which began in 1994, provides a yearlong teaching experience for newly certified teachers who are also completing a specially designed master's degree program. The structured first year teaching experience includes a broad variety of professional learning experiences designed to assist CADRE teachers in reaching a level of professional skill and judgment that characterizes a well-qualified teacher.

This experience provides practical teaching techniques and strategies, along with feedback on the classroom application of teaching strategies. The CADRE teacher has access to formal mentoring, as well as, graduate work focusing on the synthesis of various learning theories. The project also provides opportunities for veteran classroom teachers, CADRE Associates. The CADRE Associates are master teachers selected by their respective districts to serve in this role for two to three year period. They assume alternative responsibilities, which include mentoring two of the CADRE teachers, district-designated roles, and university related work.

Linking beginning teachers to veteran master teachers while incorporating university coursework specifically targeted to first year teachers' needs, collaborative inquiry, professional conversation with peers and mentors, and reflection about teaching experience, has proved to be a powerful combination. It is not enough just to bring a novice and experienced teacher together. Effective induction of beginning teachers must be linked to a vision of good teaching, guided by an understanding of teacher learning, and supported by a professional culture that favors collaboration and inquiry.

Methodology

Purpose of the Study. The goal of our research was to examine the perceptions of teaching practice early in the induction program and again at the conclusion of the induction program of first year science and mathematics teachers. Essential to new science and mathematics teacher development is the ability for the new teacher and mentor to engage in reflective dialogue about the teaching and learning experience as well as the ability for the mentor to know and understand the teaching and learning situation from the perspective of the new teacher. This study provided opportunity to examine the reflections and perceptions of both the beginning teachers and their mentors at key intervals in the induction program.

Study Participants. The study followed 12 mathematics and 12 science teachers during their first year of teaching practice. Also during this first year of teaching these 24 science and mathematics teachers were, at the time of the study, participating in the CADRE Teacher Induction Project. The CADRE Project provided the new teachers with a year-long induction experience and a mentor teacher assigned to assist them in their classrooms.

Research Questions. We examined the reflections completed by the beginning teacher (BT)-mentor pairs. The reflections were focused on teaching experiences in the fall and we compared it to the reflections on teaching experiences the following spring of the beginning teachers' first academic year. Specifically, we addressed the following questions:

- What did beginning science and math teachers perceive as going well in the observed lessons?
- What did mentor teachers perceive as going well in the observed lessons?
- What did beginning science and math teachers perceive as areas for change/ and goals for change?
- What did mentor teachers perceive as areas for change/ and goals for change?

- Was the Plus /Delta useful to beginning science and mathematics teachers and their mentors? If so, how or why? If not, why not?

The purpose of this paper is to report the findings of this Plus/Delta instrument used to assist beginning science and mathematics teachers and their mentors examine teaching experiences and discuss practice and set goals for future growth.

Study Plus/Delta Methodology

The data examined included all beginning mathematics and science teachers participating in the CADRE Induction Program from 2007 to 2013.

The reflections of the first teaching experiences were gathered using The Plus/Delta. These reflections occurred in the fall of the teacher's first year and again in the spring of that academic year for all years. Each BT (Beginning Teacher) and mentor pair recorded what went well and suggestions for change regarding lessons during the fall and again during the following spring. These observations were recorded immediately after a lesson as written comments on a one-page Plus/Delta Chart. Items recorded in the Plus section of the chart indicated what went well and items recorded in the Delta section of the chart indicated a suggestion for change. After the BT and mentors shared and discussed their comments, the BT wrote a goal at the bottom of the chart.

In the fall and spring, all the written comments were read and re-read separately by two researchers. The researchers used constant-comparative analysis to identify categories of similar comments and devise rules that described the properties of each category. (Glaser & Strauss, 1965; Goetz & LeCompton, 1981; Lincoln & Guba,1985; Bogdan & Biklen, 2007)). Each researcher attached a descriptive label to each of the categories. The comments were then re-read individually to make sure each comment was included in one of the categories we each individually identified. Then the two researchers met together to compare how each had categorized all the comments.

The researchers found they had identified six similar categories which were: a) management, b) student engagement, c) instruction, d) assessment, e) preparation, and f) differentiation. The researchers agreed upon the properties for all but the "instruction" category. The "instruction" was too broad to clearly identify comments. So the researchers then re-read the relevant coded comments in order to refine and re-label the "instruction" category. The defining properties became more limited and it was labeled the "teacher input" category. Complete agreement was then reached as to the labels and properties of all six categories. Agreement was also reached as to how to categorize each of the mentor and beginning teacher comments within the categories.

Each semester the analysis was repeated. All the written comments were read and re-read and categorized using the same categorization scheme determined the previous fall. The comments fit into the same categories except for specific teaching strategies such as : a) singing, b) utilizing the SMART Board, and c) power teaching. During the spring of 2009, three of the researchers met to review the data. We agreed to combine the comments on "teaching strategies" with the comments on "teacher input" and re-labeled all such comments under the category of "instruction." We re-instated the category of "instruction." We reached consensus that instruction included teacher input and teaching strategies. Agreement was re-affirmed as to the labels and properties of all categories.

Using the categories, frequency counts were made for both fall and spring to determine the number of lessons during which each area (category) was noted by either beginning teacher or by mentor. Frequencies were tallied for "What went well" and for "Suggestions for change."

Plus/Delta Findings

Qualitative analysis resulted in the following six categories: a) Student Engagement, b) Management, c) Instruction, d) Preparation, e) Assessment, and f) Differentiation.

Student Engagement was defined as students mentally engaged in the learning process. It included incorporating activities demonstrating higher level thinking, making connections with students, building upon prior knowledge, providing appropriate review, motivating students to engage in the learning process, recognizing evidence of student understanding/learning, and engaging all students in a lesson by giving them an opportunity to participate.

Management included class and time management, as well as self-management. Class/time management included pacing, movement, teacher/student transitions, alternate activities for early finishers, clearly defined routines, grouping students, using student names, and utilizing a paraprofessional.

Self-management included the teacher remaining calm, confident, enthusiastic, articulating expectations of the students, and establishing student rapport.

Instruction included both teacher input and teaching strategies. Teacher input included teacher modeling, use of materials, providing explanation/directions to include visuals, as well as providing examples or posting directions on the board before students began seatwork.

Teaching strategies included specific activities such as labs, using the SMART Board, the Elmo projector, showing a video, integration of manipulatives, power teaching, , and other science activities.

Preparation included the teacher demonstrating an organized lesson, stating clear objectives, as well as a lesson that integrated a variety of activities.

Assessment included the teacher's ability to use student response to formulate and give feedback or provide specific praise during questioning. Assessment also included the teacher's demonstration of wait time, appropriate work time, the teacher walking around, and/or providing learning opportunities that included feedback to students and/or guided practice.

Differentiation included lessons that were appropriately planned, lessons prepared in advance for struggling to advanced learners, lessons that included student-centered decision-making, and/or working one-on-one with students, or self- paced stratified lessons taking into account different learning styles.

All of the data presented in the following sections are summarized in charts located in Appendices A, B, C and D.

Areas Most Often Mentioned as Going Well:

Fall Semesters

Beginning Science Teachers Perspectives. The beginning science teachers overwhelmingly focused on student engagement and management followed by preparation, instruction and assessment. These areas form the main areas of teaching skill the beginning science teacher reported as going well in the identified lessons.

The beginning mathematics teachers focused on management with instruction a close second. Student engagement was third and assessment, differentiation and preparation were mentioned less frequently as going well.

Mentors Perspectives. Mentors of the science teachers also focused on student engagement and management as their top two areas identified as going well. But they depart from the beginning science teacher by mentioning assessment of student learning as a third area going well. Instruction was fourth, followed by preparation and differentiation

Mentors of mathematics teachers also focused on management, but to a greater degree than their mentees. Student engagement was second, followed by assessment, instruction, preparation and differentiation.

Spring

Beginning Teachers Perspectives. In the spring the beginning science teachers focused on student engagement, instruction and assessment in about equal emphasis. Most districts are focused on state and districts assessments in the spring and this may account for the attention given instruction and assessment. Management fades to fourth and differentiation and preparation are mentioned less frequently.

Mentors perspectives. Mentors of the science teachers still focused on student engagement and instruction as their top two areas with management a close third. Assessment was fourth on the list followed by preparation and differentiation.

Differences Between Mathematics and Science Teachers

For the beginning science teachers and their mentors the top two most frequently mentioned items as going well were student engagement and management, These areas have shown to be major areas of concern for beginning teachers as they are initially establishing classroom management systems and developing lessons and labs that hopefully engage students.

For the beginning mathematics teachers and their mentors the top two areas most frequently mentioned as going well were management for both BMT (beginning math teachers) and mentors. The second category was instruction for BMT and student engagement for the mentors.

Areas Most Often Mentioned as Challenging or Needing Change:

Fall

Beginning Teachers Perspectives. For the beginning science teachers, classroom management was the most challenging area of teaching needing the most change. Second was student engagement followed by instruction, assessment, differentiation and preparation.

Mentors Perspectives. Mentors of science teachers agreed with their mentees placing management as the clear number one area for change. Management was followed by student engagement, instruction, assessment, preparation and differentiation

Spring

Beginning Teachers Perspectives. Management is still a concern, but not to the degree expressed in the fall. Student engagement is second and differentiation is now third on the list of areas needing change. Assessment instruction and preparation are further down the list of concerns.

Mentor Teacher Perspectives. Mentors of science teachers agree with the beginning teachers and list management as their primary concern followed by student engagement. The mentors select assessment practices as needing change. Followed by instruction, differentiation and very few mention preparation as still a concern.

Chart 1: What About the Lessons Went Well: Beginning Science Teachers and Mentors

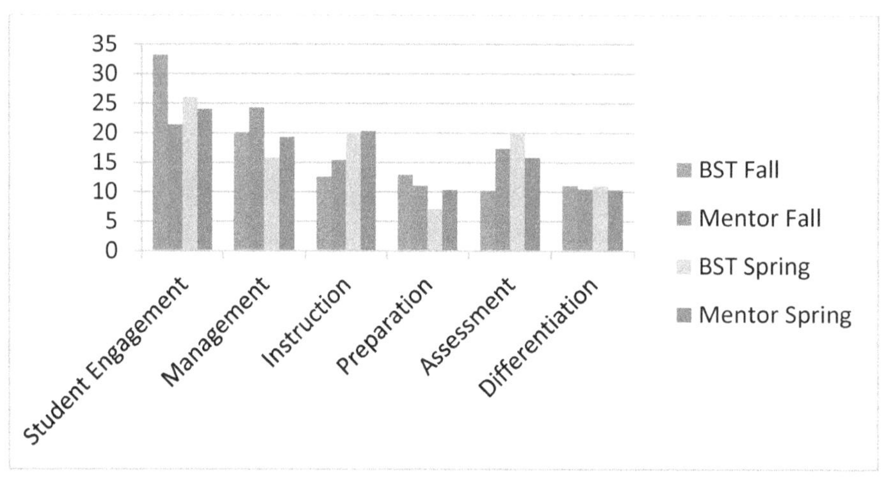

Chart 2: Suggestions for Change: Beginning Science Teachers and Mentors

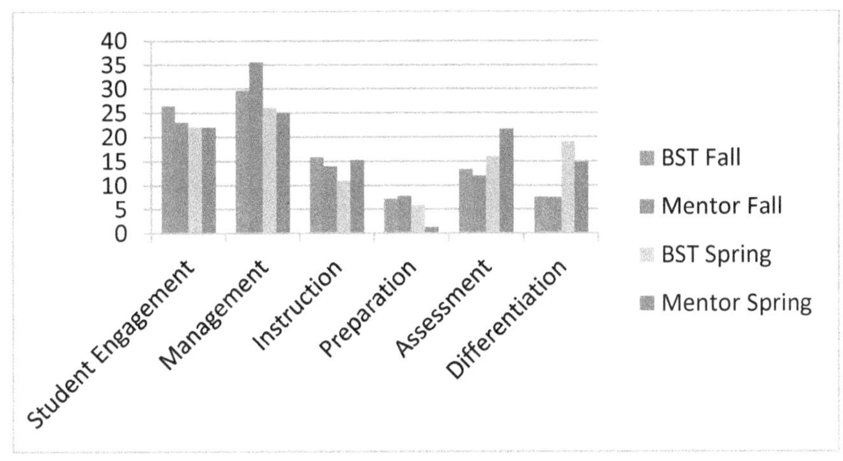

Chart 3: Areas of the Lessons that Went Well: Beginning Mathematics Teachers and Mentors

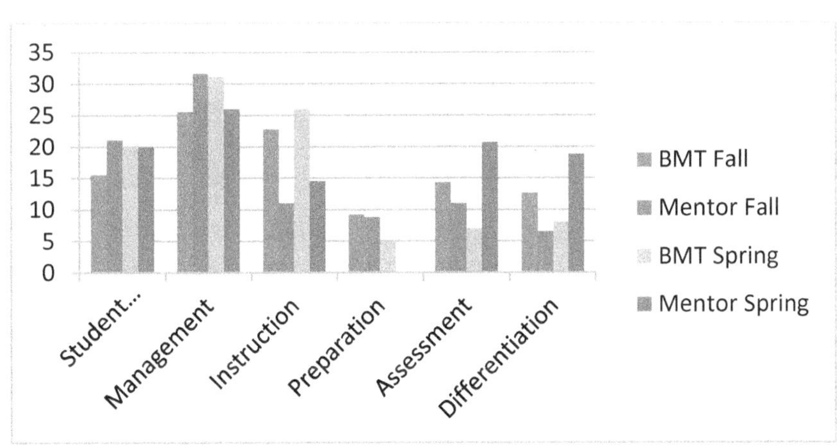

Chart 4: Suggestions for Change: Beginning Mathematics Teachers and Mentors

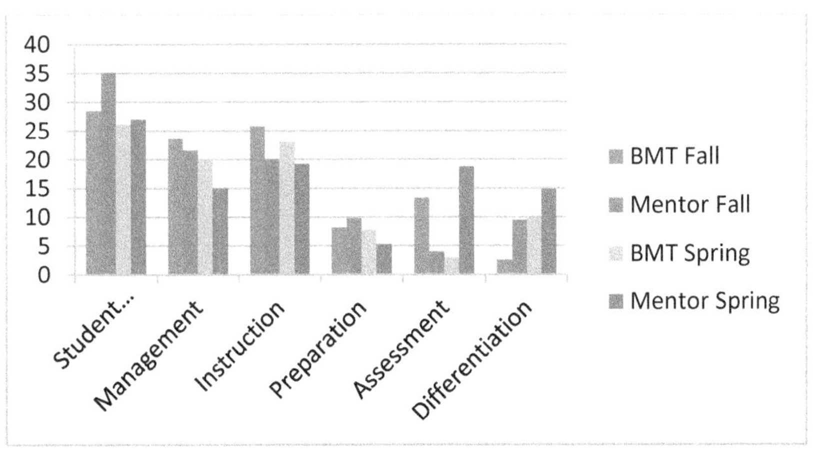

Differences between Science and Mathematics teachers

The science mentors and beginning science teachers found the area needing the most change was classroom management. In terms of areas needing change both mentors and beginning mathematics teachers mentioned student engagement as the number one area of concern.

Reflection Cycle Observed in the Plus Delta Sessions:

Both the mentor and mentee found the observation and analysis of the lessons helpful. The process was cyclic and involved observation, reflection, discussion, and goal setting.

Reflection Cycle Plus/Delta:

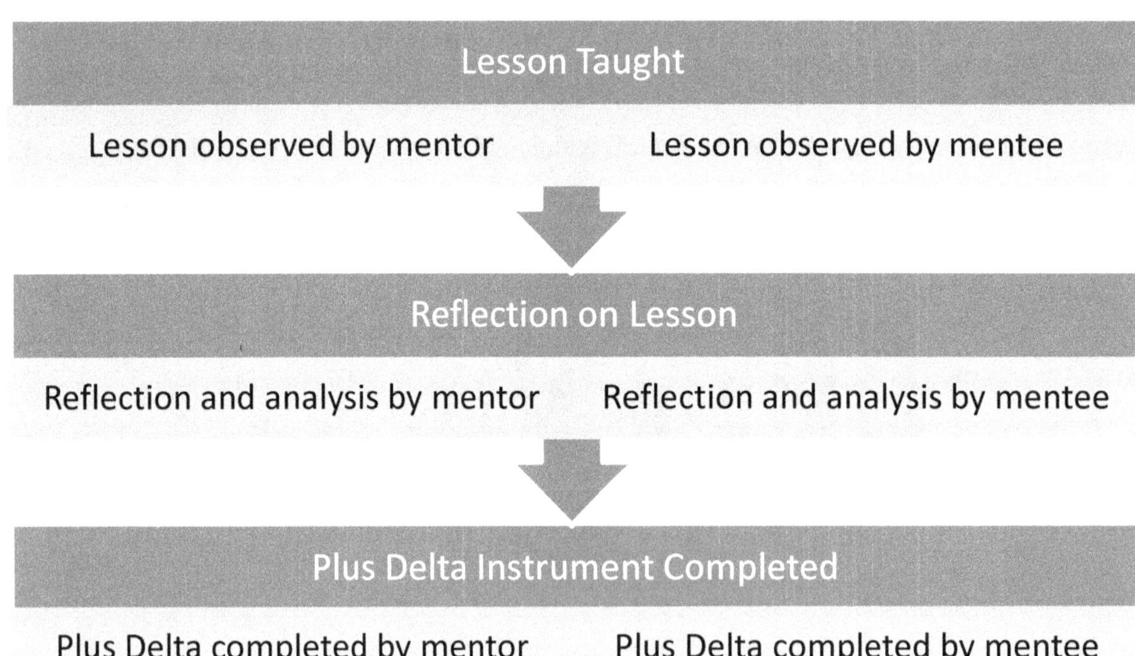

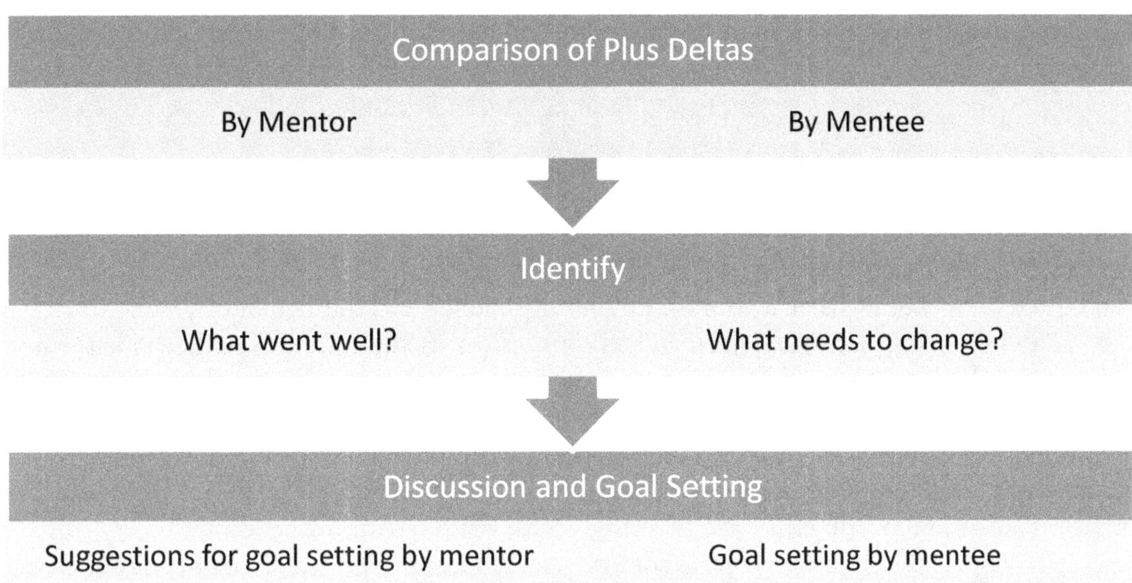

Discussion

Mathematics and science teachers have some of the same concerns but in different order of priority. The concerns were expressed by both mentors and beginning teachers, Mentor 1 expressed her experience assisting her mentee as follows: "Jason had some of the same concerns as the other science teachers. He lacked some skill in managing the labs, so we looked at some options and he set some instructional goals. The sessions were very helpful." Both mentors and beginning teachers agreed on the areas needing the most work.

Beginning teachers need help focusing on their practice. They have so many distractions and demands on their time. The mentors and beginning teachers report the usefulness of the Plus/Delta reflections. "I really have trouble getting time to think about my teaching…the students start coming in and it's so hard to have time to think about how I need to address a problem or rework a lab." (Science Teacher, 8)

Beginning teachers need assistance reflecting on their practice and setting realistic goals. One beginning math teacher stated: "My mentor was very helpful and supportive of the goals I wanted to pursue. She advised me on some strategies I might consider and how to best go about making the changes in my teaching I wanted to make." (Mathematics Teacher,11) The reflective exercise was helpful in providing focus and direction to the beginning math and science teachers

Science and mathematics teachers looked at two different areas for change. The beginning science teachers focused on **management;** while the beginning mathematics teachers focused on **student engagement**. These differences may be attributed to the nature of the subjects and the needs of the specific content areas.

For example, mathematics teachers often focus on problem solving which requires students to focus on the task at hand for extended periods. Often this task focus demands more strategies for sustained student engagement.

In science, the engagement issues are not as pressing. Most students readily engage in labs and activities required in learning science. The issues arise when trying to manage labs and activities that use equipment and require the use of chemical reagents and flames.

Management issues remained, even to the end of the year for most of our beginning science teachers.

Conclusions/Implications

Impact on the Program:

What do we know about what works for beginning science and mathematics teachers?

The beginning teachers need to have a mentor in their field whether science or mathematics. The content specific issues raised during the Plus/ Delta sessions about how to teach specific content and what activities, labs, and pedagogy to use demonstrates why content familiar mentors are most useful. BT brought up the questions posed by their students, for example, "When will I ever use this information? or "Why do we have to learn this?" or "When in real life will I see this used"? All valid questions needing to be addressed. This is best dealt with by a content savvy mentor who can assist his or her mentee in responding appropriately.

Beginning teachers need to be given support to reflect on practice. Increasing the reflection time shortens the time needed to identify areas of improvement and begin working on them. All the mentor teachers agreed that more reflection and discussion about teaching and learning issues brought out the issues faster and expedited the changes in practice put in place by the beginning teachers.

Beginning teachers need to know that change takes time and effort. "BT's believe that perhaps change comes quickly. When they find resistance in their students and discomfort in themselves they tend to recoil from change. Having a mentor who can reassure them that change takes time is helpful." Mentor Teacher, 6

Positive feedback from mentors is essential to teacher growth. "Professional development is work and we all need encouragement to stay with it." Mentor Teacher, 7

The mentors found the Plus part of the Plus/Delta to be a great place to encourage their mentees efforts and to acknowledge their strengths as teachers. It also provided a venue for the beginning teachers to learn to realistically evaluate their own performance in the classroom.

Suggestions for change/feedback must be targeted and constructive when given. Mentors reported that a detailed plan of strategy is most helpful to the beginning teacher. Mentors must avoid comments like "tighten up the discipline." Preferring instead to give beginning teachers specific instructions about how to accomplish a task, mentors found the direct and specific approach to be best. Further, mentors noted: "The more input the beginning teacher has in the goal setting and planning process, the better the result. The full participation of the beginning teacher is the best way to assure progress." Mentor Teacher, 4

Further, the mentors agreed that too much negative feedback can overwhelm the beginning teachers and cause them to lose motivation and give up. Both mathematics and science mentors agreed that with the Plus/Delta, it is better to pick the top two areas for improvement and start there.

"Many beginning math teachers struggle with student engagement, management and differentiation, and many other things. But, it is just too much to address everything at once, pick two areas, or just one. Start with encouragement and move to one suggestion, discuss it and make a goal that is short term, immediate and doable in the next few weeks. Come back and discuss the results of the instructional change…do this often…. and you will see progress. It's the incremental growth of teaching skill the Plus/Delta supports through reflection and goal setting." Mentor Teacher, 5

The data supports the need for teacher induction programs to increase the opportunities for beginning science and mathematics teachers to reflect on their teaching and discuss setting goals. Reflection done regularly will increase the rate of professional growth.

"The more times we used Plus/Delta, the more progress my mentee made. Sometimes it is hard to take the time during the school day to sit down and reflect on practice…most times it doesn't happen. But when we did take the time to teach and reflect, things came up, it started conversations that needed to happen." Mentor Teacher, 2

"I needed the time with my mentor to help me decide how to teach the math concepts coming up. We not only talked about the current lesson I reflected on, but on what I should do next. Goal setting assisted me in plotting a course toward improvement." Mathematics Teacher 7

The reflection done with plus/delta increases the ability of the mentor to have or address difficult areas. The conversation was started during a plus /delta session and often ended with an instructional goal being set. The mentors agreed that the use of the Plus/Delta instrument after observing their mentee teacher teach gave more opportunity for discussion and resulted in more growth.

"I personally found the Plus/Delta sessions with my mentor very useful and helpful. We had the opportunity to discuss in depth my strengths as a teacher. Also, the teaching skills I needed to address we discussed. There was no pressure to agree, we just talked out a strategy, maybe a new way of presenting the material I hadn't considered. We had a formal time to do this…a time for really reflecting on practice. It was very beneficial for me." Science Teacher 9

"The opportunity to reflect together made the difference for me and my mentee. The Plus /Delta opened the door to discuss areas of teaching my mentee wasn't sure about. She wanted to talk about the inquiry lab that didn't go as planned. We had a reason to stop and reflect…and she wasn't being singled out, everyone in CADRE was doing a Plus/Delta. It lowers the stress and allows the mentor-mentee to just talk about practice and discuss issues, set goals and move on." Mentor Teacher, 4

References

Adams. G. J. & Dial, M. (1994). The effects of education on teacher retention. *Education,* 114 (3), 358-365.

Berliner, D. C. (1988). *The development of expertise in pedagogy*. Washington, D.C.: American Association of Colleges of Education.

Bogdan,R.C., & Biklen, S.K. (2007). *Qualitative research for education: An introduction to theory and methods* (5rd ed.). Boston, MA: Allyn & Bacon.

Brooks, M. (1999). Mentors matter. In M. Scherer (Ed.), A Better Beginning (pp. 53-59), Alexandria, VA; Association for supervision and curriculum Development.

Cochran-Smith, M. (199 1). Learning to teach against the grain. *Harvard Education Review,* 6(10), 279-310.

Costa, A.L. & Garmston, R.J. (1994). *Cognitive coaching: A foundation for renaissance schools*. Christopher-Gordon Publishers, Inc., Norwood, MA.

Daloz, L. (1986). *Effective teaching and mentoring.* San Francisco: Jossey-Bass

Darling-Hammond, L., & Bransford, J. (2005). *Preparing teachers for a changing world: What teachers should learn and be able to do.* John Wiley and Sons, N.Y., N.Y.

Darling-Hammond, L. (1997). The quality of teaching matters most. *Journal of Staff Development,* 18, 38-41.

EunJin, B., Kern, A. L., Luft, J. A., & Roehrig, G. H. (2007). First-year Secondary Science Teachers. *School Science & Mathematics, 107*(6), 258-261.

Evey, G.G. (1956). *The new teacher comes to school*. New York, NY: Harper.

Feiman-Nemser, S. (2001). From preparation to practice: Designing a continuum to strengthen and sustain teaching. *Teachers College Record*, 103(6), 1013-1055.

Feiman-Nemser, S. (1996). Teacher mentoring: A critical review. *Eric Digest*, ED 397060. ERIC product 071 ERIC Digest 073.

Feiman-Nemser, S., Parker, M.B., & Zeicher, K. (1993). Are mentor teachers teacher educators? In D. McIntyre, H. Hagger, & M. Wilkin (Eds.), *Mentoring: Perspectives on school-based teacher education* (pp. 147-165). London: Kogan Page.

Fox, S.M., & Singletary, T.J. (1986). Deductions about supportive induction. *Journal of Teacher Education,* 17(l), 12-15.

Gilles, C., Davis, B., & McGlamery, S. (2009). Induction programs that work. *Phi Delta Kappan, 91*(2), 42-47.

Glaser, B. & Strauss, A. (1965). Discovery of substantive theory: A basic strategy underlying qualitative research. *American Behavioral Scientist*, 8(6), 5-12.

Gregory, A. (1998). In through the out door? *Works Management*, 51(2), 16-19.

Huling-Austin, L. (1990). Teacher induction programs and internships. In W.R. Houston (Ed.), *Handbook of Research in Teacher Education* (pp. 535-548). New York: Macmillan.

Kram, K.E. (1983, December). Phases of the mentor relationship. *Administrative Science Quarterly, (p.* 26).

LeCompt, M. & Goetz, J. (1982). Problems of reliability and validity in ethnographic research. *Review of Educational Research*, 52(1), 31-60.

Lincoln, Y. & Guba E. (1985). *Naturalistic inquiry*. Beverly Hills, CA: Sage Publications.

Luft, J. A., Lee, E., Fletcher, S., & Roehrig, G. (2007). Growing or Wilting?. *American Biology Teacher (National Association Of Biology Teachers)*, *69*(6), 341-346.

Luft, J. A., Roehrig, G. H., & Patterson, N. C. (2002). Barriers and Pathways: A Reflection on the Implementation of an Induction Program for Secondary Science Teachers. *School Science & Mathematics*, *102*(5), 222.

Luft, J.A., Roehrig, G.H., Patterson, N.C. (2003).Contrasting landscapes: A comparison of the impact of different induction programs on beginning secondary science teachers. *Journal of Research in Science Teaching,* 40(1), 77-97.

Luft, J.A. (2009). Beginning secondary science teachers in different induction programs: The first year of teaching. *International Journal of Science Education*, 31(17), 2355-2384.

McDonald, F.J. (1980). The teaching internship and teacher induction. In C.C. Mackey, Jr. (Ed.), Assuring qualified educational personnel in the eighties (pp. 91-117). Proceedings of the annual convention of the National Association of State Directors of Teacher Education and Certification (52 d), Boston, MA.

Odell, S.J., & Huling, L. (2000). *Quality mentoring for teachers*. Washington, D.E.: Association of Teacher Educators.

Ostroff, C., & Kozlowski, S. (1993). The role of mentoring in the information gathering processes of newcomers during early organizational socialization. *Journal of Vocational Behavior,* 42,_170-183.

Pultorak, E. G. (1993). Facilitating reflective thought in novice teachers. *Journal of Teacher Education,* 4(4), 288-295.

Richardson, V. (1990). Significant and worthwhile change in teaching practice. *Educational Researcher*, 19, 41-45.

Schulman, J.H., & Colbert, J.A. (1985). *The mentor teacher casebook.* San Francisco: Far West Laboratory for Educational Research and Development.

Shulman, L. S. (1987). Knowledge and teaching: Foundations of the new reform. *Harvard Educational Review*, 57, 1-22.

Simmons, P. E., Emory, A., Carter, T., Coker, T., Finnegan, B., Crockett, D., & Labuda, K. (1999). Beginning teachers: Beliefs and classroom actions. *Journal of Research in Science Teaching*, *36*(8), 930-954.

Smith, T. & Ingersoll, R. (2004). What are the effects of induction and mentoring on beginning teacher turnover? *American Educational Research Journal*, 41(3), 681-714.

Tisher, R.P. (1982). *Teacher induction: an international perspective on research and programs.* Paper presented at the annual meeting of the American Educational Research Association, New York, NY.

Yasin, S. (1998). *Teacher shortages across the nation: implications for SCDEs*. AACTE [American Association of Colleges for Teacher Education] Briefs, 19(12), 1.

Chapter Authored By

Sheryl McGlamery, is currently a professor of Science Education in the Department of Teacher Education at the University of Nebraska of Omaha. She completed her doctoral work at Florida State University in Science Education with an emphasis in biological oceanography. Her research interests are focused on science pedagogy, educational foundations, and assessment for the classroom teacher.

Saundra Shillingstad Ph.D. is a professor of Education in the Department of Teacher Education at the University of Nebraska at Omaha. Her teaching interests include the preparation of pre-service teachers, assessment of student learning in P-16 classrooms, and technology integration in pre-service education.

Chapter 8

Research in the Development of Scientific Thinking

ABSTRACT: The article at hand provides a focused look at research on the early development of science concepts. Many of the research findings from contemporary literature suggest that young learners are interested, eager, and sensitive to statistical patterns in their observations. These early learners can infer causal relationships, and test informal "hypotheses." Research also indicates that at very young ages, children demonstrate an impressive array of scientific behaviors, suggesting they are capable of learning a great deal about the physical, biological, and psychological worlds around them. The primary focus of the research contained herein is related to the questions of, why when we assess what young children have learned as a result of science instruction in the United States, is their performance relatively poor in international comparisons.

Introduction

Research in the development of scientific thinking: What is relevant for science teachers? Consider these two contrasting observations about children's scientific abilities: 1) Babies watch an adult pull several combinations of four balls out of a large bin that contains both pink and yellow balls, but in differing proportions (e.g., mostly pink balls with a few yellow ones, or mostly yellow with a few pink). The babies consistently show surprise and increased interest when the ratio of pink to yellow balls selected by the adult is statistically improbable based on the ratio in the larger container. The babies are 6 months old (Denison, Reed, & Xu, 2012). Young children are shown a "blicket detector"—a box that plays music when some blocks, but not others, are placed on top of it. Several blocks, in various combinations, are placed on the box; some cause the box to play music while others do not. The children are then asked to make the machine go or to turn it off. Even at 24 months of age, they use the pattern of co-variation between the blocks and the activation of the music to infer which combinations will turn the music on or off. By age 4, they can explain the effect, and systematically play with the machine in ways that test these informal "hypotheses" (Gopnik, 2010). 2) On the NAEP (National Assessment of Educational Progress) Science Assessment, performance at the Proficient level indicates "solid academic performance and competency with challenging subject matter." High school students need to perform at least at the Proficient level if they are to be successful in college-level science courses. In 2009, scores on the Science Assessment were at the Proficient level for 34% of 4th graders, 30% of 8th graders, and 21% of 12th graders (NAEP, 2009). Performance at the advanced level, indicating superior understanding of science content, was achieved by only 1% of 12th graders.

Contrasts Raise Questions

American students' performance in science has been a source of concern to educators for decades. At a time when more scientists are urgently needed to address social and economic problems, our educational system does not produce enough students who are well trained in the sciences and interested in pursuing scientific careers. Results from the NAEP Science Assessment (2009) illustrate this concern, but they also show an interesting age-related trend, with markedly lower proportions of Proficient-level scores in the 12th grade compared to scores in the 4th and 8th grades. A similar pattern can be observed in NAEP Science Assessment scores from 1996 to 2009 (see Table 1), even though overall performance improved slightly between 2005 and 2009. At the time when they most need to perform well in science if they are to have a chance at scientific careers, secondary students appear to be losing ground.

These troubling statistics raise a number of questions. First, why has the performance of high school students been consistently lower than that of other grades in the last four national science assessments? Second, why does the combination of maturation and added years of science instruction not produce better science skills by 12th grade, rather than what appears to be a decline in skills? Finally, why is science performance not better in the other grades as well? Despite nationwide efforts to improve science instruction, at no grade level tested do even half of American students show a Proficient level of science skill.

Research on the early development of science concepts paints a picture of eager "little scientists" who show sensitivity to statistical patterns in their observations, infer causal relationships, and test informal "hypotheses." At very young ages, children demonstrate an astounding array of scientific behaviors, suggesting they are capable of learning a great deal about the physical, biological, and psychological worlds around them. Why then, when we assess what they have learned as a result of science instruction in the United States, is their performance relatively poor?

A Developmental Perspective

Results such as those observed on the NAEP Assessment undoubtedly motivate science educators to seek better ways to teach science. Studies of the development of scientific thinking may be a valuable resource in this endeavor. Why might a developmental perspective be particularly useful in the area of science education? One reason is that developmental researchers assess science understanding with different kinds of questions and different research tasks from those used in educational research. For instance, questions asked on standardized tests and other achievement measures are designed to assess primarily content knowledge of the science curriculum; they show what students have learned, or their acquired knowledge at the mastery level. As such, they tap children's recall of facts, and sometimes their ability to apply procedures, but may not tap either deeper levels of understanding or concepts that are only partially understood. As developmental psychologist James Byrnes (2008) has observed, developmental researchers typically ask questions that require deeper understanding, such as, Can a molecule be weighed by a scale? or, Does a molecule get bigger when it is heated? Also, developmental studies often use more open-ended questioning methods.

Development of scientific thinking provides additional insights into students' thought processes. Finally, much developmental research is aimed at exploring the understanding of general concepts rather than specific objectives.

The primary reason a developmental perspective is useful, however, is that skilled performance in science requires specific kinds of cognitive activity, and children (as well as some adults) do not necessarily think in the ways practicing scientists do. Some aspects of typical cognitive development make it possible for scientific thinking to develop as well, but other aspects, when not understood, may interfere with teachers' attempts to foster science understanding. This chapter will discuss the developmental research that illustrates both of these aspects of development. For example, it will describe misconceptions about science that result not from a lack of knowledge, but from young children's own developing reasoning about scientific questions. It will also discuss the brain development (and accompanying change in mental processing ability) that enables older children to use the formal scientific thinking skills practiced by professional scientists. Finally, the chapter will address the role of other academic skills, such as reading and mathematics, in the development of mature scientific reasoning.

Over the years, developmental psychologists have produced a truly vast body of research on the development of skills and concepts related to scientific reasoning. A comprehensive review of this research is beyond the scope of this chapter; the reader is referred to Zimmerman (2007) who compiled an extensive review of studies to that date. The studies described here are examples relevant to the points made, but in no way represent a complete portrait of the development of scientific reasoning.

Taking a developmental perspective means looking not only at what children learn through direct instruction and classroom experiences, but also at the changes in their cognitive abilities that occur naturally, and that make different kinds of learning experiences possible. The research presented here will focus on the role of these changes in young children's early understanding of scientific concepts, as well as the more formal science knowledge acquired by older children and adolescents.

The Child as a Developing Scientist

Ever since Piaget's (1930) characterization of young children as "little scientists," researchers have explored the emergence of scientific thinking skills. Precursors to scientific thinking can be observed in infancy. Babies can detect statistical patterns in nonsense syllables, infer probabilities from samples, and exhibit experimentation on many objects (Gopnik, 2010). Developmental psychologists who advocate a position called "theory theory" argue that cognitive development in children is very similar to the process of scientific discovery (Gopnik & Meltzoff, 1997), and that children use their rudimentary ideas about how the world works (called naïve theories) to predict, interpret, and explain the world, just as scientists do. When their experiences contradict their existing views, they change their theories in a process referred to as "conceptual change."

Naïve Theories: The Development of Folk Science

Children's rudimentary ideas about science reflect their everyday experiences in play and exploration—the "natural" ways in which they come to understand how the world works. For example, they perceive the moon as bigger than the stars, rather than understanding the relations among these celestial bodies the way scientists do. Research suggests these ideas coalesce into naïve or "folk" theories about the social, biological,

Development of scientific thinking and physical worlds children are discovering. Over the course of childhood, they modify these theories so that their understanding becomes more like that of adults (e.g., they come to understand that stars are bigger than the moon; they just look smaller because they are much farther away from the earth). For the past three decades, the majority of studies have focused on three areas: folk psychology, folk biology, and folk physics.

Folk Psychology and "Theory of Mind"

Children live in a social world, and some of their earliest understandings of that world have to do with concepts of mental activity, especially that of other people. Theories of mind help children understand why people behave as they do, especially with regard to what they believe and what they desire. They also help children understand various kinds of mental activity, such as memories, dreams, imagination, and reasoning. Theory of mind has its origins in infancy, when children begin to understand others as intentional agents, that is, people who cause things to happen, and do so "on purpose." Very young infants quickly learn to look at their parents' faces, and by about 9 months they gaze in the direction adults are looking or pointing, and point or hold up objects to another person (Tomasello, 1999). By 12 to 18 months, they will point to alert others to events they are not aware of, and point to objects that adults are searching for (Liszkowski, Carpenter, & Tomasello, 2007). At 14-18 months they are more likely to imitate behavior that appears to be intentional than behavior that appears accidental (Carpenter, Akhtar, & Tomasello, 1998), and by 18 months they discriminate between intentional and unintentional actions when deciding whether to help another person (Warneken & Tomasello, 2006).

Once children understand people as intentional agents, they begin to understand that the people in their world may be motivated by beliefs and desires. A crucial part of such understanding, and one necessary for functioning in the social world, comes when children realize that others may have different beliefs and desires from their own. Many researchers have used the famed "false belief" tasks to discover at what age children really understand this. In these tasks, a child and another person (or doll, or puppet) both observe an object being hidden. When the other person is out of the room, the object is taken from its hiding place and moved to another one. The child is then asked where the other person will look for the object when he/she returns to the room. Four-year-old children typically answer correctly that the person, not knowing about the switch, will look where the object was first hidden. Three-year-old children typically fail the task and assume that the person entering the room has the same knowledge they do. The phenomenon has been explored (with many variations on the task) in hundreds of studies; a meta-analysis conducted by Wellman, Cross, & Watson (2001) concluded that it reflects genuine change in children's concepts of persons between the ages of three and four. Later developments related to theory of mind include more advanced forms of perspective-taking, as well as understanding how to use mental processes, such as the different study methods one might use for different materials (Bjorklund, 2012). Early biological concepts have to do with distinguishing between things that are alive and things that are not. These concepts are based on movement; infants as young as three months old look longer at light patterns generated by a walking person than at randomly generated patterns (Bertenthal, Proffitt, & Cutting, 1984).

Equating movement with living eventually becomes part of children's early biological theories, and they continue to think plants are not alive because they do not move independently until they are between 7 and 9 years old (Hatano et al., 1993). Studies of children's knowledge of the living world reveal that despite some limitations, young children have an impressive degree of biological understanding. For example, many 3-year-olds and most 4- and 5-year-olds attribute intention appropriately to both predator ("The lion wants to eat the zebra") and prey ("The zebra wants to escape from the lion") animals (Barrett, 2004). Four- and five-year-old children also understand that children who are undernourished are more likely to get sick, and that eye color, heartbeat, and breathing are not under voluntary control (Inagaki & Hatano, 1993; 2002).

Their understanding has limits, however; preschool children often generalize what they know about people to animals (Carey, 1985), and as late as second grade are likely to believe that people are more likely to catch a cold from a stranger than from a relative or friend (Raman & Gelman, 2008). Carey (1985) argued that this is because prior to age 7, children's understanding of the natural world is acquired as a series of isolated pieces of knowledge, and only gradually becomes more organized and coherent. In contrast, Inagaki and Hatano (2006) proposed that most children have acquired enough experience before they start school to organize their ideas into a naïve biological theory that helps them to understand both animal behaviors and bodily functions, especially those related to health. But they still require a good deal of instruction to understand such concepts as the role of germs in

Like all people, children live in a world of objects, and they learn much about that world through exploration and play. Geary (2005) proposed that children have an adaptive bias toward object-oriented play in order to determine how those objects can be used as tools. Besides exploring objects, however, children need to understand their own orientation in space and time, so they can navigate their environments and act on, and in, those spaces. Moving (or being carried) in space, looking at objects moved by others, and experiencing daily events such as waking, changing, and feeding in sequence all contribute to infants' early representations related to the physical world. Because important aspects of time and space appear to be understood very early in life, some developmental researchers argue that infants are born with "core knowledge" in domains related to objects, people, and numbers (Spelke & Kinzler, 2007).

Bjorklund (2012) has noted that in order for us to understand that objects follow the basic Newtonian laws of physics, we need to understand that objects remain the same despite changes in how they are viewed (object constancy), that objects are cohesive wholes with distinct boundaries (object continuity and cohesion), and that objects continue to exist even if they are out of our sight (object permanence). Based on laboratory research, object constancy is present in newborns, at least for smaller objects such as toys (Slater, Mattock, & Brown, 1990). Object continuity and cohesion develop gradually over the first year of life (Baillargeon & DeVos, 1991; Hespos & Baillargeon, 2001; Wang, S., Baillargeon, R., & Paterson, S., 2005; Baillargeon, 2008). Evidence of object permanence is reliably observed in laboratory studies between 3.5 and 4.5 months of age, though it is seen somewhat later on tasks requiring a search for a hidden object (Newcomb, 2002).

Other early-developing skills include dead reckoning (tracing one's path back to an initial starting point without landmarks), which is present in 1- to 2-year-olds (Newcombe, Huttenlocher, Drummey, & Wiley, 1998), and a rudimentary awareness of temporal sequence between 4 and 8 months (Lewkowicz, 2004). The combination of innate core knowledge, movement in space and time, and experience with objects leads children to construct a naïve theory of physics that includes an early sense of causality. When two events co-vary, young children are likely to infer that there is a causal relationship between them, and that the first event causes the second event. This is especially true if the events co-occur frequently, if the time gap between the events is short, and if the objects or people involved make physical contact. Inferences of this sort are well established by the end of the preschool period, but knowledge of the underlying mechanisms responsible for consistent co-variations develops more gradually (Byrnes,

Searching for these causal mechanisms is the basis for early hypothesis testing. Piaget did not think preschool children understood objects in terms of their causal capacities (Piaget, 1929). More recent research, however, suggests that young children understand at least some of the principles of "billiard ball" mechanical causality, e.g., when one billiard ball strikes another, the first one put the second one in motion (Bullock, Gelman, & Baillargeon, 1982). An interesting way of exploring the early understanding of causality is to allow children to work with a marble-and ramp apparatus, providing them with rules, such as, "If the light is off, the marble rolls straight down," and then asking them to predict various outcomes. Rule-based causal reasoning develops rapidly between the ages of 3.5 and 4 years (Hong, Chijun, Xuemei, Shan, & Chongde, 2005). With a variety of other object tasks, Gopnik and Sobel (2000) demonstrated that 3-year-olds (and even some 2.5-year-olds) will "easily and swiftly learn about a new causal power of an object and spontaneously use that information in classifying and naming the

Science Misconceptions

As Bjorklund (2012) noted, "theory" implies a coherent framework for organizing facts and making predictions, and the research suggests that children do indeed operate this way with their folk theories of psychology, biology, and physics. But coherent does not necessarily mean correct, and children may operate from knowledge, based on their theories, that is not consistent with current scientific knowledge. Although they are capable of revising their theories in the face of new information, if they do not encounter new input, their constructed knowledge may go unchallenged (Byrnes, 2008).

If young children are capable of constructing and evaluating their own scientific theories, why do so many students have difficulties understanding scientific concepts later in life? One reason is that the very qualities that make them "little scientists" result in children's construction of their own explanations about many things, and because they lack experience and access to all the relevant information, they develop misconceptions. Once they have adopted those misconceptions, it can be difficult for teachers to help them understand scientific concepts correctly, especially if teachers are unaware that the misconceptions exist. The difficulty is not that children lack knowledge, but that they have knowledge that is inaccurate, and must be discarded before more accurate information can be acquired. Another reason for later difficulties is that when young children demonstrate their early, remarkable scientific intuitions, they do so unconsciously, simply as a part of playing and exploring the world, rather than deliberately, as an effort to test formal theories, the way scientists do. Consequently, they are usually unaware of how they constructed their naïve theories, making conceptual change more difficult.

Younger students have many different kinds of misconceptions about science (Griffiths & Preston, 1992; Howe & Tolmie, 2003). These ideas range from misunderstandings about electricity (e.g., electricity is stored in batteries) to inaccurate ideas about the past (e.g., dinosaurs and cavemen lived at the same time). Misconceptions persist beyond early childhood; Kelemen (1999) observed that until they are in the fourth grade, it is common for children to evaluate the properties of animals and objects on a teleological basis (i.e. the properties exist for a purpose, such as rocks being pointy so people can use them as tools). Venville and Treagust (1998) found that it required a 10-week genetics course to shift tenth graders from a belief that genes are passive particles passed down from parents to offspring to an understanding of genes as active particles that control characteristics.

Students often come to their science courses with naïve or inaccurate conceptualizations, and this can interfere with their learning. Educators may not realize students have these incorrect beliefs, and students can often score well on tests by rote learning of vocabulary and facts without really understanding the concepts behind the information. This creates problems in higher-level science classes when they are expected to understand more complex information and think critically about it. Misconceptions about science, which hinder solid reasoning, also occur in college-level students. Kendeou and van den Broek (2005) observed that misconceptions lead to comprehension failures among college students while reading science texts. Further, they concluded that readers are often unaware of the contradictions between their prior knowledge (the inaccurate beliefs they hold) and the text they are reading.

Countering or remediating students' misconceptions about science is difficult, because there appear to be multiple reasons why students develop them. Byrnes (2008) offers one important factor that is likely related to difficulties experienced in the upper grades: many science concepts are about abstractions or nonobservable entities. Young children may be very capable of constructing folk theories about the objects, people, and other living things they observe or act on in their daily lives. They can infer causality, for example, when they observe two events happening close together in time, or when two objects or people come into close proximity with each other. But what happens when the cause of something we observe is not observable? Byrnes (2008) offers an example: if you put a 12-ounce can of Coke and a 12-ounce can of Diet Coke in a tub of water, the Diet Coke floats and the regular Coke sinks. By sight and feel, the cans appear to be the same, but the result occurs because Diet Coke has less density (less mass per unit volume) than water, whereas regular Coke has greater density than water. Understanding concepts like density, which cannot be seen or felt directly, requires a different kind of thinking, and discovering such concepts required a different kind of science (formal science) from that which the "young scientists" practice with folk theories.

How do folk science and formal science differ? For one thing, the concept of folk theories captures well the knowledge constructed by children, as well as untrained adults, in specific domains (e.g., psychology, biology, physics). But practicing scientists, besides working to explain domain-specific phenomena, practice with a set of skills that can be used in a variety of different domains (domain-general skills). These skills allow scientists to generate abstract concepts (such as density) and to test out the ability of those concepts to explain observed phenomena. Domain-general abilities such as hypothesis-generation, experimentation, and evidence evaluation make it possible for humans to revise the misconceptions they have constructed informally, and provide a process by which they can change their folk theories in response to new evidence. This is useful because many of the ideas generated by folk theories are, from the perspective of formal science, wrong.

The Transition from Folk to Formal Science

Young children, using their naïve theories of psychology, biology, and physics, may construct a large knowledge base as they interact with the worlds of people, objects, and living things. Their apparently inherent ability to detect patterns, make causal inferences, and test informal hypotheses would suggest that most of them have the capacity to make the transition from folk science to formal science easily. Yet this does not appear to be the case, at least if we consider performance on national science assessments. The transition from folk to formal science does not happen easily for most students, and happens not at all for some of them. Even many adults, while they may not retain the naïve scientific thinking of early childhood, make little progress in developing the cognitive processes used by practicing scientists. Without scientific thinking, acquiring content knowledge in science becomes an exercise in memorizing—learning the results of the past decades of scientific discovery without truly understanding how scientists arrived at those results, and also how the new evidence scientists continue to gather could change what we think now. Even though standards of modern science education (National Research Council, 1996) require that students be familiar with many scientific processes (e.g., hypothesis generation and testing, model-building) students are often able to perform acceptably, if not exceptionally, in their science classes by memorizing facts. Yet some of them do acquire the ability to reason and solve problems the way professional scientists do. How did such ability come about in the first place? Why are some humans able to think in this way?

On the Origin of Scientific Thinking

According to evolutionary psychologist David Geary (2005, 2012), humans use two cognitive systems, one that evolved in the entire species through selection pressures (a biologically primary system) and one that is culturally specific and built from the primary system (a biologically secondary system). Children's development of folk scientific knowledge derives from the primary system and includes modules for understanding the social, biological, and physical environments in which they function.

Folk psychology includes affective, cognitive, and behavioral systems; these make it possible for people to read nonverbal communication signals, make inferences about other people's emotional states, and negotiate social interactions with both individuals and groups of people. Folk biological modules support humans' ability to categorize plants and animals for food or medicine, and to understand other animal species' behavior, either for hunting or for self-defense. Folk physical modules guide people's movement in three-dimensional space, their tool use, and their early concepts of number Folk theories, and the explanations they provide, are often adequate for people's day-to-day functioning. They provide heuristics, experience-based "rules" that require minimal cognitive effort and are not always accurate, but allow people to make quick decisions and are therefore adaptive.

But our hominid ancestors lived in rapidly changing social and physical environments, and heuristics were not sufficient for them to cope with, as Geary (2012) put it, the "fluidity of social dynamics and social competition." Humans developed another kind of thinking, one that involved explicit, attention-driven mental representations of past, present, and future states. This kind of thinking was triggered when people encountered novel situations or behaviors that were inconsistent with commonly used heuristics. By focusing attention on the details of the new situation, and creating a representation of those details in working memory, people were able to engage in conscious, explicit problem solving. They used language, images, or memories of personal experiences to support this kind of thinking. It was much more effortful than heuristic thinking, but it enabled them to generate and rehearse strategies to achieve goals, to plan activities, and to solve unique problems. Sometimes, it required them to inhibit the heuristics derived from their folk knowledge and generate abstract representations of the problem at hand, especially when the heuristics were not effective for novel problems. Eventually, people also developed the ability to operate on those abstract representations, using formal, logical processes (such as deduction from premises) that could be applied to many different problems. This, Geary argues, is the foundation for the development of the scientific method and for all subsequent scientific discoveries (Geary, 2005).

Generating hypotheses, designing experiments, and evaluating evidence, as well as other skills used in the practice of formal science, all require this effortful, consciously controlled kind of thinking, as does understanding the many abstract, non-observable concepts scientists use to explain what we observe. Many names have been given to this kind of mental activity. Geary (2012) calls it the autonoetic mental model. Dual-processing theorists (Stanovich and West, 2000; Klaczynski (2000, 2005) call it analytic thinking, in contrast to the less effortful heuristic thinking. They argue that cognitive development involves the parallel development of two distinct systems of thought. The heuristic system (also sometimes called the experiential system) is the one predominantly used in daily life. It is useful because it is rapid and automatic; without it, information processing would be overburdened. With increasing age, however, people are more conscious of their own thinking and more able to invoke analytic processes. In recent years cognitive researchers (Evans, 2008; Stanovich, West, & Toplak, 2011) have simply referred to heuristic thinking as Type 1 processing and analytic thinking as Type 2 processing. They note that Type 2 processing involves not only conscious, explicit problem solving, but also inhibitory mechanisms that allow us to interrupt, and suppress, Type 1 processing when it is not helpful. Thus, recognizing one's assumptions and setting them aside is sometimes necessary before more logical, rational thought processes can be used.

The scientific method, as practiced and learned in science classes, is an example of what Geary (1995) describes as a biologically secondary ability. Unlike biologically primary abilities, which evolved in our ancestors through selection pressure, biologically secondary abilities are culturally determined and reflect skills that are important in specific cultures (such as reading in literate cultures). Primary abilities, such as language, are universally acquired in the course of human interactions. Secondary abilities, such as reading, must be purposefully taught. Bjorklund (2012) observed that children typically have high motivation to perform tasks that require biologically primary abilities. But tasks that require biologically secondary abilities, such as reading and mathematics, are not intrinsically motivating for most children, and often require tedious repetition to be mastered. Likewise, young children do not have to be trained to engage in the kinds of questioning and exploratory play that enables them to construct folk theories; indeed, much of their early science-related activities seem effortless. This sometimes causes educators to wonder why science learning becomes so effortful in later years. The answer is that they are not doing the same thing; the science they must learn later on is genuinely more difficult. Most children do have to be trained to learn the scientific skills that will allow them to revise their folk theories and form accurate scientific concepts. Formal science at higher levels is particularly challenging because it also requires the coordination of other biologically secondary skills, such as reading and math. The combination of secondary skills and effortful thought processes required to function as a scientist mean that a student choosing this career path will need both explicit training and motivation. What are the cognitive activities practiced by mature scientists? How, and when, do they develop in school-aged children and young adults? What underlying maturational factors make this development possible?

Famed cognitive developmental psychologist Jean Piaget had a (relatively) simple explanation for the development of scientific reasoning. He characterized the skills involved in understanding and using scientific methods as "formal operational," meaning skills that required the use of abstract, logical operations. In Piaget's view, cognitive development proceeds in stages, and the development of the stage of Formal Operations begins at around age 11 and solidifies across the adolescent years (Inhelder & Piaget, 1958). Students who have not yet moved into the formal operational stage are likely to experience difficulty with scientific practice, since they have not yet developed the cognitive structures to support hypothetico-deductive reasoning. In recent years, developmental research has produced a much more complex picture of the development of scientific reasoning than the one proposed by Piaget. Even as children continue to acquire domain-specific knowledge, their formal and informal educational experiences focus their attention on the domain-general skills of the practicing scientist. The research suggests that the tasks involved in formal science are many, varied, and develop asynchronously. Regarding domain-general scientific skills, two broad areas of focus will be discussed here: the development of scientific experimentation skills, such as the control of variables, and studies describing evidence evaluation, or the coordination of theory and evidence.

Experimentation

Many studies of experimentation have focused on the control of variables strategy (systematically varying one variable while holding all others constant). Understanding this strategy is crucial, because without it people design studies where variables are confounded, with no way to be certain which one is responsible for the effect observed. Using such classic problems as the pendulum task (where students must decide whether variables such as the heaviness of a weight or the length of a string affect how fast a pendulum swings), Inhelder and Piaget (1958) reported that the ability to control variables does not emerge until age 11-12. Later researchers have found slightly better performance by using different tasks, short training sessions, or feedback (Kuhn, Amsel, & O'Loughlin, 1988), but these interventions have little effect on children younger than ten (Byrnes, 2008). The ability to design un-confounded experiments, while absolutely necessary for a practicing scientist, is not common in children or adults without instruction. Chen and Klahr (1999), for example, found that prior to instruction, second graders produced an average of 26% un-confounded experiments, while fourth graders averaged 48% un-confounded experiments. Toth, Klahr, & Chen (2000) found fourth graders to average only 30% accuracy in designing un-confounded experiments prior to.

With explicit, hands-on training in the control of variables strategy, combined with experimental probe questions, Chen and Klahr (1999) found that 2nd, 3rd, and 4th grade children could learn to use the control of variables strategy (although the effects for 2nd graders were marginal). Providing only probes without training was ineffective, and only the 4th graders were able to generalize the skill to problems with different formats and domains after a long delay. These results suggest that designing a controlled experiment, while necessary for true scientific inquiry, is a very complex task, possibly representing the end point of skill development in experimentation, rather than the emergence of such skill. Even among adults, only about 40% of people spontaneously demonstrate the control of variables strategy, though more are able to do so with prompting (Kuhn et al., 1988; Linn, Pulos, & Gans, 1981). Clearly this is an example of a biologically secondary skill that requires training.

A number of researchers have explored easier tasks, such as requiring students to recognize or select a fair experiment; for example, at what age can students recognize that comparing a short thin rod with a long fat rod is not a "fair" test of the role of length in the rod's flexibility? Studies using this kind of task have demonstrated something of a developmental trajectory in that some 4-year-olds will choose a conclusive experiment if the evidence is consistent with their prior knowledge (Croker & Buchanan, 2011), some 6-year-olds can differentiate between a conclusive and an inconclusive experiment (Sodian, Zaitchik, & Carey, 1991), and 8-year-olds can reliably select a conclusive experiment among inconclusive experiments (Bullock & Ziegler, 1999).

In an effort to detect even more preliminary experimentation skills, Piekny and Maehler (2013) used a "mouse task" in which children were shown two "mouse houses" (boxes), one with a small door and one with a large door. They were told that a big mouse could enter only the house with the large door, while a small mouse could enter both houses. To assess their understanding that testing a hypothesis involves a different strategy from producing an outcome, children were then asked which house should be used to make sure the mouse obtains food that will be placed in one of the houses (house with large door, since both a big and a small mouse could get in), and which house should be used if the goal is to find out whether a mouse is big or small (house with small door, since if the food is not eaten, they will know the mouse was too big to get in the door). Few preschoolers or first-graders (15-28%) could reliably make the distinction, but 60% of 3rd-graders and 75% of 5th graders showed understanding of this concept.

Evidence Evaluation

The ability to make a decision based on evidence, whether or not that evidence is consistent with one's prior beliefs, is seen as an essential component of scientific reasoning. If we cannot let go of (or at least revise) our theories in the face of disconfirming evidence, then we are not really practicing science. But in order to make such decisions, we must first be able to evaluate evidence accurately. Tasks used to assess this ability often involve presenting students with covariation evidence; a widely used task developed by Koerber, Sodian, Thoermer, and Nett (2005) asks children which kind of chewing gum (red or green) makes teeth fall out, and presents them with evidence illustrating perfect covariation (10 pictures showing children with red chewing gum and bad teeth, and 10 pictures showing children with green chewing gum and healthy teeth). With evidence of perfect covariation, preschoolers can easily decide that red gum makes teeth fall out, but their performance is not reliable with evidence that is less than perfect (e.g. an unequal number of combinations of two gum colors and healthy or decayed teeth, but predominantly favoring one of two hypotheses), or with non-covariation evidence. On this task, Piekny and Maehler (2013) found the ability to evaluate perfect covariation and non-covariation evidence emerges during the preschool and early primary years, but observed sporadic, non-linear development during the same years in the ability to evaluate imperfect covariation.

Another aspect of evidence evaluation involves the understanding of experimental error, an inescapable aspect of empirical science. Understanding different types of error and how to deal with them is an important part of the practice of formal science and the training of scientists, but when do children become aware of the role of error in experiments? Interestingly, Masnick and Klahr (2003) observed such awareness in 2nd and 4th grade children long before they were capable of using the formal procedures necessary to control error, such as control of variables. In experiments to determine the effects of different factors on how far, or how fast, a ball travels after rolling down a ramp, children who were not very successful at designing unconfounded experiments could nonetheless propose and recognize many potential sources of error. They proposed both measurement and execution errors to explain non-identical times on identical replications of balls being rolled down ramps; significant age differences were observed for both kinds of errors, with more 4th graders than 2nd graders able to name sources of error.

Some aspects of experimentation, particularly those involving evidence evaluation, are developing during the preschool and early elementary years. But the ability to organize these concepts into a broader framework, such that children can actually design unconfounded experiments and generalize the skill to new contents, does not appear spontaneously before adolescence, and efforts to train students in this skill are not very effective until about the 4th grade (Chen & Klahr, 1999). Even among adolescents and adults, however, other aspects of scientific reasoning are not well developed and do not become so without conscious effort and training. This is particularly evident when we consider people's ability to evaluate hypotheses based on evidence. The work of Deanna Kuhn and colleagues (Kuhn, Amsel, & O'Loughlin, 1988; Kuhn, Garcia-Mila, Zohar, & Anderson, 1995) has illustrated that both adolescents and adults fall prey to their own biases when evaluating evidence. If evidence is not consistent with their beliefs, they tend to ignore it. Preexisting beliefs interfere not only with the evaluation, but also with the development of hypotheses, and people commonly construct belief-consistent hypotheses with the intent of confirmation rather than Developmental psychologist Paul Klaczynski and his colleagues (Klaczynski, 1997, 2000, 2005; Klaczynski & Lavalle, 2005; Klaczynski & Narasimham, 1998) Klaczynski observed this effect of prior belief in adolescents. In addition to a domain-general progression in analytic reasoning between 13 and 16 years of age, these researchers found that adolescents were less stringent in their analysis of evidence that was consistent with their beliefs. They tended to use heuristic processing when examining such evidence, with the information processed at a cursory level.

Justifications for accepting belief-consistent evidence were derived from personal experiences, category exemplars, positive stereotypes of in-groups, and negative stereotypes of out-groups. On the other hand, presenting adolescents with evidence that was potentially threatening to their identities and sense of self (such as showing highly religious youth fictional evidence that drug use is common among religious young people) prompted them to evaluate that evidence using the analytical thinking described by the dual-process model. Such evidence was scrutinized closely for flaws, and often rejected based on principles of logic, argumentation, and scientific reasoning (Klaczinski, 2005).

It is clear that the domain-general scientific thinking skills required for the practice of formal science also require this careful, analytic thought processes. But what maturational and developmental processes facilitate the transition from folk to formal science? A significant contributor to the process is the physical maturation of the brain.

Adolescent Brain Development

The "grey matter" of the brain is composed of closely packed neurons in the cerebral cortex. The adolescent brain experiences a wave of overproduction of this kind of matter at puberty, which is then followed by a reduction, or "pruning" of neuronal connections that are not used. The "white matter" of the brain is largely composed of the myelinated axons that connect neurons in different parts of the brain. White matter increases in adolescence as myelination (which insulates axons, causing neurons to fire more efficiently) is enhanced, and the increased insulation of established neuronal connections improves their efficiency (Giedd et al., 1999). The result is that by middle to late adolescence, teenagers have "fewer, more selective, but stronger and more effective" neuronal connections than they had during childhood (Kuhn, 2006, p. 59).

Consistent with these changes, many researchers have concluded that, compared with children just entering adolescence, older adolescents and young adults are better at monitoring and managing their own processes of learning and knowledge acquisition (Keating, 2004; Kuhn & Franklin, 2006). Regarding science performance specifically, Kwon and Lawson (2000) found evidence that prefrontal lobe maturation, along with both physical and social experience, influences students' scientific reasoning ability, including the ability to reject scientific misconceptions and accept widely supported scientific concepts. Why might this be? One possibility is that the kind of scientific reasoning involved in formal science, as opposed to folk science, requires the use of executive functions, and executive functions improve as the brain matures.

Executive functions (EF), broadly defined as the cognitive processes that underlie goal-directed behavior (Best & Miller, 2010), are more specifically identified as the processes used in regulating attention and in determining what to do with information just gathered or retrieved from long-term memory (Bjorklund, 2012). Three such processes have been widely studied: working memory, inhibition, and shifting. Working memory refers to the ability to maintain and manipulate information over brief periods of time without reliance on external aids or cues. Inhibition is an active suppression process, such as the removal of task-irrelevant information from working memory. Shifting refers to the ability to shift between mental states, rule sets, or tasks; shifting requires both inhibition and various working memory processes, depending on the task (Best & Miller, 2010).

Much of the developmental research in executive function has focused on the preschool years, because rapid improvements occur during this time on EF tasks. But as Best and Miller (2010) observed, performance on more complex EF tasks does not mature until adolescence or even early adulthood. In a review of research with a variety of EF tasks across a wide age range, they concluded that inhibition shows rapid improvement in early childhood, followed by slower but significant improvements through adolescence. Performance on complex working memory tasks, such as those requiring the maintenance and manipulation of information, improves at least through adolescence in a linear trajectory. And shifting between task sets follows a protracted developmental trajectory through adolescence. Preschoolers can shift between simple task sets; older children can handle unexpected shifts between increasingly complex task sets. Because they can monitor their own errors, teens can perform task switching on complex shift paradigms as well as adults by middle adolescence (Crone, Somsen, Zanolie, & Van der Molen, 2006; Davidson, Amso, Anderson, & Diamond, 2006).

As Best and Miller (2010) concluded, changes in executive function do not all occur in early childhood; several aspects of EF that are relevant to science reasoning continue to develop during adolescence. Improvements in working memory provide the processing space for inhibition (needed to inhibit the heuristics derived from folk knowledge), generating abstract representations of problems, and drawing inductive and deductive conclusions. All these processes are needed to evaluate evidence, especially when it is inconsistent with a theory that is being tested.

Other relevant information-processing skills that improve as the brain matures include processing speed (Luna et al., 2004) and performance on tasks that require self-regulation and management of processing, such as an organized search for objects in multiple locations (Luciana, Conklin, Hooper, & Yarger, 2005). Finally, metacognition, or awareness of one's own thinking, improves with age in a number of domains, including arithmetic (Carr & Jessup, 1995), memory (DeMarie, Miller, Ferron, & Cunningham, 2004), and scientific reasoning (Kuhn et al., 1988). Performing scientific research requires metacognition at many levels, but the most important is the core of what it means to do science at all, namely, the ability to distinguish between one's theory and the evidence that could be used to support or disconfirm it (Moshman, 1998). Kuhn (2006) noted that as metacognitive ability improves, adolescents increasingly choose what to think about and how to allocate their mental effort. They also choose the activities, including academic tasks, in which they will invest effort, based on their developing sense of personal identity. Since the pruning of unused connections in the brain is guided by an individual's experiences, the extent to which adolescents value particular intellectual activities and choose to practice them will shape their minds in increasingly specialized ways.

Klaczinski (2000) explored this issue of individual differences by examining epistemological dispositions along with reasoning biases. Using several measures of knowledge-related beliefs (the Need for Cognition scale, the Belief Defensiveness scale, the Need for Closure scale, and the Head over Heart scale), he distinguished adolescents based on their tendencies to seek challenging intellectual experiences, enjoy the pursuit of knowledge, to be open to belief revision, to be comfortable with uncertainty, and to rely on rationality rather than intuitivity. On the basis of these measures, he found that some adolescents were "knowledge-driven;" they were open-minded, willing to scrutinize their own knowledge, and able to reevaluate their opinions, postpone closure, and recognize that theories must sometimes be relinquished or revised in order to acquire knowledge. Other adolescents were "belief-driven;" they treated their beliefs as facts, devalued objectivity, and had their self-esteem tied to the truth of their theories.

These differences in the mental dispositions of adolescents were related to the choice to use the more effortful analytic system of thinking. "Knowledge-driven" adolescents were more competent reasoners than "belief-driven" adolescents, and used analytic processing to evaluate evidence, whether or not it was congruent with their personal beliefs. To these young thinkers, preserving existing theories was less important than acquiring knowledge. "Belief-driven" adolescents were more likely to use the less effortful heuristic processing for evidence that was congruent with their own beliefs, and analytic processing for evidence that was not (Klaczinski, 2000).

Mathematics and Reading in Science Understanding

Skilled scientific performance requires conscious coordination of mathematics, reading, and scientific reasoning. Both mathematics and reading skills have their own developmental trajectories, and describing these fully is beyond the scope of this chapter. A few examples presented here, however, will illustrate how reading and mathematics skills interact with developing understanding of science. Scientific activities involve many mathematical skills, such as counting, measuring, interpreting graphed information, and modeling relationships. Research studies on the development of these skills have described the early ability of infants to differentiate between arrays of objects with different numbers of items in them (Feigenson, Carey, & Hauser, 2002) as long as the numbers are small (three or less).

Infants also show the ability to keep track of small changes in quantities (Wynn, 1992) by looking longer at "impossible" addition events. The counting skills of children aged 3-5 include a rudimentary understanding of cardinal and ordinal relations of small sets, as well as procedural knowledge of counting (Gelman & Gallistel, 1978; Gelman & Meck, 1983; Wynn, 1990). Volumes of research have explored the various ways in which children respond to formal instruction in mathematics, and the levels of achievement they reach on standardized tests, but one observation stands out as related to science, and that is that children experience more conceptual and procedural problems as the mathematics curriculum becomes more abstract (Byrnes, 2008).

Of more direct relevance to science is an observation made by Kanari and Millar (2004) that, since real science involves reasoning from data, studies that only report people's performance with categorical outcomes (one car is faster than another, or two objects sink at the same speed), tell us more about logical reasoning than scientific reasoning. The development of number skills relating to data evaluation is therefore particularly pertinent to the development of scientific reasoning. Zimmerman (2007) has noted that authentic scientific inquiry requires the use of statistical procedures and statistical reasoning. Although many science studies do not require children to evaluate numerical data, children's understanding of data has become a fruitful area of study in

As described earlier, Masnick and Klahr (2003) found that 2nd and 4th grade children could propose and recognize both measurement and execution errors to explain non-identical times on replications of balls being rolled down ramps. Understanding measurement error appears to vary with task demands, however. On a more complex task that included controlling variables and collecting data, and that required the students to perform the experiments and take the measurements themselves, Kanari and Millar (2004) described only a minority of students as showing any awareness of measurement error, even though they were 10, 12, and 14 years old. Masnick and Klahr (2003) also made an interesting observation regarding children's ability to find a representative number for variable outcomes. When asked which time (out of five trials) they would give their teacher if asked how long it takes a ball to go down a ramp, NO child suggested using the mean of the five times, and only about a third of children in either 2nd or 4th grade chose a time between the minimum and the maximum time observed. Although some children appeared to have an intuition that a time in the middle is the most representative, none of them thought to apply the common statistic that is used for this purpose (even though calculating the mean is likely to be part of the math curriculum for the fourth grade).

Masnick and Morris (2008) explored people's intuitive sense of data characteristics, asking whether there are properties of data sets that help reasoners induce trends in data without using formal statistics. In several experiments, they found that both children (9- and 12-year-olds) and adults attended to both sample size and between-group variability when drawing conclusions from data, but they also observed significant age-related increases in the ability to use this "intuitive t test" to compare approximate means that include information on the variability of observations. Finally, a number of studies have looked at children's ability to record data while working on scientific experiments. Awareness of one's own memory limitations and the need therefore to keep track of one's observations, is not an early-developing skill. Spontaneous use of notebooks, even when they were provided, was observed in virtually all adults, but only half of 4th-grade children over a 10-week investigation, and adults made three times more notebook entries than children did (Garcia-Mila & Anderson (2007). Prior to being instructed to do so, 7th-grade students did not spontaneously keep records of a science experiment (Carey et al., 1989), and even some undergraduate students failed to use a notebook function when solving scientific reasoning problems in a computer environment (Trafton & Trickett, 2001). These and other studies illustrate the crucial role of metacognition in scientific thinking; scientists must recognize the memory load of complex tasks and compensate with accurate record-keeping.

Secondary level science reading is increasingly about thinking; readers must understand logical arguments, test hypotheses, and evaluate claims made by authors on the basis of evidence and convincing reasons. They must also deal with more complex language than what they usually encounter, either in conversation or in narrative texts. In his discussion of the language demands of science reading in middle school, Fang (2006) observed the many ways in which the specialist language of school science is distinct from the everyday language of ordinary life. This specialized language contains a technical vocabulary and uses ordinary words with non-vernacular meanings (e.g., school of fish, geological fault). Science text makes frequent use of subordinate clauses, as well as abstract nouns (e.g. process, situation) that build abstractions, generalizations, and arguments. It frequently includes lengthy noun phrases, complex sentences, and the passive voice. These characteristics can make it difficult for even proficient readers to understand, let alone those who are struggling. The effort involved in comprehending this different language can result in adolescent readers' turning away from science at a time when strong performance in science classes increasingly requires just such effort.

Fang (2006) offers a number of strategies for helping students to understand and use the language of science texts, including vocabulary building, analyzing the structure of expanded noun phrases, paraphrasing, and understanding the connectives (e.g., if, as, because, nonetheless) that scientists use to construct arguments. Many of these strategies involve students in deep analysis of words, phrases, and sentences. While this is vital to text comprehension, the language of science texts is not the only thing students need to analyze. It is also critical for them to evaluate science content—the conclusions presented in science texts. Science texts offer explanations of observed phenomena; the explanatory arguments they make must be analyzed carefully, with close attention paid to predictions, hypotheses, and the implications of results. To carry out such evaluations, students need both understanding of scientific methods and the ability to reason about what they read.

In this process, metacogntion, or thinking about one's own thinking, is crucial. Baker (2004) noted that metacognition is not only important to successful application of science process skills, but also is critical to successful interpretation of science texts. The National Science Education Standards (NRC, 1996, p. 45) call for children "to access scientific information from books . . . and evaluate and interpret the information they have acquired." Baker further notes that students must learn to take a critical stance with respect to what they read, and that monitoring one's understanding of what is read is an inherent aspect of such evaluation and interpretation. Why is evaluation so important in science? One reason can be seen in another section of the National Science Education Standards (NRC, 1996, p. 42), on the subject of students' opportunities to assess and reflect on their own scientific accomplishments. "The interactions of teachers and students concerning evaluation criteria help students understand the expectations for their work, as well as giving them experience in applying standards of scientific practice to their own and others' scientific efforts. The internalization of such standards is critical to student achievement in science."

In order to compare the content of scientific texts with their own internalized standards, students must exercise metacognition. The importance of evaluation in the development of metacognition and science comprehension is illustrated by a number of computer-based educational systems designed to improve these skills in science contexts. Gautam-Biswas and colleagues have experimented with "teachable agents," software programs in which students teach a computer agent to understand a concept (Biswas et al., 2005). With the program known as "Betty's Brain," students use a concept map representation to teach the computer agent, Betty. They monitor, reflect on, and evaluate Betty's answers, and in the process improve both their metacognitive skills and their science content knowledge.

As Biswas et al. (2005) described the process, teachable agents simulate the behavior of a person's thoughts about a system; this is important because the goal of learning is to simulate an expert's reasoning processes about a domain, not the domain itself. Learning empirical facts may be important, they noted, but it is equally important that students learn to think with the expert problem solving theory that organizes those facts. Such expert-level thinking is not always modeled or trained in science classrooms, where teachers may feel pressured to "cover" large amounts of content in a short time. But modeling this kind of thinking is crucial, especially if students harbor misconceptions about key concepts. As noted below, this modeling can come from texts as well as from

Much remains to be discovered about the role of metacognition in the understanding of science texts. How does metacognition develop, and what is its relation to understanding both science and science texts? According to Deanna Kuhn (2000), metacognition emerges early in life, but follows an extended developmental course during which it becomes more explicit, powerful, and effective as it comes to operate more and more under the individual's conscious control. Scientific thinking, she noted, is a form of higher-order thinking whose roots lie in early metacognitive achievements. Awareness of the sources of one's knowledge is critical to understanding evidence as distinct from and bearing on theories. In skilled scientific thinking, existing understandings are coordinated with new evidence; new knowledge is gained in a highly deliberate, rule-governed, and therefore metacognitively controlled process (Kuhn, 2000).

In order to understand the science they are reading about, students need to understand the self-constrained, rule-governed reasoning upon which science is based; if they do not, science texts become merely collections of "facts." Because scientists need to think critically and evaluatively about what they read, science text comprehension is an important aspect of the interaction of reading and scientific reasoning.

The Role of Reading in Dispelling Misconceptions

Reading well-structured text information can help students overcome science misconceptions. The use of refutation texts, which explicitly mention common misconceptions about science and then explain why they are wrong, is an effective way to bring about conceptual change (Dole, 2000; Guzzetti et al., 1993). Some science educators believe that students only overcome misconceptions through hands-on activities such as lab experiments. But using refutational texts alone may actually bring about longer-term changes in misconceptions than using hands-on activities (Hynd, Alvermann, & Qian, 1997). These texts are effective for students as young as the 6th grade and at higher age levels as well (Diakidoy, Kendeou, & Ioannides, 2003). Thus, independent reading of text information may be a key strategy for overcoming science.

One concern related to reading as a mechanism to foster conceptual change is that there are clear individual differences in reading skills. Some research has shown that less-skilled readers read refutational texts and do not comprehend them deeply enough to overcome misconceptions about science (Guzzetti, 2000). These readers may need very explicit texts that describe common misconceptions clearly, as well as other forms of support such as class demonstrations.

Misconceptions about science and its evolving nature are common among adolescent students, and may remain even in the college years (Tsai, 2006). A factor that contributes to the longevity of misconceptions is the perception held by many adolescents that science knowledge is certain. That is, students believe that science is factual, and that knowledge is unchangeable, rather than an evolving collection of theories. This is particularly true in the area of physics, where the majority of older adolescents show that they view physics knowledge as being less tentative than in other sciences (Tsai, 2006).

In summary, a developmental perspective on scientific thinking paints very different pictures of the first and the second decades of life. Infants (albeit under laboratory conditions) display a high level of awareness and perception of concepts related to science. As they move into early childhood, they are active explorers of the world, and perform some of the same activities (experimentation, hypothesis testing) that professional scientists do. Although preschoolers are more capable at such activities than Piaget thought they were, these "little scientists" perform with a minimum of conscious effort. In other words, young children show an affinity for scientific behavior without purposely doing science. They develop naïve theories and use them in some of the ways scientists use theories (e.g., to explain and predict) and they sometimes make revisions in light of evidence. But they are often unaware of their misconceptions, and ignore evidence that is inconsistent with their theories without realizing they are doing so. Their scientific understanding tends to be domain-specific, and they lack many of the domain-general skills used by scientists. They are not able to understand certain essential concepts related to scientific method, such as control of variables, and do not respond well to training in this concept until they reach the upper elementary grades. Their early science activity involves the use of a primary cognitive system, and they lack the working memory capacity and executive functions required for the secondary cognitive system used in formal science.

Young children's theories about science are largely based on their own experiences, as well as adults' explanations of the world and how it works. But this changes once they enter school. In formal educational settings, adults are not just explaining events and information from the day-to-day world; they are now purposely teaching students about the discipline we call "Science," how it is practiced, and what scientists have learned. The first difficulty children experience with science instruction is that a significant portion of what they learn may be contrary to what they have constructed using their naïve theories. Their misconceptions may interfere with their ability to acquire formal science concepts, but their teachers may not be aware of this.

Another difficulty is that science instruction involves new vocabulary and much factual information, the understanding of which is assessed through testing. The amount of material that must be formally studied, and sometimes memorized, increases. As children move into early adolescence, changes in the brain, as a result of both maturation and experience, gradually bring them the skills needed for a more mature understanding of science. Executive functions improve, and so does metacognition. But as their capacity for the kind of thinking required by formal science increases, so do the demands of science training. The need for effortful analysis, metacognition, and coordinating math and reading skills along with science content places science courses among the most demanding of academic subjects, especially in high school. The students who are likely to pursue advanced science training must not only be motivated and skilled in reading and math as well as science, but they also need to be open-minded, intellectually curious, and able to reevaluate their own opinions in light of new evidence.

They must also have the opportunity to take science classes that provide them with genuine inquiry experiences. Classes wherein students invest most of their time in test preparation and laboratory activities where the outcome is already known will not tap the kind of cognitive skills needed for the professional practice of science. Using predominantly heuristic thinking will not shape the brain of a scientist, though it might create a good test-taker. How can educators help students to acquire and maintain the analytic thinking skills their maturing minds are capable of?

As Kuhn (2006) has noted, the increased role of choice and preference in the activities of teenagers means their choices will shape their brains more than their class requirements will. If secondary students experience science as difficult and boring, they may select out of science courses whenever possible. As high school science requirements increase in the U. S., schools that are able to offer science courses that reflect a variety of interests (engineering, health, anatomy) along with more traditional classes will meet the adolescent need for independent decision-making. Again, however, those courses must offer genuine opportunities for analytic thinking. It is also true that this kind of thinking is not limited to the practice of formal science. Many of the same thought processes used by biologists and physicists are also used by historians, economists, and literary scholars. Programs that encourage analytical thinking in many different real-life areas, such as the "Think Like a Scientist" program developed by the Cornell Institute for Research on Children (Williams, Parierno, Makel, & Ceci, 2004) would also increase the chances that students maintain the capacity for analytic thinking.

A variety of science classroom activities and demonstrations are designed to show students the fun and excitement of science. While beneficial for generating interest in the short run, this is not enough to sustain students' interest in the long run, because the real practice of science is and will always be challenging. Understanding the development of scientific reasoning, especially at advanced levels, can help teachers to understand why the challenges will always be there, to have realistic expectations about the effort students need to make, and to design meaningful learning experiences.

References

Baillargeon, R. (2008). Innate ideas revisited: For a principle of persistence in infants' physical reasoning. Perspectives on Psychological Science, 3, 2-13.Baillargeon, R., & De Vos,J. (1991). Object permanence in young infants: Further evidence. Child Development, 62, 1227-1246.

Baker, L. (2004). Reading comprehension and science inquiry: Metacognitive connections. In W. Saul (Ed.), Crossing borders in literacy and science instruction: Perspectives on theory and practice (pp. 239-257). Newark, DE: International Reading Association.

Barrett, H. D. (2004). Descent versus design in Shuar children's reasoning about animals. Journal of Cognition and Culture, 4, 25-50.

Bertenthal, B. I., Proffitt, D. R., & Cutting, J. E. (1984). Infant sensitivity to figural coherence in biomechanical motions. Journal of Experimental Child Psychology, 37, 213-230.

Best, J. R., & Miller, P. H. (2010). A developmental perspective on executive function. Child Development, 81, 1641-1660.

Biswas, G., Leelawong, K., Schwartz, D., Vye, N., & The Teachable Agents Group at Vanderbilt (2005). Learning by teaching: A new agent paradigm for educational software. Applied Artificial Intelligence, 19, 363-392.

Bjorklund, D. F. (2012). Children's Thinking: Cognitive Development and Individual Differences (5th Edition). Belmont, CA: Wadsworth/Cengage Learning.

Bullock, M., Gelman, R., & Baillargeon, R. (1982). The development of causal reasoning. In W. J. Friedman (Ed.), The developmental psychology of time (pp. 209-254). New York: Academic Press.

Bullock, M., & Ziegler, A. (1999). Scientific reasoning: Developmental and individual differences. In F. E. Weinert & W. Schneider (Eds.), Individual development from 3 to 12: Findings from the Munich Longitudinal Study (pp. 38-54). Cambridge: Cambridge University Press.

Byrnes, J. P. (2008). Cognitive Development and Learning in Instructional Contexts (3rd Edition). New York: Pearson Education Inc.

Carey, S. (1985). Conceptual change in childhood. Cambridge, MA: MIT Press.

Carey, S., Evans, R., Honda, M., Jay, E., & Unger, C. (1989). "An experiment is when you try it and see if it works": A study of grade 7 students' understanding of the construction of scientific knowledge. International Journal of Science Education, 11, 514-529.

Carpenter, M., Ahktar, N., & Tomasello, M. (1998). 14- through 18-month-old infants differentially imitate intentional and accidental actions. Infant Behavior and Development, 21, 315-330.

Carr, M., & Jessup, D. L. (1995). Cognitive and metacognitive predictors of mathematics strategy use. Learning and Individual Differences, 7, 235-247.

Chen, Z., & Klahr, D. (1999). All other things being equal: Acquisition and transfer of the control of variables strategy. Child Development, 70 (5), 1098-1120.

Crone, E. A., Somsen, R. J. M., Zanolie, K., & Van der Molen, M. W. (2006). A heart rate analysis of developmental change in feedback processing and rule shifting from childhood to early adulthood. Journal of Experimental Child Psychology, 95, 99-116.

Croker, S., & Buchanan, H. (2011). Scientific reasoning in a real-world context: The effect of prior belief and outcome on children's hypothesis-testing strategies. British Journal of Developmental Psychology, 29, 409-424.

Davidson, M. C., Amso, D., Anderson, L. C., & Diamond, A. (2006). Development of cognitive control and executive functions from 4 to 13 years: Evidence from manipulations of memory, inhibition, and task switching. Neuropsychologia, 44, 2037-2078.

DeMarie, D., Miller, P. H., Ferron, J., & Cunningham, W. R. (2004). Path analysis tests for theoretical models of children's memory performance. Journal of Cognition and Development, 5, 461-492.

Denison, S., Reed, C., & Xu, F. (2012). The emergence of probabilistic reasoning in very young infants: Evidence from 4.5- and 6-month-olds. Developmental Psychology, 49, 243-249.

Diakidoy, I., Kendeou, P., & Ioannides, C. (2003). Reading about energy: The effects of text structure in science learning and conceptual change. Contemporary Educational Psychology, 28, 335-356.

Dole, J. (2000). Readers, texts and conceptual change learning. Reading & Writing Quarterly, 16, 99-118.

Evans, J. St. B. T. (2008). Dual-processing accounts of reasoning, judgment and social cognition. Annual Review of Psychology, 59, 255-278.

Fang, Z. (2006). The language demands of science reading in middle school. International Journal of Science Education, 28 (5), 491-520.

Feigenson, L., Carey, S., & Hauser, M. (2002). The representations underlying infants' choice of more: Object-files versus analog magnitudes. Psychological Science, 13, 150-156.

Garcia-Mila, M., & Anderson, C. (2007). Developmental change in notetaking during scientific inquiry. International Journal of Science Education, 29, 1035-1058.

Geary, D. C. (1995). Reflections of evolution and culture in children's cognition: Implications for mathematical development and instruction. American Psychologist, 50, 24-37.

Geary, D. C. (2005). The origin of mind: Evolution of brain, cognition, and general intelligence. Washington, DC: American Psychological Association. Doi: 10.1037/1087-000

Geary, D. C. (2012). The evolved mind and scientific discovery. In S. M. Carver & J. Shrager (Eds.), The Journey from Child to Scientist (pp. 87-115). Washington, D. C.: American Psychological Association.

Gelman, R., & Gallistel, C. R. (1978). The child's understanding of number. Cambridge, MA: Harvard University Press.

Gelman, R., & Meck, E. (1983). Preschoolers' counting: Principles before skill. Cognition, 13, 343-359.

Giedd, J., Blumenthal, J., Jeffries, N., Castellanos, F., Lui, H., Zijdenbos, A., Paus, T., Evans, A., & Rapoport, J. (1999). Brain development during childhood and adolescence: A longitudinal MRI study. Nature Neuroscience, 2, 861-863.

Gopnik, A. (2010). How babies think. Scientific American, 303, 76-81.

Gopnik, A., & Meltzoff, A. (1997). Words, thoughts and theories. Cambridge, MA: MIT Press, p. 32.

Gopnik, A. & Sobel, D. M. (2000). Detecting blickets: How young children use information about novel causal powers in categorization and induction. Child Development, 71, 1202-1222.

Griffiths, A. K., & Preston, K. P. (1992). Grade-12 students' misconceptions relating to fundamental characteristics of atoms and molecules. Journal of Research in Science Teaching, 29, 611-628.

Guzzetti, B., Snyder, T., Glass, G., & Gamas, W. (1993). Promoting conceptual change in science: Meta-analysis of instructional interventions from reading education and science education. Reading Research Quarterly, 28, 116-161.

Guzzetti, B. (2000). Learning counter-intuitive science concepts: What have we learned from over a decade of research? Reading & Writing Quarterly, 16, 89-98.

Hatano, G., Siegler, R., Richards, D., Inagaki, K., Stavy, R., & Wax, N. (1993). The development of biological knowledge: a multinational study. Cognitive Development, 8, 47-62.

Hespos, S. J., & Baillargeon, R. (2001). Reasoning about containment events in very young infants. Cognition, 78, 207-245.

Hong, L., Chijuna, Z., Xuemeia, G., Shan, G., & Chongde, L. (2005). The influence of complexity and reasoning direction on children's causal reasoning. Cognitive Development, 20, 87-101.

Howe, C., & Tomie, A. (2003). Group work in primary school science: Discussion, consensus, and guidance from experts. International Journal of Educational Research, 39, 51-72.

Hynd, C., Alvermann, D., & Qian, G. (1997). Preservice elementary school teachers' conceptual change about projectile motion: Refutation text, demonstration, affective factors, and relevance. Science Education, 81, 1-27.

Inagaki, K., & Hatano, G. (1993). Young children's understanding of the mind-body distinction. Child Development, 64, 1534-1549.

Inagaki, K., & Hatano, G. (2002). Young children's naïve thinking about the biological world. New York: Psychology Press.

Inagaki, K., & Hatano, G. (2006). Young children's conception of the biological world. Current Directions in Psychological Science, 15, 177-181.

Inhelder, B., & Piaget, J. (1958). The growth of logical thinking from childhood to adolescence. New York: Basic Books.

Kanari, Z., & Millar, R. (2004). Reasoning from data: How students collect and interpret data in science investigations. Journal of Research in Science Teaching, 41,

Keating, D. (2004). Cognitive and brain development. In R. Lerner & L. Steinberg (Eds.), Handbook of adolescent psychology (pp. 45-84). Chichester, England: Wiley.

Keleman, D. (1999). Why are rocks pointy? Children's preference for teleological explanations of the natural world. Developmental Psycholgy, 35, 1440-1452.

Kendeou, P., & van den Broek, P. (2005). The effects of readers' misconceptions on comprehension of scientific text. Journal of Educational Psychology, 97, 235-

Klaczynski, P. A. (1997). Bias in adolescents' everyday reasoning and its relationship with intellectual ability, personal theories, and self-serving motivation. Developmental Psychology, 33, 273-283.

Klaczynski, P. A. (2000). Motivated scientific reasoning biases, epistemological beliefs, and theory polarization: A two-process approach to adolescent cognition. Child Development, 71, 1347-1366.

Klaczynski, P. A. (2005). Metacognition and cognitive variability: A dual-process model of decision making and its development. In Jacobs, J. E., & Klaczynski, P. A. (Eds.), The Development of Judgment and Decision Making in Children and Adolescents. Mahwah, New Jersey: Lawrence Erlbaum Associates.

Klaczynski, P. A. & Lavallee, K. L. (2005). Domain-specific identity, epistemic regulation, and intellectual ability as predictors of belief-biased reasoning: A dual-process perspective. Journal of Experimental Child Psychology, 92, 1-24.

Klaczynski, P. A., & Narasimham, G. (1998). Development of scientific reasoning biases: Cognitive versus ego-protective explanations. Developmental Psychology, 34, 175-187.

Koerber, S., Sodian, B., Thoermer, C., & Nett, U. (2005). Scientific reasoning in young children: Preschoolers' ability to evaluate covariation evidence. Swiss Journal of Psychology, 64, 141-152.

Kuhn, D. (2000). Metacognitive development. Current Directions in Psychological Science, 9, 178-181.

Kuhn, D. (2006). Do cognitive changes accompany developments in the adolescent brain? Perspectives on Psychological Science, 1, 59-67.

Kuhn, D., Amsel, E., & O'Loughlin, M. (1988). The development of scientific reasoning skills. New York: Academic Press.

Kuhn, D., & Franklin, S. (2006). The second decade: What develops (and why)? In W. Damon & R. Lerner (Series Eds.) & D. Kuhn & R. Siegler (Vol. Eds.), Handbook of child psychology: Vol. 2. Cognition, perception, and language (6th Ed.). Hoboken, NJ: Wiley.

Kuhn, D., Garcia-Mila, M., Zohar, A., & Andersen, C. (1995). Strategies of knowledge acquisition. Monographs of the Society for Research in Child Development, 60,

Kwon, Y. J., & Lawson, A. E. (2000). Linking brain growth with the development of scientific reasoning ability and conceptual change during adolescence. Journal of Research in Science Teaching, 37, 44-62.

Lewkowicz, D. J. (2004). Perception of serial in infants. Developmental Science, 7, Linn, M. C., Pulos, S., & Gans, A. (1981). Correlates of formal reasoning: Content and problem effects. Journal of Research in Science Teaching, 18, 435-447.

Liszkowski, U., Carpenter, M., & Tomasello, M. (2007). Pointing out new news, old news, and absent referents at 12 months of age. Developmental Science, 10, F1-F7.

Luciana, M., Conklin, H., Hooper, C., & Yarger, R. (2005). The development of nonverbal working memory and executive control processes in adolescents. Child Development, 76, 697-712.

Luna, B., Garver, K., Urban, T., Lazar, N., & Sweeney, J. (2004). Maturation of cognitive processes from late childhood to adulthood. Child Development, 75, 1357-1372.

Masnick, A. M., & Klahr, D. (2003). Error matters: An initial exploration of elementary school children's understanding of experimental error. Journal of Cognition and Development,

Masnick, A. M., & Morris, B. J. (2008). Investigating the development of data evaluation: The role of data characteristics. Child Development, 79, 1032-1048.

Moshman, D. (1998). Cognitive development beyond childhood. In W. Damon (Series Ed.), D. Kuhn & R. S. Siegler (Vol. Eds.), Handbook of child psychology: Vol. 2. Cognition, perception and language (pp. 997-1016). New York: Wiley.

National Assessment of Educational Progress: Science (2009). National Center for Education Statistics, Institute of Education Science, U. S. Department of Education.

National Research Council (1996). National Science Education Standards, Washington, DC: National Academies Press.

Newcombe, N. (2002). The nativist-empiricist controversy in the context of recent research on spatial and quantitative development. Psychological Science, 13,

Newcombe, N., Huttenlocher, J., Drummey, A. B., & Wiley, J. (1998). The development of spatial location coding: Use of exernal frames of reference and dead reckoning. Cognitive Development, 13, 185-200.

Piaget, J. (1930). The child's conception of physical causality (London: Kegan Paul) [La causalite physique chez l'enfant (1927)]

Piaget, J. (1929). The child's conception of the world. London: Routledge and Kegan.

Piekny, J., & Maehler, C. (2013). Scientific reasoning in early and middle childhood: The development of domain-general evidence evaluation, experimentation, and hypothesis generation skills. British Journal of Developmental Psychology, 31,

Raman, L., & Gelman, S. A. (2008). Do children endorse psychosocial factors in the transmission of illness and disgust? Developmental Psychology, 44, 801-813.

Slater, A. M., Mattock, A., & Browne, E. (1990). Size constancy at birth: Newborn infants' responses to retinal and real size. Journal of Experimental Child Psychology, 49, 314-322.

Sodian, B., Zaitchik, D., & Carey, S. (1991). Young children's differentiation of hypothetical beliefs from evidence. Child Development, 62, 753-766.

Spelke, E. S., & Kinzler, K. D. (2007). Core knowledge. Developmental Science, 10,

Stanovich, K. E., & West, R. F (2000) Individual differences in reasoning: Implications for the rationality debate? Behavioral and Brain Sciences, 23, 645-665.

Stanovich, K. E., West, R. F., & Toplak, M. E. (2011). The complexity of developmental predictions from dual process models. Developmental Review, 31, 103-118.

Toth, E. E., Klahr, D., & Chen, Z. (2000). Bridging research and practice: A cognitively based classroom intervention for teaching experimentation skills to elementary school children. Cognition and Instruction, 18, 423-459.

Tomasello, M. (1999). The cultural origins of human cognition. Cambridge, MA: Harvard University Press.

Trafton, J. G., & Trickett, S. B. (2001). Note-taking for self-explanation and problem solving. Human-Computer Interaction, 16, 1-38.

Tsai, C. (2006). Biological knowledge is more tentative than physics knowledge: Taiwan high school adolescents' views about the nature of biology and physics. Adolescence, 41, 691-703.

Venville, G. J., & Treagust, D. F. (1998). Exploring conceptual change in genetics using a multidimensional interpretive framework. Journal of Research in Science Teaching, 35, 1031-1055.

Wang, S., Baillargeon, R., & Paterson, S. (2005). Detecting continuity violations in infancy: A new account and new evidence from covering and tube events. Cognition, 95, 129-173.

Warneken, F., & Tomasello, M. (2006). Altruistic helping in human infants and young chimpanzees. Science, 311, 1301-1303.

Wellman, H. M., Cross, D., & Watson, J. (2001). Meta-analysis of theory-of-mind development: The truth about false belief. Child Development, 72, 655-684.

Williams, W. M., Papierno, P. B., Makel, M. C., & Ceci, S. J. (2004). Thinking like a scientist about real-world problems: The Cornell Institute for Research on Children science education program. Journal of Applied Developmental Psychology, 25, 107-126.

Wynn, K. (1990). Children's understanding of counting. Cognition, 36, 155-193.

Wynn, K. (1992). Addition and subtraction by human infants. Nature, 358, 749-750.

Zimmerman, C. (2007). The development of scientific thinking skills in elementary and middle school. Developmental Review, 27, 172-223.

Chapter Authored By

Bridget Franks, Ph.D. is an Associate Professor of Teacher Education at the University of Nebraska at Omaha. She has expertise in brain research, human development and learning theory. She currently teaches classes in educational foundations and graduate research design and evaluation.

Chapter 9

STEM Education in Progressive Classrooms: A Practitioner's Approach

ABSTRACT: The article at hand provides … a detailed account of the development and implementation of a middle school course focused on Invention and Innovation. The chapter is written from an a personal account of the challenges and benefits and uses an informal voice in the writing to better represent the nature of communication, research, and development in middle school education settings. Specifically, content and outcomes from a practical Design Cycle are overviewed.

Introduction

The idea of Invention and Innovation in my school started in 2005. I had previously taught in an alternative education program for two years. Within the alternative education program, which was called *School Within a School*, I was responsible for 8th Grade Language Arts, Social Studies, Science, Mathematics, and Study Skills. In teaching Science and Mathematics, I would try to share different views and ideas on how science and mathematics applied to the students' everyday lives. I would also draw on my background as an Electrical Engineer, Field Engineer, and Project Manager to show how science and math concepts were used in a greater capacity. However, due to the required pacing of the Science and Mathematics curriculums, I never had the time to provide meaningful projects for students to experience the application of their learned knowledge of science and math concepts in real-world applications. So for those first two years of teaching, I was able to do a lot of talking about how whatever they learn could be used, but unable to give them a hands-on real world application of the concepts.

Engineering in the Classroom

During those two years, Lewis and Clark Middle School in Omaha, Nebraska did offer Industrial Technology as an elective, but the teachers were inexperienced and overwhelmed and the course was generally ineffective. Unfortunately, a great deal of equipment, computers, and various other resources were basically wasted. Add to that new budgetary concerns and the Industrial Technology course was being considered for cancellation before it was even off the ground.

The summer before the start of my third year of teaching, I thought about implementing a way to provide science and math applications through relevant classroom projects. I presented an idea to my principal, generally that I would like to offer a course that would expose students to real-world applications or self-discovery projects based on grade-appropriate science and math concepts. She granted me permission to conceptualize and develop a course that would provide students such an opportunity.

Prior to the start of each school year and several times during the school year, teachers attend content-specific professional development sessions sponsored by the district. Although I was endorsed in Mathematics, the fact that I had done teaching in an alternative education program, I often had an option of attending a particular subject areas offered in the program, that is, Language Arts, Mathematics, Science, or Social Studies. Oftentimes, I did attend the mathematics professional development; however, this particular summer I planned on attending the science professional development sessions. Now, I had also shared my intentions of a new course offering with fellow colleague who taught science by the name Lisa Showalter. At this particular science profession development session, the district presented a new partnership it formed with professors from the University of Nebraska at Omaha (UNO) and the Peter Kiewit Institute (PKI) to introduce a program to teachers that would involve educational robotic platforms. So after hearing the professors' presentation on how robotics may be used to visualize and provide hands-on experience for mathematics and science concepts, I immediately introduced myself during a break to the UNO professors.

I introduced myself as an alternative education teacher with a mathematics endorsement and a degree in Electrical Engineering. The reaction I received from the professors was one that I will never forget. They were all amazed, and Dr. Bing Chen, the department chair for Computer Engineering and Electronics Engineering at the Peter Kiewit Institute, threw his hands up in the air and exclaimed, "My prayers have been answered!" He shared with me (along with confirmation from his colleagues) that he had been said to roll out this program to the school district, it would be great to have a math and science teachers working with these educational robotics platforms, but it would be all the more wonderful to have an engineer who was a teacher who could utilize the robots in such a way as to expand understanding of the robots, how they work, and their application of mathematics and science. So with that encounter, an invaluable resource — even to this day — served as the beginning of the foundation for Invention and Innovation. Now I had to develop curriculum around ideas regarding what hands-on education would look for science and mathematics.

In developing the curriculum for Invention and Innovation, one thing I knew was that I did not want it to look like your standard Industrial Technology class in that students would not have prescribed projects where they followed the given directions and either recorded results and/or compared their finished project to a known finished product. Also, I did not want it to be so much subject content that the necessary time for research, design, and creation would be limited. I had ideas, but I needed some proven practices.

I began my research online and came across the International Technology and Engineering Educators Association (ITEEA), formerly ITEA (International Technical Educators Association). ITEA proved to be a great reference for the ideas I had in mind. It offered a variety of hands-on activities ranging in required resources and rigor through its Engineering by Design™ (EbD) program. Within EbD, ITEA had a course guide entitled Invention and Innovation to which I can go on record to say and that was always the intended title of this course — conceptualized and presented to my Principal — before I found out about ITEA. The intent of the course was to expose students to the *process of invention* and the *process of innovation* to show students how they can be producers in their world as opposed to only being consumers.

Implementation

In the fall of 2005, Invention and Innovation began as a year-long elective course open to eighth grade students. The very first class had 12 students enrolled. That year we began with some basic challenges as well as with information or lessons from the ITEA handbook. The students, Ms. Showalter, and I had a great time provided that the class was small and that the students were definitely able to work on projects individually as well as in pairs. The resources for projects were not hard to procure, and Ms. Showalter and I had the necessary in-class time to instruct and support students' learning. We did not utilize the engineering design process the first year, but basically followed a scientific method approach (two Science teachers) and required that the students use inquiry and problem solving skills to address the given challenges whether in research or in creating the product.

Some of the projects over the first couple of years included: Product Disassembly — student pairs would disassemble an inoperable desktop computer followed by identification and labeling of components. Students included descriptions of each component. The components where then cross-referenced to human organ systems. Upon completion of cross-referencing and presentations, student pairs reassembled their respective desktop computer; and Howlin' Wolf — students individually designed and built a scaled shelter (1 cubic foot, max.) based on one of three randomly chosen shelter types (i.e., straw, wood, or brick) and their respective specifications (e.g., broom straw and string, twigs and marshmallow creme, and river peebles and toothpaste). The completed shelter must withstand wind from a standard leaf blower at a distance of two feet for one minute. Turn off the Lights — student pairs were challenged to turn off a standard wall-mounted, toggle light switch using a Rube Goldberg invention that comprised of a minimum of five stages.

The class was effective in exposing students to STEM by providing them with solid applications of their learning in other courses. The first class of twelve doubled the next year to 24, which would serve as the class-size limit for subsequent years. Through advising at the end of the seventh graders' year, the number of students interested in enrolling in Invention & Innovation averaged 68 students — for the 24 seats. I requested from administration to analyze the list of interested students for the purpose of selecting students that would accurately represent our student body as a whole. Therefore, the students were queried by ethnicity, gender, grades in science and math, and district math scores. This was aligned to school demographics and course/test data. The first full course of 24 students provided a representative group of the school as a whole. This became a standard for years to follow. Nevertheless, by the end of the first year, I knew that some more educational structure was needed. Again, help came from UNO.

The following summer, in 2006, UNO and PKI began the Silicon Prairie Initiative on Robotics in Information Technology (SPIRIT) program. The SPIRIT program's goal was to get as many educational robots into classrooms through teacher training and lesson planning. As a result, UNO and PKI partnered with Omaha Public Schools to train middle school science and math teachers how to build and use robots in the classroom. Teachers received training using the Oregon State University Tekbot Platform for Learning (PFL) and a Tekbot for classroom use. The trainings were held once a month and included training in robotics concepts, sample lessons utilizing the robots, and the use of the Engineering Design Process. The Engineering Design Process was the educational structure I needed for Invention and Innovation. Admittedly, I was frustrated that I didn't think of it as concretely as the process by name. If one has ever tried to create something, the basic stages of the Engineering Design Process are applied along with its iterative steps. Now, on a college, or real-world, level, the Engineering Design Process has numerous stages and iterative steps between those stages which are as complex as the product, process, or system to which it pertains. Therefore, to ensure it's used within the SPIRIT program and in the teachers' classroom, the SPIRIT staff condensed the process to five stages. These five stages were based on the Museum of Science, Boston's Engineering is Elementary (EiE) design process. The EiE design process requires students to "Ask", "Imagine", "Plan", "Create", and "Improve". With that, I was prepared to provide the educational structure I had imagined. And given my (as well as most teachers') fascination with alliteration, I customized the engineering design process for Invention & Innovation as "The Five I's of I & I" — Inquire, Idealize, Illustrate, Invent, and Innovate.

Along with challenges from the previous year, robotics was added to the curriculum. One point I stressed to the students and parents was that robotics would be used in its total capacity as an educational platform, as opposed to an activity or opportunity for students to "play" with them. With that, students were exposed to basic electrical engineering principals such as Ohm's Law, circuitry, and soldering. Students were taught the "physical" comparison of circuitry components to plumbing devices such as a battery is akin to a water tower (potential energy), wire is akin to a water pipe or hose (conduit), a switch is akin to a faucet (regulator), a resistor is akin to a valve or filter (regulator), a capacitor is akin to a rain barrel (potential energy, storage), and a transistor is akin to a back flow preventer (regulator). The students were challenged to design and build a "plumbing model" of a basic circuit containing the given circuitry components using basic materials such as cups, paper, straws, cotton balls, craft sticks, etc. Students filled their "battery" with water, then demonstrated each model's components' function within the "circuit" as the water flowed through the "wire".

Then, students learned soldering concepts and techniques and were tasked to complete and demonstrate the function of a basic LED flasher kit (Apogee Kits AMK102B). The soldering was completed step-by-step according to the kit's instructions: I modeled the soldering technique via an ELMO and projector, checked for understanding, then I guided each student, as needed, with her/his technique for that step. Upon successful completion of the soldering lesson/challenge, students demonstrated their understanding of the use of variable resistors to adjust the flashing "frequency" of the LEDs. Afterward, students were introduced to robotics.

Students were given a history of robotics and their use in science, industry, medicine, and households. Oregon State University PFL robots were used in the classroom through the support of UNO. Students were paired to assemble and operate a Tekbot. Students were guided to use their acquired soldering skills to assemble their Tekbots. Assembly was done as a group, step-by-step to ensure each step is done correctly. Soldering work was checked first by student pairs, then by me. After a step was deemed success, or after corrections were made, the class would begin the next step. After the Tekbots' soldering and assembly was completed, students used the robots to demonstrate basic science concepts of speed, velocity, friction, force, and inclined planes, along with geometry concepts of slope, angle, and the Pythagorean Theorem through various challenges. Student pairs completed data collection and analysis for the challenges and reported their respective results and summaries.

As the program grew, the focus became STEM (Science, Technology, Engineering, and Mathematics) Education. Challenges were intentionally based on one of the four subject areas and grade appropriate. Given that the course was yearlong, each subject area of STEM was given a full quarter to utilize the engineering design process. Additionally, when the CEENBoT replaced the Tekbot as the educational robotic platform, it allowed for a more enriched learning experience for the students in regard to soldering, assembly, performance, and added programming.

Innovation

In 2011, Lewis & Clark Middle School became an approved International Baccalaureate Middle Years Program (IB MYP) school. IB MYP categorizes subject areas into six areas and Invention & Innovation would fall within "Technology" — currently "Design". IB MYP required that each student complete 50 hours of Technology through qualified course offerings. The school would be unable to fulfill that requirement under its established course offerings. The other Technology courses: CAD, Digital Media, Family Consumer Science, and Entrepreneurship were all semester courses offered to both 7th and 8th Graders. Invention & Invention would have to be scheduled as the other Technology courses within the building. This was great! For years, Invention & Innovation was only offered to 24 students a year — with as many as 75 students expressing interest each year. Also, many students and parents made the choice to attend Lewis & Clark because of Invention & Innovation, knowing the student would have to wait a year and then may be selected. Under this new IB MYP requirement, Invention & Innovation would offer three semester sections for 7th Graders and three semester sections for 8th Graders. This required me to condense one year's worth of content into one semester. This would greatly reduce much of the detailed research, analysis, and problem-solving time that a full year afforded, but it still allowed for students to gain an understanding of not only the challenge, but of the engineering design process (Design Cycle) itself. Courses within Technology must utilize the IB MYP Design Cycle. The IB MYP Design Cycle is its engineering design process model that consisted of five stages: Investigate, Design, Plan, Create, and Evaluate. This transition was seamless given "the Five I's of I&I" were essentially the same, just different names. Also, Invention & Innovation would remain the 8th Grade course. The 7th Grade course would be Invention & Innovation - Foundations. The focus for Foundations would be to explicitly stress the Design Cycle and its particulars during each unit challenge. Invention & Innovation would allow for more focus on the challenge with the Design Cycle as a guide.

With the semester classes each unit was now four weeks long and each stage of the Design Cycle would last approximately one week. The first week was given for investigation (Investigate), which would include an introduction of the challenge itself, the challenge's design specification (requirements and restrictions), and research by the student to build a starting knowledge to solve the challenge. The second week was reserved for drafting and materials/schedule planning (Design/Plan) of the solution to the challenge. Students were required to create sketches, then final drafts of their solution prior to work on the product, process, or system. They were also required to develop a materials list and time schedule that would detail the project's completion from start to finish based on the given "build" timeframe. The third week of the unit was reserved solely for creating (Create). The students worked according to their respective schedules and used only from their materials list. If they were unable to maintain their schedule or required revisions to their materials list, they were required to justify either set of modifications with me. The fourth week would provide testing, presentation, and evaluation (Evaluate). Students would test their product to see that it met the challenge according to the design specification, present their solution/product to the class based on meeting the design specifications. Finally, the solution/product would to be evaluated against the design specification of the challenge, as well as their evaluation of their own work during each stage of the Design Cycle in a reflective essay.

Invention & Innovation challenges were given to provide context or relevance to the students learning. Challenges were directly related to students' content standards in their other classes, or to real world events, organizations, or competitions. Invention & Innovation challenges included: Science - *The Scientists* (design and conduct a science experiment adhering to the Metropolitan & Engineering Science Fair guidelines for entry into the metro-wide science fair), Technology - *Sunshine Bakery* (design and create a functional solar oven from recyclables that can maintain and internal temperature of 100° C), Engineering - *The Bean Dispenser* (design and create a functional bean dispenser than dispenses 5-10 dry beans — coincides with U.S. History Industrialization and Labor unit) or *Future City Competition* (compete in the Future City Competition), and Mathematics - *Curiosity Scale Model* (design and create a 15:1 scale model of the Mars Science Laboratory "Curiosity" Rover — coincides with World Space Week and community Space Celebration Night) or *Nebraska Robotics Expo* (compete in one of the six events of the Nebraska Robotics Expo).

Invention & Innovation Foundations challenges were tied to the students' core courses. Challenges included: Science - *From Caves to Space* (design a two meter banner that highlights 24 great discoveries — discoveries are based on Science units' topics), Technology - *Renewable Energies* (design and create a functional wind turbine model that generates 0.5-1 W), Engineering - *Innovation Nation* (design and create a functional innovation to a current product), and Mathematics - *ISS Module Scale Model* (design and create a 25:1 scale model of a module of the International Space Station — coincides with World Space Week and community Space Celebration Night).

Invention & Innovation, along with Foundations, is effective because it is project-based, student-driven and educationally structured - using the engineering design process. It applies prior knowledge yet requires new knowledge through adequately paced critical thinking, creative, hands-on manipulation of resources to create a solution/product to a challenge. Students continuously display growth in confidence, knowledge, and skills through meeting the challenges of the four units. Several students have shared that they enrolled in STEM-based elective courses in high school because of their experience in Invention & Innovation. Many have also continued into higher education in STEM majors with a few who have chosen engineering because of the class.

One story in particular is of an African-American female student who I ran into shortly after she graduated with a Bachelor's degree in Nursing. She is proud to share that she "still has" her robot that she soldered, assembled, and programmed. She said, that although she never saw herself as an engineer, she knew that she would be successful in college because of the confidence she developed in the course through the challenges and the process. She concluded by saying, "I told myself, 'You built a robot. You can get this degree!"

Chapter Authored By

Derrick Nero, M.S. is an Engineering Education instructor at the University of Nebraska at Omaha. He is a licensed Electrical Engineer and has rededicated his knowledge of engineering, mathematics, and science to the success of k-12 STEM students. In particular, he research interests lie in the pedagogies and curricular issues that create successful students from underrepresented populations.

Chapter 10

Broadening the Perspectives of Science and Mathematics Teachers: Integrated STEM Education and Real World Experience

ABSTRACT: The article at hand provides suggests that the fundamental content differences in the STEM disciplines have created differences in academic training that STEM teachers receive in order to gain their certification. The literature reviewed herein suggests that mathematics and science teachers tend to have well defined coursework leading to professional certification, particularly at the secondary level. Engineering and technology teacher training, however, has traditionally been more focused on applications of the curricular principles of engineering and technology within mathematics and science courses, and does not universally lead to teaching certification. The variations within the STEM disciplines and how they are taught makes the integration of these subjects difficult and yet, it seems that for most STEM practitioners the perception of a natural connection between the STEM disciplines exists. This natural connection has become one emphasis in current educational reform; namely, the push for integration of the STEM disciplines at all educational levels where STEM is viewed as a meta-discipline.

Introduction

Teachers of the science, technology, engineering, and mathematics (STEM) disciplines take very specialized programs of study to gain their professional certification. The U.S. Department of Education has conducted the School and Staffing Survey (SASS) six times most recently in 2011 – 2012. The most recent data related to teacher certification to be published was from the 2007-2008 report. This report details what teachers have certification and teach in their subject area and what certification means according the U. S. Department of Education.

When reading the report, the following information can be identified. To receive certification to teach mathematics at a particular level, extensive courses that cover both the appropriate content and pedagogy must be successfully completed. Science certification is similar with appropriate science content and instructional pedagogy and even more specialization of discipline (physics, chemistry, biology, etc.) at the higher levels. Teachers of educational technology have their own certifications, which require knowledge gained in coursework related to how can you apply current and future technology in the classroom to facilitate learning. Currently, it appears that not many certification programs for teachers of engineering K – 12 exist (U.S. Department of Education, 2009).

The differences in the STEM disciplines have created differences in training that STEM teachers receive to gain their certification. Mathematics and science teachers tend to have well defined coursework related to their curriculum with the appropriate pedagogy for the related content. Engineering and technology teacher training tends to be more application of the curricular principles, again with appropriate pedagogy. The variations within the STEM disciplines and how they are taught makes the integration of these subjects difficult and yet, it seems that for most STEM practitioners a natural connection between the STEM disciplines exists. This natural connection has become one emphasis in current educational reform; namely, the push for integration of the STEM disciplines at all educational levels.

If we are to begin to truly integrate the STEM disciplines, I propose that we are going to need to look at the strengths and weaknesses of the disciplines and use each of the disciplines to bolster the others. Engineering and technology as disciplines are going to need to be carve out a content area where they can stand alone or be integrated at a more intimate level with other disciplines. While the mathematics and science disciplines have their own challenges.

The definition of engineering found in the on-line Merriam Webster's Dictionary is "the application of science and mathematics by which the properties of matter and the sources of energy in nature are made useful to people". Likewise, the definition of technology according to the same dictionary is "the practical application of knowledge especially in a particular area". Technology and engineering are application oriented. Their purpose is to solve problems and improve our lives through the application of tools in novel ways. Mathematicians and scientists develop those tools. However, the application and usage of those tools by teachers of mathematics and science teacher is not part of their formal training. How many science and mathematics teachers with K – 12 certification have real world experience in a business where the content they teach is in application? How many mathematics teachers have spent formal time in a laboratory using the most advanced tools to solve real problems? How many mathematics or science teachers have worked to develop new ideas that move their discipline forward above the basic experiences that they received in the required diverse coursework?

Research says that students learn best when the content that they are being taught can be related to real world problems (Strobel & van Barneveld, 2009; Riechert & Post, 2010; Berkeihiser & Ray, 2013; MacEwan, 2013; Taylor & Hutton, 2013; Worker & Mahacek, 2013). I would argue that the strength of the technology and engineering disciplines (that of application) can be used to improve mathematics and science teacher preparation by providing them with STEM discipline application experiences that they currently are not receiving. If these types of experiences were to become commonplace in science and math teacher training preparation programs, I think a sound argument could be made that the integration of the STEM disciplines in K – 12 education would be closer to reality.

Working from this view with the promise of integrated STEM education becoming a reality, the purpose of this chapter is build the argument for having mathematics and science teachers receive real world STEM experiences as part of their training program. This argument will be supported by examining: 1) a history of integrated STEM education, 2) Conflicts, Challenges, and Rationale related to STEM education, 3) Examining some STEM education projects, 4) What is seen as integrated STEM education, and 5) Evidence in literature that supports STEM education.

Support from a Historical Perspective

If integrated STEM is ever going to come to fruition, we as potential teachers of integrated STEM, must have enough experiences to draw from to successfully guide our students. Where are those experiences going to come from? As I begin to look at integrated STEM and build the argument for real world applications as part of STEM teacher training, I think that it is useful to look historically at education and show that real world application has been a part of education for a long time, real world application is what drives educational change, and real world application is critical for integrated STEM to become a reality.

A well-known quote often attributed to Plato states, "necessity is the mother of invention" which means that when humans encounter challenges, they respond with new ideas to address those challenges. When looking at the history of education in general and STEM education in specific, it seems that problem (necessity) causes innovation and change (invention) to occur. Sometimes the change is a direct result of a problem that needs to be solved or a watershed event; other times it is a result of changing perceptions and political ideas.

The history and origins of STEM education that you encounter in research depends on the researcher. Questions that they might have considered were: What did they see as fundamental to the development of STEM education? What events precipitated a need for a change in STEM education? What were the causes for the change in focus? I am going to outline a history of STEM education by combining several researchers' works to show that problems that we faced as a society tend to be answered with an attempted improvement in application.

If problems are indeed addressed by improvement in applications, and I believe that this is true, does it not follow that our educational processes should incorporate application as part of the instruction. This is one of the key components of an integrated STEM model. It gets students to work on and wrestle with real world applications and problems in order engage them, to drive a deeper conceptual understanding, and to increase transfer of knowledge. If we are going to ask students to students to work with and solve real world problems in the classroom and in life, the teachers of integrated STEM should have some experience base to draw from as they help prepare their students.

This increased interest in application is important to note because it is applications that are at the center of current integrated STEM education initiatives. Peter Senge, argues that students are engaged by real world problems (2012, pp. 294 - 295). STEM courses should focus learning on creative exploration, projects, problem solving, and innovation rather than rote memorization of current curriculum (Stearns, Morgan, Capraro, & Capraro, 2012). Problem-based approaches have shown that students learn better when they are authentically engaged in activities that are meaningful (Fortus, Dershimer, Krajcik, Marx, & Mamlok-Naaman, 2004). When students are engaged with real-world problems it makes knowledge more relevant to them and increases their ability to transfer skills and information from school to the world (Bransford, Brown, & Cockling, 2000). Stephanie Pace Marshall (2010) agrees, stating that "STEM education must engage students in understanding and experiencing the human consequences of innovation and its essential value in advancing the human condition" and to do this, we must immerse student in disciplinary and interdisciplinary thinking, creative problem solving, and innovative system and process design (p. 51). I would argue that the experiences and real world problems that the above researchers refer to are applications of STEM disciplines in order to solve problems. If we are expecting our students to have these types of real-world experiences and applications as part of the curriculum, is it not logical to expect that STEM education practitioners have had those experiences, know how to create and model those real world experiences and as a result thereby, making them more effective practitioners.

A STEM educational timeline: Need leads to innovation.

With the founding of our nation and the establishment of West Point Military Academy in 1802, our country needed roads, bridges, and railroads. Jolly (2009) argues that this was the beginning of STEM education. It was the application of math and science through the realms of engineering and technology. As our nation continued to grow STEM education continued to gain importance when the Morrill Act of 1862 was passed by congress. The purpose of the Morrill Act was to improve agriculture and work skills, but it had the additional consequence of developing science and engineering programs in all states (Butz & Science and Technology Institute (Rand Corporation), 2004). In 1958 with the launch of Sputnik by the Russians, it created an outcry for improving proficiency in the STEM areas in the United States. The National Defense Education Act of 1958 mandated specific educational courses and strengthening of instruction related to mathematics, science, and foreign language (Public Law 85-864, 1958). Education continued to be impacted through governmental action with the Elementary and Secondary Education Act of 1965 (Public Law 89-10) being passed by the Johnson administration. With data showing that students in upper grades did substantially worse in mathematics in 1970 than in 1963, the 1970's again presented a change in educational philosophy with the "back-to-basics" movement that was different from the "new math" movement of the 1960's (Kolata, 1977).

In 1983, the National Commission on Excellence in Education released the report, "A Nation at Risk". This report outlined a national crisis in American Schools related to mathematics and science and changed the educational landscape (National Commission on Excellence in Education, 1983). It called for higher graduation requirements in core subjects including math and science and recommended that K-12 and higher education adopt more "rigorous and measureable standards" and that expectations for student performance and conduct be raised (Graham, 2013). The standards movement stemmed from this report with National Council of Teachers of Mathematics creating the *Curriculum and Evaluation Standards for School Mathematics* (NCTM, 1989) and the National Research Council creating *Benchmarks for Science Literacy, National Science Education Standards* (National Research Council, 1996).

Near the end of the last century, the U. S. Department of Education published a report that underscored, "the rapid pace of change in both the increasingly interdependent global economy and in the American workplace demands widespread mathematics- and science-related knowledge and abilities" (Glenn, 2000, p. 7). This report stressed the need for children to achieve competency in mathematics and science (Glenn, 2000).

In 2002, the Bush administration passed the No Child Left Behind (NCLB) law (*NCLB Legislation*, 2001). While there are no references in the law to STEM specifically, it does call for increased performance in the areas of mathematics and science for American students (*NCLB Legislation*, 2001). Numerous other reports issued by government education, and business groups have argued for the expansion of STEM education and the improvement of instruction in STEM (Council on Competitiveness, 2005; National Governor's Association, 2007; National Science Board, 2007; National Research Council, 2007; Carnegie Corporation, 2009; President's Council of Advisors on Science and Technology, 2012).

One theme presented in these varied reports is that STEM education can lead an individual to employment that is valuable and important to the nation's ability to be innovative. Another concept is that people need to have a degree of technological literacy to be productive citizens whether they work in STEM fields or not (National Academies of Engineering [NAE], 2014). In today's science and technology-rich society, such literacy is important to being a smart consumer and thoughtful participant in democratic decision making and to making sense of the world more generally. Thus, STEM education serves to prepare a scientific and technical workforce, where integration is becoming increasingly common in cutting-edge research and development as well as a scientifically and technologically literate and more informed society (NAE, 2014, p. 28).

These highlights of the origins of the STEM education movement bolster the argument that problems or crises lead to change ("necessity is the mother of invention"). The causes of the changes are varied but the response is almost unilateral; we attempted to change STEM education to make it better able to solve the problem that precipitated the change. Usually, this was accomplished with more applications in some form of STEM concepts. West Point and

The Morrill Act created more engineers and education programs related to engineering and science. Sputnik launched the space race that produced much application of STEM principles and ultimately lead to a man being placed on the moon in 1969. Later changes were more policy related but called for more accountability, more competitiveness, and more innovation to meet the ever-changing world's needs.

How are we as educators to meet these lofty requirements? I would argue that the answer lies in the work of Senge; Stearns, Morgan, Capraro, & Capraro; Fortus, Dershimer, Krajcik, Marx, & Mamlok-Naaman; Bransford, Brown, & Cockling, Marshall and others that believe that student learning in the STEM disciplines must be real world based and authentic. These researchers believe the type of real world applications will engage students in ways that traditional classroom instruction will not and allow them to develop the skills to invent the solutions to tomorrow's problems.

This will require the teacher (maybe better called facilitator of learning) to be able to provide these experiences to their students. Since current teacher preparation programs for mathematics and science teachers often do not have these experiences, the question becomes how are those facilitators of learning going to be able gain the necessary experiences to adequately guide their students?

History of the integrated STEM movement.

When looking specifically at the history of the Integrated STEM movement for support of mathematics and science teachers having additional hands on real world experiences as part of professional training, I found the three-pronged structure that Todd Kelley (2012) outlined about how the current STEM subject integration approach has come to be useful. The integrated STEM education initiative attempts to incorporate all STEM disciplined into one course or to have heavy collaboration and interdisciplinary efforts between two or more STEM courses. Kelley (2012) argues that Design-based education, Project-based education, and Subject Integration from three legs of a tripod that have made the current integrated STEM education initiative to be in the form in which it currently exists. I would argue that Kelley's "tripod" is heavily laden in application experiences of its students and practitioners.

Design-based Education

Design-based education based on the works of Heinrich Pestalozzi in the early 1800's, who believed children should be educated in a wide range of real-life situations using a hands on approach is one of the structures that lead to the current integrated STEM movement (Kelley, 2012). Later in the 1800's, Fredrick Froebel, who was the father of modern day kindergarten, (Kelley, 2012) built on Pestalozzi's work saying that Pestalozzi greatly influenced and inspired Froebel's initial thoughts and practices (Adelman, 2000). Froebel created a line of children's toys that were boxed sets of blocks that were designed to teach children about symmetry and beauty (Coleman, 2008). Frank Lloyd Wright played with Froebel blocks and recalled them as formative. Wright believed that the Froebel blocks were critical to helping develop his design abilities (Brosterman, 1997; Coleman, 2008). Design based education was further championed by Frederic Bonser and Lois Coffey Mossman in the early 1900's when both of them emphasized the need for students to design their own projects (Kelley, 2012).

The premise of design-based education is that students should gain their knowledge through real world experiences. If you think of Frank Lloyd Wright playing with Froebel blocks as a formative educational experience, he went on to use that experience to develop some of the most unique and recognized architectural structures in the last 100 years. His experiences gave him the added ability to create innovative designs. Without a teacher who gave him the opportunities to have those experiences, Wright's life might have been very different. Should we not only provide but also ensure that the teachers of today have real world experiences with the content that they teach so that our children can have the same advantages?

Project-based Education

Kelley's second prong of the history of the integrated STEM education movement was project-based education. Its roots can be discovered at the Van Rensselaer Polytechnic Institute where practical applications of science and mathematics lead to the founding of Mathematical Arts in 1935 "for the purpose of giving instruction in Engineering and Technology" (Mann, 1918, p. 12). Another American school of engineering that combined the theory and practice of engineering was the Worchester Technical Institute in Worchester, MA. It introduced the use of vocational skills to complete projects as part of the curriculum (Kelley, 2012). Problem-Based learning continued to grow during the 20th century with the work of Kilpatrick and Dewey. Their approaches to learning argue for a meaningful task-like case-based instruction and Problem-Based Learning (Kilpatrick 1918, 1921; Dewey, 1938). Problem-Based Learning has continued to remain a focus in education with authors Dym, Agonino, Eris, Frey, and Leifer (2005) studying the complexity of engineering design and how it is best taught. These authors deemed Project-Based Learning as the most favorable approach for teaching design in engineering education and further indicated that the best context for Problem-Based Learning is first year engineering education because it provides the opportunity for students to transfer learning from one experience to another (Dym et al., 2005).

Problem-based learning is based on the premise that students will learn when challenged with meaningful tasks that form the instructional process. As the evidence above suggests, problem-based learning is a foundational part of teaching engineering. In fact, the engineering design process is specifically designed to solve a problem. Much past and current vocational education is founded in problem-based learning. Educational giants like Kilpatrick and Dewey saw the need for problem-based learning nearly a century ago and when looking at successful programs in integrated STEM education today, problem-based learning is a vital component. It engages students on a different level than most other instruction. Problem-based learning requires past experiences to help develop solutions and to see where new applications might fit into future problems. For problem-based learning to be effective, both teachers and students need to have real world experiences that they can use to filter new problems and search for new solutions.

Subject Integration

The third leg of the STEM integration platform is subject integration pioneered by Lois Coffey Mossman who wrote that integration of school subjects could be accomplished through practical classroom activities (Kelley, 2012). Subject integration again came to the forefront in the Math/Science/Technology (MST) movement of the 1990's with Laporte and Sanders (1993) stating that the MST approach would improve the status of technology education by incorporating into the core subjects. By integrating subjects together, connections that are not otherwise noticed start to come to the forefront of learning. Past and current experiences are all brought to bear on solving the tasks and real authentic engaging learning starts to take place.

These three prongs, design based education, project based education and subject integrated education, can all be seen in the current initiative of integrated STEM education as proposed by Mark Sanders (2012). His view of integrated STEM education refers to a designed based learning approach that integrates the concepts of mathematics and science education intentionally with the concepts and practices of technology and engineering education. He believes that Integrated STEM education can be further improved by integrating it with other subjects like language arts, art, and social studies (Sanders, 2012).

Sander's view of integrated STEM education very much requires the teacher (facilitator) of learning to have a sound grasp of the content that they are trying to instill in students. From personal experience and observations, some of the best innovative teachers come to education from experiences in life like business, industry, design, etc. They can use their real world experiences to engage students, to capture their imaginations, and to frame problems that students can enjoy and solve. They can make connections for students and provide relevance to the content at a much higher level than another teacher with less real world application experiences.

Support from Conflicts, Challenges, and Rationale of STEM Education

Support for mathematics and science teachers having real world experience can be garnered from many different aspects of STEM education. When considering integrated STEM education, there are many differing voices as to what integrated STEM education is and how to accomplish integrated STEM education. However, the combination of these voices can lead to educational changes for both our students and practitioners including more real world experiences for both groups.

Conflicts

In the literature, there is little consensus about what STEM education is among practitioners and sometimes conflicts exist between the STEM disciplines. In the article *Blurring the Boundaries – STEM Education and Education for Sustainable Development,* James Pitt (2009) argues that STEM in an educational context is problematic. For some, STEM education is seen as pre-vocational learning or training to encourage the pursuit of STEM careers. Others view STEM education as a different way to learn, where boundaries between subjects blur and students are encouraged to develop transferable knowledge and skills (Pitt, 2009). If integrated STEM is pre-vocational training or if we are encouraging students to develop transferable knowledge and skills, real world applications and experiences for students and teachers would help bring this vision to reality.

When discussing STEM education, Pitt (2009) believes that there is no consensus as to what STEM education is or how to best teach STEM education. He says that many people see STEM education as anything that involves a STEM discipline where others believe that STEM education must link the STEM areas.

According to de la Paz & Cluff, (2009), the concept of STEM originated in the 1990's at the National Science Foundation (NSF) when it started funding the development of instruction that integrated mathematics, science, and technology. Bybee (2010) states that "STEM" has been used to label any policy, program or practice that involves any or all of the STEM disciplines. He goes on to say that a recent survey on the perceptions of STEM indicate that professionals in STEM fields often do not understand what is meant by the STEM acronym (Bybee, 2010).

STEM education is often viewed as dominated by the mathematics and science discipline considerations and with technology and engineering considerations playing a lesser role (Kelley, 2012). In fact, during the Mathematics/Science/Technology (MST) movement when math and science educators started to use the term MST in their vernacular, Foster (1994) claimed that MST looked less like a coordinated effort between mathematics, science, and technology and more like technology education wishing that it was a coordinated effort. Many speculated if technology would become a stepchild to math and science (Kelley, 2012). He warns that as engineering education struggles to enter the K–12 educational system, it must attempt to define itself so that engineering education will not face the unclear purpose and division within its practitioners that technology education faced in the past and currently still does. This is affirmed by in the article *The Time is Now: Are We Ready for Our Role?* in which the authors argue that engineering education must form partnerships that allow all involved parties at all levels in the educational process to feel like they "win" (Haghihi, Smith, Olds, Fortenberry, & Bond, 2008). The need for an equal partnership between the STEM curricular areas is affirmed in the report, *The*

Overlooked STEM Imperatives: Technology and Engineering K–12 Education by the International Technology Education Association (de la Paz & Cluff, 2009). This report states, "more importantly, to seek to understand the importance of ensuring that the "T and E" are equal partners within STEM in order to adequately prepare the next generation workforce and produce valued contributors to our communities and society" (de la Paz & Cluff, 2009, p. 2).

These differing opinions and ideas about what integrated STEM education point out the real challenge with STEM education. There is not clear definition of what STEM education looks like. Is it or should it be integrated or is it anything related to a STEM discipline? Is it more than the traditional approach to education? Should all the STEM disciplines be equal players or some be dominant while others play a lesser role? Regardless of the answers to these questions, real world problems found in design-based education and problem-based learning scenarios enhance student's creativity, problem solving skills and transfer of knowledge. We as STEM educators need to provide these types of experiences to our students where they can develop skills and practice in the safety of a controlled environment. We must broaden their experiences by providing them with real world applications for the knowledge that they are learning. This ultimately means that STEM teachers must have an experiential base from the real world from which to draw.

Challenges

There are many challenges to implementation of integrated STEM education regardless of the form that it will ultimately take. When looking at STEM program evaluation, it appears that there are not enough qualified evaluators for STEM education projects and programs as well as a shortage of reliable and valid instruments to measure outcomes, teacher knowledge and skills, classroom practices and student understanding of STEM content (Katzenmeyer & Lawrenz, 2006).

Looking back at Kelley's (2012) three-prong structure for integrated STEM education, one of the key components is problem-based learning. However, STEM Problem-Based Learning (PBL) has been defined as having a well-defined outcome with an ill-defined task within an interdisciplinary framework (Caparo, Capari, & Morgan, 2013). This is problematic, as ill-defined tasks can be complex and messy by nature and are challenging for students to initially accomplish at high level (Torp & Sage, 2002).

Additional challenges with implementing STEM education include: (a) the unchallengeable curriculum (the rigidity and resilience of the school curriculum structure when proposing reform); (b) lack of clarity of the movement (there does not seem to be any clarity about what STEM education might look like in schools in terms of how the STEM subjects should relate to each other); (c) vocational vs. general education (explicit vocational approach in the STEM agenda, mainly related to science and engineering); and (d) dominance of mathematics and science over technology and engineering (Williams, 2011). Williams (2011) goes on to argue that when examining the projects developed and available on-line to help teachers implement STEM activities into their classrooms, the projects do not integrate science, technology, engineering and mathematics but do parts of a few disciplines and primarily to advance the goals of mathematics and science.

With these almost overwhelming challenges to the implementation of STEM education, it seems that professional development for teachers is of paramount importance.

We must have our practitioners be experts in the fields that they are teaching. It appears that if integrated STEM education is to become a reality, practitioners might need to be experts in more than one field or to heavily collaborate with other teachers. Professional development for teachers and pre-service teachers in the areas of how the content relates to one another and how it applies in the world should help integrated STEM education overcome some of the challenges outlined above.

Rationale

There is a large body of literature that provides rationale for an integrated STEM educational approach. Mark Sanders, a strong proponent of an integrated STEM education approach states that "there is sufficient evidence with regard to achievement, interest, and motivation benefits associated with new integrated STEM instructional approaches to warrant further implementation and investigation of those new approaches" (Sanders, 2009, p. 22). Sanders explains that veteran teachers understand the importance creating classrooms that are interesting and motivating to improve learning for students and that integrated STEM instruction can greatly increase interest in STEM fields. Ultimately STEM literacy may be of greater benefit than the current STEM preparedness for college entrance tests (Sanders, 2009).

Research shows students in STEM-focused high schools outperformed their peers at institutions where STEM disciplines were not integrated (Scott, 2012). Scott's research on the performance of STEM focused schools shows that high school students in STEM focused schools had much higher rates of passing mathematics and English than students that attended other schools. Additionally, Scott found that all of the STEM focused schools in the study that participated in state testing performed better than the state average in mathematics and English (Scott, 2012).

Proponents of integrated STEM education claim that the United States of America is not producing enough STEM graduates because there is a lack of social and economic incentives for pursuing STEM careers, and that increases in STEM courses taken in high school have not sparked interest in post-secondary STEM (Stearns, Morgan, Capraro, & Capraro, 2012). The authors argue that quality and integration of STEM education should be the focus rather than just having students take more STEM classes.

Building a stimulating curriculum that links across all STEM subjects is important to teachers and students alike (Pitt, 2009). Pitt believes that STEM learning has an intrinsic educational value and as such deserves a place in general education much the way that people agree that physical education is valuable in itself even though very few students become professional athletes (Pitt, 2009).

If an integrated STEM educational approach is beneficial for students and from the research it appears that this is borne out, schools and teachers must be prepared to deliver STEM content in a new way. Currently, our teacher preparation programs make each content teacher at the high school level a specialist. Each STEM discipline has specific coursework that gives a prospective teacher the skills to teach in one of the STEM areas. The research above implies that STEM teachers need to have a more broad experience base in order to be able to bridge the STEM areas. This will require additional (or different) preparation and professional development opportunities for teachers. They must be given the skills and experiences to be able to explain and apply their particular discipline across the other disciplines in order to solve real world problems.

Support from STEM Educational Projects

STEM education projects are varied in both scope and content. However, one commonality between nearly all STEM education projects is that there is a hands-on, inquiry based approach to students learning the STEM content. Often the engineering design process (or similar) is used as the over-arching structure for the educational process (Berkeihiser & Ray, 2013; MacEwan, 2013; Riechert & Post, 2010; Taylor & Hutton, 2013; Teo, 2012; Worker & Mahacek, 2013; Zhe, Doverspike, Zhao, Lam, & Menzemer, 2010). By looking at a few exemplary STEM education projects, I will continue the argument that to create integrated STEM education mathematics and science teachers must have real world experiences.

The article *Think 3d! Training Spatial Thinking Fundamental to STEM Education,* correlates spatial learning with STEM learning success. The authors claim that spatial learning is lacking in elementary school (Taylor & Hutton, 2013). In this STEM implementation, students use origami and pop-up paper engineering to strengthen visuospatial thinking. Results show that the program shows promise for improving spatial thinking and engagement in the content (Taylor & Hutton, 2013). Spatial learning is critical for careers in STEM fields. As teachers are trying to teach these types of skills, it is important to bring relevant examples of where and how they are used in the world. This is only possible if the teacher actually has an experience base that allows them to do this.

Interdisciplinary approaches to STEM projects inspire both students and teachers Berkeishiser & Ray (2013). In their project, which connected calculus students to engineering Computer Aided Design (CAD) students, students use experience from both disciplines to explore the same problem from different perspectives. Each group learns a little about how the other discipline functions and the benefits of a multidisciplinary approach to a problem (Berkeihiser & Ray, 2013). CAD is a mainstay in many STEM fields. By providing students with experience using the tools of real world STEM, teachers can not only teach STEM content; they can also show the relevance of what they are teaching and how it can apply to a student's future.

In *Skeletons to Bridges & Other STEM Enrichment Exercises for High School Biology*, the authors connect STEM concepts to biology, which is done less often than other sciences (Riechert & Post, 2010). In this project, three different examples of connecting engineering to biology were identified. First, Skeletons as Bridges had students compare mammal skeletons to bridges in a hands-on activity. Students were introduced to the principles of bridge construction by investigating tension, compression, and bending as they apply to bridges and other engineering structures as well as to animal bones and spinal columns. Second in Sound Communication, Animal and Engineered Speakers, students discuss sound and how it is formed and then compare that to how animals communicate compared to human and mechanical means of producing sound (computers, speakers, etc.). Third, Aerodynamics and Dispersal, students explore drag with respect to mass and cross sectional area of objects. Students make a helicopter out of paper and try to build one that will stay aloft the longest. Their final design is compared to seed and flight dispersal characteristics of the propeller-like seeds produced by maple, ash and sycamore trees

(Riechert & Post, 2010). These unorthodox STEM projects engaged students, encouraged them think about the world from multidisciplinary perspectives, and made STEM learning more interesting (Berkeihiser & Ray, 2013; Riechert & Post, 2010; Taylor & Hutton, 2013). A project like this is replete with real world STEM examples. As students work through these curricular units, both the teacher and students gain experience with what practitioners of STEM in the real world do on a daily basis. These kinds of experiences are invaluable for students in terms of content learned, transfer of knowledge and motivation and engagement.

In *Getting Intentional about STEM Learning,* MacEwan (2013) outlines an afterschool project where students in elementary school worked in enrichment clubs with each having its own STEM theme. The goal of these clubs was for students to use critical thinking and problem solving skills to understand broad STEM concepts. MacEwan (2013) spends much time discussing the nature of professional development for the instructors, which utilizes the same hands-on, inquiry-based activities as those used with the students. Ultimately, the project wanted students and staff to recognize STEM as a common factor in many activities that they already enjoy and to realize that STEM does not have to be intimidating (MacEwan, 2013). The push by the project director is for professional development of the instructors to make them comfortable with the content that they are teaching. MacEwan provides his instructors the same experiences that the students will get to give them the experience base to become better teachers of STEM.

The 4-H Youth Development Program has been engaging youth outside of the formal school setting to reach their fullest potential since 1902 (Worker & Mahacek, 2013). One project that 4-H sees as part of its STEM mission mandate is "4-H Junk Drawer Robotics". In this project, students are given a drawer of parts and tools to utilize in solving a problem. There are three levels that students progress through (To Learn, To Do, and To Make) which mimic the engineering design process. The author suggests that by infusing science into engineering and technology a synergy exists in situations where students are engaged and have fun learning (Worker & Mahacek, 2013). This type of project is based in the messy real world of problem solving. Student are given a task to accomplish with limited resources. By combining STEM disciplines and real world experiences, project facilitators are able to provide an environment where students learn STEM content, problem solving skills, and are engaged.

These types of STEM projects engage students in thinking about the world from a multidisciplinary perspective, and to make STEM learning more interesting (Riechert & Post, 2010; Berkeihiser & Ray, 2013; MacEwan, 2013; Taylor & Hutton, 2013; Worker & Mahacek, 2013). In an integrated STEM educational environment, I see these types of programs becoming the norm for students. They force students to deal with problems that are not textbook cases and have real relevance to their lives. As teachers in an integrated STEM environment, we must be able to guide our students in these settings. As MacEwan and others have realized, teachers must have the professional development and skills to direct student learning. Part of these skills can be gained by having and understanding of where and how their particular STEM expertise can be applied in the world.

Support from a View of Integrated STEM Education

As discussed earlier, there is a rise in interest in providing students with learning that makes connections across STEM disciplines; however, there is little research and/or consensus on how to create integrated STEM offerings for student learning (Brown, Brown, Reardon, & Merrill, 2011; Householder & Hailey, 2012; NAE, 2014). The challenge of having little research about what integrated STEM education is has great implications for potential practitioners of STEM education. It is difficult to prepare teachers to teach in integrated STEM environments when you do not really know what that integrated environment looks like. Our teacher preparation programs and staff developers are speculating about what might be important for teachers to know and what the best practices are. On the other hand, consider a teacher that has real world STEM experience. This teacher will have an innate understanding of STEM content and how it can be applied. This teacher will have a good idea about the overall goal and the processes that will allow students to achieve that goal. Real world STEM experience should server as quality professional development for teachers.

The difficulty with specifically defining what integrated STEM education is lies in the fact that there are many different definitions of STEM education (Brown, 2012). Merrill (2009) believes that STEM education is a standards-based, meta-discipline where <u>all</u> teachers use integrated practices to teaching and learning so that specific content is not divided but treated as one dynamic and fluid curriculum. Mark Sanders (2012) defines STEM education to include teaching and learning among two or more of the STEM curricular areas or between one STEM discipline and another subject. The U. S. Department of Education (2007) defines STEM education as programs intended to support or strengthen STEM education at any level including adult education. All these definitions contain one common theme; collaboration between STEM disciplines is essential (Brown, 2012).

In today's world, collaboration is of paramount importance. Looking back at the history of what integrated STEM can be as outlined by Kelley (2012), problem-based learning, subject integration, and design based education will have a large collaboration component by the very nature of the types of problems with which students and teachers will be concerned. If indeed integrated STEM has a strong collaboration component and it appears that it would, teachers that have worked in real world STEM settings or have had real world STEM experiences will have an advantage over colleagues that do not have those experiences. This should help make the case that teacher preparation programs and professional development should include some real world experiences for teachers.

Essential components of Integrated STEM Education

In the literature, research identifies many essential components for the successful implementation of integrated STEM education and most of these essential components can be bolstered by STEM education professionals having real world experiences.

<u>Effective STEM instruction</u> is identified in research as a critical for student achievement. This type of instruction utilizes student's interests and experiences. It identifies and builds on their prior knowledge and gives them educational experiences that engage them in STEM coursework and sustains their interest (National Research Council, 2011; Herschbach, 2011; National Academy of Engineering, 2014). Effective instruction

as defined in the research uses student's interests and experiences to engage them and sustain their interest. What will compose that effective instruction? I propose that a key component would be a teacher having an experience base with applications of the content that they teach.

A clear and understandable set of standards and curriculum where there are strong course offerings in all STEM areas. Engineering and technology are explicitly and intentionally integrated into STEM and non-STEM subjects (National Research Council, 2011; Brown, 2012; Peters-Burton, Lynch, Behrend, & Means, 2014). This component identifies integration of STEM and non-STEM areas specifically. Real world experiences by STEM teachers will facilitate this integration.

Teachers with a high capacity to teach their discipline is a key component of integrated STEM education that is identified by many researchers. Teachers must teach in ways that inspire all students increase their understanding of STEM content and practices (National Research Council, 2011; Scott, 2012). Teachers must have advanced STEM content knowledge and/or practical experience in STEM career fields and they must be well prepared (Monk & King, 1994; Rowan, Chiang, & Miller, 1997; Brewer & Goldhaber, 2000; Ejiwale, 2012; Peters-Burton et al., 2014). This component stands without further explanation. It specifically cites practical experience for STEM teachers.

Equal access to high-quality STEM learning opportunities is cited as another critical component for integrated STEM education. These learning opportunities must have an inclusive STEM mission where goals are stated clearly to prepare students for STEM careers, support students from minority and underrepresented population groups, and have an emphasis on recruiting students from these underrepresented population groups (National Research Council, 2011; Stone, 2011, DeJarnette, 2012; Peters-Burton et al., 2014). Equal access to high quality STEM learning for all to prepare students for STEM careers can be accomplished through STEM teaching practitioners having real world experience. Teachers with that experience can guide students into particular careers. They know and can articulate exactly what is needed to be successful in STEM careers and through that knowledge, they can support all students including minority students.

High quality integrated STEM educational settings utilize varied technology. Integrated STEM institutions use a wide variety of instructional technology like computers, graphing calculators, calculator-based laboratories, and other digital data instruments to deliver inquiry based lessons, engage in research, and to produce and present projects. The use of technology has the potential to change the interactions and relationships between students, teachers, and the knowledge that teachers are trying to convey (Scott, 2012; Peters-Burton et al., 2014). Technology as a key component of integrated STEM can also be served by teachers having real world STEM experience. If teachers have this type of experience, they likely will have utilized the tools and technology that students would be required/asked to utilize in and integrated STEM program.

Collaboration between teachers of all disciplines is seen as a critical integrated STEM component. Teachers from all disciplines should meet to analyze lesson plans and student work to improve future learning (Peters-Burton et al., 2014). STEM education requires collaboration since teachers have not been trained in all STEM curricular areas. The time allocated to teacher training needs to be dedicated and collaborative (Brown et al., 2011; Peters-Burton et al., 2014; Sanders, 2009; Scott, 2012). Collaboration has been mentioned before as a clear theme in all definitions of integrated STEM education. Teachers that have worked in real world STEM settings or have had real world STEM experiences will have an advantage over colleagues that do not have those experiences and should be better able to deliver a quality integrated STEM educational program.

Integrated STEM education needs to have real world partnerships, research opportunities, and internships. In the literature, identified STEM schools provide extensive research opportunities for students. These opportunities allow students to connect with businesses, industry, and the world of work via internships, mentorships, and projects both within the school day and outside the school day/school year. These research experiences provide hands-on experience for students and have the possibility of increasing interest in STEM career fields (Ejiwale, 2012; Pfeiffer, Overstreet, & Park, 2010; Peters-Burton et al., 2014; Scott, 2012). If real world partnerships, research opportunities, and internships are critical for a quality integrated STEM education program for students, we can expect nothing less for the teachers of the integrated STEM program.

Professional development/teacher support is another key component of integrated STEM education identified in the literature. There is much research related to professional growth and this key component of integrated STEM education. According to the National Academy of Engineering, (2014) very few teacher education programs are preparing prospective teachers with appropriate knowledge in more than one STEM curricular area. Rockland, Bloom, Carpinelli, Burr-Alexander, Hirsch, & Kimmel (2010) claims that to increase the presence of engineering in the K–12 classroom, pre-service teachers must be exposed to training on engineering concepts and how to integrate those concepts into the classroom. Professional development of teachers allow them to become more comfortable with their own knowledge of STEM and as teachers learn more about math and science they become more comfortable teaching STEM (Nadelson, Seifert, Moll, & Coats, 2012). The implementation of integrated STEM education in all educational settings will require additional content and pedagogical knowledge beyond that which teachers currently are trained. Therefore, schools currently attempting to have an integrated STEM curriculum must provide professional development for its teachers and leaders (Rockland et al., 2010; National Research Council, 2011; Nadelson et al., 2012; Sterns et al., 2012; Scott, 2012; National Academy of Engineering, 2014). Regardless of how you view professional development, real world experience for teachers of STEM will fit into this key component.

Engineering design/Problem-Based Learning as mechanism

As outlined previously related to the history of where integrated STEM came from and could be, problem-based learning is a key function of the STEM integration process. Problem-based learning along with design based education and subject integration require confident practitioners with a high knowledge of their STEM content. Coincidently, these characteristics are identified as key components to a successful integrated STEM program. There is much evidence in the literature that supports engineering design and Problem-Based Learning as a mechanism for integrated STEM education. Engineering design and engineering design challenges in the classroom expand on traditional Problem-Based Learning (PBL), which is a highly researched instructional technique (Rockland etal., 2010). Strobel & van Barneveld (2009) performed a qualitative synthesizing meta-analyses of PBL and determined that PBL is significantly more effective than traditional instruction to train competent and skilled practitioners and to promote long-term retention of knowledge and skills acquired during the learning experience or training session. Inquiry learning, Problem-Based Learning, and project-based learning are teaching methods that are proposed for use in engineering education (Prince & Felder, 2006).

Teachers that use problem-based learning must teach differently than traditional instructional methods. PBL has the potential to engage students; however, teachers have to be willing to allow students to have freedom to experiment to solve the problem. They have to be willing to let students fail while helping guide them to a successful outcome. Householder & Hailey (2012) issue a caution related to using engineering design as the vehicle for integrated STEM education. They point out that engineering design problems are ill-structured with many different solutions, developmental sequences have not been identified for high school engineering education, and there needs to be clarity concerning the outcomes that may be expected along with the arrangement of developmental sequences. Realizing these concerns and understanding what they imply can inform innovation and facilitate the early adoption of the most effective strategies for infusing engineering design into the high school STEM curriculum (Householder & Hailey, 2012). If schools are going to implement these types of problems as part of an integrated STEM curriculum, the teachers must have some knowledge of how the engineering design process functions. Real world experiences for teachers will provide them with the knowledge and skills to teach using techniques that allow students to work with and solve these ill-structured problems.

Additional research also advocates for leveraging the natural connections in the STEM disciplines and the engineering design process to engage students in integrated STEM educational settings. The National Academy of Engineering report, *Engineering in K-12 education: Understanding the status and improving the prospects* (2009) identified symbiotic relationship between mathematics, science and engineering, where engineers use mathematics and science in their work and mathematicians and scientists use the results from engineering in their work. The committee that authored this report found that due to this symbiotic relationship engineering could be the vehicle for the development of integrated STEM education (National Academy of Engineering, 2009). Rockland, Bloom, Carpinelli, Burr-Alexander, Hirsch, & Kimmel (2010) believe that the engineering design process can provide a context that supports teachers in teaching scientific inquiry to students because scientific inquiry and engineering design are parallel processes with both having similar problem solving characteristics. Kimmel, Carpinelli & Rockland (2007) argue that when engineering and science are taught together, they extend and reinforce each other. The integration of engineering principles into science instruction, presented through problem-solving inquiry/discovery pedagogy, can stimulate students as well as enable them to recognize links between their lessons and tasks performed by engineers in the real world (Harwood & Rudnistsky, 2005). If we are going to implement integrated STEM in our schools it appears that the research shows that engineering design and problem-based learning will be a function of that implementation. Teachers must be prepared to teach in these settings.

Support from Other Research-Based Literature

The theme of professional development as a mechanism to support STEM education continues throughout the literature. Many authors call for STEM teachers to develop professionally in order to support and improve STEM education (Mason et al, 2012; Page,

Lewis, Autenrieth, & Butler-Purry, 2013; Reynolds, Yazdani, & Manzur, 2013; Zollman, Tahernezhadi, & Billman, 2012). The Research Experience for Teachers (RET) project funded by the National Science Foundation supports the active involvement of K-12 teachers in STEM areas including computer and information science in research projects to bring knowledge of engineering, computer science, and technological innovation into their classrooms. One of the goals of RET is professional development of teachers to build collaborative partnerships and help them translate their research experiences and new knowledge into classroom activities ("Research Experience for Teachers," 2010). Professional development to support and improve STEM education is critical for integrated STEM to become a reality. Much of that professional development should focus on broadening a teacher's personal experience with their STEM curriculum.

One project that provided teachers with real world STEM experiences was Project SHINE conducted at Central Community College in Columbus, NE. This project had teachers complete two business externships where they gained real world STEM experience. As part of the project, each teacher had to write lessons related to their externships to bring that experience into the classroom. Overwhelmingly, the teachers and students felt that having this real world experience benefited their teaching and student learning (D. Davidchick, personal communication, July 10, 2014).

Two RET projects that have strong STEM teacher professional development components are *Enrichment Experiences in Engineering (E^3) for Teachers Summer Research Program: An Examination of Mixed-Method Evaluation Findings on High School Teacher Implementation of Engineering Content in High School STEM Classrooms* from Texas A & M university, and from the University of Texas at Arlington: *STEM High School Teaching Enhancement Through Collaborative Engineering Research on Extreme Winds*. Both of these projects have an emphasis on teachers having a hands-on research experience where they develop inquiry based engineering projects for their classrooms. Teachers learn about engineering career opportunities for students and develop an overall engineering career awareness. They are encouraged to participate in active sharing of the knowledge gained in the professional development experience. These programs and others like them support high quality professional development for teachers interested in STEM education with the overall goal of making them better teachers in the STEM disciplines (Page et al., 2013; Reynolds et al., 2013).

Benefit to Students

Research identifies support for integrated STEM education from many different sources. The National Academy of Engineering report chair Margaret Honey stated that the committee does not produce an unequivocal endorsement for integrated STEM but notes that there is a very exciting potential for using the connections that come naturally between the STEM disciplines to help students (National Academy of Engineering, 2014). Hurley (2001) conducted a meta-analysis of 31 studies, which compared integrated science and mathematics instruction to non-integrated student performance. In this meta-analysis, it was determined that there was a positive effect for integration in both mathematics and science (Hurley, 2001). Scott (2012) found that students in STEM schools outperformed their peers at other high schools on end of course finals and hand higher proficiency on state tests. Becker & Park (2011) also conducted a meta-analysis of 28 studies to see if the integration of STEM subjects is beneficial to student achievement. They note that it was a small sample size and there are not a lot of studies to analyze. However, their findings revealed positive effect for student achievement when using integrated approaches for STEM learning (Becker & Park, 2011). The report by the National Academy of Engineering, *Engineering in K-12 education: Understanding the Status and Improving the Prospects,* (2009) found that STEM disciplines should not be treated as "silos" rather they should be integrated and that engineering could serve as a motivating context to integrate the STEM disciplines. One of the believed benefits of integrated STEM education is that students can solve real-world problems and make connections to STEM fields that can increase interest in STEM fields (Brown, Brown, Reardon, & Merrill, 2011). While the support of integrated STEM is not unequivocal, there does appear to be enough evidence to warrant implementing STEM in an integrated approach. This change will cause a need for quality professional development as identified as a key characteristic of integrated STEM. That professional development will need to take many forms and projects like RET and Project SHINE where teachers gain real world STEM experience should play a role.

Increased Knowledge/Conceptual Learning

Like the benefits to student found in research, evidence in the literature shows that integrated STEM has the potential to increase knowledge and conceptual learning. The National Academy Report, *STEM Integration in K-12 Education: Status, Prospects, and an Agenda for Research* (2014), found that the integration of STEM concepts and methods has the ability to lead to increased conceptual learning in the STEM disciplines. Some caution is advised because of the small number of studies with small sample sizes, however the authors of the report see potentially promising findings. Pfeiffer, Overstreet, and Park (2010) argue that well orchestrated Problem-Based Learning (PBL) activities improve learning. Pfeiffer et al. (2010) further argues that when school curriculum is focused on STEM PBL, PBL projects improve student understanding by helping students to make the connections between content taught in other classes. Sherrod, Dwyer and Narayan (2009) claim that integrating mathematics into the science curriculum will not only improve students understanding of mathematics but show how it can be used. Wilhelm and Walters (2006) found that when mathematics is integrated into science, the curricular content complements each other causing student learning in both mathematics and science to be enhanced.

Notice the emphasis on problem-based learning. As stated before, PBL requires different teaching methods than more traditional instruction. The problems are often open-ended and not well defined, which are a challenge for students to complete and for teachers to facilitate. From research it appears that there is a benefit to students' motivation and understanding when working in this type of environment. The challenge is to produce teachers with the knowledge and skill set, both content and pedagogy, that will allow for quality instruction. Real world experience in STEM disciplines will provide a natural connection for teachers to bring into the classroom to empower students.

Goals for students and teachers

The National Academy of Engineering report, *STEM Integration in K-12 Education: Status, Prospects, and an Agenda for Research* (2014) has outlined several goals for students and teachers that integrated STEM education should address. The first goal is STEM literacy, which includes awareness of the roles of STEM fields in society, familiarity with the basic principles of each STEM area, and a basic level of understanding of how to apply each discipline. This goal requires a broad knowledge of STEM disciplines that current teacher preparation programs do not necessarily provide. A more diverse pre-professional preparation program for pre-service teachers and professional development program for current teachers would help achieve this goal. Real world experiences as part of these programs would provide some of that diversity in STEM knowledge.

The report sets other student goals: (a) developing 21st century competencies, (b) preparing a STEM ready workforce, (c) increasing interest and engagement in STEM fields, and (d) the ability to make connections between STEM disciplines. (National Academy of Engineering, 2014). This report advocates more integration of STEM curricular areas in the K–12 education system by teaching STEM using real world problems and issues, which can enhance motivation for learning and improving student achievement. If we chose to integrate STEM curricular areas as this report and other research suggests, teachers must be ready to answer the challenge. Professional development with incorporated real world experiences will be a key component in whether this movement will be successful.

Conclusion

As outlined in this chapter, research shows that integrated STEM could be of benefit for students in many ways including: more engagement, better understanding of content, test scores of integrated STEM students tend to be higher, and more interest in STEM careers. This research appears to have merit when looking at some of the implementations of integrated STEM education as part of the projects in which students take part. If integrated STEM education is to come to fruition, teachers must be knowledgeable and properly trained. Professional development is one of the critical pieces that must be present if teachers are to apply the project-based, problem-based, subject integrated content that can become integrated STEM education for students. This professional development can take many forms from development of multiple subject expertise, collaboration, problem-based learning, curriculum development, assessment and many others. Regardless of the professional development available to teachers, we can only teach students what we know and have experienced. Teachers and students can learn problem-based learning together as part of an open-ended problem but where does that problem come from? I would argue that it comes from the real world and the real world experiences of STEM practitioners will be of benefit to helping students solve those problems. Teachers and students must be exposed to where the STEM content applies in the world if successful transfer of knowledge and skills is to be accomplished. Part of the problem solving process is to look back at the problem after a solution has been attempted to see if it applies anywhere else or could be adapted to fit a similar but different problem. Quality learning occurs when past experience meets with current skills to develop new knowledge and solve a different problem. These scenarios are messy and often cumbersome but the world is made up of these types of problems. It has been said that we are nothing more than the sum of our experiences. If teachers are to be effective in teaching in an integrated STEM environment, they must have experiences to draw from or they, and their students, will flounder in the messy, chaotic problems that are supposed to be the vary the vehicle for learning in an integrated STEM curriculum. If we are to teach our children well, we must first give the teachers the real world experiences to allow them to do so.

References

Adelman, C. (2000). Over two years, what did froebel say to pestalozzi? *History of Education, 29*(2), 103-114. doi:10.1080/004676000284391

Becker, K., & Park, K. (2011). Effects of integrative approaches among science, technology, engineering, and mathematics (STEM) subjects on students' learning: A preliminary meta-analysis. *Journal of STEM Education: Innovations & Research, 12*(5), 23-37. Retrieved from http://search.ebscohost.com/login.aspx?direct=true&db=a9h& AN=72320466&site-ehost-live

Berkeihiser, M., & Ray, D. (2013). Bringing STEM to life. *Technology & Engineering Teacher, 72*(5), 21-24. Retrieved from http://search.ebscohost.com/login.aspx?direct=true& db=a9h&AN=85194704&site-ehost-live

Bransford, J. D., Brown, A. L., & Cockling, R. R. (2000). How people learn: Brain, mind, experience, and school. Washington, DC: National Academy Press.

Brewer, D., & Goldhaber, D. (2000). Does teacher certification matter? High school teacher certification status and student achievement. *Educational Evaluation and Policy Analysis*, 22, 129–145.

Brosterman, N. (1997). Child's play. *Art in America, 85*(4), 108-111, 130.

Brown, R., Brown, J., Reardon, K., & Merrill, C. (2011). Understanding STEM: Current perceptions. *Technology & Engineering Teacher, 70*(6), 5-9. Retrieved from http://search.ebscohost.com/login.aspx?direct=true&db=aph&AN=59221439&site-ehost-live

Brown, J. (2012). The current status of STEM education research. *Journal of STEM Education: Innovations & Research, 13*(5), 7-11. Retrieved from http://search.ebscohost.com/ login.aspx?direct=true&db=a9h&AN=89166314&site-ehost-live

Butz, W. P., & Science and Technology Policy Institute (Rand Corporation). (2004). *Will the scientific and technology workforce meet the requirements of the federal government?*. Santa Monica, CA: RAND.

Bybee, R. W. (2010). Advancing STEM education: A 2020 vision. *Technology & Engineering Teacher, 70*(1), 30-35. Retrieved from http://search.ebscohost.com/login.aspx?direct=true&db=a9h&AN=57388131&site=ehost-live

Capraro, Robert Michael., Capraro, Mary Margaret., Morgan,James R.,. (2013). STEM project- based learning an integrated science, technology, engineering, and mathematics (STEM) approach.

Coleman, D. (2008). Long before Legos, wood was nice and did suffice. The New York Times, 11.

Carnegie Corporation of New York. 2009. The Opportunity Equation: Transforming Mathematics and Science Education for Citizenship and the Global Economy. Available at http://opportunityequation.org/uploads/files/oe_report.pdf (retrieved January 31, 2014).

Council on Competitiveness. 2005. Innovate America. Available at www.compete.org/images/uploads/File/PDF%20Files/NII_Innovate_America.pdf (retrieved January 31, 2014).

Davidchick, D. (2014, July 10). [Personal interview by the author].

DeJarnette, N. K. (2012). America's children: Providing early exposure to stem (science, technology, engineering and math) initiatives. *Education, 133*(1), 77-84. Retrieved from http://search.ebscohost.com/login.aspx?direct=true&db=a9h&AN=79776864&site=ehost-live

de la Paz, K., & Cluff, K. (Eds.). (2009). *The overlooked STEM imperatives: Technology and engineering K–12 education*. Retrieved February 23, 2014, from http://www.nbtschools.org/nbts/Schools/Linwood%20Middle%20School/Curriculum%20Resources/Announcements/Technology%20Education/STEM%20%26%20Technology%20Resources/Teachers%20Resources/STEM%20Resources/STEM%20Guide.pdf

Dewey, J. (1938). Experience and Education, Macmillan, New York.

Dym, C. L., Agogino, A. M., Eris, O., Frey, D. D., & Leifer, L. J. (2005). Engineering design thinking, teaching, and learning. *Journal of Engineering Education, 94*(1), 103-120. doi:10.1002/j.2168-9830.2005.tb00832.x

Ejiwale, J. A. (2012). Facilitating teaching and learning across STEM fields. *Journal of STEM Education: Innovations & Research, 13*(3), 87-94. Retrieved from http://search.ebscohost.com/login.aspx?direct=true&db=a9h&AN=79468731&site=ehost-live

Fortus, D., Dershimer, C. R., Krajcik, J., Marx, R. W., & Mamlok-Naaman, R. (2004). Design-based science and student learning. *Journal of Research in Science Teaching, 41*(10), 1081-1110. Retrieved from http://search.proquest.com.leo.lib.unomaha.edu/docview/ 61996811?accountid=14692

Foster, P. (1994). Must we MST? *Journal of Technology Education*, *6*(1). Retrieved from http://scholar.lib.vt.edu/ejournals/JTE/v6n1/foster.jte-v6n1.html

Glenn, J. (2000). *Before it's too late: A report to the nation from the national commission on mathematics and science teaching for the 21st Century.* The National Commission on Mathematics and Science Teaching for the 21st Century.

Graham, E. (2013, April 25). 'A nation at risk' turns 30: Where did it take us? Retrieved February 19, 2014, from NEA Today website: http://neatoday.org/2013/04/25/a-nation-at-risk-turns-30-where-did-it-take-us/

Haghighi, K., Smith, K. A., Olds, B. M., Fortenberry, N., & Bond, S. (2008). The time is now: Are we ready for our role? *Journal of Engineering Education, 97*(2), 119-121. doi:10.1002/j.2168-9830.2008.tb00961.x

Harwood, J., & Rudnitsky, A. (2005). Learning about scientific inquiry through engineering. *Proceedings of the 2005 ASEE Annual Conference,* Portland, OR.

Herschbach, D. R. (2011). The STEM initiative: Constraints and challenges. *Journal of sTEm Teacher Education, 48*(1), 96-122.

Householder, D. L., & Hailey, C. E. (2012). *Incorporating engineering design challenges into STEM courses*. National Center for Engineering and Technology Education. c/o Department of Engineering Education Utah State University, 4160 Old Main Hill, Logan, UT 84322. Retrieved from ERIC Retrieved from http://search.proquest.com.deo.lib.unomaha.edu/docview/1312417823?accountid=14692

Hurley, M. M. (2001). Reviewing integrated science and mathematics: The search for evidence and definitions from new perspectives. *School Science and Mathematics, 101*(5), 259-68.

Jolly, J. L. (2009). The national defense education act, current STEM initiative, and the gifted. *Gifted Child Today, 32*(2), 50-53.

Katzenmeyer, C., & Lawrenz, F. (2006). National science foundation perspectives on the nature of STEM program evaluation. *New Directions for Evaluation, 2006*(109), 7-18. doi:10.1002/ev.175

Kelley, T. R. (2012). Voices from the past: Messages for a STEM future. *Journal of Technology Studies, 38*(1), 34-42.

Kilpatrick, W. H. (1918). The project method. Teach. Coll. Rec. 19: 319–335.

Kilpatrick, W. H. (1921). Dangers and difficulties of the project method and how to overcome them: Introductory statement: Definition of terms. Teach. Coll. Rec. 22: 282–288.

Kimmel, H., Carpinelli, J., & Rockland, R. (2007, September). *Bringing engineering into K-12 schools: A problem looking for solutions?* Paper presented at International Conference on Engineering Education, Coimbra, Portugal.

Kolata, G. B. (1977). Aftermath of the new math: Its originators defend it. *Science, 195*(4281), 854-857.

LaPorte, J., & Sanders, M. (1993). The T/S/M Integration Project: Integrating technology, science, and mathematics in the middle school. *The Technology Teacher, 52*(6), 17-21.

MacEwan, M. (2013). Getting intentional about STEM learning. *Afterschool Matters,* (17), 58-61.

Mann, C. R. (1918). *The carnegie foundation for the advancement of teaching: A study of engineering education* (Vol. 11). Retrieved from http://books.google.com/books?id=V98mAQAAIAAJ&pg=PA12&lpg=PA12&dq=%22the+purpose+of+giving+instruction+in+engineering+and+technology%22&source=bl&ots=2TbCK9sr92&sig=obhqXpzHKphiuT1Bz3i5TOGpZB8&hl=en&sa=X&ei=NikKU6OFD8mb2QWRg4CgAQ&ved=0CDcQ6AEwBA#v=onepage&q=%22the%20purpose%20of%20giving%20instruction%20in%20engineering%20and%20technology%22&f=false

Mason, K., Brewer, J., Redman, J., Bomar, C., Ghenciu, P., LeDocq, M., & Chapel, C. (2012). SySTEMically improving student academic achievement in mathematics and science. *Journal for Quality & Participation, 35*(2), 20-24. Retrieved from http://search.ebscohost.com/login.aspx?direct=true&db=a9h&AN=83071407&site=ehost-live

Marshall, S. P. (2010). Re-imagining specialized STEM academies: Igniting and nurturing decidedly different minds, by design. *Roeper Review, 32*(1), 48-60. doi:10.1080/02783190903386884

Merrill, C. (2009). The Future of TE Masters Degrees: STEM. Presentation at the 70th Annual International Technology Education Association Conference, Louisville, Kentucky.

Monk, D., & King, J. (1994). Multilevel teacher resource effects on pupil performance in secondary mathematics and science. In R. G. Ehrenberg (Ed.), *Choices and consequences* (pp. 29–58). Ithaca, NY: ILR Press.

Nadelson, L. S., Seifert, A., Moll, A. J., & Coats, B. (2012). I-STEM summer institute: An integrated approach to teacher professional development in STEM. *Journal of STEM Education: Innovations and Research, 13*(2), 69-83.

National Academy of Engineering and National Research Council. (2009). *Engineering in K-12 education: Understanding the status and improving the prospects.* (Katehi, L., Pearson, G., & Feder, M., Eds.). Washington, DC: National Academies Press.

National Academy of Engineering and National Research Council. (2014). *STEM Integration in K-12 Education: Status, Prospects, and an Agenda for Research* (Honey, M., Pearson, G., & Schweingruber, H., Eds.). Washington DC: National Academies Press.

National Commission on Excellence in Education. (1983). *A nation at risk*. Retrieved on February 12, 2014 from http://www2.ed.gov/pubs/NatAtRisk/risk.html

National Council of Teachers of Mathematics. (1989). *Curriculum and Evaluation Standards forSchool Mathematics* Reston, VA: NCTM.

National Governors Association. 2007. Innovation America: A Final Report. Available at www.nga.org/files/live/sites/NGA/files/pdf/0707INNOVATIONFINAL.PDF (retrieved January 31, 2014).

National Research Council. (1996). *National Science Education Standards* . Washington, DC: The National Academies Press.

National Research Council. (2007). Rising Above the Gathering Storm: Energizing and Employing America for a Brighter Economic Future. Available at www.nap.edu/catalog.php?record_id=11463 9 (retrieved January 31, 2014).

National Research Council. (2009). *Engineering in K-12 education: Understanding the statusand improving the prospects.* Washington, DC: The National Academies Press.

National Research Council. (2011). *Successful K-12 STEM Education: Identifying Effective Approaches in Science, Technology, Engineering, and Mathematics*. Committee on Highly Successful Science Programs for K-12 Science Education, Board on Science Education and Board on Testing and Assessment, Division of Behavioral and Social Sciences Education. Washington, DC: The National Academies Press.

NCLB legislation [PDF]. (2001). Retrieved October 13, 2013, from U. S. Department of Education website: http://www.ed.gov/policy/elsec/leg/esea02/index.html

National Science Board. 2007. National Action Plan for Addressing the Critical Needs of the U.S. Science, Technology, Engineering and Mathematics Education System. Available at www.nsf.gov/nsb/documents/2007/stem_action.pdf (retrieved January 31, 2014).

Page, C. A., Lewis, C. W., Autenrieth, R. L., & Butler-Purry, K. (2013). Enrichment experiences in engineering (E3) for teachers summer research program: An examination of mixed-method evaluation findings on high school teacher implementation of engineering content in high school STEM classrooms. *Journal of STEM Education: Innovations & Research, 14*(3), 27-33. Retrieved fro mhttp://search.ebscohost.com/login.aspx?direct=true&db=a9h&AN=91248346&site=ehost-live

President's Council of Advisors on Science and Technology. 2012. Report to the President. Engage to Excel: Producing One Million Additional College Graduates with Degrees in Science, Technology, Engineering and Mathematics. Available at www.whitehouse.gov/sites/default/files/microsites/ostp/pcast-engage-to-excel-final_feb.pdf. (retrieved January 31, 2014).

Peters-Burton, E., Lynch, S., Behrend, T., & Means, B. (2014). Inclusive STEM high school design: 10 critical components. *Theory into Practice, 53*(1), 64-71. Retrieved from http://search.ebscohost.com/login.aspx?direct=true&db=eoah&AN=31912149&site=ehost-live

Pfeiffer, S. I., Overstreet, J. M., & Park, A. (2010). The state of science and mathematics education in state-supported residential academies: A nationwide survey. *Roeper Review, 32*(1), 25-31. doi:10.1080/02783190903386579

Pitt, J. (2009). Blurring the boundaries--STEM education and education for sustainable development. *Design and Technology Education, 14*(1), 37-48.

Prince, M. J., & Felder, R. M. (2006). Inductive teaching and learning methods: Definitions, comparisons, and research bases. Journal of Engineering Education, 95(2), 123.]

Public Law 85-864. (1958). National Defense Education Act (NDEA). *United States Statutes at Large*, 72,1580 – 1605. Retrieved on February 18, 2014 from http://wwwedu.oulu.fi/tohtorikoulutus/jarjestettava_opetus/Troehler/NDEA_1958.pdf

Public Law 89-10. (1965). Elementary and Secondary Education Act of 1965. Retrieved from http://search.proquest.com/docview/64435107?accountid=14692

Reynolds, D., Yazdani, N., & Manzur, T. (2013). STEM high school teaching enhancement through collaborative engineering research on extreme winds. *Journal of STEM Education: Innovations & Research, 14*(1), 12-19. Retrieved from http://search.ebscohost.com/login.aspx?direct=true&db=a9h&AN=89173556 &site=ehost-live

Research experiences for teachers (RET) in engineering and computer science. (2010, November 30). Retrieved March 9, 2014, from National Science Foundation website: https://www.nsf.gov/funding/pgm_summ.jsp?pims_id=5736

Riechert, S. E., & Post, B. K. (2010). From skeletons to bridges & other STEM enrichment exercises for high school biology. *American Biology Teacher (National Association of Biology Teachers), 72*(1), 20-22. doi:10.1525/abt.2010.72.1.6

Rockland, R., Bloom, D. S., Carpinelli, J., Burr-Alexander, L., Hirsch, L. S., & Kimmel, H. (2010). Advancing the "E" in K-12 STEM education. *Journal of Technology Studies, 36*(1), 53-64.

Rowan, B., Chiang, F., & Miller, R. (1997). Using research on employee's performance to study the effects of teacher on students' achievement. *Sociology of Education*, 70, 256–284.

Sanders, M. (2009). STEM, STEM education, STEMmania. *Technology Teacher, 68*(4), 20-26.

Sanders, M. (2012, December 8). *Integrative STEM education as "best practice"*. Retrieved February 23, 2014, from http://www.teachmeteamwork.com/files/sanders.terc-paper.pdf

Scott, C. (2012). An investigation of science, technology, engineering and mathematics (STEM) focused high schools in the U.S. *Journal of STEM Education: Innovations and Research,* *13*(5), 30-39.

Senge, P. (2012). Context and engagement [Systems Thinking]. In P. Senge, N.

Cambron-McCabe, T. Lucas, B. Smith, J. Dutton, & A. Kleiner (Authors), *Schools that Learn (Updated and revised): A fifth discipline fieldbook for educators, parents, and everyone who cares about education* (Revised ed., pp. 293-297). New York, NY: Crown Business.

Sherrod, S. E., Dwyer, J., & Narayan, R. (2009). Developing science and math integrated activities for middle school students. *International Journal of Mathematical Education in Science & Technology, 40*(2), 247-257. doi:10.1080/00207390802566923

Stearns, L. M., Morgan, J., Capraro, M. M., & Capraro, R. M. (2012). A teacher observation instrument for PBL classroom instruction. *Journal of STEM Education: Innovations & Research, 13*(3), 7-16. Retrieved from http://search.ebscohost.com/login.aspx?direct=true&db=a9h&AN=79468725&site=ehost-live

Stone, J.R., III. (2011). D*elivering STEM education through career and technical education schools and programs.* Paper presented at the National Research Council Workshop on Successful STEM Education in K-12 Schools. Available at: http://www7.nationalacademies.org/bose/STEM_Schools_Workshop_Paper_Stone.pdf. doi:10.1080/02783190903386553

Strobel, J. & van Barneveld, A. (2009) When is PBL more effective? A meta-synthesis of meta-analyses comparing PBL to conventional classrooms. Interdisciplinary Journal of Problem-based Learning, 3(1), 44-58.

Taylor, H. A., & Hutton, A. (2013). Think3d!: Training spatial thinking fundamental to STEM education. *Cognition and Instruction, 31*(4), 434-455. doi:10.1080/07370008.2013.828727

Teo, T. W. (2012). Building potemkin schools: Science curriculum reform in a STEM school. *Journal of Curriculum Studies, 44*(5), 659-678. doi:10.1080/00220272.2012.689356

Torp, Linda, Sage, Sara. (2002). *Problems as possibilities : Problem-based learning for K-16 education.* Alexandria, Va.: Association for Supervision and Curriculum Development.

United States Department of Education, Academic Competitiveness Council (U.S.),. (2007). *Report of the academic competitiveness council.* Washington, D.C.: U.S. Dept. of Education.

U.S. Department of Education National Center for Education Statistics. (2009, June). *Characteristics of public, private, and Bureau of Indian education elementary and secondary schools in the United States: Results from the 2007-08 schools and staffing survey* (Report No. NCES 2009321) (A. Keigher, Author) [PDF]. Retrieved from http://nces.ed.gov/pubs2009/2009321.pdf

Wilhelm, J. A., Walters, K. L. (2006). Pre-service mathematics teachers become full participants in inquiry investigations. *International Journal of Mathematical Education in Science & Technology, 37*(7), 793-804.

Williams, J. P. (2011). STEM education: Proceed with caution. *Design and Technology Education, 16*(1), 26-35.

Worker, S., & Mahacek, R. (2013). 4-H out-of-school-time STEM education. *Children's Technology & Engineering, 18*(2), 16-20. Retrieved from http://search.ebscohost.com/login.aspx?direct=true&db=a9h&AN=92976301&site=ehost-live

Zhe, J., Doverspike, D., Zhao, J., Lam, P., & Menzemer, C. (2010). High school bridge program: A multidisciplinary STEM research program. *Journal of STEM Education: Innovations & Research, 11*(1), 61-68. Retrieved from http://search.ebscohost.com/login.aspx??direct=true&db=a9h&AN=53171854&site=ehost-live

Zollman, A., Tahernezhadi, M., & Billman, P. (2012). Science, technology, engineering and mathematics education in the united states: Areas of current successes and future needs. *International Journal of Science in Society, 3*(2), 103-111. Retrieved from http://search.ebscohost.com/login.aspx?direct=true&db=a9h&AN=91821674&site=ehost-live

Chapter Authored By

Brian Sandall, M.S. is a mathematics teacher in the Blair Public Schools in Blair, Nebraska. He is currently a doctoral candidate in Educational Leadership. His research includes defining the critical factors that are used to define STEM education including how those factors contribute to the instructional environment in STEM classrooms.

Chapter 11

Framing Professional Development that Promotes Mathematical Thinking

ABSTRACT: Several studies have shown that when teachers teach for conceptual and procedural understanding, rather than focusing solely on computational fluency, student achievement improves (Haycock, 2001; Knapp, 1995; Newmann & Associates, 1996). But because teachers themselves learned mathematics through a system that emphasized procedural fluency, many teachers currently lack the conceptual basis to teach in this manner. There is thus a need for high-quality professional development that gives teachers both the knowledge and the pedagogical tools to teach for deep mathematical understanding. This chapter describes one successful effort to develop and implement a professional development framework that models what teaching for understanding looks like while deepening teachers' own conceptual content knowledge.
In order to build a model for teaching mathematics with understanding and conducting professional development to promote this type of teaching in mathematics, we researched and identified instructional practices we wanted to observe in teachers' classrooms. From this theoretical framework for developing mathematical thinking, we proceeded to build a professional development model that helps teachers put these instructional structures into practice.

Background

Funded by a Mathematics Science Partnership (MSP) grant, the Developing Mathematical Thinking (DMT) framework for teaching was implemented and then examined and evaluated in schools over a three-year period. The project demonstrated positive changes in teachers' knowledge and beliefs regarding mathematics, changes in instructional practices, and increased student achievement over two successive three-year grants in seven Title 1elementary schools and one middle school (Jonathan L. Brendefur, Thiede, Strother, Bunning, & Peck, 2013; Jonathan L. Brendefur, Thiede, Strother, Jesse, & Sutton, In Review).

Because of the demonstrated success, the state of Idaho commissioned a five year mathematics education initiative to provide all elementary certified teachers, secondary mathematics teachers and administrators (including district office personnel) to take the initial course from the DMT project and provide additional professional development opportunities, including webinars, short workshops, and embedded professional development, to interested individuals. Over the five year implementation period, teachers demonstrated changes in beliefs and knowledge (Michele B. Carney, Jonathan L. Brendefur, Keith Thiede, Gwyneth Hughes, & John Sutton, In Review).

The purpose of this chapter is to highlight the underpinnings of the DMT framework, demonstrate how professional development opportunities were created, and provide an example that exemplifies the professional development and parallels suggested classroom activities.

Teaching for Understanding - Conceptual Definition

Our concept of teaching for understanding is grounded in a cognitive (structural) and social (functional) perspective (Hiebert et al., 1996). From a cognitive perspective on understanding, teachers aim to create classroom experiences that press students to *incorporate and organize* new information into a well-connected network of foundational mathematical ideas. For example, when initially studying multiplication, students show a structural understanding when they can connect the operation to their previously (or concurrently) developed understandings of addition, patterning, and area. From a social perspective, teachers should provide tasks and activities that place students in situations where they *reflect* on how they solve problems and *articulate* relationships between different strategies or concepts. For example, a teacher might ask a class to determine the number of carrots in five bags of baby carrots, each containing 17 carrots, long before students are familiar with a standard multiplication method. Students demonstrate functional understanding when they are, for example, able to explain their own solution method and analyze the solution methods of others.

In order for students to develop understanding, teachers must attend to both the cognitive and social aspects of teaching the content within their classrooms. As Carpenter and Lehrer (1999) claim, "For learning with understanding to occur, instruction needs to provide students the opportunity to develop productive relationships, extend and apply their knowledge, reflect about their experiences, articulate what they know, and make knowledge their own" (p. 32). These components became a foundation for our theoretical framework for instruction – Developing Mathematical Thinking (DMT).

DMT Instructional Theory

This section frames an approach to teaching mathematics for understanding. We describe this type of instruction as Developing Mathematical Thinking or DMT. This instructional model builds on Carpenter and Lehrer's (1999) elements listed above, and in addition incorporates notions of "progressive formalization" and "mathematizing" (Freudenthal, 1973, 1991; Treffers, 1987). As Gravemeijer and van Galen (2003) describe, progressive formalization is a process of first allowing students to develop informal strategies for solving contextual problems and ways to model these approaches, and then, by critically examining both these strategies and models, teachers press students to develop more sophisticated, formal, conventional and abstract strategies and algorithms. By comparing solution strategies and examining the relationship among enactive, iconic and symbolic models (Bruner, 1964), students learn which manipulations make sense for given contexts and are encouraged to develop more generalizable procedures.

Students are pressed to make connections between existing knowledge (informal ideas) and new knowledge (more formal mathematical ideas) required by Hiebert & Carpenter's (1992) concept of conceptual or structural understanding through solving novel problems. By critically examining their own and others' strategies and models, students build social or functional understanding, which exemplifies the importance of social interactions in classrooms. "By thinking and talking about similarities and differences between arithmetic procedures, students can construct relationships between them. … the instructional goal is not necessarily to inform one procedure by the other, but rather, to help students build a coherent mental network in which all pieces are joined to others with multiple links"

(Hiebert & Carpenter, 1992, p. 68). Through these interlinked processes of modeling situations mathematically and analyzing/comparing different methods, teachers press students to progressively formalize towards more abstract mathematical ideas. For example, pre-algebra students might initially solve a problem in which they are solving for an unknown value by drawing pictures or guessing and checking. By asking students to connect between methods and generalize their thinking with questions or problem variations, a teacher can move students to abstract towards algebraic thinking and using symbols – i.e. to progressively formalize.

Closely related to progressive formalization, the DMT instructional framework also incorporates Treffer's (1987) notions of horizontal and vertical mathematization. Horizontal mathematization occurs when students represent a contextualized problem mathematically in order to find a solution strategy. Vertical mathematization involves taking the mathematical matter to a higher level, and occurs when students make their representations and strategies objects of mathematical examination. Mathematizing covers such activities as generalizing, justifying, formalizing, and curtailing – including, but not limited to, developing an abstract algorithm (Gravemeijer & van Galen, 2003). By focusing on both types of mathematizing in their classrooms, teachers must maintain a focus on the inherent structure of the mathematical ideas that are emerging. In addition, they must address students' misconceptions as they arise so these misconceptions do not hinder the mathematizing progression. One outcome of mathematizing is that teachers connect students' informal ideas, many of which may be developed outside of school, with more formal mathematical ideas. An assumption made as part of the DMT process is that students' informal ideas, conceptions, and strategies anticipate more formal mathematics to be learned later in the students' classroom experience. "One would predict that if children possessed internal networks constructed both in and out of school, and if they recognized the connections between them, their understanding and performance in both settings would improve" (Hiebert & Carpenter, 1992, p. 79).

Such a process starts with carefully chosen tasks – typically contextualized (Doerr, 2006; Larsen & Bartlo, 2009; Simon & Tzur, 2004). To solve these problems, students must model the situation to some degree. Rather than beginning with the standard algorithms and attempts to concretize them, teaching begins with students' commonsense solutions to contextual problems that are real for them. By reflecting on the solution procedures they have used, students develop and are introduced to more sophisticated models and procedures that they can also use in other situations (Gravemeijer & van Galen, 2003, p. 114).

Modeling is a key component of developing mathematical thinking. Mathematical knowledge originates from students' attempts to model contextual situations. These models then become the basis for solving related problems as well as a means of support for more formal mathematical reasoning (Gravemeijer & van Galen, 2003). As Cobb (2000) described, this use of modeling "…implies a shift in classroom mathematical practices such that ways of symbolizing developed to initially express informal mathematical activity take on a life of their own and are used subsequently to support more formal mathematical activity in a range of situations" (p. 319). In this way, modeling is a fundamental process in learning mathematics. However, this view of models and modeling contrasts with current practices in mathematics instruction in which models are used to "concretize expert knowledge" (Gravemeijer & van Galen, 2003, p. 118), such as when students are taught to model the traditional borrowing algorithm for subtraction with base-10 blocks. Likewise, contextual problems are traditionally presented only after students have mastered standard algorithmic ways of solving problems. Progressive formalization is the process of taking students' ways of modeling through enactive, iconic, and symbolic representations (Bruner, 1964) to become more formalized, without making huge leaps. This process is addressed through both horizontal and vertical mathematizing. In turn, the focus is toward students' ways of using models rather than on teacher or curriculum dictated ways of using models. Through enacting aspects of 'progressive formalization' and 'mathematizing' teachers develop a classroom practice based on the tenets of teaching for understanding. We believe their practice hinges on five key elements of classroom practice – the DMT framework (Brendefur, 2008):

- The centrality of students' ideas
- Encouraging multiple solution strategies and models
- Pressing students conceptually
- Addressing misconceptions
- Maintaining a focus on the structure of the mathematics.

By focusing their teaching practices on these five key elements, teachers shift their attention toward students' informal strategies for solving problems and the mathematical connections to and among multiple mathematical models and formal solution strategies. By encouraging students to use informal knowledge and experiences, student misconceptions are bound to arise. By acknowledging and addressing them, teachers encourage students to make sense of and correct their flawed ways of thinking, rather than glossing over them or ignoring them completely. Maintaining a focus on structure entails helping students see how foundational ideas extend across grade levels and topics. For example, students are often taught specific, unconnected algorithms for working with similar figures, calculating percents, and determining the slope of a line, when in fact all these topics use the basic concept of ratio. By emphasizing the connection across the different topics, students need not be limited to memorized procedures for each special case, and can instead problem solve in any ratio-related context. These five key elements grow out of the concept that (a) mathematics is comprised of underlying, inherently related constructs and (b) students learn mathematics by creating web- like or hierarchical organizations for these constructs.

Example of Professional Development Task Facilitation

Based on the DMT framework we developed a professional development model that could be implemented on a variety of scales for different mathematical topics. We wanted teachers to walk away understanding the DMT framework by experiencing it authentically themselves, thus building both their content knowledge and their understanding of what the DMT framework looks like pedagogically in a classroom. Mirroring the structure of progressive formalization, we engage teachers in carefully selected tasks that can then be debriefed both in small groups and whole class discussions in which certain ideas (both content and pedagogical) are emphasized, connected, and formalized. This section provides an example of the DMT professional development task facilitation structure in practice. Table 1 is an overview of a task facilitation process from the initial professional development planning that involves task creation or selection, followed by the actual facilitation structure with accompanying focus.

Table 1. Overview of the Task Facilitation Process

Focus		Research Connection
Professional Development Task Planning		
Task Creation or Selection	*Task Features* --Typically a contextual problem where a range of informal to formal modes of representation can be utilized to solve the problem --Must build specialized and pedagogical	--Enables mathematizing and progressive formalization through a task that provides multiple opportunities to examine informal to formal representational modes
Task Facilitation Structure		
Individual & Small Group Discussion	--Participants cognitively engage in the task at their level of mathematical understanding --Builds participants' awareness of their knowledge and understanding of a topic --Allows instructor time to find and when	--Enables horizontal mathematizing through individuals cognitive engagement with a contextual problem that they must represent
Whole Group Discussion	--Provides a pedagogical example of how to lead a whole-class discussion --Presses understanding of and connections between multiple models to build specialized content knowledge	--Presses horizontal mathematizing and progressive formalization through examination of multiple solution methods with a facilitation focus on building connections between and progressively formalizing multiple ways of
Extension Task or Situated Application	--Provides practice of the newly developed specialized content knowledge by asking participants to apply a newly learned model or strategy to an extension problem or new	--Provides a simple example of vertical mathematizing by pressing participants to attempt slightly more
Pedagogical Implications	--Explicitly discuss modeling the pedagogical approach to use in the classroom with students through examination or review of the DMT	-- Provides an opportunity for them to explicitly process ideas around progressive formalization and

Task Creation or Selection

The following task is utilized early in the 4-8 and 6-12 MTI courses due to (1) the accessible nature of the contextual situation, (2) the spontaneous presentation of a trajectory of informal to formal solution methods from course participants with minimal instructor press, (3) its ability to highlight important aspects of specialized and pedagogical content knowledge, and (4) the active engagement of participants due to the cognitive press that occurs throughout the task facilitation. We have found these four elements imperative to successful task facilitation and it mirrors the elements teachers need to consider when utilizing these types of tasks in their classroom.

Joey is in science class and is told that his group will be given 8 packages of seeds containing a total of 76 seeds. Pumpkin seeds come in packages of 12 and sunflowers seeds come in packages of 8. How many pumpkin packages and how many sunflower packages will Joey's group be given? The task is modified by from an original task from the CGI material. *Solve as a 2nd grader, middle school student, and high school student.*

Individual and Small Group Discussion

The task is presented without any further whole-class 'guidance' from the instructor. Course participants typically begin working individually, but after a 2-5 minute period begin discussing approaches to solving the task in their small groups. In the meantime the instructor is walking around the room facilitating small group discussion by asking the following types of questions:

- For individuals who are struggling to figure out how to approach solving the problem
    - *Is there a way to draw a picture or mathematical diagram of the situation?*
- For individuals who approached the problem with an "educated" guess and check strategy
    - *Is there a way for you to notate your thinking process in order to communicate it to others?*
- For individuals who have solved the problem symbolically using either a table or linear system
    - *How do you think a 2nd grader or middle school student would approach solving the problem?* This sometimes involves convincing participants that the problem *can* be solved be a 2nd grader.
- For groups that have multiple solution strategies within their group –
    - *How are the various approaches related?*
    - *Find an element of your solution process in someone else's drawing?*

The goal for this portion of the task facilitation is to cognitively engage all course participants in a solution path for the task. This allows them to take ownership in the process of solving the problem and builds their explicit awareness of their knowledge and understanding for the topic. This in turn makes them more open to establishing connections to other solution paths further into the facilitation. In addition, it provides the important perspective that anyone no matter their level of mathematics content knowledge can access a problem when it is presented in a manner where multiple solution strategies, including informal methods, are both possible and encouraged.

In addition to asking probing questions during the individual and small group portion of the task facilitation, the instructor plans which participant-generated models will be used for the whole-class discussion of the problem. For this particular problem, the instructor is looking for a range of models including (1) informal iconic drawings, (2) 'educated' guess-and-check strategies, (3) organized tables, (4) systems of linear equations, and occasionally (5) a graph of the linear equations. As the instructor finds a model that is going to highlight an important idea or relationship, they ask the course participant or group to recreate the model on poster paper for whole-class discussion. These models are posted around the room during the small group discussion time. Many groups begin analyzing and discussing the various solution strategie within their small group as they are posted. When the instructor does not see a particular model while monitoring participants' work, they look to see whose thinking trajectory lends itself to the 'missing' model and will work individually with a participant by asking probing question in order to generate the model based on the work they have already completed. For example, a participant may have listed several combinations of packets and total seeds without actually building a table. A few questions about organizing work can lead the participant to build a table that still reflects his or her thinking. In this way, the model is still based in the participant's initial understanding and provides an example later during the whole-class discuss of how to facilitate the emergence of particular models during classroom instruction.

Whole Group Discussion

The following examples represent four of the solutions debriefed in one 6-12 MTI course for this particular task. While other models were also included in the discussion, these four provide a representative progression of informal to formal solution strategies that are discussed. The examples are presented in the typical order of facilitation with the initial focus on describing the solution path depicted by the model, followed by establishing connections to previous models when applicable. We tend to start the facilitation with the informal iconic drawing of the situation to ensure everyone has access to a solution path and to progressively formalize understanding as we move to increasingly symbolic models. Figure 1 provides an example of an informal iconic representation of the seeds task. The course instructor will typically ask the individual who created the model (the model creator) to describe his or her thinking process involved in solving the problem. However, occasionally other course participants are asked to describe how they think the model's creator approached the problem. The original model creator is then asked to confirm or disconfirm the analysis of his or her thinking. In the case of the model presented in Figure 1, another course participant was asked to describe the thinking of the model's creator. The quote below details how the first person described the

Figure 1: Informal iconic representation for the seeds task

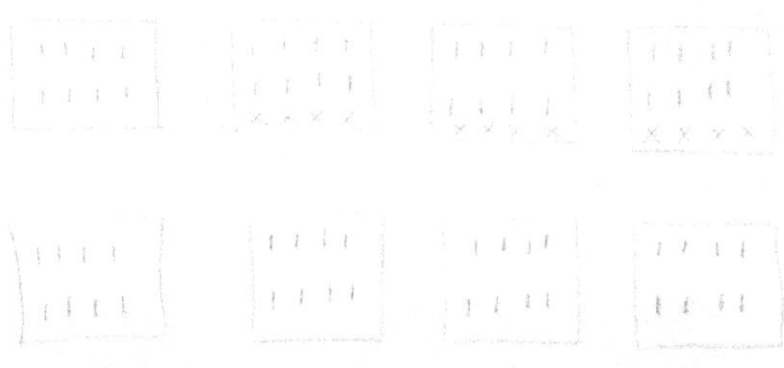

anticipated thinking of the original model creator (transcripts slightly modified for ease of reading):

> *That's actually kind of how I started. I had my little bubble of 76 total and then I gave everybody 8 [seeds], knowing that there had to be at least 8 [in each package]. And then I had my 12 [seeds] left over. Which I'm thinking - what is a kid going to do here - well there's 8 packages, I've got 12 seeds, they could give everybody another seed. Now there are 9 [in each package]. But then they have to go back to the problem and realize that I can't have 9 in a package - how do I have to divvy up my remaining 12 so that it fits the problem? So then they have to [realize] that the 12 [seeds] have to be separated into groups of 4, so that I can take a pack of seeds that has 8 add 4 to it and I then I've got another group of 4 and then I've got another group of 4 and now I'm out of seeds but I've got everything divided equally between the packets.*

From here the instructor asks other course participants to think about and discuss whether the description provided matches what is seen in the drawing. The goal is to have participants examine the model for evidence of the thinking represented in the description. For example, in this situation the person described something that was a part of his thinking originally giving every packet a 9th seed – but was not actually evidenced in the model that was drawn. While an important idea to discuss, because this is a common mistake, it is also important for the instructor to draw out the idea that as teachers we often place our thinking on students' models. A significant focus of the whole group discussion is the understanding that when provided meaningful contextual problems with multiple solution paths, students will demonstrate dramatically different strategies and models. Teachers thus need to have the specialized content knowledge to anticipate and analyze students' thinking based on the students' models in order to press them to more sophisticated ways of modeling.

Following the description, the original drawer typically adds to, confirms, or corrects some aspects of the description of their thinking. Many ah-ha's are typically shared during the debrief of the informal iconic representation. In particular, many individuals who solved the problem via symbolic methods tend to appreciate the simplicity of the solution strategy. In addition, the idea of examining a representation to determine how students (or other course participants) thought about the problem is a relatively novel idea for many individuals. However, particularly in classes with secondary mathematics teachers, comments are also brought up regarding how this approach works for this problem, but would not work for all linear system problems. Depending upon the group and the instructor, the conversation around the ideas of progressive formalization and learning trajectories can occur here but participants tends to have a much broader perspective by the end of the problem so it is typically left until that time.

The discussion of the informal iconic model is typically followed by examination of 'educated' guess and check strategies. We use the term educated to indicate there is some form of mathematical reasoning involved that can be expressed. A participant's explicit awareness of the reasoning they utilized often comes through probing questions from the instructor during the individual or small group work time. For example – *why did you start with that particular number*? Figure 2 provides an example of utilizing the minimum and maximum values as the starting place for the guess-and-check strategy.

The quote below provides a brief description by the course participant who created the model in Figure 2:

What's the minimum possible number you could have? So that's 8 times 8 is 64. What's the maximum number you could have? (Points to 8 times 12 is 96) Okay so that…kind of bracketed my guess and check. Because then it's… 76, not close to 64, not really close to 96, it's right about in the middle. So, now that I know it's right about in the middle I'll just go to the standard guess and check technique. But that way, maybe in a slightly harder problem, I wouldn't get lost I would have a good place to start.

Figure 2: 'Educated' guess and check strategy for the seeds task

Following a brief discussion of this solution strategy – the instructor begins to press connections between this model (Figure 2) and the previous model (Figure 1) by asking the following questions:

- *Where is the minimum, 8 x 8 = 64, represented in the drawing (Figure 1)? How would the original word problem be modified to represent this idea?*
- *Where is the maximum, 8 x 12 = 96, represented in the drawing (Figure 1)? How would the original word problem be modified to represent this idea?*
- *How could the guess of 4 x 8 and 4 x 12 be represented in the drawing?*

Each probing question is followed by a class discussion with participants often coming to the board to point out the connections they observe between the models and other participants asking them to more fully articulate what they are seeing.

Once a few other 'educated' guess and check models are debriefed and connections established, a table model is typically discussed to (a) present a more formal model for keeping track of the guess and check methodologies, and (b) provide a basis for numerous connections that can be established between the original problem, the models presented so far, and the linear system model that is debriefed last.

Figure 3: Original table model for the seeds task

8	12	
8-64	0-0	64
7-56	1-12	68
6-48	2-24	72
5-40	3-36	76
4-32	4-48	80
3-24	5-60	84
2-16	6-72	88
1-8	7-84	92
0-0	8-96	96

During the discussion of the table(s), we initially focus on the organization of the table itself and make clear connections to the original word problem, such as – *where can you see the idea of 8 packets?* There is often a second table to debrief in which the 76 seeds are maintained but the number of packages varies. The dual table representations allow the instructor to ask probing questions about what each table is keeping constant from the word problem and what is varying. Once the meaning and structure of the table (or tables) is established, the instructor typically focuses on making connections to previous models and, in particular for this problem, begins to focus intently on what happens when we replace a sunflower packet with a pumpkin seed packet or vice-versa. One can see that for the original table (Figure 3) this information is not clearly highlighted. But as the table is debriefed the instructor or a course participant will typically notate on the table where the change in seeds between packets occurs (Figure 4). In addition, participants focus on where that rate of change can be seen in the models previously analyzed. The following quote highlights the articulation of this concept:

Figure 4: Modified table model following discussion of changing from packet type to another.

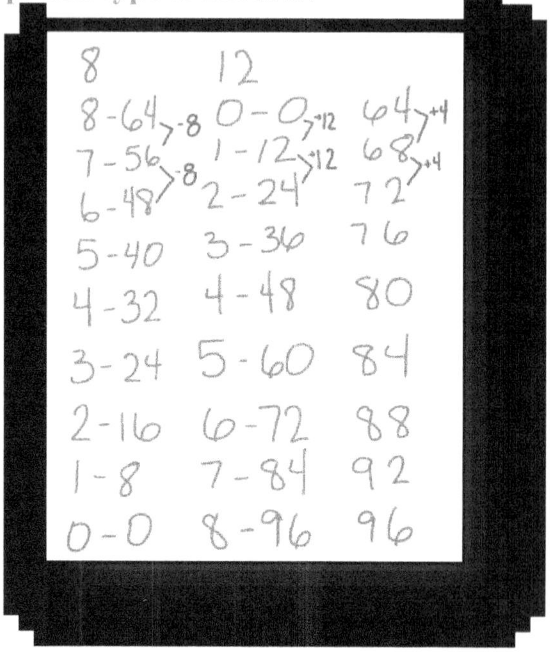

8	12	
8-64 ⟩-8	0-0 ⟩+12	64 ⟩+4
7-56 ⟩-8	1-12 ⟩+12	68 ⟩+4
6-48	2-24	72
5-40	3-36	76
4-32	4-48	80
3-24	5-60	84
2-16	6-72	88
1-8	7-84	92
0-0	8-96	96

If you want to alter one package to another package, that choice makes a difference of 4. You can't make a smaller difference, you can make differences in increments of 4, so that's kind of your choice. So swapping out a sunflower for a pumpkin leads to a difference of 4.

Lastly, the linear system model is debriefed (Figure 5). For many course participants who have been able to understand the various models to this point, the switch to a formal discussion of the linear system solution causes palpable anxiety. Often times the person who describes the model will do a good job of contextualizing the two equations.

$$p + s = 8$$
$$12p + 8s = 76$$

Clear connections are established regarding the meaning of p – number of pumpkin packets, s – number of sunflower packets, 12p – number of pumpkin seeds, and 8s – number of sunflower seeds. Other course participants, who are unfamiliar with linear systems, are also asked to articulate the relationship to ensure that initial understanding is common across the class.

However, when the course participant begins discussing the process of solving the two equations – either by elimination or substitution – the solution method often becomes what we refer to as 'math magic'. Decisions about how to operate with the equations are based solely on the conventions of the solution strategy rather than on the context of the problem. The instructor typically focuses on the fact that up until this point we have been able to make sense of each of the models from the perspective of the original task that was presented. However, solving the system appears to represent a pro that occurs in a black box with the answer just popping out at the end. At this point in the debrief, the instructor will ask course participants to discuss in detail the solution process with a particular focus on explaining the contextual meaning of certain lines such as 4p = 12. The goal is to have the participants make sense – contextually – of what is occurring algebraically.

Figure 5: Systems of Equations model, solved by elimination

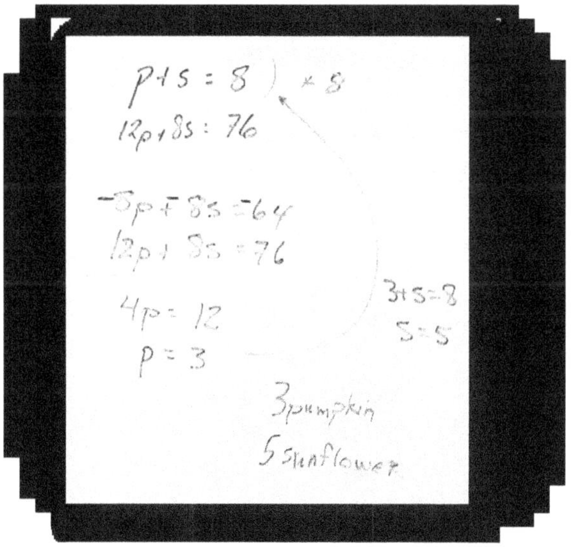

This section is perhaps the most powerful portion of the task debrief because it presses individuals to make connections between iconic representations and extremely formal mathematics solution paths. For individuals who are not strong in mathematics, the process presses them to make connections between formal mathematics and the problem context, allowing them access to what was previously perceived as a mess of numbers and symbols on the board. For individuals who have secondary mathematics backgrounds - and found the linear solution method to be easy – the process forces them to articulate connections to iconic models and context that most have never seen. They are pressed to articulate how the technical mathematical process of solving a linear system relates to the actual packets and seeds in the problem. Participants discover that depending on how one sets up the system one either starts at the minimum (64 seeds – seen in Figure 5) or the maximum (96 seeds) and builds up or down in

increments of 4 to a target value - in this case 76 seeds. For many secondary teachers these ideas are a huge ah-ha.
The following text for a whole-class discussion occurred following the instructor question - *what do the equations mean within the context?*

Instructor: *Does somebody want to take a stab at what do these equations actually mean within the context? And where do these numbers come from? Where have we seen them before?*

Jane (comes to board): *It took a while, the thinking between the two of us, so I'm not taking credit for this. Because we're both high school, college level teachers. And to really go back and think - what is that meaning? This is the packages (points to $p + s = 8$ equation). And if you're multiplying those by 8 (points to $-8p + -8s = -64$ equation), where they are usually multiplied by12 and 8 (points to $12p + 8s = 76$ equation) with 12 seeds in each pumpkin package and 8 seeds in each sunflower package. If you multiply both of them by 8 (again pointing to $-8p + -8s = -64$ equation) and you get 64, it's the same thing as the model (points to the informal iconic drawing), if you have put 8 in each of the packages. And then this part when you do this elimination tells you how they differ (points to $4p = 12$ equation). How many are different (between the two types of packages), there's our 4, and how many seeds were left over (points to 12). And the solution here tells you that you've got 3 of the packages that you need to distribute those 12 seeds into.*

Instructor: *Does someone else want to explain the things they saw?*

Larry (from table): *It's a great connection to the picture, I think*

Instructor: *How is it a great connection?*

Larry: *I think that cleared up a lot of things. Because I hadn't come away thinking about it but connecting it to those original 8, everybody has to have at least 8. We start there, and then the next step of - what is the 4p equals 12 representative of? So it really was a good way of explaining each of those pieces and how it connects to that (symbolic linear system solution). So it's really concrete. You can really represent what each of those values is and where does 'that 12 come from' is the what's left over. So yeah it was nice.*

Jane: *It really was a wrench to try to... oh we've been teaching this for so long, how many decades? And what does that really mean, concretely? We talk, we talk but we don't go back to the picture all the time, and it was really hard to go back to the picture and connect it. But that visual would make a lot of sense, I think, to students, those students that don't see that.*

Instructor: *Well first - how does what Jane explained actually relate to Rich's method (minimum- maximum guess and check)?*

Instructor: *And if we combine it (minimum-maximum guess and check) with John's (linear systems solution)? Somebody want to take a stab at that? Greg?*

Greg: *I think... the 64 in that equation (points to linear systems solution) is the 64 over here in his minimum (points to minimum-maximum guess and check). Or if all 8 packages were what - sunflower seeds - then you get 64 there. But if you had eliminated the p instead of the s (pointing to the portion of the equation -8s + -8p = -64), you'd multiply by 12 (instead of 8) and you'd get the 96?*

Instructor: *If we'd done this instead? (Instructor notates)*

$$12p + 12s = 96$$

$$12p + 8s = 76$$

Greg: *Right.*
Followed by murmurings from course participants as they briefly discuss in their group.

Instructor: *So you're saying if that - what was that 96 again?*

Greg: *That was if all of the packages were 12 each (pumpkin packages).*

Instructor: *What would that look like in a picture format?*

Kim: *Starting with all 12 and then*

Rob: *You'd start with 12*

Kim: *And then taking away seeds from each*

This dialogue serves to highlight the cognitive press that occurs throughout the task facilitation in terms of building connections between multiple models to encourage specialized content knowledge (e.g., solving two linear systems algebraically often involves using the minimum or maximum value of one of the variables under consideration) and pressing the contextual understanding of mathematical procedures. By solving the initial problem as though they were students at different grade levels, participants actively engage in horizontal mathematizing from several perspectives. By analyzing multiple solution strategies and models for a contextual task, participants mimic the process of progressive formalization, beginning with an informal representation and connecting progressively to increasingly formal methods. Building a full trajectory from drawings to formal linear systems with students would take days or even weeks, but through this single professional development activity, participants begin to see how horizontal mathematizing and the DMT framework might look in the classroom.

Extension Task or Situated Application

In order to further participants' understanding of the content at hand and to model the DMT practice of *pressing students conceptually*, participants are typically given a series of problem extensions or additional problems that press participants to apply or extend ideas developed during the task facilitation. Given this framework is used across multiple professional development settings and groups, this aspect of the framework is adjusted to the needs of the specific professional development situation. The following extension questions or tasks are utilized either throughout or following the initial seeds task facilitation. Each one provides a different area of focus and facilitators make the judgment based on their participants which of the extension tasks to utilize.

Pedagogical Implications

The professional development task facilitation structure models the components of the Development Mathematical Thinking (DMT) framework. The final aspect of task facilitation involves the explicit discussion of the parallels between the DMT framework, the Joey-Seeds task facilitation, and connections to participants' classroom instruction. Participants are asked to articulate where the components of the DMT framework were utilized throughout the task facilitation and to make connections to how this could be applied to their classroom. This final section provides our brief description of each of the components, followed by related examples from two questions on the end of course evaluation survey for MTI participants regarding new mathematics and instructional practices learned. We feel the participants' actual responses illuminate how they are framing their instruction through the DMT framework following participation in our professional development.

(Table 2. Overview of Task Extensions May be found on the following page)

Table 2. Overview of Task Extensions

	Extension Task or Situated Application	Focus	Research Connection
Extension 1	1. There are 76 seeds, what are all the possibilities of packages. 2. There are 8 packages, what are all the possibilities of seeds?	These extension situations are commonly utilized during the task facilitation to encourage multiple models and to press participants that have solved the original problem but struggle to model it another way. It often presses them to make an organized table of their guess-and-check solution	This extension focuses on important aspects of progressive formalization and horizontal mathematizing by pressing participants within the bounds of the current context – but implicitly asking for a more formal organization to their work in order to solve the extensions.
Extension 2	Analysis of a graph of the equations in the linear systems model and the connections to linear systems.	This typically follows the debrief of the formal linear systems solution and is primarily utilized in the 6-12 MTI course. It provides a more formal iconic method of examining the problem and allows for extensions into linear inequalities.	This extension continues to focus on Treffers (1987) horizontal mathematizing by pressing participants to contextually explain a formal iconic model for the problem.
Extension 3	Application to a new problem: Lizzie collects lizards and beetles. She has 8 creatures in her collection so far. All together they have 36 legs. How many of each kind of creature does she	Following the seeds task debrief, the Lizzie problem is utilized to press participants to apply the knowledge from the previous problem to a new situation. Participants understand that practice is important but should connect to foundational mathematical ideas rather consist of rote	This extension focuses on Treffers (1987) vertical mathematizing by pressing participants to generalize the mathematics from the previous problem to solve the new task (e.g., starting at the minimum and seeing the change of 2).

Taking Students' Ideas Seriously. In classrooms where students' ideas are taken seriously, the instructional focus is on valuing and building upon students' intuitive understanding of mathematical concepts.

Encouraging Multiple Models and Strategies. In classrooms where students are encouraged to use multiple strategies and models, the instructional focus is on developing students understanding of various approaches to solving problems.

Pressing Students Conceptually. In classrooms where students are pressed conceptually, the instructional focus is on building connections between mathematical strategies and models and progressively formalizing those ideas and methods for solving problems.

Addressing Misconceptions. In classrooms where student misconceptions are meaningfully addressed, the instructional focus is on using mistakes and misconceptions as valuable tools to build mathematical understanding.

Focusing on the Structure of the Mathematics. In classrooms where students focus on the structure of the mathematics, the instructional focus is on facilitating students' understanding of fundamental mathematical concepts.

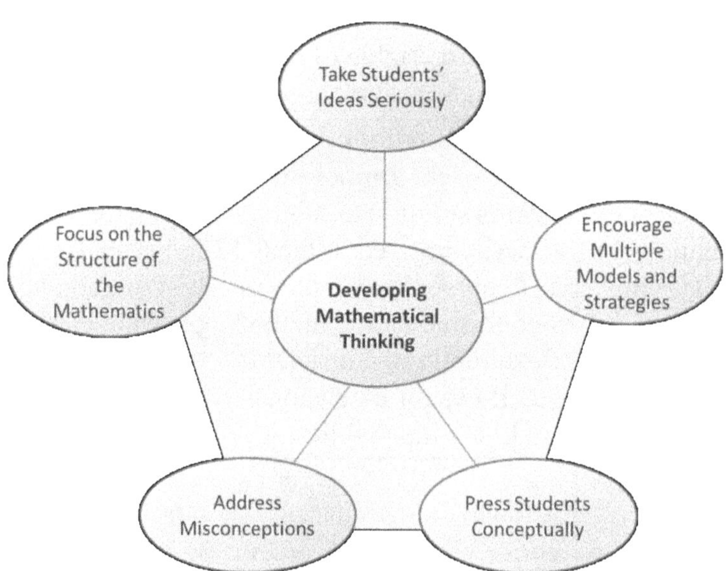

I will focus on the process NOT the answer. I won't be doing all the talking either. I will ask guided questions and let my kids think about the process. I have come to understand that talking, and communicating, and listening are VERY important. Also, real stuff that they are interested in solving - not textbook problems. I plan on making each TASK something that is meaningful to my students.

I learned 1. modeling, 2. teacher questioning to lead the students to a desired outcome, 3. student group participation which increased learning through sharing of ideas, 4. interconnection between tasks and algorithms demonstrated a wide variety methods, and 5. the desire to change me (my) teaching style to what I now believe will facilitate a greater and deeper understanding of math and the role math plays in the real world.

To listen to the students more and find out what they know and build from there.

I would definitely let the students explore in small groups or with a partner how they would solve a problem and then press them into taking it further by explaining it to me and the class.

Having children explore solutions to problems and do their own thinking!! Also making sure students have time to share their ideas and discuss why the different ways to solve a problem work! Taking students ideas seriously and using their thinking to guide instruction!

Having students share their math ideas/models first to guide our discussions. Making mistakes (teacher or student) are powerful teaching tools.

I learned better questioning strategies to help students explain how they thought through a problem. I intend to have students present their methods for solving a problem and question them to connect their method to other student' (sic) methods and to think about why they did each step.

I will use group discussion, notate student thinking, and go from informal to formal.
Be less helpful. :) That is, ask more questions and answer fewer. That seems to be the key. To allow the children to brainstorm and work on the problem first and then get together and discuss the different ways they solved that problem. The instruction should be guided but student led! Students should be allowed to think for themselves but also get others view as well.

Final Considerations

The DMT professional development task facilitation structure provides a model that parallels the pedagogical shifts we are asking teachers' to make. Through the use of this model we have seen large-scale shifts in participants' beliefs and knowledge (M. B. Carney, J. L. Brendefur, K. Thiede, G. Hughes, & J. Sutton, In Review) and changes in instructional practices and student achievement at the local level (J. L. Brendefur, 2007; Jonathan L. Brendefur et al., In Review). As we have utilized the framework across multiple professional development settings (e.g., 45-hour courses, after school workshops, one-day trainings) and groups (e.g., teachers, paraprofessionals, administrators) we have a final important consideration.

Though presented as a 'pentagon', one lens through which to view the DMT instructional practice framework is as a continuum with individuals who are first being introduced to a student-centered approach to instruction focusing on (1) taking students' ideas seriously, (2) encouraging multiple strategies and models, and (3) addressing misconceptions. For many participants, what is being asked for by these three components is such a large shift in practice it is difficult for them to fully conceptualize the components of (4) pressing students conceptually and (5) focusing on the structure of the mathematics, despite their centrality within the DMT framework. Without continued support – either through explicit or embedded professional development – teachers may continue to focus on these horizontal mathematizing components, treating mathematics discourse as "show-and-tell" (Stein, Engle, Smith, & Hughes, 2008) and without moving to a very necessary focus on the vertical mathematizing components. It is vital that teachers press students conceptually and emphasize major mathematical concepts because otherwise students are left with only their own initial solution methods, which may be informal, inefficient, and perhaps not applicable in all circumstances. In our experience, follow-up or embedded professional development built consistently upon the task facilitation structure and the DMT framework does enable teachers to understand the importance of vertical mathematization and the implementation of all five DMT framework practices. Typically, this process takes two to three years for many teachers (Jonathan L. Brendefur et al., 2013).

References

Brendefur. (2008). Connecting elementary teachers' mathematical knowledge to their instructional practices. *The Researcher, 21*(2), 1-18.

Brendefur, J. L. (2007). Developing Mathematical Thinking: Final Technical Report. Idaho: BoiseState University: Center for School Improvement and Policy Studies.

Brendefur, J. L., Thiede, K., Strother, S., Bunning, K., & Peck, D. (2013). Developing mathematical thinking: Changing teachers' knowledge and instruction. *Journal of Curriculum and Teaching, 2*(2).

Brendefur, J. L., Thiede, K., Strother, S., Jesse, D., & Sutton, J. (In Review). A longitudinal study on the effects of professional development on elementary students' mathematics achievement. *Journal of Mathematics Teacher Education.*

Bruner, J. S. (1964). The course of cognitive growth. *American Psychologist, 19*(1).

Carney, M. B., Brendefur, J. L., Thiede, K., Hughes, G., & Sutton, J. (In Review). Analysis of a mandatory statewide mathematics professional development course on teacher knowledge, self-efficacy, and beliefs. *Educational Policy.*

Carney, M. B., Brendefur, J. L., Thiede, K., Hughes, G., & Sutton, J. (In Review). Analysis of a Mandatory Statewide Mathematics Professional Development Course on Teacher Knowledge, Self-Efficacy, and Beliefs.

Carpenter, T. P., & Lehrer, R. (1999). Teaching and learning mathematics with understanding. In E. Fennema & T. Romberg (Eds.), *Mathematics Classrooms that Promote Teaching for Understanding* (pp. 19 - 32). Mahwah, NJ: Lawerance Erlbaum Associates.

Cobb, P. (2000). Conducting classroom teaching experiments in collaboration with teachers. In R. Lesh & A. Kelly (Eds.), *Handbook of research design in mathematics and science education* (pp. 307-334). Mahwah, NJ: Lawrence Erlbaum.

Doerr, H. M. (2006). Examining the tasks of teaching when using students' mathematical thinking. *Educational Studies in Mathematics, 62*(1), 3-24.

Freudenthal, H. (1973). *Mathematics as an educational task*: Springer.

Freudenthal, H. (1991). Revisiting Mathematics Education: China Lectures.

Gravemeijer, K., & van Galen, F. (2003). Facts and algorithms as products of students' own mathematical activity. In J. Kilpatrick, W. G. Martin & D. Schifter (Eds.), *A research companion to principles and standards for school mathematics* (pp. 114-122). Reston, VA: NCTM.

Haycock, K. (2001). Closing the achievement gap. *Educational Leadership, 58*(6), 6-11.

Hiebert, J., & Carpenter, T. P. (1992). Learning and teaching with understanding. In D. A. Grouws (Ed.), *Handbook of Research on Mathematics Teaching and Learning* (pp. 65-97). New York: Macmillan.

Hiebert, J., Carpenter, T. P., Fennema, E., Fuson, K. C., Human, P., Murray, H., . . . Wearne, D. (1996). Problem solving as a basis for reform in curriculum and instruction: The case of mathematics. *Educational Researcher, 25*(4), 12-21.

Knapp, M. (1995). *Teaching for meaning in high-poverty classrooms*. New York, NY: Teachers College Press.

Larsen, S., & Bartlo, J. (2009). The role of tasks in promoting discourse supporting mathematical learning. In L. Knott (Ed.), *The role of mathematics discourse in producing leaders of discourse* (pp. 77-98). Charlotte, NC: Information Age Publishing.

Newmann, F. M., & Associates. (1996). *Authentic achievement: Restructuring schools for intellectual quality*. San Francisco, CA: Jossey Bass.

Simon, M., & Tzur, R. (2004). Explicating the role of mathematical tasks in conceptual learning: An elaboration of the hypothetical learning trajectory. *Mathematical thinking and learning, 6*(2), 91-104.

Stein, M. K., Engle, R. A., Smith, M. S., & Hughes, E. K. (2008). Orchestrating productive mathematical discussions: Five practices for helping teachers move beyond show and tell. *Mathematical Thinking and Learning, 10*(4), 313-340.

Treffers, A. (1987). *Three dimensions: A model of goal and theory description in mathematics instruction* – The Wiskobas Project. Dordencht, The Netherlands: Reidel.

Chapter Author(s)

Dr. Jonathan Brendefur is a mathematics education Professor in the Department of Curriculum, Instruction, and Foundational Studies in the College of Education at Boise State University. He has a Ph.D. from the University of Wisconsin at Madison, focusing on assessment, mathematics curriculum, and professional development with specific emphasis on student thinking and learning trajectories. He has spent the last 24 years teaching mathematics and mathematics pedagogy to K-12 students and preservice and inservice teachers though grants, courses, and workshops.

Dr. Carney is an assistant professor of mathematics education in the Department of Curriculum, Instruction, and Foundational Studies in the College of Education at Boise State University. She has a Ph.D. from University of Idaho. Previously she worked as a K-12 mathematics curriculum coordinator, coach, and teacher for several years. Her research focuses on mathematics professional development, educational leadership, and measuring and scaling mathematics education efforts. She works with teachers, schools, and district to improve mathematics instruction and student achievement.

Dr. Gwyneth Hughes is currently the online math specialist for the Initiative for Developing Mathematical Thinking at Boise State University and an instructor for middle school math teachers through the University of Wisconsin. Previously she taught high school mathematics in Washington DC. She went on to study volcanology at Stanford University, focusing on using mathematics in studying and modeling volcanism at different scales. After completing a PhD in Geological Sciences and an MS in Geophysics, she returned to mathematics education at Boise State University as part of the Initiative for Developing Mathematical Thinking.

Sam Strother is a mathematics education specialist for the Initiative for Developing Mathematical Thinking at Boise State University. He has a Master's degree in Curriculum and Instruction with a mathematics education focus from Boise State University. He is an instructor for pre-service educators as well as a professional development facilitator for in-service teachers. He has worked closely with students and teachers in the field to improve instructional, assessment and curriculum. Currently he is working with colleagues to research predictive assessment in the primary grades, basic fact fluency in elementary school and understanding of rational number in middle schools.

Chapter 12

On Axiomatic Systems in Semiotic to English Language Translation

ABSTRACT: The manuscript at hand is a brief manifest relating the notation, syntax, and semantics of mathematics to the notation, syntax, and semantics of natural written English. Semiotics is the context used to describe the similarities in the processes and goals of both systems as methods of communication. The discussion of semiotics falls within three categories: 1) examining the parallel structures of written language and mathematics (syntax), 2) translating mathematical symbols, notation, and processes into meaning (semantics), and 3) exploring the nature and differences of mathematical versus standard written vocabulary and notation (pragmatics). Finally, the manuscript concludes by defining the term "STEMiotics" as a way to define the interplay in symbols used for communication between the STEM disciplines using natural language as an intermediary context.

Introduction

As a communication tool, mathematics is commonly seen as a substrate of some *natural* language (e.g. English) but having its own notation, technical terms, and conventions. While this may be true depending on how one perceives the temporal precedence of various language structures, it can also be logically argued that mathematics not only subsumes the formal structure, notation, and use of all written and spoken language, it is, itself, the most precise mechanism we have for explaining the universe and all it contains (Devlin, 2000). In essence, mathematics is the purest, most concise, and most comprehensive language system known to humankind. From the complex vocal sounds by which we transmit our individual thoughts and feelings, to the various permutations of the alphabetic symbols used to make words and sentences, to the geometric translations of sign language into meaning; all forms of language are, and must naturally be, mathematically structured. Thoughtful consideration on a much broader scale even suggests that if we ever receive a message from intelligent life outside our own solar system, it will likely be a mathematical one. Yet with all of its elegant communication potential, mathematics is typically only utilized as a *common* language by mathematicians, scientists, and engineers despite the obvious parallels to how our natural written language is structured and used by non-mathematicians (Etsy, 2014).

The unfortunate fact is that traditional American schooling only exposes students to the most trivial facets of mathematics from their earliest contact with the subject; and very little of this exposure involves recognizing the language and communication aspects of mathematics

(Jamison, 2008). This is not to say that opportunities for more communication based applications are not available in the instruction of mathematics, but rather that the concept of mathematics as a language is overshadowed by the procedural fluency aspects of the discipline as we learn about it (NRC, 2001). This fact is ironic considering that procedural fluency is actually a component of mathematical communication but is rarely described as such. Specifically, the National Council of Teachers of Mathematics (NCTM) highlights mathematical *communication* as a critical element of the mathematics curriculum (NCTM, 2000). Yet, mathematical communication is still conceptualized and taught in a way that represents mathematical syntax as a communication structure that is largely independent of natural language.

The narrative provided hereafter will make the case that secondary school mathematics curriculum would benefit from a reconceptualization of computation and procedural fluency as syntactic communication tools aimed at better leveraging semantic concepts in the sciences, engineering, and technology. This argument will be made in the context of semiotics which is roughly defined as, "…the science of communication studied through the interpretation of signs and symbols as they operate in various fields, esp. language" (Oxford English Dictionary, 2003). The relevance of studying mathematics as a communication protocol within the context of semiotics will be made evident through the following discussions: examining the parallel structures of written language and mathematical notation (syntax), using mathematical symbols, notation, and processes to establish meaning in natural language (semantics), and finally, exploring the nature and differences of mathematical versus standard written vocabulary and notation (pragmatics).

Parallel Structures of Written Language and Mathematical Notation (Syntax)

The statements from the previous section are not merely suggestions that if we look hard enough, we can find subtle connections between written language and mathematics, but rather that communication itself exists within the structure of mathematics and that mathematics is primarily a communication based discipline. To demonstrate this idea, let us examine some structural and syntactic similarities between written language and mathematics. We can do this by comparing a few basic postulates that are common in all written systems of language to the processes and symbols mathematicians use. In mathematics, a postulate (or axiom) is a statement that is assumed to be true without the burden of formal proof, usually because these assumptions are necessary for defining a starting point for the mathematical system, and also because they are often self-evident. For example, the ancient mathematician Euclid built an entire system of two-dimensional geometry, which is still studied and taught worldwide, based on five simple postulates. We might now generate some basic postulates to redefine our natural written system of language, which can be directly compared to the numeric processes and notation with which we are already familiar. Note that the same mathematical structures could be applied to any syntactic system, but also that the structure does not automatically carry over to issues of semantics. There is, however, a unique semantic aspect of mathematics that applies to the development of mathematical communication, which will be discussed later. The following postulates for language will be used to demonstrate that natural written language exists within a system that is very similar to how mathematical notation is structured:

1. Postulate 1: Semiotic languages have individual, uniquely identifiable symbols that can be arranged to create semantic systems of varying size and complexity. Written language uses permutations of a finite set of alphabetic symbols (letters), which exist in a hierarchical form to express meaning (words and sentences). Mathematics uses permutations of a finite set of numeric symbols (digits) that exist in a hierarchical form to express quantity (place value and exponential notation). The permutation (or rearrangement) of symbols is critical to the operation of both systems. For example, the letters in the word "cat" give us a completely different meaning when rearranged as "act" or no identifiable meaning when arranged as "tca" because a specific meaning or idea has not been universally assigned for the arrangement "tca." Likewise, the arrangement of the digits 123 give us a different value than if we rearrange them as 231, or no identifiable value if rearranged as $1^3 2$ because exponential notation within an array of digits has not been universally defined.
2. Postulate 2: Semiotic languages all include a specific set of delimiters. In natural written language, delimiters (punctuation) are used to organize thoughts into manageable subsections and provide order and nuance to ideas. The symbols of mathematics include a specific set of delimiters (mathematical operators) to organize expressions and provide order and nuance to quantities. For example, there is an old joke about how a comma can save a life: "Let's eat Grandma." versus "Let's eat, Grandma." One small delimiter changes the meaning of an otherwise identical permutation of letters. The mathematical system is a bit more obvious. For example, it is clear that 314 is an expression of a different value than 3.14. Again a small delimiter completely changes the value of an otherwise identical permutation of digits.
3. Postulate 3: Semiotic languages use a mathematical process of substitution. Written language uses different symbol combinations (e.g. words or phrases) that exhibit a degree of congruence or equality to other words or phrases. These equivalent word and phrase combinations can be substituted for one another to simplify communication or clarify meaning. Mathematics uses different symbol combinations (called expressions) that may exhibit congruence or equality and can be substituted for one another to simplify communication or clarify meaning. For example, we might substitute the phrase, "Those shoes stink." for the phrase, "Those shoes smell bad." We may do this to make the phrase more efficient (four words to represent the idea versus three words for the same idea) or to emphasize an aspect of our idea (the intensity of the smell of the shoes). In mathematics, this idea is captured by a formal mathematical property called the transitive

property of equality. This property states that if A = B and B = C, then A = C, and allows the three variables to be used interchangeably. An extremely simplified example of this property might be illustrated by substituting an improper fraction into an expression in place of a mixed number. The symbol representations look different but hold the same value and can, therefore, be used interchangeably. The ability to substitute equivalent values (expressions) within a communication system is perhaps the most critical operational structure of both of these systems. For instance, expository writing is not simply a matter of choosing appropriate words, but choosing the best words to convey the writer's meaning. A mathematician does the same thing by distilling a complex expression through a set of successively simplified equivalences. This will be demonstrated in more detail in the next section.

4. Postulate 4: All languages and numeric systems are interdependent. We use numbers and mathematical constructs in written language and letters and words in numeric systems. Clearly no kind of quantity or ordinal relationship can be expressed in written language without the underlying mathematical concepts supporting them. Conversely, generalizable algebraic and geometric relationships could not be stated without the use of letters as variables, or without the description of conditions using precise written language. It is therefore inaccurate to call mathematics a substrate of natural language given that any natural language must exist within a mathematical structure and which also requires the capacity to express mathematical constructs to be complete.

Translating Mathematical Symbols, Notation, and Processes into Meaning (Semantics)

The Second Edition of the 20-volume Oxford English Dictionary contains definitions for over 171,000 words in the English language. Other sources cite over a million words when considering the non-official elements related to obsolete words, special jargon, slang and dialect. Factor in the knowledge that written language allows for many words to hold multiple meanings and you have a system of immense power to transmit ideas; however, such complexity comes with a much greater potential for ambiguity in the interpretation (semantics) of ideas. The mechanism by which the transmission of ideas can be made more efficient and more precise is mathematics. Applying a mathematical process to language whereby we simplify a written expression through the substitution of a more concise statement reduces the ambiguity. As an exercise in a mathematical substitution process applied to writing, let us interpret the following paragraph:

> "It would certainly be most auspicious if you would evince a design, for which I would be abundantly grateful, whereby it would be resolved that the canine, currently residing in the immediate vicinity, be escorted from the premises; this

pursuant to the beast's immediate biological need to vacate copious amounts of extraneous fluid due to an exceedingly high internal pressure index."

Many readers may appreciate various aspects of word usage in the previous narrative, or perhaps interpret it as an example of ironic overstatement of the intended message, or maybe even as the sarcastic tirade of a pseudo-intellectual. In reality, any interpretation may constitute a deviation from the writer's true intention because this passage is subject to the nuances of individual perception as readers digest each component to determine the meaning. By applying mathematical thinking to a written process or notational system we can reduce or even eliminate the interpretive ambiguity of a passage if we so choose. Let us try it with the passage above. Politely stated, a mathematician might generate a final equivalence that looks something like, "Thank you for taking the dog outside. He needs to tinkle." This would be done through a series of substitutions using simplified equivalencies until a distilled message emerges. Let us dissect the passage by identifying important components and making substitutions of reasonably congruent but simplified phrases:

1. Component 1: "It would certainly be most auspicious if you would evince a design" = "it would be favorable to consider a way"
2. Component 2: "for which I would be abundantly grateful" = "and I would be very thankful."
3. Component 3: "whereby it would be resolved that the canine, currently residing in the immediate vicinity" = "where we decide that the dog living here"
4. Component 4: "would be escorted from the premises" = "would be taken outside"
5. Component 5: "this pursuant to" = "based on"
6. Component 6: "the beast's immediate biological need to vacate copious amounts of extraneous fluid" = "the dog's need to get rid of extra water"
7. Component 7: "due to an exceedingly high internal pressure index" = "because of uncomfortable bladder pressure"

We can now reassemble the passage with the substitutions and possibly have a more concise and efficient statement although, in this form, it may appear to be somewhat awkward:

> It would be favorable to consider a way… and I would be very thankful… where we decide that the dog living here… would be taken outside… based on… the dog's need to get rid of extra water… because of uncomfortable bladder pressure.

Now, let us consider a few more mathematical procedures that could be applied to this revised passage. There is a property in mathematics referred to as *commutativity*, which states that, when certain conditions are true, the order of some mathematical operations within an expression does not influence the value of the expression. An example would be the Commutative Property of Addition applied thusly, $2 + 3 = 3 + 2$. The placement of the digits in the expression does not impact the simplified value of the expression. We can apply this property to the phrase, "and I would be very thankful" because the placement of this phrase within the message does not critically impact the meaning of the message. Additionally, we could combine components 3 and 4 into a single new reasonably equivalent component. The same could be done with components 5, 6, and 7. If we simply started with the phrase, "Thank you" and continued to simplify the revised expression with reasonably congruent substitutions, the next iteration of the passage may look something like the following:

Component 2	Component 1	Components 3 and 4	Components 5, 6, and 7
Thank you…	for considering…	taking this dog out…	because he needs to go to the bathroom

This passage can be simplified even farther based on the need for precision or specific attention to various details. The most basic message may end up reading something like, "Thanks for taking the dog out. He needs to tinkle."

Let us now examine a mathematical translation of meaning with an eye focused on the same procedural mechanism but using mathematical notation. As complex as mathematical communication appears to be, the Encyclopedia of Mathematics (2013) reports that there are fewer than 100 symbols in all of mathematics. Factor in that mathematical symbols hold more consistently to a single function rather than having multiple meanings the way that words do, and the system appears comparatively simple. So how does mathematical language have the ability to be so concise and so robust with so little notation relative to natural written language? The answer is fairly straight forward in that a unique permutation of mathematical symbols typically has a single, exact meaning; moreover, the purpose of mathematical notation is ultimately intended to distill numbers, expressions and relationships down to their most elegant, readable, or otherwise useful form. Theoretical constructs such as irony or sarcasm, good or evil, do not exist in mathematical notation even though those constructs can still be defined mathematically within a system. By eliminating the ambiguity of the notation, logic prevails because there is no opportunity to interpret the meaning past what is specifically stated by the symbols. Semantics is then a function of expression through a series of exacting statements. As an exercise, let us examine the following simple relationship:

$$A = B$$

This is a statement equating the values associated with the variables A and B. Though we do not know the values, or even the nature of the values, we know they are the same because it has been explicitly stated. The relationship is absolute and does not allow for parameters, conditions, provisos or special circumstances the way that natural language does. This notion of absolute equality tends to offend our natural intuition about the world because so much of how we interpret communication is dependent on other contextual factors. For example, suppose a ship approaching a rocky shoreline in foggy conditions sees the single pulse of a lighthouse beacon. This single flash of light, repeated at regular intervals as the light rotates, carries a message of warning. The environmental conditions create a context for the communication. Now put the same ship in clear conditions on still water. A single repeating pulse of light would simply inform the ship's crew that the lighthouse was working. Successive flashes would need to be emitted in some other kind of mathematical pattern for a message of danger to be successfully transmitted.

Context is important in mathematics as well but it is generally supplied by additional notation. The absence of this additional notation often creates ambiguity in mathematical explanations. For example, at some point we have all learned that the sum of the interior angles of a triangle is 180 degrees. However, without more contextual communication, this equivalency may not be true. If the triangle is constructed on the surface of a convex manifold, say, the surface of the earth, then the sum of the angles would be different. Try it. Place one vertex of a triangle at the North Pole of a globe. Draw a *straight* line due South until you intersect the equator (note that for the purposes of this example we ignore the curvature of the manifold over which the line is constructed and assume that *straight* is only considered in the two topical dimensions of the surface of the manifold). Make a right angle turn (90 degrees) to define the second vertex and follow the equator due East one fourth of the way around the globe. Define the third vertex by turning back due North and draw your last side as a *straight* line that ends at the North Pole. You have made three right angles in constructing this triangle, the sum of which is 270 degrees, not the 180 that you have been taught. Is the fabric of our mathematical system breaking down because of this contradiction? Of course not. We have simply failed to communicate the conditions under which our 180 degree relationship holds true, and this is one of the great oversights of mathematics instruction at the secondary level.

The previous example is evidence of why looking at the notation of mathematics as a language is so important. Critical parts of messages cannot be omitted while maintaining an expectation that the intended meaning will be accurately relayed. Let us suppose that we want to describe a *rational* number. Most math teachers adopt a shorthand approach to this kind of description by suggesting that a rational number is basically a number that can be written as a ratio of a whole number over a whole number. The description seems fairly complete, but consider the precision of the following notation:

$\mathbb{N}$ defines the Natural Numbers: 1, 2, 3…

$\mathbb{Z}$ defines the Integers: 0, ±1, ±2, ±3…

$\mathbb{Q}$ then defines the rational numbers thusly: $\left\{\frac{a}{b} \mid \forall a \in Z, b \in N\right\}$

The notation of Q can be translated to English as follows: *Rational Numbers* are the *set* of numbers expressed in the form *a* over *b* such that *every* value of *a* is an *element* of the *Integers*, *and every* value *b* is an *element* of the *Natural Numbers*.

Admittedly, the formal notation defining a rational number looks intimidating, and maybe even seems excessive, but the message being conveyed requires an explicit notation to eliminate ambiguity. The qualifying statements defining the Integers and the Natural Numbers is tantamount to providing *situational context* in natural language. If we were to simply say that a rational number is a number over a number or an integer over an integer, we would have to consider zero to be a possible character in the denominator of a fraction, which in computational mathematics defies definition as a constant value.

The message here is that equivalence relationships are only factual if we are meticulous about how we communicate them. For this reason, mathematical notation is not a language system intended to describe truth, but rather, to define fact, irrefutable and absolute within a given context. This, of course, begs the question how are facts determined?

If we can get past the notion that fact is only as pure as the postulates on which we base our system, we can begin to focus on the goals of our communication. The language of computational mathematics, as taught in secondary schools, has only four broad procedural goals in the determination of fact, and the goals occur in a hierarchy:

1. to define known values as contextualized constants/measurements
2. to define unknown values as mathematical expressions in terms of identified and contextualized variables and constants/measurements
3. to establish relationships between and among different combinations of expressions and constants in the form of equations
4. to create concrete notions of equality from abstract situations that occur numerically, algebraically, and geometrically.

If you were to examine the contents of an algebra textbook, you would discover that every section of every chapter involves procedures focused on one or more of the goals stated above. Mathematical instruction, then, often conceptualizes "doing math" as procedural applications, or simply completing the steps necessary for reaching a solution to a problem. This is a misrepresentation of mathematical process. These so called "steps" of a problem are merely restatements of equivalent expressions. Successive substitutions (what appears to be steps of a problem) of these equivalent expressions allow us to remove the ambiguity of the original expression. Each *step*, in reality, is a simpler restatement of the initial expression using very similar protocols as we did when we simplified the written passage in the last section. Though the written versus mathematical problems look different, the processes needed to simplify or interpret them are nearly identical. Suppose, for example, that we want to derive a popular relationship stating that the area of a circle is equivalent to the product of the constant Pi and the numeric square of the measurement of the circle's radius. Many of us know this formula by rote memorization ($A = \pi r^2$). This familiar formula is an elegant, factual statement connecting two expressions from a complex relationship, but how was the relationship established? There are many different notational approaches to establishing this equivalence relationship, but perhaps the purest notation can be found in calculus. Note that each "step" of this process is a notational restatement or translation of a previous expression, beginning with an equivalence relation for the algebraic representation of a circle.

$$x^2 + y^2 = r^2$$

$$y = \sqrt{r^2 - x^2}$$

$$\int_0^r \sqrt{r^2 - x^2}\ dx$$

$$\frac{u}{2}\sqrt{a^2 - u^2} + \frac{a^2}{2}\sin^{-1}\frac{u}{a}$$

$$\frac{x}{2}\sqrt{r^2 - x^2} + \frac{r^2}{2}\sin^{-1}\frac{x}{r}\Big|_0^r$$

$$\left[\frac{r}{2}\sqrt{r^2 - r^2} + \frac{r^2}{2}\sin^{-1}\frac{r}{r}\right] - \left[\frac{0}{2}\sqrt{r^2 - 0^2} + \frac{r^2}{2}\sin^{-1}\frac{0}{r}\right]$$

$$\left[\frac{r}{2}(0) + \frac{r^2}{2}\sin^{-1}1\right] - \left[\frac{0}{2}(r) + \frac{r^2}{2}\sin^{-1}0\right]$$

$$\left[0 + \frac{r^2}{2}\cdot\frac{\pi}{2}\right] - \left[0 + \frac{r^2}{2}(0)\right]$$

$$\frac{\pi r^2}{4}$$

Just as the goal of a written document somewhat determines the language style and composition appropriate for representing the idea, mathematical processes are determined by the nature of the solution being sought. In the area formula derivation illustrated above, the final expression allows us to determine the relationship between a circle's area and its radius. The purpose is to determine a complex measured value (the area of the circle) by relating it to a value that is easier to obtain by measurement, that being the radius. In this example, a non-mathematician only needs to know that each statement provides an equivalent representation in successively less complex terms under given conditions, exactly as we did when simplifying the written passage. In considering only the outcome, which is a simple formula involving two variables, it is easy to overlook the precision of the communication protocol and notation that allows the formula to exist.

Using the four procedural goals stated above, we can define a notational system of mathematical rules which seem complex relative to the written English rules we use almost every day, but in reality, are just an application of the same logical principles under two different communication paradigms. The mathematical procedures that we have used for the both the written passage and formula derivation also apply to sign language and voice patterns. In fact, they are so simple that even a computer can understand them! Of course our instincts may tell us that if we need a computer, our task must be difficult. Consider, however, that a computer can only function by being told *exactly* what to do. The communication protocol that a computer uses must be simple enough to be distilled down into a finite number of combinations using only ones and zeros. Let us conclude this section by exploring a modern application of computers and the mathematical language that helps illustrate a translational phenomenon.

There are approximately 44 sounds (phonemes) in the English language depending on the linguistic source we choose to consider (Chomsky & Halle, 1968). Each sound combination in a spoken word is analogous to the letter combinations used to make written words. Our brains recognize and interpret sounds in spoken language similarly to how they recognize and interpret words in written language. Amazingly enough, a computer can be *taught* to do the same thing. By analyzing a range of values for the variables of pitch, duration, frequency, volume, pacing, intonation, etcetera, the computer can begin to *recognize* the vocalization of different words and phrases by comparing strings of binary digits. Of course this is a bit of an oversimplification. The actual programming model must be significantly more complex because an English word may be spoken a number of different ways by the same individual, not to mention, many different ways by the English speaking world. Mathematics helps the computer estimate what the sounds of words and phrases should digitally look like by using a mathematical model called a *Markov Chain*. When we speak, the sounds our voices make are converted to binary code (numbers consisting of only ones and zeros). A mathematical analysis can then be applied to compare the numeric code to a database of existing codes for possible written word substitutions. The Markov model is a Stochastic modeling process that relies on the idiosyncrasies of a given language to help determine the intended order of words based on how the language is commonly structured. For example, the words "happy birthday" have a higher probability of being spoken in sequence than "aptly earth pay," which might sound similar to the computer depending on who is speaking. The mathematical model would help the computer select the most likely translation based on the context of the surrounding phrase combinations. Under this paradigm, dialects and other sound protocols are highly mathematically predictable.

Exploring the nature and differences of mathematical versus standard written vocabulary and notation (pragmatics)

Although we know that English words can potentially have several meanings, many of us may not fully appreciate how the meaning of a word is established by the context of the surrounding language. For example, when we use the word "root" in English, we might mean the underground part of a plant or tree, the fundamental cause of a problem, or even a *root*-word extraction. In each option, the surrounding words provide context for how we interpret "root" but note that each of the interpretive contexts fall under an organizational system for written words. In short, with words having multiple meanings, we must use the context of surrounding language to accurately interpret which possible meaning is most appropriate, but consider what occurs when there is a crossover of English words into mathematical language contexts.

The word *root* has a unique mathematical meaning that is written the same way as other English language notation, but has a very different semiotic notation in the language of mathematics. Suppose we wanted to evaluate the root of an expression to find the hypotenuse of a right triangle in two dimensions. In English, we would simply use the phrase, "evaluate the *root* of the expression to determine the length of the hypotenuse." Translated into semiotic notation for mathematical language, it might read as follows: $h = \sqrt{a^2 + b^2}$. The notation is relatively simple in this example, but with a more complex expression the notation not only assumes we know what the *root* symbol means in the language of mathematics, but also how the surrounding contextual nuances affect the process of simplifying it. As an exercise in English to mathematics language, translate into words, the following mathematical notation: $\sqrt[3]{x}$. Syntactically, this expression is simple translate into English, "... the third root of x." Semantically, it is more difficult to capture, which is exactly why the study of mathematics needs to be taught beyond the aspects of procedural fluency (Thompson & Rubenstein, 2000). Semantically, the expression translates to, "...identify a number such that the *product* of three identical *factors* of the variable *x* results in the number." Given this semantic description, we must also understand the definition and context of the terms *product* and *factors*, as well as understanding that the index value of the root determines the number of identical factors of *x* that must be present to determine our numeric restatement of the expression. It is logical to surmise that every syntactic notation of mathematics can be translated to natural written language but we cannot make assumptions about the meaning of the English words that describe a mathematical process without increasing the ambiguity so let us now turn our attention to some inconsistencies in translating from English to mathematics language using a few of the previous ideas.

Some words are shared between English description and mathematical notation and can be translated directly from one system to the other without ambiguity. Also, as we have seen using the word "root," the translations can be more difficult and require some contextual information. In a third scenario, there are some delimiters that are shared between the systems but have completely different meanings. In the first case, we might use the example, "five is greater than three." The phrase can easily be translated into mathematical notation, $5 > 3$. The notation $>$ can be directly substituted for the phrase, "is greater than." As a counterpoint, now consider the use of delimiters. We could make an exclamatory statement in English, "... the shoes are red!" Clearly, the writer is expressing excitement about the shoes being red. On the other hand, we could structure a syntactically similar phrase in mathematics, "... the answer is 5!" This may not be an exclamatory statement, but rather, a substitution of a numeric answer of 120 using *factorial* notation. In mathematics, an exclamation point has its own meaning, which is very different than how it is used in a standard written system. A *factorial* translates into written language as the product of all of the numbers counting down from a given number n to 1 and including n and 1 (i.e. n x (n-1) x (n-2) ... x 4 x 3 x 2 x 1). The translation of a natural language value of 120 to mathematical notation describing a specific factorial (e.g. 5!) can be expressed as follows:

$$120 = 5! = \prod_{n=1}^{5} n$$

Finally, let us briefly look at an English-to-mathematics translation of ideas that appears to be self-evident but is often interpreted incorrectly. Take the word "twenty" for example. This, of course, equates to the numeric value of 20. In reality the number 20 is a notational representation of a quantity that only exists because of place value notation, not because of a single word that denotes the quantity. That is to say the digits zero through nine are each represented by a single word. The number 20 is also represented by a single word, "twenty" but the quantity of 20 is actually not a single number in the way that the digits zero through nine are. The number 20, in essence, a quantity represented by two digits (mathematical letters if you please) and place value notation to create the equivalent of a mathematical *word* meaning 20. The place value notation of the number 20 says we have two sets of a place value worth 10 and zero sets of the place value worth 1. Understanding how numbers follow this rule within an algebraic system is critical to understanding how polynomial operations in algebra can be used to create useful expression and equations. Unfortunately our assumptions about how words represent quantities may mislead us when we attempt to draw meaning from a mathematical expression.

Semiotics to "STEMiotics"

Up to this point, our focus has been on examining the parallel syntactic structures of natural language versus mathematical notation, exploring how mathematical notation translates into meaning, and looking at some basic misconceptions of the interplay between natural language and mathematical language. The purpose of these investigations was to help us consider a broader view of communication using mathematical systems and natural language. Hopefully reflecting on communication in this way can help us make better sense of large semiotic systems and apply mathematical communication techniques to a broader spectrum of technical language instruction in the STEM disciplines.

Semiotic systems are not limited to translating mathematics to natural language. There are a myriad of semiotic systems within the STEM disciplines, each with its own unique "vocabulary" but all with a mathematical communication-based foundation. The Bohr Model for atomic structures, circuit diagrams for electronics, computer programming languages, free body diagrams in statics, and even musical compositions are all semiotic representations of much larger semantic communications (i.e. nuclear fusion, electronic billboards, computer applications, stresses on bridge members, and Beethoven's fifth symphony). Each semantic system is represented by its own syntax, and each can be defined mathematically by the postulates previously outlined in the first section of this manuscript.

Students studying the STEM disciplines can better understand the nature of technical communication through the use of symbols by relating all of these syntactic modalities to how they already use natural language. Early on in this manuscript, semiotics was broadly defined as the science of communication studied through the interpretation of signs and symbols as they operate in various fields, esp. language. The generation and interpretation of symbols in the STEM disciplines, leveraged for the purpose of communication, is critical to expressing ideas in a concise and accurate manner irrespective of the field. An integration of topics in the STEM disciplines takes this idea to the next level by representing technical semantic systems with diagrammatic symbols. For example, if we examine a simple circuit diagram we will find a page of information using very little text from which we can interpret an exact result. The point is that each symbolic system in the STEM disciplines and beyond has its own unique language but carries a specific meaning when translated to natural language. We can now create a new word for the Oxford English Dictionary! STEMiotics: the science of communication in the STEM disciplines studied through the interpretation of signs, symbols, and diagrams and related to natural communication.

Conclusion

Capturing the idea of how language is used in everyday communication is tremendously difficult. It is hard to imagine that the 26 alphabetic symbols we use can be permuted into 171,000 meaningful words, which, in turn, can be arranged to make sentences and stories with more possible symbolic permutations than there are atoms in the known universe. But within all of this complexity, there are some very simple underlying mathematical structures that define the use of all languages including the communication aspects mathematics itself. Recall the four postulates that govern the syntax of written and mathematical communication. Letters and digits create the symbols we understand as words, numbers, and abstract expressions. Punctuation and mathematical notation help organize and provide nuance. Equivalent expressions can be substituted for one another in both systems to clarify meaning or model efficiency. Written language and mathematical language are, and will remain, interdependent. Recall also that the mathematical processes of substitution and simplification are designed to reduce ambiguity and misinterpretation in the transmission and presentation of ideas. Finally, consider that vocabulary and symbolic notation is not universally defined between these two interdependent communication systems. These concepts are important to remember in the instruction of all STEM and language-based subjects. As mathematics teachers, in particular, strive to define mathematical processes, it may be effective to consider drawing parallels to how students communicate in written English. As language teachers try to reinforce the idea of clarity in their students' writing, they can draw parallels to simple mathematical processes. At any rate, we should reinforce what we all know about transmitting messages to solve problems, particularly in the modern age of texting, tweeting, and emailing where abbreviations, shorthand, and colloquial symbolism reign supreme.

References

Chomsky, N., & Halle, M. (1968). *The Sound Pattern of English.* Harper & Rowe: New York

Devlin, K. (2000). *The Language of Mathematics: Making the Invisible Visible*. Holt Paperbacks: New York

Mathematical Symbols. *Encyclopedia of Mathematics*. Retrieved from URL: http://www.encyclopediaofmath.org/index.php?title=mathematical_symbols&oldid=31085.

Etsy, W.W. (2014). *The Language of Mathematics*. 19th Ed: Author

Jamison, R.E. (2000). Learning the language of mathematics. *Language and Learning across the Disciplines*, 4(1), 45-54.

National Council of Teachers of Mathematics. (2000). *Principles and Standards for School Mathematic*s. Reston, VA: Author

National Research Council. (2001a). Adding it up: Helping children learn mathematics. In J. Kilpatrick, J. Swafford,& B. Findell (Eds.), *Mathematics Learning Study Committee, Center for*

Education, Division of Behavior and Social Sciences and Education: Washington DC: National Academies Press.

Thompson, D.R., & Rubenstein, R.N. (2000). Learning mathematics vocabulary. Potential pitfalls and instructional strategies. *Mathematics Teacher*, 93, 568-574

Chapter Author(s)

Elliott Ostler is a Professor of Educational Leadership specializing in STEM Education at the University of Nebraska at Omaha. He has taught courses in mathematics, physics, statistics, pedagogical methods, and research design. His research interests are primarily focused on the paradigms of integrated STEM education and the use of mathematics as a language.

Chapter 13

Shifting the Paradigm: STEM Teachers and Real World STEM Experience

ABSTRACT: At some point in their careers science, technology, engineering, and mathematics (STEM) teachers all face the same question from their students; "When am I ever going to use this?" This question is relevant to students and deserves an answer that is credible and based in the real world. If an educator can answer this question, student engagement and learning is enhanced. This article reports on a professional development program for teachers of STEM called Project SHINE. Project SHINE addressed the paradigm related to teachers of STEM and their experiences with real world STEM applications by giving them the real world experience that they often lack.

Introduction

Peter Senge, argues that students are engaged by real world problems (2012, pp. 294 - 295). STEM courses should focus learning on creative exploration, projects, problem solving, and innovation rather than rote memorization of current curriculum" (Stearns, Morgan, Capraro, & Capraro, 2012). This problem-based approach has shown that students learn better when they are authentically engaged in activities that are meaningful (Fortus, Dershimer, Krajcik, Marx, & Mamlok-Naaman, 2004). When students are engaged with real-world problems it makes knowledge more relevant to them and increases their ability to transfer skills and information from school to the world (Bransford, Brown, & Cockling, 2000). Stephanie Pace Marshall (2010) agrees, stating that "STEM education must engage students in understanding and experiencing the human consequences of innovation and its essential value in advancing the human condition" and to do this, we must immerse student in disciplinary and interdisciplinary thinking, creative problem solving, and innovative system and process design (p. 51). Problem-based or real world problems engage learners in ways that other teaching methods do not. This clearly shows that curricular content must be shown to be relevant for students to take an interest.

When I, a veteran teacher of mathematics for 18 years, have been faced with this question from my students, I often provided answers that satisfy most students; but at other times like many STEM educators, a satisfactory answer was not always forthcoming. The content educators teach which has been selected by individual districts and/or mandated by various government agencies is well known by educators but the connection to the real-world application that it sustains is often lost to the teaching practitioner and student alike.

This situation creates an existing paradigm and related instructional problem in STEM education; namely, that the teachers of STEM do not often have real world STEM experiences on which to base their teaching practices. It is hard for STEM teachers to provide the relevant connections between their content and the STEM fields where it applies (N. Grandgenett, personal communication, May 17, 2014)

To address and change this paradigm, a National Science Foundation (NSF) grant was awarded to Central Community College in Columbus, Nebraska entitled, *Shaping High-quality Integrated Nebraska Education* (Project SHINE) which was funded as DUE #0903157 within the Advanced Technological Education Program. This project received several different national recognitions including being a finalist for the Bellwether Award and being recognized in a Report to the President on Capturing Domestic Competitive Advantage in Advanced Manufacturing by the President's Council of Advisors on Science and Technology. Project SHINE served as professional development for teachers of STEM to give them access to the critical real-world STEM experiences that they can employ in their classrooms.

Project SHINE had three objectives that specifically addressed increasing STEM teacher awareness/experiences with practical STEM implementation. These objectives were clearly present in all three cohort groups and were measured with a series of self-rating assessments and pre/post workshop surveys. The three relevant objectives related to improving STEM teacher knowledge of practical STEM implementation are as follows.

Objective 1. Provide STEM-related professional development opportunities for secondary and college faculty from across the state of Nebraska.

Objective 2. Develop a heightened awareness of applied technical skills and an interest in STEM careers for students of Project SHINE educators.

Objective 3. Develop long-lasting, collaborative relationships between business mentors and education participants through coordinated experiential learning activities and curricular program development.

The formal project began in the summer of 2010 and continued through the summer of 2012 with a no cost extension granted by the NSF for the summer of 2013. Sixty-eight Nebraska teachers (mostly teachers in the STEM disciplines) were recruited for professional develop workshops that consisted of 14 days over the summer and an additional five days during the school year. Each teacher participated in two externships with local businesses that were two days in length (included in the 19 days). Businesses that teachers completed their externships with include:

- Abengoa Bioenergy
- Archer Daniels Midland Company
- BD Medical-Medical Surgical Systems
- BD Medical-Pharmaceutical Systems
- Behlen Mfg. Co.
- Cargill Meat Solutions
- Conductix-Wampfler
- Duo-Lift Manufacturing Company, Inc.
- Gottberg Auto Company
- Green Plains Renewable Energy
- Katana Summit
- Kawasaki Motors Manufacturing Corp., USA
- Lincoln Machine
- Loup Power District
- Nebraska Machine Company NMC CAT
- Nebraska Public Power District
- Nucor Steel
- Parker Hannifin
- Tri-V Tool & Mfg. Co.
- Valero Renewable Resources
- Valmont Industries
- Vishay Dale Electronics

The purpose of the externships was to provide teachers with real world experience related to their curricular content. Teachers attended the business, observed the work environment, asked questions, and explored connections between the business that served as their externship and their curriculums. Participants were expected to develop two Problem-Based Learning (PBL) lessons surrounding their externships (for a total of four) that applied what they learned about the business and how it applied to their curricular area.

These externship experiences gave teachers real-world examples and experience in how STEM is applied in the realms of energy, biofuel, food-processing, and manufacturing industries. In addition to the externships, teachers were given intensive training and experience in developing PBL lessons by faculty and consultants from the University of Nebraska at Omaha. All developed lessons have a strong Science, Technology, Engineering, and Mathematics (STEM) focus in addition to the real-world business connection. A total of 207 lessons and supporting material were developed by the participants over the three year grant timeframe and are now electronically posted in the SPIRIT (http://spirit.unomaha.edu/spirit/index.html) and Project SHINE and (http://www.mechatronics-mec.org/igsbase/igstemplate.cfm?SRC=DB&SRCN=&GnavID=8&SnavID=45) databases.

These lessons were in a modular format that was originally conceptualized for another Nebraska-based NSF grant, the Silicon Prairie Initiative for Robotics in Education (DUE #0733228). The modular format of the lessons is based on the AEIOU acronym, which allows lesson components that share the same instructional component to be interchanged in order to make different lessons. The AEIOU components include A - Asking Questions, E - Exploring Concepts, I - Instructing Concepts, O - Organizing Learning, and U - Understanding Learning (or assessment). With this AEIOU strategy, a well-established base of critical and thoroughly vetted lesson components allows for a flexible retrieval of existing lessons and customized design of new lessons, as desired by a teacher using the curriculum.

The AEIOU lesson components are further detailed in the following description.

SPIRIT Lesson Format:

A – Asking questions: Designed to facilitate an initial classroom interchange of questions and ideas. An A component may include a prompt-type question in an engineering or scientific format as a model of good questioning.

E – Exploring concepts: This component helps students to study, experiment, conjecture, and to instructionally play with the robotics equipment in the context of the questions that were asked in the A component.

I – Instructing: This component is the key component of the lesson plan and is designed to instruct students in the formal core processes of the STEM topic that they are studying.

O – Organizing learning: Designed to allow students to participate in a guided practice environment where they might create graphs, develop charts, solve problems, and make decisions based upon what they have learned from the I components as well as what they have observed from their questions and explorations in the A and E phases.

U – Understanding: Designed around effective ways to assess how well the various I components have been addressed for students. The U components include a number of unique assessment instruments that range from short quizzes, games, to tests and worksheets, to projects, to interpretive writing.

The modular interactive lessons have been introduced to more than 2,000 secondary and community college students in Nebraska classrooms, and additional students across the country resulting from four years of dissemination activities at regional and national conferences by the project leadership team.

Project SHINE participants were competitively selected through an application process and served a mix of new participant educators and experienced educators over the life of the project with the breakdown of participants shown in Table 1.

Table 1: Project SHINE Participants per Cohort Year

PARTICIPATION	Year 1	Year 2	Year 3	Entire Project
New Participant Educators	23	20	12	55
Experienced Participant Educators	0	7	6	13
TOTALS	23	27	18	68

Fifty-five secondary and community college participant teachers were drawn from 33 different academic institutions throughout Nebraska. Each teacher entered into a year-long mentoring relationship with the business with which they completed their externships. Participant business primarily fit into four categories: energy, biofuels, food-processing, and advanced manufacturing environments. Additional hands-on STEM experiences were provided to the teachers at Central Community College using industrial equipment such as mills, lathes, and presses to fabricate catapults and fluid power arms.

The results of Project SHINE indicate that many teachers found the business externship experience was beneficial for their understanding of STEM in practice and their ability to bridge the academic world of STEM with the real world of STEM practice. In Table 2, participants across all Cohorts rated their experiences regarding STEM and Project SHINE.

**Table 2: Compiled End of SHINE Workshop Summaries for All Cohorts
Periods Covering June 7-17, 2010; June 6-16, 2011; June 4-14, 2012**

	Strongly Disagree	Disagree	Neutral	Agree	Strongly Agree
1) So far, this workshop is increasing my knowledge of applied STEM.	☐	☐	☐	24%	76%
2) So far, this workshop is increasing my knowledge of STEM in business.	☐	☐	2%	23%	75%
3) So far, this workshop is providing me with some instructional ideas.	☐	☐	☐	24%	76%
4) So far, I found this workshop to be interesting and fun.	☐	☐	2%	43%	72%
5) So far, I found this workshop to be useful or practical for me as a teacher.	☐	☐	4%	26%	70%
6) So far, I believe that this workshop will help me improve my instruction with my students.	☐	☐	7%	21%	72%
7) So far, I would recommend this workshop to other teachers.	☐	☐	4%	24%	72%

At the end of each project year, a survey was given to participants related to how Project SHINE changed their teaching related to STEM and how their externship experiences changed/improved what they did in the classroom. In Table 3, participant rankings are summarized and show that Project SHINE participants believe that their teaching practices and students responses changed in a positive way because of their Project SHINE experiences.

**Table 3: End of Year Educator Survey: Summary of Project Lessons Section
June 1 to May 31 – All Cohorts (2010-11, 2011-12, 2012-13)**

	Strongly Disagree	Disagree	Neutral	Agree	Strongly Agree	Not Applicable
1) I introduced my students to new instructional ideas because of Project SHINE.	☐	☐	2%	37%	56%	5%

2) Students responded favorably to new ideas I introduced from Project SHINE.	2%	□		49%	41%	5%
3) My Project SHINE lessons helped students understand applied STEM.	□	□	12%	46%	37%	5%
4) My students learned more about STEM in business than in previous years.	□	□	7%	32%	54%	7%
5) Project SHINE lessons helped improve my instruction with students.	□	□	7%	39%	49%	5%
6) I will continue to use the lessons I developed in Project SHINE next year.	□	□	5%	32%	63%	□

Participating educators were also surveyed regarding their business mentor experiences throughout the school year following their summer Project SHINE professional development workshop. The business mentor that worked with them as part of their externships was to provide support to their classroom as the teacher and mentor mutually agreed. The teacher response to this survey can be found in Table 4. This data shows that most participant educators found the connection to business that their mentor provided to the classroom during the school year was a benefit to students and student learning.

Table 4: End of Year Educator Survey: Summary of Business Mentor Section
June 1 to May 31 – All Cohorts (2010-11, 2011-12, 2012-13)

	Strongly Disagree	**Disagree**	**Neutral**	**Agree**	**Strongly Agree**	**Not Applicable**
1) Working with my business mentor helped me during the school year.	24%	2%	12%	15%	32%	15%
2) My business mentor was involved with my class	7%	10%	17%	32%	12%	22%

during the school year.						
3) My business mentor helped my students appreciate applied STEM.	2%	10%	10%	34%	24%	20%
4) My students understand how STEM is used in the business that mentored me.	2%	7%	7%	41%	27%	15%
5) My students are better aware of technical careers using STEM.		2%	12%	37%	37%	12%
6) I plan to continue working with my business mentor after this year.	4%	10%	10%	22%	44%	10%

During the summer professional development workshop, each cohort was given a series of daily surveys that captured formative feedback. In addition, a pre/post workshop survey was administered to better understand educator opinions and perceptions. An analysis of that data is in Table 5 and revealed significant increases in responses to the following questions.

Table 5: Educator Pretest/Posttest Opinion Survey – Significant Increases:

Cohort #1 - 2010-11 **Cohort #2 - 2011-12** **Cohort #3 - 2012-13**

Survey Question	**Pretest/Posttest**	**N**	**Mean**	**Comment**
I am comfortable designing Project-Based Learning.	Pretest Group Posttest Group	21 20	2.10 2.70	Significant: $P < .05$
I know how to pace students learning in long term projects.	Pretest Group Posttest Group	21 20	2.19 2.55	Significant: $P < .05$
I would advise my students to take as many STEM courses as they can.	Pretest Group Posttest Group	21 20	3.33 3.85	Significant: $P < .005$
Minority students are less likely to succeed in STEM subjects than White students.	Pretest Group Posttest Group	21 20	1.57 1.20	Significant: $P < .05$
Connecting to businesses is a useful context	Pretest Group	21	3.52	Significant:

for learning STEM concepts.	Posttest Group	20	3.85	P < .005
Business connections can be easily integrated into many STEM courses within middle school context.	Pretest Group Posttest Group	21 20	2.86 3.50	Significant: P < .005
I have strategies for assessing my students work in groups.	Pretest Group Posttest Group	24 21	2.79 3.10	Significant: P < .05
I am comfortable designing Project-Based Learning.	Pretest Group Posttest Group	24 21	2.58 2.85	Significant: P < .05
I know how to pace students learning in long term projects.	Pretest Group Posttest Group	24 21	2.29 2.76	Significant: P < .05
Students with a solid grasp of STEM subjects are better prepared for the future than those who are not.	Pretest Group Posttest Group	24 21	3.17 3.43	Significant: P < .05
My teaching often includes group activities for students.	Pretest Group Posttest Group	17 13	2.412 3.000	Significant: P < .05
I am comfortable designing project-based learning activities.	Pretest Group Posttest Group	17 13	2.118 2.769	Significant: P < .01
I know how to pace student learning in long-term projects.	Pretest Group Posttest Group	17 13	2.176 2.692	Significant: P < .05
I intend to take more professional development with a STEM focus.	Pretest Group Posttest Group	17 13	3.176 3.615	Significant: P < .05
Connecting to businesses is a useful context for learning STEM concepts.	Pretest Group Posttest Group	17 13	3.412 3.769	Significant: P < .05
Business connections can be integrated into many STEM courses within middle school.	Pretest Group Posttest Group	17 13	2.706 3.308	Significant: P < .01

Mean scale - 1=do not agree, 2=agree somewhat, 3=agree, 4=strongly agree

Project SHINE also collected data in the form of short answer comments related to the project. Below is a sampling of these responses as they relate to the paradigm of STEM teachers and real world STEM experience. Almost unequivocally, respondents stated how meaningful and powerful their experiences with the real world STEM applications that they encountered as part of the externships were to their personal understanding and for their teaching of students. The development of problem-based learning lessons with a business context has shown to be an effective technique for engaging STEM educators and energy, biofuels, food-processing, and manufacturing businesses and for them to gain real world insights to STEM in application. It is reasonable to expect the behavioral changes experienced by the educators, students, and business mentors in the project could be replicated with other business sectors and academic disciplines.

- "I liked the hands-on activities that my students participated in. They also enjoyed completing the surveys and discovering what career opportunities may be of interest to them."
- "When using a Project SHINE lesson my student's interest and intensity in learning increased. Having an understanding of how a concept or skill is used outside the classroom in a real business application truly helped to engage my students. All of the sudden what they were learning was important."
- "It has allowed me to provide real world examples to my students on where they will use math."
- "I liked being able to see first-hand what skills are needed in different workplaces so that I could help students understand why they need to learn specific skills and how they will use them in the future."
- "I liked the support from the business sector and knowing what is important to teach students to prepare them for a career or for the continuing education they will need to obtain these careers."
- "It gave me extra tools and ideas to connect business and mathematics."
- "I liked using the lessons I developed. I also appreciated that experience of visiting the different places so I could apply what is learned in the classroom with where it is used in the real world."
- "Project SHINE was enlightening in a way not many other P.D. experiences are. Instead of showing us a PowerPoint and saying "Try this in your classroom," we instead were shoved out the door to experience different parts of the world for ourselves, and had an amazing support network to help us develop our own ideas from our real-world, real-situation experiences."
- "I thought that my application of chemistry concepts to real world technology and factories helped students see connections better than I had explained it in the past."

Conclusion

While Project SHINE influenced only a small subset of educators in the state of Nebraska, the participant teachers indicated that their experiences with STEM related businesses helped with their understanding of how the content that they teach is applied in the real world. For many teachers, the experience translated to behavioral changes in the classroom. This professional development opportunity for teachers shows that it is possible to shift the paradigm that STEM teachers do not have real world STEM experience by providing them with opportunities to gain such experiences. Project SHINE shows that there is merit in projects like this and that they seem to have a positive impact on teachers as well as their students relative to practical STEM knowledge. From the success of Project SHINE, it appears that it would be beneficial for teachers to provide additional professional development that provides real world STEM connections that they can implement in the classroom or to possibly incorporate such experiences into pre-service teacher training.

As research shows, students are engaged in real world problems that have the ability to motivate students in ways that traditional instruction often does not. By providing professional development opportunities to teachers of STEM related to real world STEM applications, it gives teachers a better opportunity for helping students bridge what they are learning in the classroom and the types of real world problems that they will encounter. Shifting the paradigm and providing STEM teachers with real world experiences in addition to their other educational preparation seems like a practical way to develop a larger educational toolset.

References

Bransford, J. D., Brown, A. L., & Cockling, R. R. (2000). How people learn: Brain, mind, experience, and school. Washington, DC: National Academy Press.

Fortus, D., Dershimer, C. R., Krajcik, J., Marx, R. W., & Mamlok-Naaman, R. (2004). Design-based science and student learning. *Journal of Research in Science Teaching, 41*(10), 1081-1110. Retrieved from http://search.proquest.com.leo.lib.unomaha.edu/docview/

Grandgenett, N. (2014, May 17). [Personal interview by the author].

Marshall, S. P. (2010). Re-imagining specialized STEM academies: Igniting and nurturing decidedly different minds, by design. *Roeper Review, 32*(1), 48-60. doi:10.1080/02783190903386884

Senge, P. (2012). Context and engagement [Systems Thinking]. In P. Senge, N. Cambron-McCabe, T. Lucas, B. Smith, J. Dutton, & A. Kleiner (Authors), *Schools that learn (Updated and revised): A fifth discipline fieldbook for educators, parents, and everyone who cares about education* (Revised ed., pp. 293-297). New York, NY: Crown Business.

Stearns, L. M., Morgan, J., Capraro, M. M., & Capraro, R. M. (2012). A teacher observation instrument for PBL classroom instruction. *Journal of STEM Education: Innovations & Research, 13*(3), 7-16. Retrieved from http://search.ebscohost.com/login.aspx?direct=true&db=a9h&AN=79468725&site=ehost-live

Chapter Author(s)

Brian Sandall, MS
Candidate for a Doctorate in Educational Leadership
University of Nebraska at Omaha
Omaha, Nebraska
USA

Dan Davidchik, MS
DOL/NSF Project Manager
Central Community College,
Columbus Nebraska
USA

www.ingramcontent.com/pod-product-compliance
Lightning Source LLC
Chambersburg PA
CBHW082113230426
43671CB00015B/2692
* 9 7 8 0 9 9 6 6 7 4 1 1 9 *